Working Memory
in Second Languag
Acquisition and Pro   ...g

SECOND LANGUAGE ACQUISITION

Series Editor: **Professor David Singleton**, *University of Pannonia, Hungary* and Fellow Emeritus, *Trinity College, Dublin, Ireland*

This series brings together titles dealing with a variety of aspects of language acquisition and processing in situations where a language or languages other than the native language is involved. Second language is thus interpreted in its broadest possible sense. The volumes included in the series all offer in their different ways, on the one hand, exposition and discussion of empirical findings and, on the other, some degree of theoretical reflection. In this latter connection, no particular theoretical stance is privileged in the series; nor is any relevant perspective – sociolinguistic, psycholinguistic, neurolinguistic, etc. – deemed out of place. The intended readership of the series includes final-year undergraduates working on second language acquisition projects, postgraduate students involved in second language acquisition research, and researchers and teachers in general whose interests include a second language acquisition component.

Full details of all the books in this series and of all our other publications can be found on http://www.multilingual-matters.com, or by writing to Multilingual Matters, St Nicholas House, 31-34 High Street, Bristol BS1 2AW, UK.

SECOND LANGUAGE ACQUISITION: 87

Working Memory in Second Language Acquisition and Processing

Edited by
**Zhisheng (Edward) Wen,
Mailce Borges Mota and Arthur McNeill**

MULTILINGUAL MATTERS
Bristol • Buffalo • Toronto

Library of Congress Cataloging in Publication Data
A catalog record for this book is available from the Library of Congress.
Working Memory in Second Language Acquisition and Processing/Edited By Zhisheng
(Edward) Wen, Mailce Borges Mota and Arthur McNeill.
Second Language Acquisition: 87.
1. Second language acquisition–Psychological aspects. 2. Memory. 3. Psycholinguistics.
I. Wen, Zhisheng, editor. II. Mota, Mailce Borges, editor. III. McNeill, Arthur, editor.
P118.2.W667 2015
418.0071–dc23 2014047896

British Library Cataloguing in Publication Data
A catalogue entry for this book is available from the British Library.

ISBN-13: 978-1-78309-358-8 (hbk)
ISBN-13: 978-1-78309-357-1 (pbk)

Multilingual Matters
UK: St Nicholas House, 31-34 High Street, Bristol BS1 2AW, UK.
USA: UTP, 2250 Military Road, Tonawanda, NY 14150, USA.
Canada: UTP, 5201 Dufferin Street, North York, Ontario M3H 5T8, Canada.

Website: www.multilingual-matters.com
Twitter: Multi_Ling_Mat
Facebook: https://www.facebook.com/multilingualmatters
Blog: www.channelviewpublications.wordpress.com

The policy of Multilingual Matters/Channel View Publications is to use papers that
are natural, renewable and recyclable products, made from wood grown in sustainable
forests. In the manufacturing process of our books, and to further support our policy,
preference is given to printers that have FSC and PEFC Chain of Custody certification.
The FSC and/or PEFC logos will appear on those books where full certification has been
granted to the printer concerned.

Typeset by Deanta Global Publishing Services Limited.
Printed and bound in Great Britain by Short Run Press Ltd.

Contents

Final Commentary

Acknowledgements

The editors wish to thank all the contributors for making the effort to submit their chapters to the volume. In particular, we are grateful to Alan Juffs, Clare Wright and Peter Skehan for help in reviewing some chapters as well as contributing their own commentary chapters for each theme-based section. We also wish to express our special thanks to Michael Bunting, Randall Engle, Alan Baddeley, Nelson Cowan and John Williams for accepting our invitation to contribute their innovative insights into working memory second language acquisition (WM-SLA) issues at the latter stage of this volume. Their support to the WM-SLA enterprise is much welcomed and highly appreciated. Our thanks also go to the general editor of the SLA series, David Singleton, the anonymous reviewers and Laura Longworth of Multilingual Matters for their encouragement, assistance and patience at different stages of the book.

Finally, the editors gratefully acknowledge the initial support coming from the journal *Language Learning* (with its grant programme), The Center for Language Education of the Hong Kong University of Science and Technology, the Universidade Federal de Santa Catarina (UFSC) and the *Asian Journal of English Language Teaching* (AJELT) of The Chinese University of Hong Kong. Without their support, the current volume would not be possible.

Contributors

Mohammad Javad Ahmadian (PhD, University of Isfahan) is currently an assistant professor of second language acquisition at the University of Isfahan, Iran. His major research efforts and output have been in the area of task-based planning. Dr Ahmadian is interested in cognitive approaches to SLA, task-based language teaching and learning, and L2 speech production processes.

Alan Baddeley (PhD, Cambridge University) is a professor of psychology at the University of York. He graduated in psychology from University College London and after a master's from Princeton, completed a PhD at the Medical Research Council Applied Psychology Unit (APU) in Cambridge where he spent the next few years. He moved on to Sussex and then Stirling universities before returning to the APU where he followed Donald Broadbent as director. After 20 years, Alan retired from the directorship, moving first to Bristol and then to York University. Professor Baddeley is best known for his pioneering work on working memory, in particular for his multiple components model.

Melissa Baralt (PhD, Georgetown University) currently works as an assistant professor of Spanish applied linguistics at Florida International University in Miami, Florida. Her areas of research include task-based language teaching and learning, the perception and use of feedback during conversational interaction, cognitive and task design factors that affect language learning, and the ways in which teachers use tasks in the classroom – in both traditional and online settings.

Michael F. Bunting (PhD, University of Illinois at Chicago) is an associate research scientist and area director of cognitive psychology at the University of Maryland Center for Advanced Study of Language (CASL). He is a faculty affiliate of the University of Maryland's Neuroscience and Cognitive Science (NACS) Programme and the Department of Psychology. His research interests are the nature, organisation and trainability of working memory and selective attention; the structure of the inductive reasoning domain and the relationship between reasoning ability (general fluid intelligence) and working memory capacity; and the cognitive and non-cognitive determinants of human aptitude and acquired abilities, including complex skill acquisition and aptitude for foreign language learning.

Rendong Cai (PhD, Guangdong University of Foreign Studies) is currently a lecturer at the School of English and Education of Guangdong University of Foreign Studies. Dr Cai has research interests and publications in interpreting, psycholinguistics and applied linguistics.

Kiel Christianson (PhD, Michigan State University) is an associate professor at the Department of Educational Psychology and Beckman Institute for Advanced Science and Technology, University of Illinois, Urbana-Champaign. Dr Christianson's research is heavily influenced and informed by linguistic theory. Overarching themes in his present work are (mis)interpretation in sentence processing, morphological processing during reading and cross-linguistic research.

Nelson Cowan (PhD, University of Wisconsin) holds a distinguished Curators' Professor title at the University of Missouri, where he has taught since 1985. He authored *Attention and Memory: An Integrated Framework* (1995, Oxford University Press), *Working Memory Capacity* (2005, Psychology Press) and numerous journal articles on working memory and attention. He relates these interests to a curiosity about consciousness. He has broad interests in science, philosophy and current events and likes reading and film, but the non-work interests that receive a respectable amount of his time are those that involve his wife, three grown children, a grandchild, other relatives, a few close friends and a little exercise and amateur sport.

Yuncai Dai (PhD, Shanghai International Studies University) is currently a Professor and the Dean of the School of Foreign Languages at Chongqing Technology and Business University, China. Dr Dai's research interests include individual differences in second language acquisition, second language sentence processing and aptitude–treatment interaction.

Yanping Dong (PhD, Guangdong University of Foreign Studies) is a professor of psycholinguistics at the National Key Research Center for Linguistics and Applied Linguistics of Guangdong University of Foreign Studies. She has research interests and extensive publications in psycholinguistics, applied linguistics, bilingualism and interpreting. Professor Dong is also the founding president of the Chinese Association of Psycholinguistics.

Randall Engle (Randy) (PhD, Ohio State University) received his BS in psychology at West Virginia State University and his PhD in experimental psychology from Ohio State University. After positions at King College and the University of South Carolina, he served as chair of the School of Psychology at Georgia Institute of Technology (Georgia Tech) from 1995 to 2008. He was founding director of the Center for Advanced Brain Imaging from 2008 to 2009. His publications have been cited over 20,000 times and can be downloaded from http://psychology.gatech.edu/renglelab/index.htm. Dr Engle is a fellow of the American Psychological Association, the Association of Psychological Science, the American Association for the Advancement of Science, the Society of Experimental Psychology and the Memory Disorders Research Society. He has served as chair of the governing board of the Psychonomic Society, chair of the board of the Council of Graduate Departments of Psychology (COGDOP) and president of Division 3 of APA.

Sun-A Kim (PhD, University of Illinois at Urbana-Champaign) is currently an assistant professor at the Department of Chinese and Bilingual Studies, The Hong Kong Polytechnic University. Dr Kim's research interests include second language acquisition, the psycholinguistics of Chinese and of Korean and teaching Chinese and Korean as second languages.

Irina Konstantinova (MA, Ohio University) is currently involved in a major research project that investigates the relationship between cross-linguistic influence and working memory at Ohio University. Irina coordinates and leads weekly meetings, oversees the work of all students involved in this project and participates in data collection and analysis. Her interests include research in second language acquisition, working memory and transfer.

Scott Jarvis (PhD, Indiana University) holds the title of professor in the Department of Linguistics at Ohio University, where his main research interests include cross-linguistic influence, cognitive linguistics and research methods related to the investigation of language proficiency and the measurement of lexical diversity. His work in these areas has appeared in several authored and edited books, numerous book chapters and journal papers in the fields of second language acquisition and multilingualism. Professor Jarvis is also associate executive director for the journal *Language Learning*.

Alan Juffs (PhD, McGill University) is a professor of linguistics in the Department of Linguistics, University of Pittsburgh. He is the director of the English Language Institute at the University of Pittsburgh and co-editor of the Pitt Series in ESL textbooks published by the University of Michigan

Press. He is a former president of the University and College Intensive English Programs Consortium (UCIEP). Dr Juffs' research interests include the semantics–syntax interface and second language sentence processing. In addition to the more theoretical aspects of SLA, he conducts classroom research in ESL vocabulary teaching and materials development.

Shaofeng Li (PhD, Michigan State University) is currently a senior lecturer in applied language studies at the University of Auckland, New Zealand. Dr Li's research interests include form-focused instruction, the cognitive constraints of SLA (especially language aptitude and working memory) and language assessment. He has published widely in key international journals of applied linguistics and recently co-edited (with Rod Ellis) a special issue of *Applied Linguistics* (2015).

Yanbin Lu (PhD, Georgia State University) is currently an associate professor at the Department of Foreign Languages and Literatures, Tsinghua University, Beijing, China. Dr Lu's research interests include academic L2 writing assessment, working memory and L2 writing, and the teaching and learning of English for academic purposes (EAP) in EFL contexts.

Arthur McNeill (PhD, University of Wales, Swansea) is director of the Center for Language Education and associate dean of the School of Humanities and Social Science at the Hong Kong University of Science and Technology. Dr McNeill has research expertise and publications in key areas of applied linguistics, SLA, teacher education and vocabulary teaching and learning.

Anne Mitchell (MA, Ohio University) is a member of a research project at Ohio University examining the relationship between working memory, cross-linguistic influence and the language learning process. Her interests include research in working memory, second language acquisition and language transfer.

Mailce Borges Mota (PhD, Federal University of Santa Catarina) is currently a professor in the Department of Foreign Languages and Literatures at the Federal University of Santa Catarina, Brazil, and a research fellow of the prestigious Brazilian National Council for Scientific and Technological Development (CNPq). Dr Mota's research and publications have focused on the relationship between language processing and memory systems.

Michelle O'Malley (PhD, Ohio University) is currently an assistant professor in the Linguistics Department at Ohio University. Her areas of concentration are working memory and language acquisition, phonetics/phonology and dialect study. Michelle's dissertation research focused on the relative contributions of phonological and visual components of working memory to children's auditory language processing.

Jerome Packard (PhD, Cornell University) is a professor at the Department of East Asian Languages and Cultures and Beckman Institute for Advanced Science and Technology, University of Illinois, Urbana-Champaign. Professor Packard specialises in Chinese linguistics, Chinese word structure, Chinese psycholinguistics and Chinese language acquisition and pedagogy. His current research interests include sentence processing in native Mandarin speakers and learners of Mandarin as a second language, and the acquisition of reading by Chinese children in China.

Patrick Rebuschat (PhD, Cambridge University) is currently a lecturer in second language acquisition and bilingualism at the Department of Linguistics and English Language at Lancaster University. Prior to moving to Lancaster, he spent two years at Bangor University, Wales, and three years as a visiting assistant professor at Georgetown University in Washington, DC. Dr Rebuschat's research interests and extensive publications have focused on bilingual cognition, particularly the implicit and explicit learning of languages.

Kindra Santamaría (PhD, Florida State University) is now teaching French at Haltom High School in Texas. Prior to this, she worked as an assistant professor of French at Texas Christian University in Fort Worth, Texas. Dr Santamaria's research interests include working memory and classroom language acquisition.

Peter Skehan (PhD, Birkbeck College, University of London) is a professorial research fellow at St. Mary's University College, Twickenham, London, having previously worked at Auckland University, The Chinese University of Hong Kong, King's College London and Thames Valley University. Professor Skehan's research interests and extensive publications are in major areas of applied linguistics, second language acquisition, L2 task-based language teaching, learning and testing and individual differences (especially language aptitude).

Gretchen Sunderman (PhD, Penn State University) is an associate professor of Spanish linguistics at Florida State University in Tallahassee, Florida. Dr Sunderman's research interests include lexical processing and individual differences in second language acquisition.

Kaitlyn M. Tagarelli (PhD, Georgetown University) recently completed her PhD in applied linguistics and is currently a postdoctoral fellow in the Department of Psychology and Neuroscience at Dalhousie University in

Halifax, Nova Scotia. Dr Tagarelli's research focuses on the neural and cognitive mechanisms involved in second language learning, particularly which brain structures and memory systems underlie language learning, and how individual differences and learning conditions interact in ways that influence the language learning process and outcomes.

Zhisheng (Edward) Wen (PhD, The Chinese University of Hong Kong) is currently an associate professor at the School of Languages and Translation at Macao Polytechnic Institute (MPI). Dr Wen has lectured, researched and published extensively in second language acquisition, psycholinguistics and other areas of applied linguistics. His current research foci are theoretical, methodological and pedagogical issues surrounding cognitive aptitudes (e.g. working memory) in first and second language acquisition and processing. Dr Wen is a recipient of the 2012 Language Learning Roundtable Conference Grant and successfully convened the International Language Learning Roundtable on 'Memory and Second Language Acquisition' in Hong Kong (June, 2012).

John Williams (PhD, Cambridge University) is currently a reader in applied psycholinguistics at the Department of Theoretical and Applied Linguistics at the University of Cambridge. Dr Williams specialises in the cognitive mechanisms of second language learning and second language lexical and syntactic processing. His current research focuses on implicit learning of form-meaning connections and incidental learning of word order regularities. He has published numerous articles on these topics in journals such as *Language Learning, Studies in Second Language Acquisition* and *Applied Psycholinguistics*.

Clare Wright (PhD, Newcastle University) is currently a lecturer at the Department of English Language and Applied Linguistics at the University of Reading. Her main research focuses in the area of SLA with a particular emphasis on the development of grammatical accuracy and fluency in L2 English, L2 Mandarin and L2 French. Her research investigates linguistic, cognitive and contextual factors underpinning how language knowledge is acquired and processed, with special interest in how working memory can aid L2 development in and out of the classroom, as featured in her recent *TESOL Quarterly* paper and other publications.

Foreword

On a foreign language student's first trip abroad, an assignment might be asking a hotel concierge for directions to a popular café, navigating the streets and public transportation system and, at dinner, translating the waiter's dining recommendations for those companions who do not speak the language. These activities – formulating and following a plan, following directions and simultaneous translation – would be virtually impossible without the attentional and immediate memory system known as *working memory*. A convenient analogy for working memory is to think of it as the mental workspace of the mind: the small amount of memory that holds information and the capacity for attention control to manipulate that information for ongoing use. This dynamic working memory and attention system guides behaviour and permits conscious awareness of goal-relevant information. Another important function of the working memory system is to prevent potentially irrelevant or distracting information from gaining access to our consciousness. By deliberately focusing or dividing attention, that foreign language student can pay attention, make and maintain plans and engage in goal-directed behaviour.

It is for good reason that working memory processes are among the most important and widely studied components of human cognition. Working memory processes have been implicated in a variety of native language linguistic processes, such as paying attention to conversation, auditory and reading comprehension, speech planning, verbal problem solving and language use. Many aspects of first and second language comprehension rely heavily on working memory capacity: Working memory is positively correlated with first and second language vocabulary learning, reading and listening comprehension and writing proficiency (Atkins & Baddeley, 1998; Baddeley, 2000; Daneman & Hannon, 2007; Engle, 2001). Working memory is used when taking notes (Piolat *et al.*, 2005), while following directions (Engle *et al.*, 1991) or when ignoring visual and auditory distractions as well as internal distractions from one's own intruding thoughts and daydreams (Engle, 2001).

These same working memory processes are equally important outside of the verbal domain to learning, skills and abilities, including general fluid intelligence (Engle *et al.*, 1999), reasoning ability (Kyllonen & Christal, 1990), mathematical ability (Ashcraft & Krause, 2007) and spatial ability (Kane *et al.*, 2004). Because working memory plays an important role in these broader cognitive processes and abilities, it comes as no surprise that working memory is considered to be one of the most critical components of cognitive and linguistic achievement. The importance of working memory for everyday activities has been widely studied by cognitive psychologists interested in how memory works, by developmental psychologists interested in lifespan changes, by clinicians and psychiatrists interested in deficits due to illness or injury, and by educators interested in individual differences. While considerable progress has been made, the scientific study of the role of working memory in second language acquisition, by comparison to some of these other disciplines, has only just begun.

As almost anyone who has tried to learn another language can attest, second language learning can be a frustrating and time-consuming experience. This is true for adults and children alike. Despite serious effort and dedication, not all learners will achieve anything like native language proficiency. Even fewer still will learn to speak a second language without an 'accent'. For only the rarest of individuals, second language learning is easy and fast. For the vast majority of learners who want results, adult, post-critical period foreign language learning is not a casual enterprise. These observations of individual differences in ultimate attainment, as well as individual differences in the ease and rate of second language learning, suggest that there are abilities and talents that make some people better able than others to learn a second language. Hence, for these people, there is a *second language aptitude*.

Many factors complicate the scientific study of second language acquisition. For starters, the rate of learning is not a direct function of time on task, and it, as well as the way in which learners learn, varies by individual (McLaughlin, 1992). Furthermore, the greater the degree of dissimilarity between the second language a person wants to learn and his/her native language, the greater the difficulty of language learning. Some are fairly similar to the person's native language. English, for example, is one of 48 different living Germanic languages, which include Swedish, Dutch and German, and the majority of the English vocabulary is derived from Latin and French, which are members of another Indo-European language family, the Romance languages. As a result of these similarities, Swedish and French are easier for native English speakers to acquire than are languages from other more distally related language families. Learning Korean, which is a language isolate, or Arabic, a Semitic language of the Afro-Asiatic language family, represents a more significant challenge to native English speakers than learning more similar languages. Importantly, while the degree of similarity between a learner's native and target language is a determiner of the degree of difficulty of learning the language, research suggests that all languages require more or less the same aptitudes to learn (Carroll, 1985).

A fundamental tenet of cognition is that complex, high-level processes are dependent on lower-level, more elementary processes. For example, reading requires a complex interaction of lexical activation, syntactic parsing and meaning integration. If there is a deficiency in any one of these steps, the larger process fails. Some elementary processes are not specialised to any particular domain or broader skill, but are believed to be fundamental parts of all cognition.

It follows that people who possess processing advantages for these lower-level skills should also demonstrate processing advantages for more complex tasks. Variations between people for these skills are called individual differences, and there are four individual differences that are most clearly implicated as being important for understanding how well people perform high-level cognition (Kyllonen & Christal, 1990).

- *Working memory capacity*, the ability to temporarily retain information for short periods of time.
- *Declarative knowledge*, overall knowledge about the world or the domain at hand.
- *Procedural memory*, memory for automatised (non-conscious) procedures.
- *Processing speed*, how fast someone processes information.

These factors have been proposed as the primary sources of individual differences on cognitive tasks. They stem from a general outline of a standard cognitive architecture which charts the structures and processes that characterise human information processing, or the process of acquiring, retaining and using information.

This architecture is by no means comprehensive, but models used to explain performance on various cognitive and learning tasks have been developed from this framework (e.g. Anderson & Lebiere, 1998; Cowan, 1995). Individual differences may arise from any of the memory structures (procedural, working and declarative) or processing cycles (cognitive, motor and perceptual) in this framework, the key components being the type and extent of knowledge in declarative and procedural memory, working memory capacity and the speed with which one can execute the processing cycles (Kyllonen & Crystal, 1990). These are the four components of the four-sources model. Working memory capacity is thought to be the central factor in this model and is therefore considered to have the greatest influence on an individual's performance on cognitive and learning tasks.

Working memory is capacity and time limited, as is easy to see from one's own experience of memory limitations and forgetting. Who has not had the experience of meeting someone new and almost immediately forgetting his/her name, sometimes even before the conversation is over? There could be any number of reasons why this happens (inattentiveness, distractibility, information overload), but the point is that there are constraints on how much information can be managed, processed and integrated effectively all at once. Perhaps not surprisingly, people vary in their working memory capacity and in how susceptible they are to short-term forgetting.

Attention control is important to the function of the working memory system. Research indicates that attention control is one of those ubiquitous cognitive processes which operates across domains. Our view is that it is a central, limited-capacity, domain-general resource that can be voluntarily applied to holding and manipulating information in memory. The *central* aspect of attention indicates that the resource is shared among all modalities (vision, hearing, etc.) and types of information coding (phonological, orthographic, spatial, etc.). The *limited-capacity* aspect indicates that one type of manipulation or storage can be increased only at the expense of other types.

Science distinguishes between two fundamentally different forms of attention: exogenous and endogenous attention. From the amoeba that orients and moves away from bright illumination to the tourist entranced by the neon lights of Radio City Music Hall, organisms from the lowest form to the most advanced involuntarily orient towards (or sometimes away from) a stimulus that captures their attention. In contrast to exogenous attention, endogenous attention is paying attention to stimuli or locations of one's own choosing. Only the most evolved animals can voluntarily select objects to attend to. With intention and effort, the endogenous allocation of attention is under voluntary control, as when people allocate their attention according to variable instructions or pay-offs. However, attention is not completely voluntary: flashing lights, loud noises and sudden movements can involuntarily grab attention away from where it is intended, thus triggering an exogenous orienting response. Such a distraction can cause a lapse in attention to the task and, by extension, a failure to remember critical components of the task that was being completed (e.g. remembering the name of your new acquaintance or the context of the newspaper article you were just reading).

There are many diverse theoretical descriptions of the working memory system (cf. the 12 unique perspectives in Miyake and Shah [1999]). Baddeley and Hitch (1974) first described working memory as having two different subsystems or components: visuospatial working memory for manipulating and briefly maintaining information from the spatial domain; and phonological working memory for handling verbally mediated representations and processing (see also Baddeley, 1986, 2007; Baddeley & Logie, 1999). Research on structural models of working memory has addressed the further subdivision of these two primary components into subcomponents. Of relevance to the language community, Caplan and Waters (1999) suggested that verbal working memory should be differentiated for verbal (but not syntactic) processes for cognitive tasks generally versus syntactic/grammatical processes that support linguistically mediated tasks such as sentence processing and comprehension. Contrary to the approach that describes working memory in multiple task-specific processes, Kane *et al.* (2004) demonstrated that linguistic and non-linguistic (but still verbally mediated) tasks rely on a single pool of working memory resources and that working memory processes are by and large domain general.

More recent theories of working memory, such as Cowan's (1995, 2001, 2005) embedded processes model, are process oriented rather than structural. Cowan's model distinguishes a zone of privileged and immediate access – *the focus of attention* – from activated but not immediately accessible long-term memory. Information in the focus of attention is readily accessible and resistant to forgetting, but because the capacity of focus of attention is quite limited, very few items or fixed groups of items (*chunks*) can reside there. According to Cowan, that capacity may be as little as four items for the average individual. In contrast, the activated portion of long-term memory is not capacity limited, but memory in this state is prone to forgetting due to decay and/or interference (i.e. confusion with other similar information in memory). Attentional control processes are responsible for manipulating the contents of working memory. They activate, focus, update, switch and inhibit memory during information processing.

Because learning one's native language and learning a second one are both cases of language learning, the usual assumption is that information about one illuminates the other. Support for the idea that working memory plays an important role in second language acquisition comes from the Developmental Interdependence Hypothesis, which states that a learner's competence in the second language is at least partially dependent on competence in the first language (Cummins, 1979). This would be expected if working memory plays a role in ability for both first and second language processing. There is evidence showing that working memory is correlated with second language vocabulary acquisition time (Ellis, 1996), English as a second language vocabulary ability (Miyake & Friedman, 1998), second language explicit grammar learning (Tagarelli *et al.*, 2011) and second language reading and writing ability (Bergsleithner, 2010).

Linck *et al.* (2014) conducted the first comprehensive formal meta-analysis on the relationship between working memory and the products of second language acquisition: the development of second language proficiency and second language processing. They examined 748 effect sizes from 79 samples involving 3707 participants and found that working memory capacity is positively associated with both second language processing and proficiency outcomes, with an estimated population effect size (ρ) of 0.255. Not surprisingly, they found larger effective sizes when working memory capacity was measured with verbal measures than when it was measured with spatial or otherwise non-verbal measures. They also found greater effects sizes for the executive control component of working memory capacity than for measures emphasising storage capacity.

Beginning in 2007, researchers at the University of Maryland Center for Advanced Study of Language (CASL) have been examining the skills, traits and abilities that are necessary for adult, post-critical period language learning. Much of their work has been done with the help of language learners at the Defense Language Institute Foreign Language Center (DLIFLC), which is the primary language school for all four branches of the US military. The DLIFLC educates thousands of students during 30- and 60-week intensive language training courses. Students at the DLI are held to a rigorous and disciplined academic schedule. In order to graduate, DLI students must meet national proficiency standards in reading, listening and speaking, as determined by the defense language proficiency test. In a series of correlation-based studies, including two large-scale field studies at the DLIFLC (total sample exceeding 2200 students), CASL's researchers have looked for relationships between language learning success at the DLIFLC and (1) cognitive abilities including, but not limited to, general cognitive abilities (e.g. working memory, explicit induction) and specific linguistic abilities (e.g. English vocabulary knowledge, English reading abilities); (2) non-cognitive measures including surveys of personality, motivation, self-regulation, self-efficacy, ambiguity tolerance, learning orientation, ability to cope with stress and need for closure; and (3) experiential measures including early exposure to multiple languages and previous foreign language learning experience. Results of this research have been reported in technical reports for the US government (Bunting *et al.*, 2011) and a report for publication is in development. Of significance here is the fact that working memory, as measured by the running memory span task (cf. Bunting *et al.*, 2006), was more highly correlated with second language learning outcomes than any other measure of general cognitive abilities.

This recent work, including the large-scale correlation-based study and the formal meta-analysis, are strong evidence of the involvement of working memory in second language acquisition, but what has been lacking heretofore is a theoretical account of *how* working memory supports second language acquisition. What has been lacking is an *integration* of working memory theory with second language acquisition theory. This book is an attempt to bridge that divide. As the modern world becomes more economically and socially connected, it will be ever more important that people be able to communicate outside the isolated sphere of their own culture and language and this will place greater emphasis on multi-language education. This book is an attempt to apply the ideas and data of modern cognitive psychology to facilitate that endeavour.

Michael Bunting and Randall Eagle

References

Anderson, J.R. and Lebiere, C. (1998) *The Atomic Components of Thought*. Mahwah, NJ: Lawrence Erlbaum Associates.

Ashcraft, M.H. and Krause, J.A. (2007) Working memory, math performance, and math anxiety. *Psychonomic Bulletin & Review* 14, 243–248.

Atkins, P.W.B. and Baddeley, A.D. (1998) Working memory and distributed vocabulary learning. *Applied Psycholinguistics* 19, 537–552.

Baddeley, A.D. (1986) *Working Memory*. Oxford: Oxford University Press.

Baddeley, A.D. (2000) The episodic buffer: A new component of working memory? *Trends in Cognitive Sciences* 4, 417–423.

Baddeley, A.D. (2007) *Working Memory, Thought, and Action*. Oxford: Oxford University Press.

Baddeley, A.D. and Hitch, G.J. (1974) Working memory. In G.A. Bower (ed.) *Recent Advances in Learning and Motivation* (Vol. 8; pp. 47–89). New York: Academic Press.

Baddeley, A.D. and Logie, R.H. (1999) Working memory: The multiple-component model. In A. Miyake and P. Shah (eds) *Models of Working Memory: Mechanisms of Active Maintenance and Executive Control* (pp. 28–61). New York: Cambridge University Press.

Bergsleithner, J.M. (2010) Working memory capacity and L2 writing performance. *Ciências & Cognição* 15, 2–20.

Bunting, M.F., Cowan, N. and Saults, J.S. (2006) How does running memory span work? *Quarterly Journal of Experimental Psychology* 59, 1691–1700.

Bunting, M.F., Bowles, A.R., Campbell, S.G., Linck, J.A., Mislevy, M.A., Jackson, S.R., Tare, M., Silbert, N.H., Koeth, J.T., Blake, C.L., Smith, B.K., Corbett, R., Willis, R.A. and Doughty, C.J. (2011) Reinventing DLAB: Potential new predictors of success at DLIFLC: Results from construct-validation field testing for DLAB2. University of Maryland Center for Advanced Study of Language Technical Report.

Caplan, D. and Waters, G.S. (1999) Verbal working memory and sentence comprehension. *Behavioral and Brain Sciences* 22, 77–94.

Carroll, J.B. (1985) Second-language abilities. In R.J. Sternberg (ed.) *Human Abilities: An Information-Processing Approach* (pp. 83–103). New York: W.H. Freeman & Company.

Cowan, N. (1995) *Attention and Memory: An Integrated Framework*. Oxford Psychology Series, No. 26. New York: Oxford University Press.

Cowan, N. (2001) The magical number 4 in short-term memory: A reconsideration of mental storage capacity. *Behavioral and Brain Sciences* 24, 87–185.

Cowan, N. (2005) *Working Memory Capacity*. Hove: Psychology Press.

Cummins, J. (1979) Linguistic interdependence and the educational development of bilingual children. *Review of Educational Research* 49, 222–251.

Daneman, M. and Hannon, B. (2007) What do working memory span tasks like reading span really measure? In N. Osaka, R.H. Logie and M. D'Esposito (eds) *The Cognitive Neuroscience of Working Memory* (pp. 21–42). New York: Oxford.

Ellis, N.C. (1996) Working memory in the acquisition of vocabulary and syntax: Putting language in good order. *The Quarterly Journal of Experimental Psychology Section A: Human Experimental Psychology* 49, 234–250.

Engle, R.W. (2001) What is working memory capacity? In H.L. Roediger, J.S. Nairne, I. Neath and A.M. Suprenant (eds) *The Nature of Remembering: Essays in Honor of Robert G. Crowder* (pp. 297–314). Washington, DC: American Psychological Association Press.

Engle, R.W. (2002) Working memory capacity as executive attention. *Current Directions in Psychological Science* 11, 19–23.

Engle, R.W., Carullo, J.J. and Collins, K.W. (1991) Individual differences in working memory for comprehension and following directions. *The Journal of Educational Research* 84, 253–262.

Engle, R.W., Tuholski, S.W., Laughlin, J.E. and Conway, A.R.A. (1999) Working memory, short-term memory, and general fluid intelligence: A latent-variable approach. *Journal of Experimental Psychology: General* 128 (3), 309–331.

Kane, M.J., Hambrick, D.Z., Tuholski, S.W., Wilhelm, O., Payne, T.W. and Engle, R.W. (2004) The generality of working memory capacity: A latent-variable approach to verbal and visuospatial memory span and reasoning. *Journal of Experimental Psychology: General* 133, 189–217.

Kyllonen, P.C. and Christal, R.E. (1990) Reasoning ability is (little more than) working-memory capacity! *Intelligence* 14, 389–433.

Linck, J.A., Osthus, P., Koeth, J.T. and Bunting, M.F. (2014) Working memory and second language comprehension and production: A meta-analysis. *Psychonomic Bulletin & Review* 21/4, 861–883.

McLaughlin, B. (1992) *Myths and Misconceptions about Second Language Learning: What Every Teacher Needs to Unlearn.* Washington, DC: Center for Applied Linguistics.

Miyake, A. and Friedman, N.P. (1998) Individual differences in second language proficiency: Working memory as language aptitude. In A.F. Healy and L.E. Bourne (eds) *Foreign Language Learning: Psycholinguistic Studies on Training and Retention* (pp. 339–364). Mahwah, NJ: Lawrence Erlbaum.

Miyake, A. and Shah, P. (eds) (1999) *Models of Working Memory: Mechanisms of Active Maintenance and Executive Control.* New York: Cambridge University Press.

Piolat, A., Olive, T. and Kellogg, R.T. (2005) Cognitive effort during note taking. *Applied Cognitive Psychology* 19, 291–312.

Tagarelli, K., Borges Mota, M. and Rebuschat, P. (2011) The role of working memory in implicit and explicit language learning. In L. Carlson, C. Hölscher and T. Shipley (eds) *Proceedings of the 33rd Annual Conference of the Cognitive Science Society* (pp. 2061–2066). Austin, TX: Cognitive Science Society.

Introduction and Overview

Zhisheng (Edward) Wen, Mailce Borges Mota and Arthur McNeill

Working memory (WM) generally refers to our ability to briefly maintain and also operate on a limited amount of information in our mind when completing some mentally demanding tasks (Baddeley, 1992). Despite its limited capacity, WM has been found to play a key role in many human central cognitive activities such as language comprehension, arithmetic calculation, prospective planning and problem solving (Carruthers, 2013). Given its fundamental role in so many aspects of human life, WM has garnered enormous enthusiasm from scholars in multiple research fields, straddling virtually all of the six disciplines configured within George Miller's (2003) hexagon of cognitive sciences: psychology, linguistics, neuroscience, biology, computer science and anthropology.

Among these, cognitive and development psychologists have pinpointed that WM's putative storage and executive control aspects are directly implicated in diversified language learning and processing activities (e.g. Baddeley, 2000, 2003; Cowan, 2013; Gathercole & Baddeley, 1993). In light of the close links depicted between WM and first language (L1) learning, recent years have witnessed a burgeoning interest among second language acquisition (SLA) researchers to explore the potential role of WM in second language (L2) processing and learning (see Juffs & Harrington, 2011; Sagarra, 2013; Wen, 2012, 2016 manuscript under review; Williams, 2012; for recent reviews, see Linck et al. [2014] for a comprehensive research synthesis and meta-analysis).

Generally speaking, initial findings from these WM-SLA explorations have been encouraging and they mostly emulate the positive relationships evidenced between WM and L1 learning. Notwithstanding, however, another lingering theme that arises out of these literature reviews of WM-SLA studies (e.g. Wen, 2014) relates to the great difficulties encountered by SLA researchers in apprehending and operationalising this buzzword from cognitive psychology. The biggest frustrations usually stem from the lack of a consensus view of the WM construct in the face of its dozen theoretical perspectives and models (e.g. Miyake & Shah, 1999) and the controversies and debates over its nature, structure and functions (Baddeley, 2012; Carruthers, 2013; Conway et al., 2007; Cowan, 2014). Adding to this confusion is the daunting number of WM assessment tasks and procedures that are currently implemented in cognitive psychology. As a consequence, SLA researchers are often confronted with formidable challenges in their research design and methodology in WM-SLA explorations (Wen, 2012, 2014, 2016 manuscript under review; also see Gass & Lee, 2011; Juffs, 2006; Linck *et al.*, 2014, for a similar argument).

In view of these extant and emerging caveats inflicting on SLA researchers in their WM-SLA endeavours, the general editors of this volume commissioned a group of leading scholars at the forefront of WM research from cognitive psychology to join efforts with cognitive-oriented SLA researchers to address major theoretical and methodological issues concerning the 'WM-SLA nexus' (Wen, 2012). In so doing, we hope that this current volume can serve as an interactive forum to *bridge* dialogues from both fields so that WM theories can be further *integrated* into SLA theories. Towards this end, the whole volume is further organised into four sections, with each section addressing a key aspect of the WM-SLA conundrum. What follows is a synopsis of the individual chapters in each section.

Theoretical Perspectives and Models

The first section of the book contains four theoretical chapters that lay the foundations for the whole book. In the first chapter, Alan Baddeley begins with a brief autobiographical account of the evolution of his multi-component model of WM (a model that is most frequently referred to by subsequent chapters), including its early formation and more recent developments. More relevant to the themes of the current volume, Baddeley provides a succinct review of some major studies conducted by cognitive psychologists (including himself) that have explored the roles of multiple WM components (e.g. its phonological component) in more specific aspects of L2 learning (e.g. vocabulary and grammar learning). In so doing, Baddeley graciously pinpoints some possible avenues for future research that will shed light on elucidating their intricate relationships.

Taking a slightly different approach from Baddeley, Nelson Cowan in Chapter 2 first depicts a conjectured scenario where a person has to struggle to understand and use a language that is foreign to him/her, thus bringing in the key concept of WM that is pivotal to survival in these rather deplorable circumstances. Starting from here, Cowan proceeds to comment on Baddeley's multi-component model of WM. Building on Baddeley's modular view, Cowan further extends the concept of WM to an architecture of embedded processes resembling John Venn's portrayal of convergent albeit distinctively overlapping diagrams. Through this analogy, Cowan makes a cogent argument that current WM theories may need to be broadened further to accommodate and integrate essential concepts in SLA and processing.

Echoing the calls initiated elsewhere and by Baddeley and Cowan in Chapters 1 and 2, the third chapter by Zhisheng (Edward) Wen sets out to *integrate* the rather well-defined and seemingly disparate research paradigms of WM in cognitive psychology into nuanced SLA research. Towards this end, Wen first extracts three 'unifying characterisations' of the WM construct out of its many theoretical perspectives that can lend theoretical support to the formulation of a conceptual framework for understanding and measuring WM in L1 and L2 research. By further incorporating findings from L1 and L2 studies of WM effects, Wen aligns the phonological component of WM (PWM; subsuming the phonological short-term store and the articulatory rehearsal mechanism) and its executive aspects (EWM; encompassing such executive functions as information updating, task-switching and inhibitory control; Miyake & Friedman, 2012) with specific SLA activities. These WM-SLA alignments culminate in an overarching theoretical framework (i.e. the phonological/ executive [P/E] model) that subsumes specifically motivated hypotheses regarding WM effects in nuanced SLA domains and processes. As such, the main premise of the P/E model lies in its P/E dichotomy and their distinctive effects on specific SLA areas that are further modulated by learners' age and L2 proficiency. To put it succinctly, the P/E model postulates that PWM underlies those *acquisitional* and *developmental aspects* of SLA in such domains as lexis, formulaic sequences and morphosyntactic constructions; while EWM is predominantly subserving those *monitoring* and *attention-oriented processes* in L2 comprehension, interaction and production, including selective online and offline processing and performance areas.

The theoretical section ends with a commentary chapter (Chapter 4) by Yanping Dong and Rendong Cai on the theoretical models of WM and interpreting. Indeed, given its unique features that likely implicate both language comprehension (of the source language input) and production (of the target language) processes, simultaneous interpreting between two languages has been demonstrated by empirical studies to rely heavily on such cognitive resources as WM (Cowan, 2000; Christoffels *et al.*, 2006). In their commentary, the authors provide a theoretical overview of the intricate relationships between WM and interpreting training and performance. In addition, they also elaborate on such critical and thorny issues as WM effects on interpreting skills and performance, WM training and interpreter training and WM-based interpreting models. Finally, the authors also report preliminary data from empirical studies conducted in their own laboratory as support for their arguments. The authors conclude the commentary by calling for further studies to explore the arguably most complex relationship between WM and interpreting.

WM in L2 Processing

The second section of the book starts to address more focused issues that are pertaining to WM and L2 processing. It begins with an empirical chapter by Sun-A Kim and colleagues on L2 character reading (Chapter 5). They examined the influence of WM in learning to read L2 Chinese characters under two conditions. The first condition was designed to lead participants to use visual WM more, while the second condition was intended to involve more PWM. The results show that participants who have higher visuospatial WM spans are better able to learn the visually enhanced characters, while those with higher verbal WM capacities perform better in learning the regular Chinese characters belonging to the normal and the similar sets. On the other hand, WM effects seemed to disappear when participants learned to read the six groups of phonetic families whose consistency levels varied. The chapter thus contributes to the distinction between visual WM and PWM in L2 character processing.

Moving on from L2 character processing to sentence processing, Chapter 6 by Yuncai Dai investigated the processing strategies employed by Chinese learners of English as an L2 and the role played by their WM capacity in resolving the ambiguities of relative clause (RC) attachment in such sentences as 'someone shot the servant of the actress who was on the balcony'. Participants are first-year Chinese college students who took part in three experiments, of which two are concerned with online processing of L1 and L2 RC attachment, respectively. Participants' WM is measured by a computerised reading span task in L1. The third study includes two offline questionnaires. The results indicate that Chinese learners of L2 English demonstrate universal processing strategies in L2 sentence processing, and there is no L1 transfer effect in L2 RC attachment. Although the findings suggest that WM plays a substantial role in L2 RC attachment, no significant role was found in L1 RC ambiguity resolution. These findings seem to suggest that the processing of L2 RC attachment involves a multitude of factors including not only structural information but also semantic and pragmatic cues, which are then mediated by structural cues and WM. All these factors may interact to permit learners to perform a reanalysis in RC ambiguity resolution.

This section on WM and L2 processing ends with the commentary by Juffs (Chapter 7). After a brief summary and illustration of major syntactic structures that are typically involved in the WM-language processing literature, Juffs takes issue with their inconsistent findings regarding the role of WM effects in certain aspects of sentence-level processing among adult L2 learners. The author ends the commentary by reporting some pilot data from a study that investigates the effect of RCs on pronoun–antecedent links in paragraph-length texts, thus calling on future WM-L2 processing research to move beyond the sentence level and to explore effects in discourse processing.

WM in L2 Interaction and Performance

Turning away from L2 processing, the third section of the book contains both empirical and commentary chapters that address theoretical and empirical issues pertaining to the role of WM in L2 interaction and production. It begins with Chapter 8 by Shaofeng Li who examined two independent variables, language analytical ability (a subsection of the modern language aptitude test [MLAT]; Carroll & Sapon, 1959/2002) and WM (as measured by the listening span task) and their relation to the provision of implicit and explicit corrective feedback by participants at two different proficiency levels (low vs advanced). Statistical results indicate that low-proficiency learners rely more on language analytical ability, while advanced learners draw more on their WM capacity to benefit from corrective feedback. These findings suggest that both WM and language analytical ability are viable, albeit different components of language aptitude, but that their effects are less straightforward and may be sensitive to L2 learners' proficiency level and the feedback types in question.

Chapter 9 by Mohammad Javad Ahmadian reports an empirical study that looked into L2 learners' WM capacity and their self-repair behaviour within the paradigm of WM and L2 task planning research (Ellis, 2005). Fifty-one Iranian intermediate language learners participated in the study. Their WM was measured via a listening span test and the subjects were then required to perform an oral narrative task under the online planning condition. Results revealed that, under this planning condition, there was a statistically significant positive relationship between WM and the number of error repairs and appropriacy repairs. There was also a significant negative relationship between WM and the number of different-information repairs. In other words, WM directs learners' attention to different areas in the process of monitoring their own speech production and performance.

Chapter 10 by Yanbin Lu reports the results of a study which investigated the relationship between WM and L2 written performance. Contrary to expectations, no significant relationship between WM capacity (as measured by the operation span task) and L2 writing performance was found, despite a slight relationship between L2 WM capacity and L2 productive vocabulary knowledge. Subsequent stepwise regression identified productive vocabulary as the only significant predictor of L2 writing performance (but not WM), regardless of participants' L2 proficiency level. The results seem to suggest only a minimal contribution of WM capacity to timed writing performance in L2 argumentative essays when a global marking is implemented.

This section ends with the commentary chapter (Chapter 11) by Peter Skehan. With reference to the three stages conceived in the standard speech production model of Levelt (1989), Skehan postulates that WM limitations play a key role in relation to the interplay between the 'conceptualiser' and 'formulator' stages; and that L2 mental lexicon limitations spill over, in their consequences, to all aspects of speech performance. As such, L2 speech production becomes a *serial* rather than a *parallel* process. Under these circumstances, it is task characteristics and task conditions which impact upon attentional functioning, and the ways that the tendency towards serial processes is overcome. Such WM-L2 speech analysis sheds significant light on theories of L2 performance, and in particular, should serve to further illuminate the ongoing debate between the Trade-off Hypothesis (Skehan, 2009, 2014) and the Cognition Hypothesis (Robinson, 2011) in L2 task-based learning research (Révész, 2014).

WM in L2 Instruction and Development

The fourth section of the book includes three empirical studies and one commentary chapter that address more pedagogical issues pertinent to the relationship between WM and L2 instruction and development. Chapter 12 by Kindra Santamaria and Gretchen Sunderman investigated the role of WM in processing instruction of L2 French direct object pronouns. Participants are second- and third-semester learners of French and their WM capacity was measured by a reading span task. Statistical results showed no effect for WM and no interaction between WM and instruction. Production results, however, did show that higher-span participants scored higher on the post-tests as opposed to their low-span counterparts, indicating longer-term effects from WM. This interesting result led the authors to conclude that WM can serve as an effective make-up that compensates for L2 learners' inefficient processing strategies in processing instruction.

Chapter 13 by Kaitlyn Tagarelli, Mailce Borges Mota and Patrick Rebuschat explores the relationship between WM and different learning conditions in SLA. In the experiment, a group of 62 English native speakers were exposed to a semi-artificial language under two learning conditions (incidental and intentional), and their WM capacity was measured by two non-verbal complex WM span tasks (the operation-word span task and the letter-number serial order task). The results of the experiment suggest that both conditions produced a learning effect, with an advantage for the intentional group. WM capacity was not correlated with overall performance on a grammaticality judgement task for either group. Interestingly, it was found that WM capacity predicted performance on grammatical items for the intentional group, suggesting a closer link between WM and explicit learning conditions.

Chapter 14 by Melissa Baralt explores the intricate relationships between WM, cognitive complexity and L2 recasts in online language teaching. The study reported in this chapter sets out to test the hypothesis that WM capacity is related to feedback efficacy during task-based computerised chat interaction, and that the computerised environment might assist learners with lower WM capacity as they perform increasingly complex tasks. Thiry-four learners of intermediate-level Spanish carried out two interactive, story-retell tasks one-on-one with the researcher, during which they received recasts on the Spanish past subjunctive. Regarding results, contrary to expectations, WM capacity did not moderate learning outcomes in this study, for low or for high WM learners. This finding suggests that WM does not moderate feedback efficacy if that feedback is written and in the computer-mediated communication (CMC) mode, regardless of task type.

Chapter 15 by Anne Mitchell and colleagues begins with a discussion of how the results of some past WM-SLA studies could have been skewed by an over-reliance on cognitive psychology tasks that may be inappropriately implemented for SLA research. More specifically, the authors argue that a language-independent WM task paired with a reliable proficiency assessment (such as the test of English as a foreign language, internet-based test [TOEFL iBT]) will more accurately reflect the unique relationship between WM capacity and L2 proficiency. The authors also report on an empirical study to support their argument. In the study, 36 native Chinese learners of English were administered simple (digit span) and complex (operation span) WM tests in both their L1 (Chinese) and L2 (English). Their TOEFL iBT scores were used as a measure of L2 proficiency. Results indicate stronger correlations between proficiency scores and L2 WM tasks than for L1 WM scores. These findings are interpreted by the authors as evidence that WM performance is affected by proficiency in the language in which the task is performed, meaning that WM tasks constructed in participants' L2 may not be appropriate in WM-SLA research. In addition, the results of complex WM tasks indicate the presence of a more nuanced relationship between WM and L2 proficiency than previously demonstrated in past studies. This finding led the authors to argue that learners at different stages of L2 acquisition may rely on WM in different ways. That is to say, high-proficiency learners may rely more heavily on executive aspects of WM (EWM) as measured by the general-domain operation span task, while low-proficiency learners rely more heavily on phonological short-term memory (PSTM) as measured by the digit span tasks.

This section ends with Clare Wright's commentary (Chapter 16) delineating the relationship between WM and the longitudinal development of L2. The chapter first summarises and then reflects on the wider context of SLA and WM research and, in particular, it spells out the claims of the functioning of different aspects of WM (in this case, PSTM and EWM) that come into play as learners progress through developmental stages of L2 acquisition and learning. The author cogently argues that some of the challenges for SLA research are arising from the lack of consideration to theoretical and empirical evidence of WM across the lifespan of L2 development. That is to say, future WM-SLA research, in their research design and methodology, may need to take into account participants' developmental stage in the L2. Overall, these discussions will have significant implications for WM theories and assessment procedures.

Final Commentary

The last commentary chapter (Chapter 17) by John Williams reflects on the theoretical and methodological ramifications brought forth by this volume. As such, Williams first identifies potential challenges to the emerging WM-SLA enterprise as revealed by the current volume. These include, *inter alia*, that the relationship between WM and SLA is far more complex and nuanced than previously expected; and that WM tests fail to constitute the cognitive bedrock of aptitude testing. In view of these, Williams calls for a fundamental *paradigm shift* in future WM-SLA research from the current bottom-up approach to a more top-down approach that can emulate the theoretical framework of Just and Carpenter (1992). Williams ends the commentary by highlighting several avenues that are promising in future WM-SLA endeavours, such as explorations of the relationships between WM and rapid attention switching and that of implicit learning.

Summary

In this section, we aim to recapitulate the major results and findings of the empirical chapters in the current volume, with a view to further discussing their contributions to the theoretical and methodological advancement of WM-SLA research. As such, we begin by summarising in Table 1 the research design (WM components and targeted SLA domains and activities), methodology (WM measures) and major results and findings of all the nine empirical chapters.

From Table 1, we can derive three major observations. First of all, these results and findings are generally in line with the fundamental premise of the P/E model (Wen, this volume) which stipulates that different WM components are playing distinctive roles in various aspects of SLA. More specifically, Kim et al. (Chapter 5) have suggested a distinctive role for visual WM and EWM in the reading and processing of L2 characters. In another example, Mitchell et al. (Chapter 15) seem

Table 1 An overview of the empirical findings of the current volume

Author and chapter no.	WM components and measures	Targeted SLA domains and activities	Major results and findings
Kim (5)	VWM (LRT) and WM (Rspan)	L2 character processing	Positive results for a distinctive role for VWM and executive WM
Dai (6)	WM (Rspan)	L2 sentence processing	Positive results in processing L2 relative clause attachment (but not in L1)
Li (8)	WM (Lspan)	L2 corrective feedback	Advanced proficiency learners draw more on WM to receive feedback (as opposed to low-proficiency learners who draw more on language analytical ability)
Ahmadian (9)	WM (Lspan)	L2 self-repair	Positive results for error repairs and appropriacy repairs; but negative with different-information repairs
Lu (10)	WM (Ospan)	L2 written performance	Negative results with overall written performance
Santamaria (12)	WM (Rspan)	Processing L2 input	Negative results with short-term effects, but positive results with long-term effects
Tagarelli (13)	WM (Ospan, LNO)	L2 learning conditions	Positive with intentional learning; negative with incidental learning
Baralt (14)	WM (Ospan, Lspan, Rspan)	L2 recasts	Negative results with feedback efficacy (written and in the CMC mode, regardless of task type)
Mitchell (15)	PSTM (Dspan); WM (Ospan in L1 and L2)	L2 proficiency	PSTM plays bigger role at low proficiency; WM plays bigger role at high proficiency

Key: VWM=visual WM; PSTM=phonological short-term memory; Rspan=reading span task; Lspan=listening span task; Ospan=operation span task; LRT=letter rotation task; LNO=letter-number ordering task.

to further specify the P/E–L2 proficiency interaction and its empirical results suggest that PSTM plays a bigger role for low-proficiency L2 learners while EWM affects more advanced L2 learners. Besides these two chapters, other empirical chapters have also contributed to provide insights into the relationship between WM and various aspects of SLA and they are further discussed below.

The second generalisation that can be derived from Table 1 is related to EWM. As postulated in the P/E model, EWM plays an important role in many post-interpretive processing and real-time performance-related aspects of L2 comprehension, L2 interaction and production. It is clear from the table (in particular, as shown in the 'WM components and measures' column) that most empirical studies in the current volume have focused on EWM rather than PSTM. Based on the basic tenets of the P/E model, such a practice is reasonable given that most participants involved in these empirical studies are actually college-level university students who are either at their intermediate or post-intermediate L2 proficiency levels (as opposed to those at low proficiency/beginner level). As suggested by the subtitles for the three 'research' sections of empirical chapters (in the table of contents of the book), these studies have made distinctive contributions to clarifying the relationships between WM and L2 acquisition and processing domains and activities from three areas.

First, in terms of WM and L2 processing, Kim *et al.* (Chapter 5) and Dai (Chapter 6) have pointed to the closer link between WM and the processing of L2 characters and RC attachment. Second, in terms of WM and L2 interaction and performance, Ahmadian's study (Chapter 9) suggests significant WM effects on selective areas of self-repair behaviours; while Li (Chapter 8) has helped to tease out the finer-grained relationships existing between WM and L2 interaction and recasts; and finally, Lu (Chapter 10) has helped to illuminate the relationship between WM and L2 written performance. Third, in terms of WM effects on L2 instruction and development, empirical studies (Chapters 12–15) have also helped to draw a clearer picture between WM and L2 instruction (e.g. processing instruction, learning conditions, CMC) and L2 proficiency and development.

The third observation from these empirical studies, however, is a slightly surprising and even disappointing one (at least on the surface as it seems). Based on the 'results and findings' column of Table 1, it becomes clear that not all studies in the current volume have demonstrated a *positive* correlation between WM effects and L2 acquisition and processing. In some chapters, such effects are not always straightforward and are even surprising (Chapter 9 by Ahmadian; Chapter 12 by Santamaria and Sunderman; and Chapter 13 by Tagarelli and colleagues), and in other chapters (Chapter 14 by Baralt and Chapter 10 by Lu), such effects are virtually absent. Despite these somewhat disappointing results, however, when reinterpreted, they can still be considered to be in line with the hypotheses of the P/E model.

Even more so, these results are equally telling as they have actually helped to isolate the possible scenarios where WM effects are *not* present or obvious. For example, Santamaria and Sunderman's chapter (Chapter 12) suggests that WM effects are not obvious immediately after the task but will gradually emerge in the longer term. In a similar manner, Tagarelli and colleagues' chapter (Chapter 13) suggests that WM effects are not obvious for incidental learning, but will be recorded in the intentional learning condition. The same holds true for Baralt's chapter (Chapter 14) which suggests that WM effects are not present when corrective feedback (or recasts) is presented in the written mode (as opposed to the spoken mode) or in the CMC mode (as opposed to the face-to-face mode). Finally, the absence of a positive correlation between WM and L2 written performance in Lu's chapter (Chapter 10) is also thought-provoking. As the author suggests, such an absence can be attributed to the WM measures implemented or the performance measures implemented (for example, the subjective global marking of the participants' writing). It becomes obvious then that such a lack of a positive correlation between WM and L2 written performance is more tentative rather than conclusive. Therefore, more empirical studies are called for to explore the complex relationships between WM and SLA.

To sum up, it is hoped that all the individual chapters included in this book have made concerted albeit distinctive contributions to advancing the theoretical and methodological fronts of the WM-SLA endeavour. Notwithstanding, given that this interdisciplinary enterprise of WM-SLA is still in its early developmental stage, there is still a long way to go from here (Williams, this volume). In that sense, there is a dire need for much more research that can contribute to further illuminating the dynamic and complex relationships constituting the 'WM–SLA nexus' (Wen, 2012).

A Final Note on Terminology and Abbreviations

As noted earlier and also elsewhere (e.g. Wen, 2012, 2016 manuscript under review; Wen *et al.*, 2013), one stumbling block for the WM-SLA integration stems from the inconsistent use of related terms of 'working memory' and the implementation of assessment procedures in many existing SLA studies. To reduce these terminology confusions, it is argued that a clear demarcation is desirable for these closely related terms of WM so that taxonomic coherence can be achieved. To facilitate this process, the current volume aims to arrive at a unified understanding of the WM construct (e.g. Chapter 3 by Wen) by following the specifications of the extended model of WM as proposed in Coolidge and Wynn (2009: 43). It is hoped that such an extended model of WM should quite adequately incorporate and synthesise the key features of the construct as advocated by its two representative theoretical perspectives of Baddeley (this volume) and Cowan (this volume).

To begin with, a clear distinction is made between the terms 'short-term memory' (STM), 'working memory' (WM) and 'long-term memory' (LTM) in the current volume. In this sense, STM refers to the single function of *maintenance* in the memory system and it thus subsumes the putative storage components in Baddeley's WM model: the phonological short-term store which is also called phonological short-term memory (PSTM) or simply phonological memory in the volume; the visual spatial stores (including visual WM and spatial WM) and/or the episodic buffer (EB). In terms of assessment procedures, STM is usually measured by a version of the 'simple memory span test' such as the digit span, the letter span and most prevalently the non-word repetition span task.

Then, the term 'working memory' (and its abbreviation 'WM') is used in the book in two different senses. First of all, the term 'working memory' is used as a general (laymen) concept (as in the cases of its use in the book title and the chapter titles) that refers to the whole cognitive construct covering all those multiple components and functions of maintenance and executive control (Miyake & Shah, 1999). In this first sense, WM distinguishes itself clearly from both STM that is only restricted to the single function of short-term storage and LTM that involves longer-term or permanent storage of information. In contrast, the second sense of WM is conceptualised and operationalised by most chapters of the current volume. Within this second sense, WM is used more restrictedly in that it only refers to the *executive* and/or *control functions* of the general concept of WM (sometimes abbreviated as EWM to distinguish from its broad sense), thus excluding its *'storage'* function (which has been taken up by the term 'STM'). WM as used in this second sense has been adopted by most North America-based cognitive psychologists (such as Nelson Cowan, Michael Kane, Randy Engle and Ellen Bialystok). In terms of Baddeley's conception then, this second sense of WM is equivalent to its executive component (i.e. the 'central executive'). In terms of assessment, WM is generally measured by the many versions of those more 'complex memory span' tasks such as the reading span (Rspan), the operation span (Ospan), the N-back span task, etc., that are tapping into the multiple mechanisms and functions associated with the construct. Consequently, the result (usually indexed as a score) of these memory span tasks becomes the participants' 'working memory capacity' (WMC).

Finally, on the other end of the WM-SLA conundrum then, the term 'second language acquisition' (or its more frequently appearing abbreviation of SLA) is used in the book to refer to either the general field of enquiry or to the umbrella concept that contains all relevant and specific domains (lexis and/or vocabulary; formulaic sequences/formulae; morphosyntactic constructions or grammar) and sub-skills (listening, reading, speaking, writing and translation/interpreting) in the acquisition and processing of a second or foreign language. In this latter case, no distinction is made between 'second' and 'foreign' language learning or between 'acquisition' and 'learning' unless indicated otherwise. For that matter, the two terms in each pair are used interchangeably.

References

Baddeley, A.D. (1992) Working memory. *Science* 225, 556–559.

Baddeley, A.D. (2000) Working memory and language processing. In B.E. Dimitrova and K. Hyltenstam (eds) *Language Processing and Simultaneous Interpreting: Interdisciplinary Perspectives* (pp. 1–16). Amsterdam/Philadelphia, PA: John Benjamins.

Baddeley, A.D. (2003) Working memory and language: An overview. *Journal of Communication Disorders* 36, 189–208.

Baddeley, A.D. (2012) Working memory: Theories, models and controversies. *Annual Review of Psychology* 63, 1–30.

Carroll, J.B. and Sapon, S. (1959/2002) *Modern Language Aptitude Test (MLAT)*. New York: The Psychological Corporation. (Reprinted in 2002 by Second Language Testing Inc.)

Carruthers, P. (2013) The evolution of working memory. *Proceedings of National Academy of Sciences* 110 (Supplement 2), 10371–10378.

Christoffels, I.K., De Groot, A.M.B. and Kroll, J.F. (2006) Memory and language skills in simultaneous interpreters: The role of expertise and language proficiency. *Journal of Memory and Language* 54, 324–345.

Coolidge, F. and Wynn, T. (2009) *The Rise of Homo Sapiens: The Evolution of Modern Thinking*. Malden, MA: Wiley-Blackwell.

Conway, A.R.A., Jarrold, C., Kane, M.J., Miyake, A. and Towse, J.N. (eds) (2007) *Variation in Working Memory*. New York: Oxford University Press.

Cowan, N. (2000) Processing limits of selective attention and working memory: Potential implications for interpreting. *Interpreting* 5 (2), 117–146.

Cowan, N. (2005) *Working Memory Capacity*. New York and Hove: Psychology Press.

Cowan, N. (2013) Working memory and attention in language use. In J. Guandouzi, F. Loncke and M.J. Williams (eds) *The Handbook of Psycholinguistics and Cognitive Processes*. London: Psychology Press.

Cowan, N. (2014) Working memory underpins cognitive development, learning, and education. *Educational Psychology Review* 26 (2), 197–223.

Daneman, M. and Carpenter, P.A. (1980) Individual differences in working memory and reading. *Journal of Verbal Learning and Verbal Behaviour* 19, 450–466.

Ellis, R. (2005) *Planning and Task Performance in a Second Language*. Amsterdam/Philadelphia, PA: John Benjamins.

Gass, S. and Lee, J. (2011) Working memory capacity, inhibitory control, and proficiency in a second language. In M. Schmid and W. Lowie (eds) *From Structure to Chaos: Twenty Years of Modeling Bilingualism: In Honor of Kees de Bot* (pp. 59–84). Amsterdam: John Benjamins.

Gathercole, S. and Baddeley, A. (1993) *Working Memory and Language*. Hove: Lawrence Erlbaum Associates.

Juffs, A. (2006) Working memory, second language acquisition and low-educated second language and literacy learners. *LOT Occasional Papers: Netherlands Graduate School of Linguistics* 89–104.

Juffs, A. and Harrington, M. (2011) Aspects of working memory in L2 learning. *Language Teaching* 44, 137–166.

Just, M.A. and Carpenter, P.A. (1992) A capacity theory of comprehension: Individual differences in working memory. *Psychological Review* 99, 122–149.

Levelt, W.J.M. (1989) *Speaking: From Intention to Articulation*. Cambridge, MA: MIT Press.

Linck, J.A., Osthus, P., Koeth, J.T. and Bunting, M.F. (2014) Working memory and second language comprehension and production: A meta-analysis. *Psychonomic Bulletin & Review* 21 (4), 861–883.

Miller, G. (2003) The cognitive revolution: A historical perspective. *Trends in Cognitive Science* 7 (3), 141–144.

Miyake, A. and Shah, P. (eds) (1999) *Models of Working Memory: Mechanisms of Active Maintenance and Executive Control*. New York: Cambridge University Press.

Révész, A. (2014) Towards a fuller assessment of cognitive models of task-based learning: Investigating task-generated cognitive demands and processes. *Applied Linguistics* 35 (1), 87–92.

Robinson, P. (2011) Task-based language learning: A review of issues. *Language Learning* 61, 1–36.

Sagarra, N. (2013) Working memory in second language acquisition. In C.A. Chapelle (ed.) *The Encyclopedia of Applied Linguistics*. Oxford: Wiley-Blackwell.

Skehan, P. (2014) Limited attentional capacity, second language performance, and task-based pedagogy. In P. Skehan (ed.) *Processing Perspectives on Task Performance* (pp. 211–260). Amsterdam: John Benjamins.

Wen, Z. (2012) Working memory and second language learning. *International Journal of Applied Linguistics* 22, 1–22.

Wen, Z. (2014) Theorizing and measuring working memory in first and second language research. *Language Teaching* 47 (2), 173–190.

Wen, Z. (2016, manuscript under review) Working Memory and Second Language Learning: An Integrated Approach. Multilingual Matters.

Wen, Z., Mota, M. and McNeill, A. (2013) Working memory and second language acquisition: Innovation in theory, research and practice (Special Issue). *Asian Journal of English Language Teaching* 23, 1–103.

Williams, J.N. (2012) Working memory and SLA. In S. Gass and A. Mackey (eds) *Handbook of Second Language Acquisition* (pp. 427–441). Oxford: Routledge/Taylor & Francis.

Part 1

Theoretical Perspectives and Models

1 Working Memory in Second Language Learning

Alan Baddeley

Introduction

The multi-component model of working memory (WM) was developed with the dual aims of providing a framework for the basic understanding of human memory, and at the same time providing a bridge to application beyond the laboratory. One of the earliest and, in my view, most successful of such applications was to language learning, principally to the acquisition and development of vocabulary in children (Baddeley *et al.*, 1998), and also to second language learning (Atkins & Baddeley, 1998). As is clear from the current volume, research on WM and second language learning has flourished in the years since my own rather minimal involvement, and hence I was delighted to hear of the present enterprise, and to lend my support through writing this introductory chapter to express my speculative thoughts on the possible implications of the multi-component view of WM for second language learning.

While it would have been very nice to read the contributions and subsequently comment on them, the timing clashed with the process of revising and updating our memory text (Baddeley *et al.*, 2015). My initial agreement was to write a Preface that envisaged little more than enthusiastic support of this particular application of the WM model. I was, however, tempted by the editor's suggestion that I might outline the current state of the multi-component model, and in doing so thought it would be interesting to think about second language learning and speculate as to how the various current components of the model might be involved. I should emphasise, however, that what follows is simply a brief account of the current model (a more extended discussion can be found in Baddeley [2012]), together with some initial thoughts that may well be proved misguided by the chapters that follow. If so, I shall simply fall back on the observation that progress is often made by discovering points where our predictions are clearly wrong.

Evolution of the Multi-Component Model

Our WM model has its roots in the proposal that short-term memory (STM), principally verbally based, played a useful role in cognition more generally, a view first presented by Broadbent (1958) and developed much more extensively by Atkinson and Shiffrin (1968). Our own work (Baddeley & Hitch, 1974) was prompted by difficulties encountered by this approach in dealing both with links to long-term memory (LTM) and with data from patients whose impaired verbal STM had surprisingly little impact on their broader cognition. Our own studies, relying heavily on dual task methods, led us to propose the model shown in Figure 1.1, which assumes an attentionally limited control system, the central executive, aided by two temporary storage systems, one specialised for acoustic and language stimuli, and the other counterpart the visuospatial sketchpad.

Further development was spurred by the challenge of finding an evolutionary function for the phonological loop that might prove more plausible than remembering telephone numbers. Our search was helped by access to a patient, PV, with a very pure phonological loop deficit. We first tested the hypothesis that the loop was necessary for language comprehension, but found little evidence of impairment, except for certain convoluted sentences explicitly designed to rely on the phonological loop (Vallar & Baddeley, 1987). We then tested the hypothesis that the phonological loop might have evolved for language acquisition, finding that our patient was greatly impaired in acquiring vocabulary in a foreign language, Russian (Baddeley *et al.*, 1988). We went on to show that procedures interfering with the phonological loop function disrupt the acquisition of foreign language vocabulary but not memory for meaningful word pairs in healthy participants (Papagno *et al.*, 1991), and that polyglots who have acquired several languages tend to show enhanced phonological loop capacity (Papagno & Vallar, 1995), while otherwise extremely able people with a reduced verbal STM also tend to have difficulty in acquiring foreign vocabulary (Baddeley, 1993). Furthermore, extensive research by Susan Gathercole and myself has shown a clear link between native

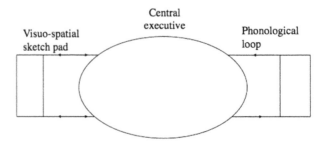

Figure 1.1 The original Baddeley and Hitch (1974) working memory model

language vocabulary learning in children and phonological memory (see Baddeley *et al.* [1998] for a more detailed account).

As a result of this line of work, we modified the basic model to that shown in Figure 1.2. The principal difference is a clear link between the phonological loop and phonological LTM, a link that operates in both directions; the phonological loop facilitates the acquisition of new words, and in due course the richer the available array of existing words, the easier it is to use these to help acquire new items. We speculate that a similar link will occur between the sketchpad and visuospatial semantics, although this has been little investigated so far.

The next version of the model was also driven by the study of language and, in particular, the very strong relationship between prose comprehension and the WM span measure originally developed by Daneman and Carpenter (1980). They presented their participants with sequences of sentences to read, subsequently asking them to recall the last word of each. This and other complex span measures, not necessarily involving language, have proved to be very powerful predictors not only of comprehension (Daneman & Merike, 1996), but also of cognitive processing more generally, including measures of intelligence (see Engle *et al.* [1999] for a review).

Daneman and Carpenter explicitly based their test on the requirement to combine the storage and processing of information, as in our original model. We were therefore delighted that it proved so successful, but worried by the implications it had for our model, as it existed at the time.

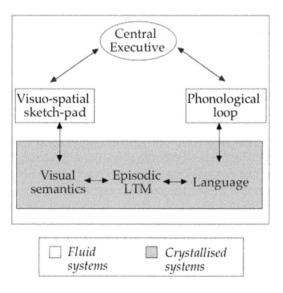

Figure 1.2 A modification of the original model to take account of the evidence of links between WM and LTM

This concerned our assumptions regarding the central executive. Initially, it had been assumed to be capable of combining both storage and attentional processing, an assumption that was so broad and unconstrained that it effectively became a homunculus, the little man who could do everything that might create problems for the model. This presented a problem. Homunculi are good servants but bad masters; if our homunculus was able to do everything, how could it be tested and how could the theory be developed? Homunculi can, however, be useful if constrained by specifying exactly what tasks they are to perform, and then attempting to explain each of these in turn. When all are explained, the homunculus can be retired.

We began by removing the storage role of the executive, assuming that it is a purely attentional system (Baddeley & Logie, 1999). Unfortunately, this assumption created difficulty in trying to explain just how our model provided the substantial storage needed by the Daneman and Carpenter (1980) WM span task, since neither the phonological loop nor the sketchpad has enough storage capacity to hold entire sentences. Faced with this dilemma, I finally added a fourth component, the *episodic buffer* (Baddeley, 2000). This is assumed to be a multidimensional storage system, capable of combining information from the visuospatial and verbal subsystems and linking it with further information from perception and LTM. It was assumed to hold a limited number of episodes (cf. Cowan, 2005), with each episode binding together information from these various sources into unified chunks. Finally, the buffer was assumed to be accessible to conscious awareness, and indeed to be the basis of conscious awareness which, like Baars (2002), I proposed serves the specific function of binding together information into consciously experienced arrays or episodes. A problem with this ambitious speculation is the danger that it simply becomes another homunculus, all powerful but untestable. The next stage in collaboration with Graham Hitch and Richard Allen has been to demonstrate that this is not the case.

The 2000 model was explicitly designed with the assumption that the episodic buffer was under the strict control of the central executive, just a short but important step from our original all-purpose homunculus. We chose to focus on the process of binding features into the chunks stored in the buffer, using our dual task methods to block the various components of the model, and in particular the central executive. Our initial speculative model predicted that without the strong support of the executive, such binding would break down. We looked at both the binding of colours and shapes into visual objects, and also at the binding of words into the chunks that occur in remembering meaningful sentences. This is a very powerful effect, with memory span for unrelated words being around 5, and for meaningful sentences around 15 words. We argued that if the executive is needed in order to perform this binding, then a demanding attentional task should interfere with binding and hence reduce the sentence advantage. This did not happen; an attentional task like concurrently counting backwards reduced overall performance, but had no impact on the difference between recall of unrelated words and sentences. We concluded that the advantage from the semantic and syntactic constraints of sentences came from LTM and was relatively automatic (Baddeley *et al.*, 2009b). An exactly equivalent story came from our study of the binding of features into objects (Allen *et al.*, 2006). We concluded that the episodic buffer is an important but passive store, capable of holding bound episodes, but not itself performing a binding function. We suggest that binding is likely to happen in different ways for language and vision, using different systems at different brain locations. It appears to function as a passive store rather than an attentionally dependent component of WM.

Our current, now rather more complex model is shown in Figure 1.3. It still has the three original basic components, with the addition of a fourth, the episodic buffer. The phonological and visuospatial subsystems feed into the buffer, and are themselves envisaged as bringing together information from a range of contributory sources. In the case of the sketchpad, these involve spatial location, colour and shape together with information from the complex systems underpinning touch and kinesthesis. The phonological loop is seen as bringing together information not only from speech, but also from language-related sources such as lip read and signed information, together with access from non-verbal sounds. Note that the loop is atypical in having a specific and very effective process for rehearsal via vocal and subvocal articulation. Rehearsal more generally within the system is assumed to be equivalent to Johnson's concept of *refreshing* (Park *et al.*, 2010), a process whereby focusing attention on an item within the episodic buffer allows continuous maintenance. This is more attentionally demanding than subvocal rehearsal, which is why we tend to use verbal rehearsal when possible.

An important issue remains however, that of how WM relates to LTM. Our current view is expressed in Figure 1.4 in which WM is seen as providing an interface between cognition and action. Our representation of cognition is intentionally kept general since the information entering WM can come from a range of different sources which themselves interact. A person in a digit span experiment for example will gain from his or her long-term knowledge of digit names; his or her span would be substantially less for digits in an unfamiliar language such as Finnish. In the case of vision, we tend to perceive the world in terms of meaningful objects, a process that itself depends on LTM. However, the function of all of this activity is to allow us to interact with the world, to take in information and to act upon it.

One final issue concerns the relationship between our version of WM and that proposed by Nelson Cowan whose chapter follows. Our theoretical views are frequently seen as in direct opposition; we focus on

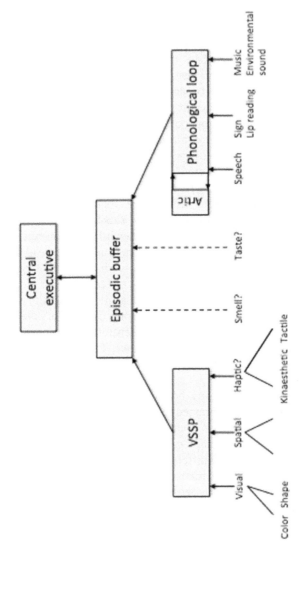

Figure 1.3 A speculative view of the flow of information from perception to WM

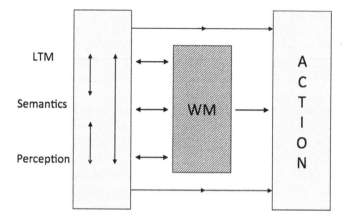

Figure 1.4 My current view of the complex and multiple links between WM and LTM

temporary storage and manipulation, while Nelson assumes a major role for activated LTM. However, as I think Nelson will agree, the differences are more apparent than real. His is a top-down approach, based initially on his interest in attention and its limited capacity. Our own approach has been essentially bottom-up, starting with memory span and only later worrying about the links with LTM. As Figure 1.4 shows, we are entirely comfortable with necessary links between WM and LTM, but regard the concept of activated LTM as a general term for a wide and complex range of processes. Such a concept acts as a place marker, allowing Nelson to focus on his principal interest, the role of attentional control. I see this as somewhat analogous to our use of the relatively broad and unspecified concept of the central executive, allowing us to focus more explicitly on the more tractable subsystems. As our models have developed, I feel they have come closer together, and would see Nelson's model within our own terms as focusing on the interface between the executive and the episodic buffer.

Do we differ? I think we do in that we assume that information is downloaded from LTM into the episodic buffer, whereas Nelson favours a system with pointers to the relevant LTM locations. We can neither of us currently think of a good way of resolving this, and whichever way it goes would not seriously challenge either of our broad theoretical frameworks. That does not mean, of course, that we will always agree on the best way of interpreting our data or choosing the next question to study, but it does mean that our approaches are sufficiently compatible to be mutually informative.

Working Memory and Second Language Learning

An important feature of the multi-component model is that it should be readily applicable to cognition beyond the bounds of the psychology laboratory. The learning of both first and second languages is an obvious area of application that has continued to interest me over the years. However, I cannot claim to have kept up with the large and expanding literature reflected in the chapters that follow. Hence, I am not able to provide an overview, but have instead agreed to offer some speculations as to how I might expect the current version of the model to apply to the learning of a second language.

It seems likely that different components of the model will be relevant to different aspects of the task of language learning, so I will go through the various subcomponents in turn and speculate as to where and how they might potentially be relevant.

The most obvious and I believe well established is the role of the phonological loop. We have argued that the loop plays a significant role in native language acquisition (Baddeley et al., 1998) with much of the evidence for this claim coming, as described earlier, from studies in which participants attempt to learn new items typically either foreign language vocabulary or non-words. Other supportive evidence has come from correlational studies based on second language learning in both children (Service, 1992) and adults (Atkins & Baddeley, 1998), with more recent evidence coming from the study of children participating in programmes involving an immersive language approach (Engel de Abreu & Gathercole, 2012; Nicolay & Poncelet, 2013).

All of this points to a link between the phonological loop and verbal LTM for language, a link that goes in both directions. Not only does the capacity of the phonological loop influence the rate of vocabulary acquisition, but also, conversely, a richer vocabulary is associated with increased verbal memory capacity, probably because the richer substrate of language habits allows elaborate and effective coding within the phonological loop (Gathercole, 1995).

In recent years, there has been considerable theoretical development in providing detailed models of how serial order is maintained in verbal STM (see Hurlstone et al. [2014] for a review). This in turn has encouraged theorists to explore ways in which information appears to be transferred from the phonological loop into LTM. Their tool of choice has been the Hebb Effect. This stems from the demonstration by Hebb (1961) of a long-term component in the standard serial verbal recall task. He presented participants with sequences of nine random digits for immediate recall. Each sequence appeared to be different, but in fact every third string was an exact repetition. Performance on these gradually improved, with no difference being found between people who noticed the repetition and those who did not. Melton (1963) interpreted this result as implying that it was only necessary to assume one type of memory, LTM; others disagreed, proposing that the task itself contained both STM and LTM components. Recent studies have supported this claim, demonstrating that factors influencing immediate verbal recall, such as articulatory suppression and phonological similarity, do not influence the Hebb Effect (Hebb, 1961). This is currently a very lively area that is likely to have long-term implications for implicit aspects of second language learning (see Page *et al.* [2013] for a recent survey of this area).

In conclusion, there appears to be considerable evidence for the importance of the phonological loop in language acquisition; however, this does not necessarily demonstrate that it is essential rather than useful. For example, SR, a graduate student who appeared to have a developmental weakness in STM, found great difficulty in acquiring new languages, but had a good vocabulary in his own, suggesting that the loop is a very helpful but not essential tool in language acquisition (Baddeley, 1993).

While the case for the acquisition of vocabulary is reasonably strong, there is to the best of my knowledge, much less on the role of the loop in acquiring grammar. Previous studies (Atkins & Baddeley, 1998; Service, 1992) of language acquisition more broadly could indeed reflect a combination of vocabulary and grammar, but in these cases it is hard to untangle the two. I know of only two studies that specifically focus on grammar, one on acquiring a specific grammatical form within Welsh (Ellis & Sinclair, 1996) and a more recent attempt to evaluate the influence of the phonological loop on the acquisition of artificial grammars (Andrade & Baddeley, 2011). I suspect, however, that this is an area that may have considerable research of which I am unaware.

In contrast to the extensive research on the phonological loop and second language learning, I know of very little concerned with a possible role of the visuospatial sketchpad. At a purely speculative level, it might conceivably play a role in the acquisition of novel script such as that used in Arabic or Hebrew, or in visually complex orthographies such as Chinese. This would seem to be an interesting area to investigate, and may indeed have already been explored.

One component of WM that one might expect to influence second language learning is the central executive. I know of very little work directly focused on this, but it would be surprising if it did not play a relatively substantial part, given the high correlation with measures of intelligence (Engle *et al.*, 1999) and its relevance to learning in general (Vicari & Carlessimo, 2002). It is unclear, however, whether the executive has any more impact on second language learning than on other types of learning. Where there are differential patterns within learning disability, such as are found in Down's syndrome, they appear to be associated with a particular deficit in the phonological loop (see Baddeley & Jarrold [2007] for a review). However, even within a syndrome, patterns of deficit may vary, with Vallar and Papagno (1993) describing a highly atypical young woman with Down's syndrome who had mastered several languages and who had a much greater phonological loop capacity than is typical in Down's syndrome.

One might also expect an interaction between the central executive and the phonological loop such that good executive capacities would potentially mitigate limitations in the phonological loop. Research by Gathercole and colleagues on the academic achievement of schoolchildren suggests that a major problem in acquiring both vocabulary and reading skills occurs when a child has poor capacity of both the loop and executive (Gathercole et al., 2006). However, evidence from our previously described graduate student, SR, suggests that even a high level of intelligence is not sufficient to overcome problems in second language learning presented by a limited phonological loop (Baddeley, 1993).

This raises the question of how SR's vocabulary and general language development managed to be apparently normal. I suspect that this may well reflect differences in the pattern of acquisition of first and second languages, with the distributed nature of the normal pattern of first language acquisition potentially relying more heavily on implicit learning procedures that differ from the WM components. As you may recall, Page et al. (2013), using the Hebb repeating sequence effect, found that variables influencing immediate verbal recall such as phonological similarity and articulatory suppression, failed to impact on the long-term Hebb Effect.

One way in which the central executive might influence language acquisition is through its impact on comprehension. As previously described, Daneman and Carpenter's (1980) measure of WM capacity was very effective at predicting prose comprehension, presumably because adequate comprehension demands the capacity to build up an argument or a scene in LTM, which in turn depends on the capacity to link ideas together in a coherent way. However, the executive contribution to comprehension may be less than one might expect; Hambrick and Engle (2002) found a significant but relatively small contribution of WM span to the capacity to remember a baseball passage compared to a much larger contribution from baseball knowledge, while work of our own suggests that there is much less interference between comprehension and concurrent tasks than one might expect (Baddeley et al., 2009).

If research on the role of the central executive is somewhat sparse, that on the episodic buffer is to my knowledge virtually non-existent. This no doubt stems partly from the problem that we still know relatively little about the buffer, other than that it appears to be essentially passive and limited in capacity, with no currently agreed methods of measuring such capacity, although we are inclined to Nelson Cowan's (2005) maximum of five episodes or chunks.

In conclusion, the development of the WM model has benefited substantially from research on both first and second language learning. The chapters that follow reflect the impressive liveliness of the field and do, I hope, bode well for our understanding of both second language learning and WM.

References

Allen, R., Baddeley, A.D. and Hitch, G.J. (2006) Is the binding of visual features in working memory resource-demanding? *Journal of Experimental Psychology: General* 135, 298–313.

Andrade, J. and Baddeley, A. (2011) The contribution of phonological short-term memory to artificial grammar learning. *Quarterly Journal of Experimental Psychology* 64, 960–974. doi: 10.1080/17470218.2010.533440

Atkins, P.W.B. and Baddeley, A.D. (1998) Working memory and distributed vocabulary learning. *Applied Psycholinguistics* 19, 537–552.

Atkinson, R.C. and Shiffrin, R.M. (1968) Human memory: A proposed system and its control processes. In K.W. Spence and J.T. Spence (eds) *The Psychology of Learning and Motivation: Advances in Research and Theory* (Vol. 2; pp. 89–195). New York: Academic Press.

Baars, B.J. (2002) The conscious access hypothesis: Origins and recent evidence. *Trends in Cognitive Sciences* 6 (1), 47–52.

Baddeley, A. (1993) Short-term phonological memory and long-term learning: A single case study. *European Journal of Cognitive Psychology* 5, 129–148.

Baddeley, A. (2012) Working memory, theories models and controversy. *The Annual Review of Psychology* 63, 12.11–12.29.

Baddeley, A.D. (2000) The episodic buffer: A new component of working memory? *Trends in Cognitive Sciences* 4 (11), 417–423.

Baddeley, A.D. and Hitch, G.J. (1974) Working memory. In G.A. Bower (ed.) *Recent Advances in Learning and Motivation* (Vol. 8; pp. 47–89). New York: Academic Press.

Baddeley, A.D., Papagno, C. and Vallar, G. (1988) When long-term learning depends on short-term storage. *Journal of Memory and Language* 27, 586–595.

Baddeley, A.D., Gathercole, S.E. and Papagno, C. (1998) The phonological loop as a language learning device. *Psychological Review* 105 (1), 158–173.

Baddeley, A.D. and Logie, R.H. (1999) Working memory: The multiple component model. In A. Miyake and P. Shah (eds) *Models of Working Memory: Mechanisms of Active Maintenance and Executive Control* (pp. 28–61). New York: Cambridge University Press.

Baddeley, A.D. and Jarrold, C. (2007) Working memory and Down syndrome. *Journal of Intellectual Disability Research* 51, 925–931.

Baddeley, A.D., Eysenck, M. and Anderson, M.C. (2015) *Essentials of Human Memory* (2nd edn). Hove: Psychology Press.

Baddeley, A.D., Hitch, G.J. and Allen, R.J. (2009) Working memory and binding in sentence recall. *Journal of Memory and Language* 61, 438–456.

Broadbent, D.E. (1958) *Perception and Communication*. London: Pergamon Press.

Cowan, N. (2005) *Working Memory Capacity*. Hove: Psychology Press.

Daneman, M. and Carpenter, P.A. (1980) Individual differences in working memory and reading. *Journal of Verbal Learning and Verbal Behaviour* 19, 450–466.

Daneman, M. and Green, I. (1986) Individual differences in comprehending and producing words in context. *Journal of Memory and Language* 25, 1–18.

Ellis, N.C. and Sinclair, S.G. (1996) Working memory in the acquisition of vocabulary and syntax: Putting language in good order. *Quarterly Journal of Experimental Psychology* 49(A), 234–250.

Engel de Abreu, P.M.J. and Gathercole, S.E. (2012) Executive and phonological processes in second language acquisition. *Journal of Educational Psychology* 104, 976–986. doi: 10.1037/a0028390

Engle, R.W., Tuholski, S.W., Laughlin, J.E. and Conway, A.R.A. (1999) Working memory, short-term memory, and general fluid intelligence: A latent-variable approach. *Journal of Experimental Psychology: General* 128 (3), 309–331.

Gathercole, S.E. (1995) Is nonword repetition a test of phonological memory or long-term knowledge? It all depends on the nonwords. *Memory and Cognition* 23, 83–94.

Gathercole, S.E., Lamont, E. and Alloway, T.P. (2006) Working memory in the classroom. In S. Pickering (ed.) *Working Memory and Education* (pp. 220–241). London: Elsevier Press.

Hambrick, D.Z. and Engle, R.W. (2002) Effects of domain knowledge, working memory capacity and age on cognitive performance: An investigation of the knowledge-is-power hypothesis. *Cognitive Psychology* 44, 339–387.

Hebb, D.O. (1961) Distinctive features of learning in the higher animal. In J.F. Delafresnaye (ed.) *Brain Mechanisms and Learning* (pp. 37–46). New York: Oxford University Press.

Hurlstone, M.J., Hitch, G.J. and Baddeley, A.D. (2014) Memory for serial order across domains: An overview of the literature and directions for future research. *Psychological Bulletin* 140(2), 339–373.

Melton, A.W. (1963) Implications of short-term memory for a general theory of memory. *Journal of Verbal Learning and Verbal Behavior* 2, 1.21.

Nicolay, A.C. and Poncelet, M. (2013) Cognitive abilities underlying second-language vocabulary acquisition in an early second-language immersion education context: A longitudinal study. *Journal of Experimental Child Psychology,* 115, 655–671. doi: 10.1016/jecp.2013.04.002

Page, M.P.A., Cumming, N., Norris, D., McNeil, A.M. and Hitch, G.J. (2013) Repetition-spacing and item-overlap effects in the Hebb repetition task. *Journal of Memory & Language* 69, 506–526.

Papagno, C., Valentine, T. and Baddeley, A.D. (1991) Phonological short-term memory and foreign language vocabulary learning. *Journal of Memory and Language* 30, 331–347.

Papagno, C. and Vallar, G. (1995) Verbal short-term memory and vocabulary learning in polyglots. *Quarterly Journal of Experimental Psychology* 48A, 98–107.

Park, S., Chun, M.M. and Johnson, M.K. (2010) Refreshing and integrating visual scenes in scene-selective cortex. *Journal of Cognitive Neuroscience* 22, 2813–2822.

Service, E. (1992) Phonology, working memory and foreign-language learning. *Quarterly Journal of Experimental Psychology* 45A (1), 21–50.

Vallar, G. and Baddeley, A.D. (1987) Phonological short-term store and sentence processing. *Cognitive Neuropsychology* 4, 417–438.

Vallar, G. and Papagno, C. (1993) Preserved vocabulary acquisition in Down's syndrome: The role of phonological short-term memory. *Cortex* 29, 467–483.

Vicari, S. and Carlesimo, G.A. (2002) Children with intellectual disabilities. In A.D. Baddeley, M.D. Kopelman and B.A. Wilson (eds) *Handbook of Memory Disorders* (2nd edn; pp. 501–520). Chichester: Wiley.

2 Second Language Use, Theories of Working Memory and the Vennian Mind

Nelson Cowan

Introduction

The parts of the title of this chapter are also the headings of its three sections. In turn, they consider what second language use may be like, how theories of working memory might be of importance in understanding second language use and how the structures of the existing theories may need to be broadened further to accommodate all of the important concepts in second language use. My expertise is not in second language use, so readers may have to cut me some slack to accept, for the sake of argument, my examples in that domain.

Second Language Use

Imagine yourself in a rather dire circumstance in the ancient world. In your home territory, a ferocious dispute has taken place and you find yourself a wandering refugee. You and your family arrive at a territory in which you are treated passably well, but with a great deal of suspicion regarding your intentions. You have had very little prior contact with the language spoken in your new refuge, and you are trying to learn the words that you urgently need to get food and shelter and put your new hosts at ease. Suddenly, your spouse and children are no longer just responsibilities to you in your troubled journey; they are assets, in that they might notice language meanings that you have overlooked. You must be careful, though. If you miss a critical meaning, your family might miss the opportunity to have warm shelter that night. If you think you have heard that you are invited to sit down but a certain word is not exactly what you thought, you might seriously offend your hosts. Slight subtleties of meaning may make a big practical difference, as in the difference between *come* and *go*. Slight sounds may matter, as in the difference between *folk* and *foe*. Idiomatic expressions might concern you; the expression *we don't mind* means *we think that it is all right*, but a foreign visitor might take it to mean *we don't pay attention* (with reference to the human *mind*). With the wrong turn of a phrase, you might accidentally insult one of their deities. (If one translates *it is raining* into a certain other language literally, might one imply that the deity is an *it* rather than a *he* or *she*, and would that be insulting?) You use everything at your disposal to try to interpret the language or give it an educated guess; tones of voice, facial expressions, gestures and the situational context.

It is easy to understand that under such a circumstance as the acquisition or use of a second language, certain properties and limitations of the human mind are critically important for success. Key among these properties and limitations are the characteristics of human working memory, the faculty that retains a small number of things at a time and allows us to work with them mentally. What sets language apart from other forms of communication is the arbitrary relations between symbols – in the form of words – and the meanings symbolised. These arbitrary relations allow a great many meanings to be expressed in symbolic form by combining the symbols in new ways. We can eventually learn many of the mappings between language and meaning but new ones are difficult to keep in mind for long; the mind is overwhelmed with new information to learn. The capacity of working memory will determine how complex can be the learned information. For example, in order to understand the meaning of the word *tiger*, one must grasp that it is a big cat with stripes. Lose any part of that definition and a different animal could fit the bill (e.g. a small cat with stripes, a zebra or a lion). This sort of mistake often happens in young children, and it may be that their small working memories compared to adults are one reason.

Theories of Working Memory

The term 'working memory' was used by Miller *et al.* (1960) to describe memory for plans one hoped to carry out, and the small goals that had to be met along the way to an ultimate goal. Such plans could easily include those of language. In a running fashion, people plan ahead when formulating sentences and then fill in the words at a later point and the phonemes within those words still later, just before actually speaking them. That process is clear, for example, in a corpus of speech transposition errors that show longer-distance swaps in the case of higher-level units (Fromkin, 1973). Any of the phases of planning can be affected by the novelties of a new language that are discrepant from one's first language.

Working memory, of course, must also come into play during language comprehension, when the words presented by mid-sentence may not add up to a sensible thought until words coming later clarify them. This is all the more important when one does not understand some of the words and must rely more heavily on the total context to help guide understanding, or an educated guess at understanding. In the sense of Miller *et al.* (1960), one must plan to construct a meaningful interpretation of the sentence, ruling out other possible meanings, or possibly keeping in mind more than one possible meaning until the situation makes clear which one was actually meant.

Miller *et al.* (1960) provided only an intuitive sketch of the idea of working memory, though. Does the actual theory of working memory make a difference for an understanding of second language acquisition and processing? I believe it does, for reasons that I will explain.

The idea of something like working memory as a storage buffer was prevalent throughout the early phase of cognitive psychology, including well-known works, especially a book titled *Communication and Perception* by Broadbent (1958), moving away from behaviourism and towards a cognitive approach; and then a book chapter by Atkinson and Shiffrin (1968), emphasising the importance of modelling processes that controlled the flow of information into and out of working memory. This view of a unified working memory changed with the seminal chapter by Baddeley and Hitch (1974), which preserved the central store but noted that there also appeared to be two dissociable, auxiliary storage units. These were specific on the one hand to phonological information (later called the phonological loop, a reference to the importance of covert verbal rehearsal of the phonological information) and on the other hand to visual, spatial information (the visuospatial sketchpad). All of the components operating together as a system were collectively termed 'working memory'.

Perhaps the most important type of evidence for this multi-component system of Baddeley and Hitch (1974) was that phonological inputs heavily interfered with other phonological information in working memory but interfered much less with non-verbal, visual or spatial information in working memory, and vice versa. That is, interference patterns were pretty domain specific, which seemed to indicate separate stores for the different kinds of information. Baddeley (1986) thought he could use only these two peripheral storage buffers, with the additional catch-all, general-purpose central storage component mentioned in passing by Baddeley and Hitch omitted for the sake of parsimony. An attention-related, central executive component to carry out processing was now conceived as being devoid of actual storage. Baddeley (2000), however, found the model unable to explain some types of memory (for example, memory for the association or binding between a verbal item and a spatial location; memory for semantic units or syntactic structures). He therefore added the episodic buffer to cover such cases. It has yet to be rigorously described but is the topic of considerable ongoing research. The seeds of the episodic buffer, however, appear to be present in the central storage component mentioned by Baddeley and Hitch, and in the earlier unified approaches to working memory.

We have already seen in my language examples that second language use must involve the coordination of many kinds of information. The language user may have to interpret orthography and spatial or visual context, as well as semantic and pragmatic context, in addition to phonological information. Consequently, from a multi-storage viewpoint, all of the storage buffers are likely to get a workout during the acquisition and processing of a second language.

One can do quite well in discussing language processing with this model, but a lot may rest on getting beyond a naïve interpretation of the model. In the naïve interpretation, each stimulus goes to a certain buffer. If the stimulus has phonological value it goes to phonological storage, if it has visuospatial value it goes to the sketchpad and if it somehow does not fit these categories it goes to the episodic buffer. That kind of interpretation has been the subject of jokes; it is like a lampoon parody I once read about how one's body is nourished when one eats a cheeseburger (the slice of cheese goes to the right arm, the top of the bun to the right leg, the meat to the head and so on). The problem with the simplistic interpretation of the multimodal working memory model is that the stimulus does not know where it should go, and it is unclear what mechanism would direct it to the right store. Instead, it seems more likely that a stimulus activates multiple features at the same time. A printed word can activate orthographic, phonological and semantic features and, in fact, focusing attention on the latter deeper features is better for long-term remembering than focusing on features close to the surface of the stimulus (Craik & Tulving, 1975). The different features allow different types of language processing to take place.

The phonological representation is presumably of special use for rote rehearsal, which may be a good way to remember or repeat new sequences of phonological material, such as ordered lists of words (as in a phrase that one doesn't completely understand) or ordered sequences of syllables (as in a new word that one is just learning). The key importance of a phonological representation for word learning is well established (Baddeley et al., 1998). However, if one can hold in mind semantic and visual information concurrently, that should be quite advantageous for the interpretation of language in real time. One might remember the sound of a word in a foreign language, a few recent visual events that may be candidates for the meaning of this new word and the context in terms of the meaning of the interaction taking place (e.g. commerce, romance, education and conflict). All of this information along with long-term knowledge that has been built up could lead to a new fusion; the fusion may be a new hypothesis about the meaning of this word, which is then stored in long-term memory.

The theoretical framework of Cowan (1988, 1999) is often viewed as a unitary framework that is devoid of the modules of Baddeley and Hitch (1974) or Baddeley (2000). That was not exactly the intent. Cowan just considered that the Baddeley and Hitch model was tailored to the types of stimuli that they used in their experiments, and taken by the rest of the world as a general model of how the human mind operates with respect to working memory. It seems unlikely that it can be taken as so general. There was an emphasis in the model on the classic finding (Conrad, 1964) that confusions between printed letters in working memory are primarily acoustic rather than visual in nature; the most common confusions between English letters are between consonants with names that rhyme (e.g. between *B, C, D, G, P, T, V, Z* except when *Z* is pronounced 'zed'). Although this is a profound finding that shows the importance of an internal phonological code, there were later findings of visual confusions between letters in working memory as well (Logie *et al.*, 2000). Moreover, there are sensory features that are activated in addition to phonological ones; memory for the end of a verbal list is typically superior with acoustic as compared to written presentation (for a review, see Penney [1989]). There are modalities that have not been included in the Baddeley model, such as tactile, olfactory and gustatory stimuli and muscle senses. It is difficult for all of these stimuli and feature types to be stuffed into the several stores in the multistore model.

What Cowan (1988, 1999) assumed instead is that a stimulus activates many kinds of features in long-term memory. Subsequent stimuli with some similar features may interfere with memory for those features in the previous stimuli. (That assumption can account for dissociations between types of memoranda and different types of interference effects.) For example, if the word *horse* is followed by a picture of a cat, there will be some interference with the semantic features of the horse but very little interference with the phonological or orthographic features. If the word *laugh* is followed by *ghost*, there may be orthographic interference because of the *gh* appearing in two different contexts (with completely different pronunciations). If *root* is followed by *route*, the interference is with phonological features, making rote verbal rehearsal risky as the meaning might not be preserved, unless there is a separate effort to remember the meaning specifically.

Instead of concluding that the many different types of features each have their own modules, Cowan (1988, 1999) assumed that the features all reflect temporary activation of long-term memory information. There is clearly a structure to the brain that implies that different kinds of stimuli activate different brain patterns. Nevertheless, the taxonomy of this activation was taken to be complex and not yet fully known, so any subdivisions into specific modules were not marked in the model by Cowan, at least for the time being.

Cowan (1988, 1999) also reserved a special role for attention in the model. A subset of the information in the activated part of long-term memory is in the focus of attention, and even the part of activation outside of the focus of attention is considered part of working memory. Historically, the activated portion of long-term memory and the focus of attention are reminiscent of the concepts of Hebb (1949) and James (1890), respectively, and something like this whole ensemble can be found, I am told, in the previous German writings of Wilhelm Wundt.

A considerable variety of studies limits the information in the focus of attention to about three to five meaningful items in normal adults (Cowan, 2001). People are assumed to be able to think about these items consciously and combine them to form new concepts. That is not necessarily true of the information that is in working memory but outside of the focus of attention. It can be fragmentary, consisting of bundles of features that can be brought into focus for further consideration, maybe a few at a time, but these activated features do not necessarily form a meaningful pattern all together.

In language learning, a key issue I see is whether the focus of attention plays a special role in combining diverse sources of information to arrive at new composites (e.g. a new word connected to its meaning in the focus of attention). This might correspond to the function of the episodic buffer in the model of Baddeley (2000), though the jury may still be out, in his view, as to how the episodic buffer relates to attention (for recent work, see Allen *et al.* [2012]).

A key difference between the two different theories of working memory is in the prediction about how much of a trade-off there will be between verbal information and non-verbal visual information when both have to be retained at the same time. The trade-off presumably comes from the use of the focus of attention to hold information about either type of stimulus, with the capacity limit applying across both types. The limit should be especially notable when there is a mask to prevent sensory information from being used as an auxiliary store and when there are precautions to prevent covert verbal rehearsal from being used. Saults and Cowan (2007) presented verbal stimuli as concurrent spatial arrays in different voices, making the voices difficult to rehearse. They found a considerable trade-off between memory for voice–digit pairing, on the one hand, and colour–location pairing, on the other hand (see also Morey *et al.*, 2011).

For language learning, one implication of this trade-off in working memory is that keeping in mind several verbal items at once and several visual items concurrently might create conflict. To learn and use language effectively, that conflict has to be managed by limiting the focus of attention. Either a teacher has to help the learner by limiting the amount of multimodal information to be integrated, or the student or learner has to learn to manage the information ideally on his or her own (e.g. when learning word referents, perhaps by adopting a strategy that involves concentrating on one spoken word at a time and trying to match it to several potential referents sequentially). For further discussion, see Cowan (2013, 2014).

There is now neuroimaging evidence supporting the existence of brain regions that support a focus of attention that includes several items at once. Cowan *et al.* (2011) found activity in the left intraparietal sulcus that increased as a function of the number of items to be held in working memory, no matter whether those items were spoken letters, coloured squares or some combination of the two. This area had previously been shown to be activated in attention tasks even when working memory was not involved, and to respond to increasing visual working memory loads in a manner mirroring capacity according to behavioural results.

Lewis-Peacock *et al.* (2012) showed that there is also brain activity specific to the item or items being used in the focus of attention. In one experiment, they used multivoxel pattern analysis to identify patterns corresponding to three different categories: words for which a synonym judgement was required, pseudowords for which a rhyme judgement was required and line segments for which a spatial orientation judgement was required. Then these items were used in a same-different task with two cues in succession, to yield some interesting information about what is active in working memory. For example, at the beginning of a trial, a word might be presented along with line segments. The first cue might indicate that the first test would be on a word. Then a word would be presented and the required response would be to indicate whether it is the same as the originally presented word. The second cue could indicate that what was coming next was another word, or a line segment. When the latter was the case, the results were especially interesting. The multivoxel pattern activity for the first-tested category was high after the first cue, and then was reduced after the second cue when it involved a switch to the other category. More interestingly, the pattern activity for the second-tested category suddenly rose after the second cue. That is to say, when the item to be tested second (the line segment in the example) was in the activated part of long-term memory and therefore was still retrievable, there was no multivoxel pattern activity for it; but when the cue indicated that it would now be tested, the multivoxel pattern activity rose. This activity thus indicates that an item is in the focus of attention. Perhaps what Cowan (1988) called activated long-term memory outside of the focus of attention is preserved through an ionic balance in the brain that is not reflected by available magnetic resonance imaging (MRI) techniques; observable activation seems to reflect the information in the focus of attention. When two items are being used at the same time, the multivoxel pattern activity for both of them can be seen concurrently, indicating that the focus of attention can hold more than one item at a time.

The multivoxel pattern activity for the items appears not in the intraparietal sulcus, but in posterior visual regions. The warranted conclusion appears to be that the sensory processing regions represent the actual information, whereas the focus of attention holds pointers to a limited number of items represented in the activated portion of long-term memory. The frontal-parietal regions do show multivoxel pattern activity reflecting not the stimulus types, but the task instructions (Riggall & Postle, 2012).

What is the special significance of the focus of attention, as compared to the information represented in working memory outside of that focus? I believe that the focus of attention may be the workshop whereby new concepts are formed, by linking together information that is currently in focus to form new information. An example is the coexistence of *big+striped+cat* in the focus of attention, to form the folk concept of a tiger. Halford *et al.* (2007) suggested that the childhood development of cognition involves the increasing amount of complexity that can be understood as the number of items that can be cross-tabulated in a limited-capacity working memory increase.

There is little direct evidence that this cross-tabulation must occur in the focus of attention, but Cowan *et al.* (2013) made a start towards that end. Participants received lists of three, six or nine items at once and were to indicate which item in the list was 'most interesting'. Later, there was a surprise test on whether pairs of words came from nearby serial positions in the same list, or from nearby serial positions in different lists. Presumably, nearby items from the same list would have coexisted in the focus of attention much more often for lists of three items (within the presumed capacity of the focus of attention) and less often for longer lists of six or nine items. Performance on the surprise associative memory task was much better for lists of three items than for lists of six or nine items, which were both not much better than chance. So it may be, as Cowan (1999) suggested, that the linking together of elements to form new concepts must take place in the focus of attention.

In short, the model of Cowan (1988, 1999, 2001) has borrowed much from the previous model of Baddeley and Hitch (1974), but has placed more emphasis on the diversity of inputs that must be handled (a point with which seems in agreement with Baddeley [2000]), and more emphasis on the role of the focus of attention in storing and recombining information.

How can humans conquer complex languages using such a minimal system, one that can only hold several items at once in the focus of attention while rehearsing a few more items outside of the focus and adding in just a little more potentially relevant visual and semantic information, in case it's needed? The key to that question was addressed by Miller (1956) in his classic article, and has been brought up again in more recent work (e.g. Cowan *et al.*, 2012). The answer is in the use of long-term memory to form new chunks. The capacity limit is in chunks, not items. Thus, if one is presented with the series of letters FBICIAIRS to be remembered, one may recognise the three-letter acronyms for three US agencies, FBI, CIA and IRS, simplifying the task from nine letter chunks down to three acronym chunks. This simplification presumably occurs in many ways during language acquisition and comprehension.

One builds a unified semantic structure as one listens to language and is forced to throw away much of the verbatim information because working memory cannot hold it (Fedorenko *et al.*, 2007; Jarvella, 1970), or one interprets a sentence in a manner that includes shorter separate parts until the whole thing can be integrated (Swets *et al.*, 2007). In some cases, people even tend to ignore the confining details of syntax and often just retain semantic gist elements that arise (Ferreira *et al.*, 2002). For example, one may encounter the sentence, *While Stuart dressed the baby played*, and retain from that sentence the propositions that (1) Stuart dressed the baby and (2) the baby played, even though there is no grammatically correct reading of the sentence that allows both of those two propositions. (Stuart had to have dressed himself, not the baby.) So in the real world, there does not seem to be a syntactic module that is used in a way that isolates it from concerns of a general working memory, as Caplan *et al.* (2007) suggested. In second language use, there presumably is an especially prevalent use of non-linguistic information to complement and support the limited linguistic information available.

The Vennian Mind

It is worth considering the structures that we have drawn upon in describing the working memory system and its relation to language. The model of Baddeley and Hitch (1974) is one in which boxes are used separately, as modules. This representation provides a nice, simple starting point for the field, but it is not easy to understand in neural terms if some of the same assemblies of cells participate in more than one type of working memory activity (cf. Hebb, 1949). Cowan (1988) introduced a different representation in which major faculties occurred in an embedded fashion, with the focus of attention embedded within the activated portion of long-term memory, which is in turn embedded in the memory system at large. This conception can be more brain-friendly in allowing embedded relations; thus, the same neurons can participate in representing information both in and out of the focus of attention, but with additional processes kicking in for the attended information.

Even this embedded structure, however, is too confining to describe the mechanisms we have discussed. We need the representation commonly attributed to Venn (1880), whose diagrams showed overlapping circles to represent sets of elements that were partly convergent and partly different. In linguistics, a given verbal stimulus can activate visual, orthographic, phonological, morphological (word-form), syntactic, semantic and pragmatic features all at once; two stimuli often overlap in some features and differ in others. The overlapping features can cause one idea or stimulus to prime or activate a related idea, but concurrently activated items with overlapping features also can cause mutual interference.

An open question is what happens to these overlapping items in the focus of attention. Cowan (2001) suggested that the focus of attention was simply limited by an absolute number of chunks but, even if that is so, our recent unpublished work suggests that the focus of attention does not stay on the job in the same way throughout a trial. Items in a set may be taken into the focus of attention only momentarily, so that a meaningful configuration of the items can be set up in activated long-term memory. This could be an important mechanism for the chunking of separate words and phrases into a coherent message that is comprehended.

In preparing an interesting sentence to express an idea, the basic idea may be held in the speaker's working memory while a configuration of colourful words might be brought to mind that, together, express that idea well. These components might be retained while a syntactic structure is mentally designed. The focus of attention may prove small enough that these components of speech (phonological, semantic, syntactic, etc.) cannot all be kept in the focus of attention at once as separate configurations; attention probably must be shuttled between them to keep the components sufficiently active (cf. Barrouillet *et al.*, 2011; Vergauwe *et al.*, 2014). Extraneous distractions (notably emotion-laden events) also compete with the linguistic elements and lead to errors. The need to aim and continually shift the focus of attention may contribute to the struggle, hesitations and slips of the tongue that can become so painfully apparent in the expression of thought, especially in a language other than one's native tongue.

References

Allen, R.J., Hitch, G.J., Mate, J. and Baddeley, A.D. (2012) Feature binding and attention in working memory: A resolution of previous contradictory findings. *Quarterly Journal of Experimental Psychology* 65, 2369–2383.

Atkinson, R.C. and Shiffrin, R.M. (1968) Human memory: A proposed system and its control processes. In K.W. Spence and J.T. Spence (eds) *The Psychology of Learning and Motivation: Advances in Research and Theory* (Vol. 2; pp. 89–195). New York: Academic Press.

Baddeley, A. (2000) The episodic buffer: A new component of working memory? *Trends in Cognitive Sciences* 4, 417–423.

Baddeley, A.D. (1986) *Working Memory*. Oxford: Clarendon Press.

Baddeley, A.D. and Hitch, G. (1974) Working memory. In G.H. Bower (ed.) *The Psychology of Learning and Motivation* (Vol. 8; pp. 47–89). New York: Academic Press.

Baddeley, A.D., Gathercole, S.E. and Papagno, C. (1998) The phonological loop as a language learning device. *Psychological Review* 105, 158–173.

Barrouillet, P., Portrat, S. and Camos, V. (2011) On the law relating processing to storage in working memory. *Psychological Review* 118, 175–192.

Broadbent, D.E. (1958) *Perception and Communication*. New York: Pergamon Press.

Caplan, D., Waters, G. and DeDe, G. (2007) Specialized verbal working memory for language comprehension. In A.R.A. Conway, C. Jarrold, M.J. Kane, A. Miyake and

J.N. Towse (eds) *Variation in Working Memory* (pp. 272–302). New York: Oxford University Press.

Conrad, R. (1964) Acoustic confusion in immediate memory. *British Journal of Psychology* 55, 75–84.

Cowan, N. (1988) Evolving conceptions of memory storage, selective attention, and their mutual constraints within the human information processing system. *Psychological Bulletin* 104, 163–191.

Cowan, N. (1999) An embedded-processes model of working memory. In A. Miyake and P. Shah (eds) *Models of Working Memory: Mechanisms of Active Maintenance and Executive Control* (pp. 62–101). Cambridge: Cambridge University Press.

Cowan, N. (2001) The magical number 4 in short-term memory: A reconsideration of mental storage capacity. *Behavioral and Brain Sciences* 24, 87–185.

Cowan, N. (2013) Working memory and attention in language use. In J. Guandouzi, F. Loncke and M.J. Williams (eds) *The Handbook of Psycholinguistics and Cognitive Processes* (pp. 75–97). London: Psychology Press.

Cowan, N. (2014) Working memory underpins cognitive development, learning, and education. *Educational Psychology Review* 26 (2), 197–223.

Cowan, N., Li, D., Moffitt, A., Becker, T.M., Martin, E.A., Saults, J.S. and Christ, S.E. (2011) A neural region of abstract working memory. *Journal of Cognitive Neuroscience* 23, 2852–2863.

Cowan, N., Rouder, J.N., Blume, C.L. and Saults, J.S. (2012) Models of verbal working memory capacity: What does it take to make them work? *Psychological Review* 119, 480–499.

Cowan, N., Donnell, K. and Saults, J.S. (2013) A list-length constraint on incidental item-to-item associations. *Psychonomic Bulletin & Review* 20, 1253–1258.

Craik, F.I.M. and Tulving, E. (1975) Depth of processing and the retention of words in episodic memory. *Journal of Experimental Psychology: General* 104, 268–294.

Fedorenko, E., Gibson, E. and Rohde, D. (2007) The nature of working memory in linguistic, arithmetic and spatial integration processes. *Journal of Memory and Language* 56, 246–269.

Ferreira, F., Bailey, K.G.D. and Ferraro, V. (2002) Good-enough representations in language comprehension. *Current Directions in Psychological Science* 11, 11–15.

Fromkin, V.A. (ed.) (1973) *Speech Errors as Linguistic Evidence*. The Hague: Mouton.

Halford, G.S., Cowan, N. and Andrews, G. (2007) Separating cognitive capacity from knowledge: A new hypothesis. *Trends in Cognitive Sciences*, 11, 236–242.

Hebb, D.O. (1949) *Organization of Behavior*. New York: Wiley.

James, W. (1890) *The Principles of Psychology*. New York: Henry Holt.

Jarvella, R.J. (1970) Effects of syntax on running memory span for connected discourse. *Psychonomic Science* 19, 235–236.

Lewis-Peacock, J.A., Drysdale, A.T., Oberauer, K. and Postle, B.R. (2012) Neural evidence for a distinction between short-term memory and the focus of attention. *Journal of Cognitive Neuroscience* 24, 61–79.

Logie, R.H., Della Sala, S., Wynn, V. and Baddeley, A.D. (2000) Visual similarity effects in immediate verbal serial recall. *Quarterly Journal of Experimental Psychology* 53A, 626–646.

Miller, G.A. (1956) The magical number seven, plus or minus two: Some limits on our capacity for processing information. *Psychological Review* 63, 81–97.

Miller, G.A., Galanter, E. and Pribram, K.H. (1960) *Plans and the Structure of Behavior*. New York: Holt, Rinehart and Winston, Inc.

Morey, C.C., Cowan, N., Morey, R.D. and Rouder, J.N. (2011) Flexible attention allocation to visual and auditory working memory tasks: Manipulating reward induces a tradeoff. *Attention, Perception, & Psychophysics* 73, 458–472.

Morey, C.C. and Bieler, M. (2013) Visual working memory always requires general attention. *Psychonomic Bulletin and Review* 20, 163–170.

Penney, C.G. (1989) Modality effects and the structure of short-term verbal memory. *Memory & Cognition* 17, 398–422.

Riggall, A.C. and Postle, B.R. (2012) The relationship between working memory storage and elevated activity as measured with functional magnetic resonance imaging. *The Journal of Neuroscience* 32 (38), 12990–12998.

Saults, J.S. and Cowan, N. (2007) A central capacity limit to the simultaneous storage of visual and auditory arrays in working memory. *Journal of Experimental Psychology: General* 136, 663–684.

Swets, B., Desmet, T., Hambrick, D.Z. and Ferreira, F. (2007) The role of working memory in syntactic ambiguity resolution: A psychometric approach. *Journal of Experimental Psychology: General* 136, 64–81.

Venn, J. (1880) On the diagrammatic and mechanical representation of propositions and reasonings. *Philosophical Magazine Series* 5, 10 (59), 1–18.

Vergauwe, E., Camos, V. and Barrouillet, P. (2014) The impact of storage on processing: How is information maintained in working memory? *Journal of Experimental Psychology: Learning, Memory, & Cognition* 40 (4), 1072–1095.

3 Working Memory in Second Language Acquisition and Processing: The Phonological/ Executive Model

Zhisheng (Edward) Wen

Introduction

Working memory (WM) generally refers to the kind of memory system(s) that allows us to maintain and manipulate a very small amount of information in our head when we are carrying out some cognitive tasks in daily life, such as language comprehension, arithmetic calculation, reasoning and problem solving (Baddeley, 2010). Over the years, a large body of research has accumulated on the conception and measurement of WM as well as on its relation to first and second language acquisition (SLA), paving the way for the formulation of a comprehensive theoretical framework. The present chapter attempts to clarify the theoretical and empirical bases on which this integrated model of WM in SLA were founded. To this end, it is organised into five sections. The first section provides a succinct commentary on the commonalities and differences between representative theoretical models of WM that are often adopted in first and second language (L2) research. These include Baddeley's multi-component model (Chapter 1) and Cowan's embedded-processes model (Chapter 2). Such a review of WM conceptions in cognitive psychology gives rise to three unifying characterisations of the WM construct embraced by most contemporary WM models.

In light of these nomothetic theories of WM, the second and third sections, respectively, synthesise empirical studies that have investigated the role of WM in first and second language acquisition. These strands of WM-related language research converge on the distinctive roles of phonological WM (PWM) and executive WM (EWM) in specific SLA domains and activities. Notwithstanding, the research syntheses in the third section also reveal some intractable theoretical and methodological issues confronting current WM-SLA studies. Given these limitations and potential caveats in current and future WM–language explorations, it becomes imperative to bring in a *more principled approach* to theorising and measuring WM in practical SLA research.

To resolve these theoretical and methodological issues in WM-SLA research, in the fourth section we propose an integrated framework for conceptualising and measuring WM in SLA. The fifth section further incorporates emerging patterns of the differential roles of PWM and EWM as they relate to specific SLA domains and activities: the Phonological Executive (P/E) Hypothesis. Couched with this P/E model is also the stipulation of adopting separate memory span tasks to measure PWM and EWM in specific WM-language research. We conclude the chapter by identifying some empirical consequences and predictions of this integrated perspective of WM in SLA.

Unifying Characterisations of WM

The advancement of cognitive psychology has led to the propagation of a dozen WM models over the past half-century (Miyake & Shah, 1999; see also Dehn, 2008). Among these, the most seminal WM model was proposed by Baddeley and Hitch (1974). In their classical tripartite model of WM, two storage (buffer) systems, that of a phonological loop and a visuospatial sketchpad, are postulated to be maintaining domain-specific materials (such as sound-based materials and visual/spatial information). Activities in the two slave buffers are coordinated by a domain-general supervisory attentional system (SAS), which is the central executive of WM. Later, Baddeley (2000) added a fourth component to the original model, the episodic buffer, which serves as a fractionated component of the central executive to store and integrate information coming from all sources (Baddeley, 2012, this volume). Ever since then, this multi-component view of WM advocated by Baddeley has become a benchmark model of WM not just in cognitive psychology, but also in many other practical areas, such as general academic learning and education (e.g. Dehn, 2008).

In spite of the general appeal of this multi-component conception of WM, some cognitive psychologists (especially those based in North America) have opted for a single-resource view on the WM construct. Subsequently, they tend to regard WM as one unitary system of storage and processing (Just & Carpenter, 1992), or alternatively, as the activated focus of attention that is embedded within broader long-term memory (LTM) processes (Cowan, 1999, 2014, this volume). In a similar vein, other cognitive psychologists (e.g. Kane & Engle, 1999) would equate WM with executive attention that is distinguished from short-term memory (STM). Overall, WM as conceived by these North America-based research groups is synonymous with the active portion of LTM, coupled with mechanisms for executive and attentional control (Conway et al., 2009).

Over the past several decades of unabated WM research, controversies and debates still linger over these multiple perspectives on the construct of WM (Baddeley, 2012; Cowan, 2014). At the same time, however, there is also a growing consensus nowadays among cognitive psychologists about its nature, its components and its signature limits (Carruthers, 2013). Take the two most representative models of WM, Baddeley's multi-component model (with its addition of the episodic buffer), has become more compatible with Cowan's embedded-process view on WM (Baddeley, 2012, this volume; Cowan, 2014, this volume). When these WM conceptions are put into perspective (Conway et al., 2007; Miyake & Shah, 1999), three 'unifying characterisations' of the WM construct can be derived to inform applications of WM in such practical areas as academic learning (Dehn, 2008) and first and second language research (Wen, 2012a, 2016 manuscript under review; see also Wen et al., 2013).

First, WM has limited capacity. Despite the fact that controversies still remain among WM camps over the source of its limited capacity and over the exact quantification of its holding capacity, most cognitive psychologists would agree to accept WM as a sub-memory system possessing limited cognitive resources (Conway et al., 2007). Such a limited capacity manifests itself first in terms of the restricted amount of information that can be maintained in our immediate consciousness (Baddeley, 1992) or in the 'focus of attention' as conceived by Cowan (1998, 2005). Over the history of WM research, various attempts have been made by cognitive psychologists to gauge this holding capacity. Initially, Miller (1956) had speculated this number to be around seven units of information (the famous 'magical number seven plus or minus two'). A more recent quantification of this capacity came from Cowan (2000), who conjectured that such a figure should be reduced to around four chunks of information (i.e. the 'magical number four plus or minus one'). Baddeley (2012) also agrees that Cowan's reduced quantification is more realistic and plausible.

The other manifestation of the limited capacity of WM is evident in the projected time-course of memory decay of information that can stay active in our trailing consciousness (Cowan, 2014). In other words, information temporarily stored in our WM usually lasts for only a few seconds and will disappear gradually (unless it is rehearsed in a timely manner). Notwithstanding, this limited capacity of our WM has proven to be a defining feature of human memory as opposed to that of other species such as primates (Carruthers, 2013; Coolidge et al., 2013).

Second, WM is better conceived as a kind of memory system that subsumes multiple mechanisms and executive functions (Miyake & Shah, 1999). Indeed, recent years have witnessed compelling evidence coming from multidisciplinary inquiries, particularly from neuropsychology and advanced brain-imaging techniques (such as event-related potentials and functional magnetic resonance images), that converges on the multifunction view of WM (Conway *et al.*, 2009). For instance, Dehn (2008: 36) has aligned the corresponding brain regions with reported activation during WM processes, such as those regions that are purported to subserve the multiple WM functions of phonological storage, rehearsal and executive process. In a similar vein, Coolidge and Wynn (2009: 43) offer a schematic portrayal of Baddeley's multi-component model that is augmented by corresponding brain areas and cortical processes.

In practice, most cognitive psychologists nowadays would be ready to accept WM as consisting of both domain-specific storage components (such as the three STM components of phonological short-term store, visuospatial store and the episodic buffer) and domain-general executive functions such as information updating, task switching and inhibitory control (Williams, 2012: 428). Among these multiple components of WM, however, only the phonological short-term store/memory (PSTM or PWM) and the central executive component of WM (EWM) will be of particular interest here as both have been shown to be most directly relevant to first and second language learning and processing (Gathercole & Baddeley, 1993; Juffs & Harrington, 2011; Linck *et al.*, 2014; Wen, 2012a, 2014; Williams, 2012).

Third, LTM forms an integral part of the WM system. As also demonstrated in the extended WM model of Coolidge and Wynn (2009: 43), LTM lies in the bottom quartile of the WM system and thus constitutes the underlying foundation for WM. In addition, it is further divided into declarative and procedural LTM, each being subserved by respective brain areas and cortical processes and is purported to store different kinds of knowledge permanently. For example, in Michael Ullman's (2012) declarative and procedural LTM model, declarative memory is believed to store individual facts, verbal materials and episodic events; while procedural LTM is deemed to be mainly responsible for maintaining those non-verbal information and motor skills.

Above all, the WM portrayal as presented here makes a clear distinction between STM components, WM functions and LTM components. As also noted from the extended model of WM by Coolidge and Wynn (2009), permanent knowledge saved in LTM is usually unconscious (or 'preconscious'), while information held in WM (the three STM components in the mid-level and the central executive at the top) is mostly conscious (aka, 'currently activated' in Cowan's terms; though see Soto and Silvanto [2014] for a disassociated view between WM and awareness). Interpreted this way, WM is a *primary* memory system (Williams, 1890; cf. LTM as 'secondary') that functions as an interactive workspace where bidirectional flow of information is actively taking place between its STM stores/buffers (the phonological store, the visuospatial sketchpad and the episodic buffer) and LTM (declarative and procedural). Therefore, it becomes clear that such a view of the STM–WM–LTM connection is largely endorsed by most contemporary theoretical models of WM (Baddeley, 2012; Cowan, 2014) and it thus lays the theoretical foundation for the integrated framework of WM in SLA to be proposed later in this chapter.

WM in First Language Acquisition and Processing

Since the inception of the WM concept in the early 1970s, cognitive psychologists have been equally intrigued by the relationship between WM and (first) language acquisition and processing (Baddeley, 2003, this volume; Gathercole & Baddeley, 1993). Inspired by the distinctive conceptions of WM across the two sides of the Atlantic, researchers in Europe and North America have respectively afforded different interpretations to the WM–language connection (Andrade, 2001, 2008). Gradually, this line of research effort has developed into two parallel albeit disparate paradigms of WM–language explorations; each has its own research focus and methodologies (Mackey, 2012; Wen, 2012a).

In most of Europe and in the UK particularly, developmental and cognitive psychologists (mainly led by Alan Baddeley and Susan Gathercole) have generally focused on the cognitive mechanisms associated with the *phonological* aspect of WM (i.e. the phonological loop in Baddeley's multi-component model). To explore the WM–language association, their research has focused on the role of the phonological loop in vocabulary learning among young children (Baddeley *et al.*, 1998; also see Baddeley, this volume). In assessing WM, they normally resort to a storage-plus-rehearsal version of memory recall tests (such as the digit span test, the non-word repetition span test; Gathercole, 2006; Gathercole *et al.*, 1994). The findings from these studies are generally affirmative, pointing to positive correlations between phonological WM (e.g. as indexed by the non-word repetition span task) and vocabulary acquisition and even grammar development in the longer term (Baddeley, 2000, 2003; Gathercole & Baddeley, 1993; see also Andrade & Baddeley, 2011). These positive findings have led these Europe-based cognitive psychologists to postulate that PWM (subsuming a phonological short-term store and an articulatory rehearsal mechanism) functions as a key *'language learning device'* and plays an instrumental role in acquiring *novel* phonological forms in both native and foreign language (Baddeley, 2003; Baddeley *et al.*, 1998).

In contrast to the British tradition that focuses on the phonological aspect of WM in language learning, dozens of cognitive psychologists in North America (*inter alia* Meredith Daneman, Patricia Carpenter, Nelson Cowan, Randall Engel, Andrew Conway, Michael Kane, David Kaplan, Gloria Waters, Akira Miyake and Ellen Bialystok) are more interested in the executive and control functions attributed to the WM construct. In line with this premise, they have sought to probe into the individual differences in the executive aspects of WM as well as their potential impacts on language processing activities, with a particular focus on those sub-level processes that are implicated in language comprehension. To tap into these individual differences in participants' WM capacity, researchers in this paradigm have usually opted for a more complex version of the storage-plus-processing type of WM span tasks (such as the reading span task constructed by Daneman and Carpenter [1980] or the domain-general operation span task advocated by Turner and Engle [1989]) which are purported to tax more of the executive functions of WM (e.g. information maintenance, updating, task switching, inhibitory control; Miyake & Friedman, 2012).

Regarding their research findings, considerable studies pursuing this more focused WM–language processing relationship have also been able to generate quite positive results, normally pointing to a moderate 0.5–0.6 correlation between WM (as indexed by complex versions of WM span tasks) and reading comprehension test scores (Daneman & Merikle, 1996). Other researchers also forge a similar link between WM and language production (Acheson & McDonald, 2009). To explain these positive results of WM effects in language comprehension, however, two rather contrastive views have been offered. On the one hand, Waters and Caplan (1996, 2003, 2005; Caplan & Waters, 1999; see also Caplan et al., 2007) have posited a two-stage interpretation process that distinguishes *initial* WM-free online syntactic processing from the *post-interpretive* WM-reliant language comprehension processes (such as anaphor resolution). On the other hand, other cognitive psychologists (*inter alia* Just & Carpenter, 1992; Macdonald & Christiansen, 2002) do not embrace such a distinction but resort to attributing multiple linguistic and non-linguistic processes to the single-resource pool of WM capacity.

Interestingly, the dispute over the WM-language processing interpretation in North America not only exists among cognitive psychologists, but it also exists among linguistic theorists. In this regard, there are two noteworthy accounts, i.e. that of the emergentist approach by William O'Grady and the 'parallel architecture' framework initiated by Ray Jackendoff. On the one hand, O'Grady (2005, 2012) argues that, among the three factors in the design and acquisition of (first) language (*inter alia* universal grammar, language experience or exposure and WM), it is the third factor (i.e. WM, which represents the general cognitive principles not specific to the faculty of language) that is the most fundamental due to its overarching constraint effects on syntactic carpentry. Such a processing view stands in sharp contrast to the mainstream generative grammar (MGG) which holds that, it is the genetic endowment specifically for language (aka, the language faculty) that is the core (Hauser et al., 2002). On the other hand, Jackendoff (2002, 2007), in his so-called 'parallel architecture' perspective on language processing, has divided linguistic WM into three separate parts, that for phonology, syntax and semantics, respectively. It is clear that both views, despite some subtle differences in research focus and scope, have posited WM as imposing fundamental constraints on language processing.

Thus, we can hereby establish a close link between WM and first language acquisition (L1A) and processing. More specifically, as demonstrated by the emerging empirical studies conducted within the two research paradigms (that of Europe and North America), two putative components of WM are found to be particularly relevant to L1A: PWM (or the 'phonological loop') and EWM (or the central executive). Furthermore, research conducted by these cognitive psychologists has pointed to the distinctive roles of these two WM components as they relate to specific L1A activities (Baddeley, 2003; Cowan, 2013; Gathercole & Baddeley, 1993). Specifically, PWM with its associated phonological short-term store and articulatory rehearsal mechanism has been found by the European cognitive psychologists to be mainly underpinning the *acquisitional* and *developmental* aspects of L1A, most evident in the acquisition of vocabulary, and possibly in the long-term development of grammar.

In contrast, the executive aspects of WM (EWM) have been demonstrated by the North American cognitive psychologists to be likely implicated in some higher-level, demanding and complex 'post-interpretive' processes in language comprehension and production (such as the detection of pronouns and antecedents, subject–verb agreement errors, resolution of ambiguities, anaphor resolution and the processing of relative clause attachment; Cowan, 2013; Gibson, 1998; Hartsuiker & Barkhuysen, 2006; Miyake & Friedman, 1998).

WM in Second Language Acquisition and Processing

Inspired by these positive results from WM-L1A studies, more and more SLA researchers have increasingly subscribed to the view that WM may play an equal if not greater role in the learning of a second or foreign language (Wen, 2012a). Such an assumption should come as no surprise given the perceived fundamental differences between L1A and SLA (Bley-Vroman, 1990; Krashen, 1981; Meisel, 2011). In the case of L1A, for example, it is largely taking place in an implicit and unconscious manner (e.g. as epitomised in children picking up their mother tongue effortlessly). In this process, the demands placed on such cognitive resources as WM should be minimal and will only be called upon when such processing becomes more demanding and/or the tasks are complex enough.

When the use of an L2 is involved, as Cowan has lively depicted in his introductory chapter (Chapter 2), the demands for such cognitive resources of WM should be much greater and sometimes can be pathetic. Under these circumstances, many language comprehension and production activities have to be carried out with a much smaller mental lexicon and with a severely restricted L2 grammar system (Skehan, this volume).

Inspired by such a basic assumption of the L1–L2 distinction, many SLA researchers are therefore ready to endorse a stronger link between WM and SLA as opposed to WM and L1A (Wen, 2012a). Indeed, recent years have witnessed a surge of interest in exploring this WM–SLA relationship, which has been further propelled by the renewed enthusiasm towards language aptitude research in SLA (Wen, 2012b; Wen et al., 2016). To that effect, some scholars have bluntly posited that WM, given its permeation in so many key aspects of SLA, will rise up to be the *apt* candidate for modifying John Carroll's foreign language aptitude theory (Harrington, 1992; Juffs & Harrington, 2011; McLaughlin, 1995; Miyake & Friedman, 1998; Skehan, 2002, 2012, 2015; Wen, 2016 manuscript under review; Wen & Skehan, 2011; see also Sawyer & Ranta, 2001).

An alternative account to forge the WM–SLA melding comes from Nick Ellis (1996, 2012). Adopting the construction- and usage-based approach to SLA, Ellis (2013) posits that L2 learning (though the same can be applied to L1A) is in essence to acquire and use an adequate range of sequences and/or constructions at different linguistic levels (e.g. phonemes, lexis, formulaic sequences and morphosyntactic constructions). More relevantly, Ellis (1996, 2012) argues that PWM, given its associated functions of phonological short-term store and articulatory rehearsal mechanism, plays an instrumental role in the *chunking* and consolidating of these newly acquired sequences, thus allowing them to transform into a long-term knowledge base in LTM. An increasing number of empirical studies have emerged to converge on this assumption, generating positive results for constructing a close link between PSTM and L2 vocabulary (e.g. Cheung, 1996; Ellis & Sinclair, 1996; French, 2006; French & O'Brien, 2008; Service, 1992); L2 formulaic sequences and collocations (e.g. Bolibaugh & Foster, 2013; Foster et al., 2014; Skrzypek, 2009); and morphosyntactic constructions or grammar acquisition and development (e.g. Martin & Ellis, 2012; O'Brien et al., 2006, 2007; Williams & Lovatt, 2003).

In addition to the explorations of WM effects on the specific L2 domains of vocabulary, formulae and grammar, other strands of empirical studies have set out to gauge the impact of WM on sub-level processes embedded within L2 comprehension, L2 interaction and L2 production. In this regard, Linck et al. (2014) have recently conducted a comprehensive meta-analysis and research synthesis of 79 studies (though it also included some of the studies described above) that involved a sample pool of 3707 participants (also see the Foreword by Bunting and Engle, this volume). Again, their results have indicated that WM is positively associated with L2 processing and proficiency outcomes at different acquisitional stages. Such WM effects are found to be impacting on L2 listening (e.g. Miki, 2012), L2 reading comprehension (e.g. Alptekin & Erçetin, 2011; Leeser,

2007; Walters, 2004), L2 interaction and noticing of corrective feedback (e.g. Mackey *et al.*, 2002, 2010; Révész, 2012), speech production and performance (Ahmadian, 2012; Fortkamp, 2003; Guará-Tavares, 2008) as well as written production and performance (Abu-Rabia, 2003; Bergsleithner, 2010).

To gain a more comprehensive picture of the intricate relationships between WM and specific SLA domains and activities, major results and findings of these strands of empirical studies are summarised in Table 3.1.

As shown in Table 3.1, results from these WM-SLA studies have converged on the separate and distinctive roles of the phonological component of WM (PWM) and its executive component (EWM) in specific SLA (Linck *et al.*, 2014). Again, they seem to corroborate WM-L1A studies that PWM generally plays a critical role in *acquisitional and developmental aspects* of vocabulary, formula and grammar (e.g. such as research conducted by N. Ellis and colleagues). On the other hand, EWM is mainly implicated in some conscious and intentional monitoring, i.e. *real-time performance* aspects of language processing activities (such as accuracy measures of speech and written performance), as well as in a number of *post-interpretive processes* beyond the sentence level (such as the noticing of corrective feedback during native and non-native interaction).

Amid these positive results regarding WM effects on SLA, the above research synthesis has also revealed some intractable issues relating to their research design and methodology that will potentially pose challenges to SLA researchers (Gass & Lee, 2011; Juffs, 2006; Linck *et al.*, 2014). For example, the use of the term 'working memory' (or 'WM' to that effect) can sometimes be confusing, as it may mean the phonological aspect of WM (i.e. PWM) in some studies, while in other studies, it refers to the executive aspects of WM (i.e. EWM). As discussed above, such confusion may arise due to the distinctive conceptions of WM as embraced by cognitive psychologists in Europe and their counterparts in North America. Such confusion, at its worse case scenario, can present formidable challenges for WM-SLA research in applied linguistics. One noteworthy practice among some WM-SLA studies is that they tend to combine participants' PWM and EWM scores to arrive at a so-called 'composite WM span'. As we have argued elsewhere (Wen, 2012, 2016 manuscript under review; Wen *et al.*, 2013), such a practice may have confounded the distinctive roles of PWM and EWM as demonstrated by many empirical studies described above.

To resolve this terminology confusion, it seems that a distinction should be emphasised between the 'multiple components' of WM (referring to its structure in the European tradition) and the 'multiple mechanisms' of WM (referring to its 'function' by the North American WM camps). In this regard, current neuropsychological evidence seems to endorse the functional view more than the multi-component view (Conway *et al.*, 2009; Cowan, this volume), though both views are incorporated into the integrated

Table 3.1 Results and findings of WM-SLA studies

SLA domains and activities	PSTM	EWM	Major SLA studies
L2 vocabulary acquisition and development	Instrumental in storing and acquiring novel phonological forms	Not yet clear	Cheung (1996); French (2006); French and O'Brien (2008); Service (1992); Speciale et al. (2004)
Acquisition and development of L2 formulae and collocations	Facilitates the storage and chunking of phonological sequences or collocations	Not yet clear	Bolibaugh and Foster (2013); Ellis and Sinclair (1996); Foster et al. (2014); Skrzypek (2009)
Acquisition and development of L2 grammar and/or morphosyntactic constructions	Facilitates the storage and chunking of morphosyntactic constructions	Not yet clear	Martin & Ellis (2012); Williams and Lovatt (2003)
L2 language comprehension (listening and reading)	Used to maintain a phonological record that can be consulted during offline language processing?	Facilitates in processing syntactic and semantic information	Alptekin and Erçetin (2011); Berquist (1997); Harrington and Sawyer (1992); Havik et al. (2009); Leeser (2007); Miyake and Friedman (1998); Walter (2004)
L2 interaction and cognitive processes (e.g. noticing)	Not yet clear	Facilitates noticing of corrective feedback during interaction	Bergsleithner and Fortkamp (2007); Goo (2012); Lai et al. (2008); Mackey et al. (2002, 2010); Révész (2012); Sagarra (2007); Yilmaz (2013)
Language production (speaking and writing)	Predicts narrative vocabulary at early stage; predicts grammatical accuracy at later stage	Is related to performance measures of L2 speech (e.g. accuracy)	Abu-Rabia (2003); Ahmadian (2012); Bergsleithner (2010); Fortkamp (1999, 2003); Guará-Tavares (2008); O'Brien et al. (2006, 2007); Payne and Whitney (2002)

Note: Updated from Wen (2012: 8).

framework, in which WM is conceptualised as a multi-component memory system that possesses multiple mechanisms and functions.

Given this and many other caveats that are confronting extant WM-SLA research (see Wen [2012, 2016 manuscript under review] for more details), it becomes imperative for the SLA field to bring *a more principled approach* to incorporating the WM construct into its mainstream research. More urgently, SLA studies desperately need a viable conceptual framework that not only allows SLA researchers to conceptualise WM but also guides them to operationalise and assess it in practical research. In view of this, we now propose an integrated framework of WM and SLA that aims to address these theoretical and methodological issues.

Towards an Integrated Framework of WM in SLA

Building on the above nomothetic and consensual theories of the WM construct and by further incorporating research insights from previous WM–language research in cognitive psychology and applied linguistics, we now propose a theoretical framework to conceptualise and operationalise the WM construct in SLA research. As schematically demonstrated in Figure 3.1, this 'so-called' integrated WM-SLA framework consists of three key components, namely: (a) a working definition of WM in SLA; (b) the language-related WM *components* as well as their associated *mechanisms* and *functions* that are most relevant to the SLA process; and (c) the proposed assessment procedure for WM in SLA. Each of these will be discussed below.

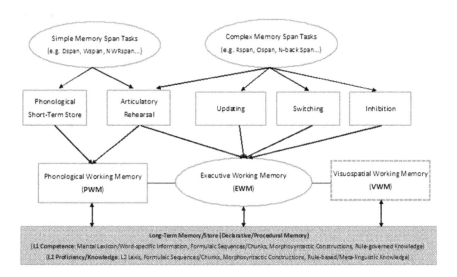

Figure 3.1 An integrated framework of WM in SLA

Firstly, the integrated framework adopts a working definition of WM as 'the limited capacity of multiple mechanisms and processes implicated in L2 domains and activities'. This conception of WM echoes the unifying characterisations of the construct from general cognitive psychology (as discussed above): possessing a limited capacity and comprising multiple components with associated mechanisms and functions. In addition, as indicated in Figure 3.1, these putative WM components are all posited to be interacting bidirectionally with LTM, the murky area inhabited by learners' L1 mental lexicon and grammar as well their L2 knowledge/proficiency; which are purportedly subserved by their declarative memory and procedural memory systems (Ullman, 2012).

Secondly, the integrated WM-SLA framework further postulates that to incorporate WM in SLA studies, it is both necessary and advisable to focus first on those key WM components and their associated functions that are already demonstrated to be most relevant to the language learning process (though it does not rule out the possible influence of other putative WM components that are currently not in focus in SLA research). Building on the research syntheses in the above sections, two WM components have been identified to be directly implicated in language learning and processing: PWM that embraces a phonological short-term store and an articulatory rehearsal mechanism and EWM that subsumes such attention-regulating and executive control functions as *updating, shifting* and *inhibition* (Miyake & Friedman, 2012). That is to say, the visuospatial WM component (VWM) is not in focus in the current WM-SLA framework (as indicated by the dotted lines in Figure 3.1) despite its plausible involvement in reading (particularly of such logographic languages as Chinese). Excluded also from this WM-SLA framework is the newly proposed WM component of the episodic buffer (Baddeley, 2000), although it may be implicated in processing syntactic and semantic information in language (Rudner & Rönnberg, 2008; see also Baddeley, 2012, this volume).

Thirdly, the integrated WM-SLA framework also attempts to offer a tentative solution to sort out the dismal array of WM span tasks frequently used in cognitive psychology and SLA research (Conway *et al.*, 2005; Linck *et al.*, 2014). As Dehn (2008: 58) has put it, 'until research and measurement tools allow us to further delineate WM processes, it might be safest to define WM as what simple and complex WM span tasks measure'. To that effect, the integrated framework proposes to implement separate memory span tasks for assessing the two distinctive WM components of PWM and EWM. Based on previous language-focused WM research paradigms by the European and North American groups, the framework stipulates the adoption of a 'simple WM span task' (such as the non-word repetition span task in Table 3.2) to measure PWM, and a 'complex memory span task'

Table 3.2 Classification of working memory span tasks

	Verbal (domain specific)	Non-verbal (domain general)
Simple	Word span	Digit span
	Non-word span	Counting span
	Letter span	Backward digit span
		Letter rotation
		Size judgement
Complex	Reading span	Operation span
	Listening span	Math span
	Speaking span	N-back span
	Writing span	AMIPB
	English opposites span	

Note: Based on Linck *et al.* (2014; Table 2).

(such as the reading span task and its variants or the operation span task, as listed in Table 3.2) for measuring EWM.

Table 3.2 (based on Linck *et al.*, 2014) provides a comprehensive list of all major WM span tasks that are currently available from cognitive psychology and neuroscience research. Clearly, the rationale for this specification of different WM span tasks to measure PWM and EWM draws on previous discussion in cognitive psychology regarding the nature of these WM span tasks. In terms of the simple WM span task, for example, Gathercole (2006) provides a lengthy discussion of the non-word repetition span task as a viable measure of PWM. In addition, Conway *et al.* (2005) provide a comprehensive and authoritative review of reliability and validity issues related to these major WM measures together with some general guidelines for test construction and administration.

Finally, the integrated WM-SLA model also specifies a two-way interaction of information flow between WM and LTM (as indicated by the double-headed arrows shown in Figure 3.1). More importantly, it posits that participants' *L2 proficiency/knowledge* (operationalised as L2 vocabulary and grammar knowledge as well as metalinguistic knowledge residing in the LTM alongside the L1 mental lexicon and grammatical competence) should be taken into full account when deciding on which WM measure to adopt in SLA research (cf. Gass & Lee, 2011; Juffs, 2006; see also Claire, this volume). For example, it is advisable that a simple memory span task (e.g. the non-word repetition span task) should be adopted for less-educated L2 learners or those with low levels of literacy, while a complex memory span task (e.g. the reading span task or the operation span task) can be implemented as an additional measure for learners with relatively high L2 proficiency (Juffs, 2006). In other words, a *developmental* perspective that takes into account of participants' L2 proficiency levels should be incorporated in future WM-SLA research design and methodology.

The Phonological/Executive Hypothesis

Indeed, such a PWM–EWM distinction is being increasingly recognised in cognitive psychology and bilingualism/SLA research as well (e.g. N. Ellis, 2012; Engel de Abreu & Gathercole, 2012; Szmalec *et al.*, 2013; Williams, 2012). Given these emerging patterns regarding the P/E dichotomy of WM in SLA, we are now ready to push it further and to formulate an overarching theoretical model with a view to further accommodating and integrating research insights discussed so far: the Phonological/Executive (P/E) Hypothesis. The P/E model as proposed here not only emulates Michael Ullman's (2012) declarative/procedural (D/P) LTM model, but it also complements it by specifying a two-way interaction manner of information flow between WM components and LTM (as indicated in Figure 3.1).

Similar to Ullman's (2012) D/P model, the P/E model comes in two versions, with a view to taking into full account SLA learners' L1–L2 scenarios from a developmental perspective: P/E for L1A and very advanced SLA learners (Figure 3.2); P/E for low-proficiency SLA learners (Figure 3.3). In addition, there are two possible scenarios in each figure. In terms of P/E for L1 (Figure 3.2), it is posited that PSTM plays a greater role at a younger age, while EWM begins to weigh in more prominently as learners become more mature. In terms of P/E for L2 (Figure 3.3), it is also hypothesised that

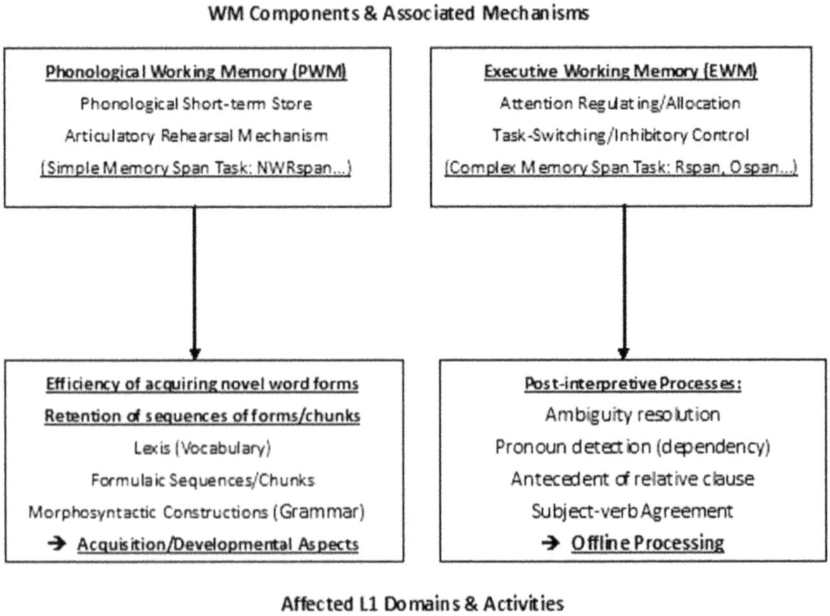

WM Components & Associated Mechanisms

Phonological Working Memory (PWM)	Executive Working Memory (EWM)
Phonological Short-term Store	Attention Regulating/Allocation
Articulatory Rehearsal Mechanism	Task-Switching/Inhibitory Control
(Simple Memory Span Task: NWRspan...)	(Complex Memory Span Task: Rspan, Ospan...)

Efficiency of acquiring novel word forms	Post-interpretive Processes:
Retention of sequences of forms/chunks	Ambiguity resolution
Lexis (Vocabulary)	Pronoun detection (dependency)
Formulaic Sequences/Chunks	Antecedent of relative clause
Morphosyntactic Constructions (Grammar)	Subject-verb Agreement
→ Acquisition/Developmental Aspects	→ Offline Processing

Affected L1 Domains & Activities

Figure 3.2 The Phonological/Executive Hypothesis for L1A & Advanced/Late SLA

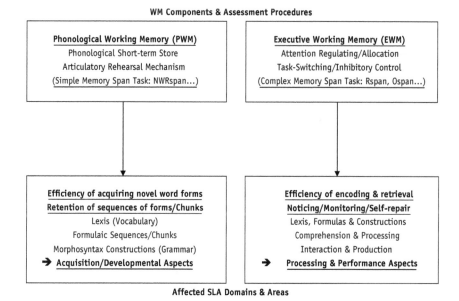

WM Components & Assessment Procedures

Phonological Working Memory (PWM)
Phonological Short-term Store
Articulatory Rehearsal Mechanism
(Simple Memory Span Task: NWRspan...)

Executive Working Memory (EWM)
Attention Regulating/Allocation
Task-Switching/Inhibitory Control
(Complex Memory Span Task: Rspan, Ospan...)

Efficiency of acquiring novel word forms
Retention of sequences of forms/Chunks
Lexis (Vocabulary)
Formulaic Sequences/Chunks
Morphosyntax Constructions (Grammar)
→ **Acquisition/Developmental Aspects**

Efficiency of encoding & retrieval
Noticing/Monitoring/Self-repair
Lexis, Formulas & Constructions
Comprehension & Processing
Interaction & Production
→ **Processing & Performance Aspects**

Affected SLA Domains & Areas

Figure 3.3 The Phonological/Executive Hypothesis for Early & Intermediate SLA Stages

PWM is more important when SLA learners are at low/beginner stage (and accordingly, the simple memory span task should be implemented at this stage; Juffs, 2006), while EWM begins to play out a greater role as learners progress to more advanced L2 proficiency. In this stage, it is conceivable that PWM effects are less obvious and sometimes even become implicit, thus making the scenario more L1A-like (Bowden *et al.*, 2013; Steinhauer, 2014).

As Figure 3.3 indicates, the P/E Hypothesis for WM-SLA consists of two layers or levels, namely: (a) an upper level of key WM components with associated mechanisms/functions as well as their respective assessment procedures; and (b) a lower level of specific SLA domains and areas that are likely to be affected by these postulated WM components. Following the basic tenet of the integrated WM-SLA framework (Figure 3.1), PWM and EWM are pinned down as the two key WM components that are most relevant to the language learning process and therefore their effects should be prioritised in WM-SLA research (see also R. Ellis, 2005; Linck *et al.*, 2014; Williams, 2012 for a similar argument). Then, the lower level depicts the specific SLA domains and areas that are likely to be affected by the two putative WM components of PWM and EWM.

As suggested by previous research synthesis of WM-SLA studies (described above), PWM is purported to affect the efficiency of acquisition of novel phonological forms and the serial-order retention of sequences/chunks of word forms (Baddeley *et al.*, 1998; Szmalec *et al.*, 2013; Williams,

2012); thus, it likely exerts an impact on the *acquisition and developmental* aspects of SLA domains such as vocabulary and formula acquisition and grammar development. On the other hand, EWM with its associated executive and attentional functions is mainly involved in *monitoring* and *self-repair* aspects of L2 learning; thus, it is likely to affect the *processing and performance-related areas* of L2 comprehension, L2 interaction and L2 production.

Again, the P/E model for WM-SLA also adopts a *developmental* perspective which further specifies the early and later stages of SLA. In that regard, it is hypothesised that in the early stage of SLA (such as among L2 beginners), PWM is assumed to play a bigger role; while at the later stage, EWM weighs in more predominantly. As their L2 proficiency progresses, their acquisition and processing resemble native speakers (Figure 3.3).

Conclusions

To sum up, it is clear from the above discussion that the formulation of the P/E model and its hypotheses gets inspiration from multidisciplinary research insights straddling cognitive and developmental psychology, neuroscience, linguistics and applied linguistics. On the one hand, the P/E model is built on the unifying characterisations of the WM construct that are generally endorsed by most contemporary WM theorists in cognitive psychology (Miyake & Shah, 1999; see also Conway *et al.*, 2007). In line with this integrative perspective (Wen, 2016 manuscript under review), WM as conceptualised by the P/E model is the primary memory system(s) comprising multiple components and mechanisms/functions that allow(s) us humans to maintain and manipulate a small amount of information in immediate consciousness when carrying out cognitive activities in daily life. This multiple component/function view of the WM construct is well studied and is increasingly established in major disciplines of cognitive sciences, ranging from anthropology, philosophy, computer science, biology and psychology to neuroscience (Carruthers, 2013; Coolidge & Wynn, 2009; Coolidge *et al.*, 2013). This consensus view of WM in cognitive psychology is thus lending a strong theoretical basis to the P/E model.

On the other hand, the P/E model also rides on the latest developments achieved in linguistic theories (in particular, the emergentist and connectionist accounts of L1A and processing; Jackendoff, 2007; O'Grady, 2005) and applied linguistics research (particularly its connectionist and constructionist perspectives on SLA and processing; N. Ellis, 2013). Viewed through these lenses, first and second language acquisition can be interpreted as learning a wide range of linguistic sequences or chunks (ranging from phonemes, lexis, formulae, to morphosyntactic constructions; Ellis, 1996, 2012) that serve as effective devices to facilitate communication, or in other words, to create meaning. In this sense, the linguistic dimension of the P/E model clearly distinguishes itself from traditional (e.g. mainstream generative) grammar and has fully incorporated the essence of these modern linguistic theories that are providing new insights into the SLA phenomena (under such terms as 'connectionism', 'emergentism', 'construction grammar' and 'usage-based learning theories'; see Dörnyei [2009] for a summary of these views in SLA).

To conclude the chapter, it becomes obvious that, when the two most language-relevant WM components of PSTM and EWM are thus pinned down and further aligned with specific SLA domains and processes, future WM-SLA studies can be designed to formulate *novel, specific* and *testable* predictions about the *representation, access* and *control* (Alterriba & Isurin, 2013) of the two languages residing in the bilingual mind of SLA learners (see Wen [2016 manuscript under review] for more details). In time, as more and more WM-SLA studies are conducted, it is conceivable that we will arrive at finer-grained juxtapositions constituting the 'WM–SLA nexus' (Wen, 2012). This also becomes the primary objective of all the succeeding chapters of this current volume. In this sense, their results and findings can be regarded as providing initial empirical evidence testing the hypotheses as laid out in the P/E model presented here.

References

Abu-Rabia, S. (2003) The influence of working memory on reading and creative writing processes in a second language. *Educational Psychology* 23, 209–222.

Acheson, D.J. and MacDonald, M.C. (2009) Verbal working memory and phonological encoding in speech production: Common approaches to the serial ordering of verbal information. *Psychological Bulletin* 135, 50–68.

Ahmadian, M.J. (2012) The relationship between working memory and oral production under task-based careful online planning condition. *TESOL Quarterly* 46 (1), 165–175.

Alptekin, C. and Erçetin, G. (2011) The effects of working memory capacity and content familiarity on literal and inferential comprehension in L2 reading. *TESOL Quarterly* 45, 235–266.

Altarriba, J. and Isurin, L. (2013) *Memory, Language, and Bilingualism: Theoretical and Applied Approaches*. Cambridge: Cambridge University Press.

Andrade, J. (2001) *Working Memory in Perspective*. Hove: Taylor & Francis.

Andrade, J. (2008) *Memory: Critical Concepts in Psychology, Volume 3: Working Memory*. London; New York: Routledge.

Andrade, J. and Baddeley, A.D. (2011) The contribution of phonological short-term memory to artificial grammar learning. *Quarterly Journal of Experimental Psychology* 64, 960–974.

Baddeley, A.D. (2000) The episodic buffer: A new component of working memory? *Trends in Cognitive Sciences* 4 (11), 417–423.

Baddeley, A.D. (2003) Working memory and language: An overview. *Journal of Communication Disorders* 36, 189–208.

Baddeley, A.D. (2010) Working memory. *Current Biology* 20 (4), R136–R140.

Baddeley, A.D. (2012) Working memory: Theories, models and controversies. *Annual Review of Psychology* 63, 1–30.

Baddeley, A.D. and Hitch, G. (1974) Working memory. In G.A. Bower (ed.) *The Psychology of Learning and Motivation* (Vol. 8; pp. 47–90). New York: Academic Press.

Baddeley, A.D., Gathercole, S.E. and Papagno, C. (1998) The phonological loop as a language learning device. *Psychological Review* 105, 158–173.

Baddeley, A.D. and Logie, R.H. (1999) Working memory: The multi-component model. In A. Miyake and P. Shah (eds) *Models of Working Memory: Mechanisms of Active Maintenance and Executive Control* (pp. 28–61). New York: Cambridge University Press.

Bergsleithner, J.M. (2010) Working memory capacity and L2 writing performance. *Ciências & Cognição* 15 (2), 2–20.

Bergsleithner, J.M. and Fortkamp, M.B.M. (2007) The relationship among individual differences in working memory capacity, noticing, and L2 speech production. *Revista Signo* 32, 40–53.

Berquist, B. (1997) Individual differences in working memory span and L2 proficiency: Capacity or processing efficiency? In A. Sorace, C. Heccock and R. Shillcock (eds) *Proceedings of the GALA' 1997 Conference on language acquisition* (pp. 468–473). Edinburgh: The University of Edinburgh.

Bley-Vroman, R. (1990) The logical problem of foreign language learning. *Linguistic Analysis* 20, 3–49.

Bolibaugh, C. and Foster, P. (2013) Memory-based aptitude for nativelike selection: The role of phonological short-term memory. In G. Granena and M. Long (eds) *Sensitive Periods, Language Aptitude, and Ultimate L2 Attainment* (pp. 203–228). Amsterdam: John Benjamins.

Caplan, D. and Waters, G.S. (1999) Verbal working memory and sentence comprehension. *Behavioral and Brain Sciences* 22, 77–126.

Caplan, D., Waters, G. and Dede, G. (2007) Specialized verbal working memory for language comprehension. In A.R.A. Conway, C. Jarrold, M.J. Kane, A. Miyake and J.N. Towse (eds) *Variation in Working Memory* (pp. 272–302). New York: Oxford University Press.

Carruthers, P. (2013) The evolution of working memory. *Proceedings of National Academy of Sciences* 110 (Supplement 2), 10371–10378.

Cheung, H. (1996) Nonword span as a unique predictor of second-language vocabulary learning. *Developmental Psychology* 32 (5), 867–873.

Conway, A., Kane, M., Bunting, M., Hambrick, D., Wilhelm, O. and Engel, R. (2005) Working memory span tasks: A methodological review and user's guide. *Psychonomic Bulletin & Review* 12, 769–786.

Conway, A.R.A., Jarrold, C., Kane, M.J., Miyake, A. and Towse, J.N. (eds) (2007) *Variation in Working Memory*. New York: Oxford University Press.

Conway, A.R.A., Moore, A.B. and Kane, M.J. (2009) Recent trends in the cognitive neuroscience of working memory. *Cortex* 45 (2), 262–268.

Coolidge, F. and Wynn, T. (2009) *The Rise of Homo Sapiens: The Evolution of Modern Thinking*. Malden, MA: Wiley-Blackwell.

Coolidge, F.L., Wynn, T. and Overmann, K.A. (2013) The evolution of working memory. In T.P. Alloway and R.G. Alloway (eds) *Working Memory: The Connected Intelligence* (pp. 37–60). New York: Psychology Press.

Cowan, N. (2001) The magical number 4 in short-term memory: A reconsideration of mental storage capacity. *Behaviour and Brain Sciences* 24, 87–185.

Cowan, N. (2005) *Working Memory Capacity*. New York and Hove: Psychology Press.

Cowan, N. (2013) Working memory and attention in language use. In J. Guandouzi, F. Loncke and M.J. Williams (eds) *The Handbook of Psycholinguistics and Cognitive Processes*. London: Psychology Press.

Cowan, N. (2014) Working memory underpins cognitive development, learning, and education. *Educational Psychology Review* 26 (2), 197–223.

Daneman, M. and Carpenter, P.A. (1980) Individual differences in working memory and reading. *Journal of Verbal Learning and Verbal Behaviour* 19, 450–466.

Daneman, M. and Merikle, P.M. (1996) Working memory and language comprehension: A meta-analysis. *Psychonomic Bulletin and Review* 3, 422–433.

Dehn, M.J. (2008) *Working Memory and Academic Learning: Assessment and Intervention.* Hoboken, NJ: John Wiley & Sons, Inc.

Dörnyei, Z. (2009) *The Psychology of Second Language Acquisition.* Oxford: Oxford University Press.

Ellis, N.C. (1996) Sequencing in SLA: Phonological memory, chunking and points of order. *Studies in Second Language Acquisition* 18, 91–126.

Ellis, N.C. (2012) Formulaic language and second language acquisition: Zipf and the phrasal Teddy Bear. *Annual Review of Applied Linguistics* 32, 17–44.

Ellis, N.C. (2013) Second language acquisition. In G. Trousdale and T. Hoffmann (eds) *Oxford Handbook of Construction Grammar* (pp. 365–378). Oxford: Oxford University Press.

Ellis, N.C. and Sinclair, S.G. (1996) Working memory in the acquisition of vocabulary and syntax: Putting language in good order. *The Quarterly Journal of Experimental Psychology* 49A (1), 234–250.

Ellis, R. (2005) *Planning and Task Performance in a Second Language.* Amsterdam/ Philadelphia, PA: John Benjamins.

Engel de Abreu, P.M.J. and Gathercole, S.E. (2012) Executive and phonological processes in second language acquisition. *Journal of Educational Psychology* 104 (4), 974–986.

French, L.M. (2006) *Phonological Working Memory and Second Language Acquisition: A Developmental Study of Francophone Children Learning English in Quebec.* New York: Edwin Mellen Press.

Fortkamp, M.B.M. (1999) Working memory capacity and aspects of L2 speech production. *Communication and Cognition* 32, 259–296.

Fortkamp, M.B.M. (2003) Working memory capacity and fluency, accuracy, complexity and lexical density in L2 speech production. *Fragmentos* 24, 69–104.

Fortkamp, M.B.M. and Bergsleithner, J.M. (2007) The relationship among individual differences in working memory capacity, noticing, and L2 speech production. *Revista Signo* 32 (52), 40–53.

Foster, P., Bolibaugh, C. and Kotula, A. (2014) Knowledge of nativelike selections in an L2: The influence of exposure, memory, age of onset and motivation in foreign language and immersion settings. *Studies in Second Language Acquisition* 36 (01), 101–132.

Gass, S. and Lee, J. (2011) Working memory capacity, inhibitory control, and proficiency in a second language. In M. Schmid and W. Lowie (eds) *From Structure to Chaos: Twenty Years of Modeling Bilingualism: In Honor of Kees de Bot* (pp. 59–84). Amsterdam: John Benjamins.

Gathercole, S. (2006) Nonword repetition and word learning: The nature of the relationship (Keynote article). *Applied Psycholinguistics* 27, 513–543.

Gathercole, S. and Baddeley, A. (1993) *Working Memory and Language.* Hove: Lawrence Erlbaum Associates.

Gathercole, S.E., Willis, C.S., Baddeley, A. and Emslie, H. (1994) The children's test of nonword repetition: A test of phonological working memory. *Memory* 2 (2), 103–127.

Gibson, E. (1998) Linguistic complexity: Locality of syntactic dependencies. *Cognition* 68, 1–76.

Goo, J. (2012) Corrective feedback and working memory capacity in interaction-driven L2 learning. *Studies in Second Language Acquisition* 34 (3), 445–474.

Guará-Tavares, M.G. (2008) Pre-task planning, working memory capacity and L2 speech performance. Unpublished doctoral thesis, Universidade Federal de Santa Catarina.

Harrington, M. (1992) Working memory capacity as a constraint on L2 development. In R.J. Harris (ed.) *Cognitive Processing in Bilinguals* (pp. 123–135). Amsterdam: North Holland.

Hartsuiker, R.J. and Barkhuysen, P.N. (2006) Language production and working memory: The case of subject–verb agreement. *Language and Cognitive Processes* 21, 181–204.

Hauser, M., Chomsky, N. and Fitch, W. (2002) The faculty of language: What is it, who has it, and how did it evolve? *Science* 298, 1569–1579.

Havik, E., Robert, E., van Hout, R. Schreuder, R. and Haverkort, M. (2009) Processing subject-object ambiguities in the L2: A self-paced reading study with German L2 learners of Dutch. *Language Learning* 59, 73–112.

Jackendoff, R. (2002) *Foundations of Language: Brain, Meaning, Grammar, Evolution*. Oxford: Oxford University Press.

Jackendoff, R. (2007) A parallel architecture perspective on language processing. *Brain Research* 1146, 2–22.

Juffs, A. (2006) Working memory, second language acquisition and low-educated second language and literacy learners. *LOT Occasional Papers: Netherlands Graduate School of Linguistics* 89–104.

Juffs, A. and Harrington, M. (2011) Aspects of working memory in L2 learning. *Language Teaching* 44, 137–166.

Just, M.A. and Carpenter, P.A. (1992) A capacity theory of comprehension: Individual differences in working memory. *Psychological Review* 99, 122–114.

Kane, M.J., Conway, A.R.A., Hambrick, D.Z. and Engle, R.W. (2007) Variation in working memory capacity as variation in executive attention and control. In A.R.A. Conway, C. Jarrold, M.J. Kane, A. Miyake and J.N. Towse (eds) *Variation in Working Memory* (pp. 21–49). Oxford: Oxford University Press.

Lai, C., Fei, F. and Roots, R. (2008) The contingency of recasts and noticing. *CALICO Journal* 26, 70–90.

Linck, J.A., Osthus, P., Koeth, J.T. and Bunting, M.F. (2014) Working memory and second language comprehension and production: A meta-analysis. *Psychonomic Bulletin & Review* 21(4), 861–883.

MacDonald, M.C. and Christiansen, M.H. (2002) Reassessing working memory: Comment on Just and Carpenter (1992) and Waters and Caplan (1996). *Psychological Review* 109, 35–54.

Mackey, A. (2012) *Input, Interaction and Corrective Feedback in L2 Learning*. Oxford: Oxford University Press.

Mackey, A., Philp, J., Egi, T., Fujii, A. and Tatsumi, T. (2002) Individual differences in working memory, noticing of interactional feedback and L2 development. In P. Robinson (ed.) *Individual Differences and Second Language Instruction* (pp. 181–209). Philadelphia, PA: Benjamins.

Mackey, A., Adams, R., Stafford, C. and Winke, P. (2010) Exploring the relationship between modified output and working memory capacity. *Language Learning* 60 (3), 501–533.

Martin, K.I. and Ellis, N.C. (2012) The roles of phonological STM and working memory in L2 grammar and vocabulary learning. *Studies in Second Language Acquisition* 34 (3), 379–413.

McLaughlin, B. (1995) Aptitude from an information processing perspective. *Language Testing* 11, 364–381.

Meisel, J.M. (2011) *First and Second Language Acquisition: Parallels and Differences*. Cambridge: Cambridge University Press.

Miki, S. (2012) Working memory as a factor affecting L2 listening comprehension sub-skills. *Kumamoto University Departmental Bulletin Paper* 10, 119–128.

Miller, G. (1956) The magical number of seven, plus or minus two: Some limits on our capacity for processing information. *Psychological Review* 63, 81–97.

Miyake, A. and Friedman, N.P. (1998) Individual differences in second language proficiency: Working memory as language aptitude. In A.F. Healy and L.R. Bourne (eds) *Foreign Language Learning: Psycholinguistic Studies on Training and Retention* (pp. 339–364). Mahwah, NJ: Erlbaum.

Miyake, A. and Shah, P. (1999) *Models of Working Memory: Mechanisms of Active Maintenance and Executive Control*. New York: Cambridge University Press.

Miyake, A. and Friedman, N.P. (2012) The nature and organization of individual differences in executive functions: Four general conclusions. *Current Directions in Psychological Science* 21 (1), 8–14.

Oberauer, K., Süß, H.-M., Wilhelm, O. and Wittmann, W.W. (2003) The multiple faces of working memory: Storage, processing, supervision, and coordination. *Intelligence* 31, 167–193.

O'Brien, I., Segalowitz, N., Collentine, J. and Freed, B. (2006) Phonological memory and lexical, narrative, and grammatical skills in second language oral production by adult learners. *Applied Psycholinguistics* 27, 377–402.

O'Brien, I., Segalowitz, N., Collentine, J. and Freed, B. (2007) Phonological memory predicts second language oral fluency gains in adults. *Studies in Second Language Acquisition* 29, 557–582.

O'Grady, W. (2005) *Syntactic Carpentry: An Emergentist Approach to Syntax*. Mahwah, NJ: Erlbaum.

O'Grady, W. (2012) Three factors in the design and acquisition of language. *Wiley Interdisciplinary Reviews: Cognitive Science* 3, 493–499.

Payne, J.S. and Whitney, P.J. (2002) Developing L2 oral proficiency through synchronous CMC: Output, working memory, and interlanguage development. *CALICO Journal* 20, 7–32.

Révész, A. (2012) Working memory and the observed effectiveness of recasts on different L2 outcome measures. *Language Learning* 62 (1), 93–132.

Rudner, M. and Rönnberg, J. (2008) The role of the episodic buffer in working memory for language processing. *Cognitive Processing* 9 (1), 19–28.

Sagarra, N. (2007) From CALL to face-to-face interaction: The effect of computer-delivered recasts and working memory on L2 development. In A. Mackey (ed.) *Conversational Interaction in Second Language Acquisition: A Series of Empirical Studies* (pp. 229–248). Oxford: Oxford University Press.

Sagarra, N. and Abbuhl, R. (2013) Optimizing the noticing of face-to-face recasts via computer-delivered feedback: Evidence that oral input enhancement and working memory help L2 learning. *Modern Language Journal* 97, 196–216.

Sawyer, M. and Ranta, L. (2001) Aptitude, individual differences, and instructional design. In P. Robinson (ed.) *Cognition and Second Language Instruction* (pp. 319–353). New York: Cambridge.

Service, E. (1992) Phonology, working memory and foreign-language learning. *Quarterly Journal of Experimental Psychology* 5, 21–50.

Skehan, P. (2002) Theorising and updating aptitude. In P. Robinson (ed.) *Individual Differences and Instructed Language Learning* (pp. 69–94) Amsterdam: John Benjamins.

Skehan, P. (2012) Language aptitude. In S. Gass and A. Mackey (eds) *Routledge Handbook of Second Language Acquisition* (pp. 381–395). New York: Routledge.

Skehan, P. (2015, in press) Foreign language aptitude and its relationship with grammar: A critical overview. *Applied Linguistics*.

Skrzypek, A. (2009) Phonological short-term memory and L2 collocational development in adult learners. *EUROSLA Yearbook* 9, 160–184.

Soto, D. and Silvanto, J. (2014) Reappraising the relationship between working memory and conscious awareness. *Trends in Cognitive Sciences* 18, 520–525.

Speciale, G., Ellis, N.C. and Bywater, T. (2004) Phonological sequence learning and short-term store capacity determine second language vocabulary acquisition. *Applied Psycholinguistics* 25, 293–321.

Steinhauer, K. (2014) Event-related potentials (ERPs) in second language research: A brief introduction to the technique, a selected review, and an invitation to reconsider critical periods in L2. Applied Linguistics 35 (4), 393–417.

Szmalec, A., Brysbaert, M. and Duyck, W. (2013) Working memory and (second) language processing. In J. Altarriba and L. Isurin (eds) *Memory, Language, and Bilingualism: Theoretical and Applied Approaches* (pp. 74–94). Cambridge University Press.

Turner, M.L. and Engle, R.W. (1989) Is working memory task dependent? *Journal of Memory and Language* 28, 127–154.

Ullman, M.T. (2012) The declarative/procedural model. In P. Robinson (ed.) *Routledge Encyclopedia of Second Language Acquisition* (pp. 160–164). London: Routledge.

Waters, G.S. and Caplan, D. (1996) The measurement of verbal working memory and its relation to reading comprehension. *Quarterly Journal of Experimental Psychology* 49A, 51–74.

Waters, G.S. and Caplan, D. (2003) The reliability and stability of verbal working memory measures. *Behavior Research Methods, Instruments, and Computers* 35, 550–564.

Waters, G.S. and Caplan, D. (2005) The relationship between age, processing speed, working memory capacity, and language comprehension. *Memory* 13, 403–413.

Wen, Z. (2012a) Working memory and second language learning. *International Journal of Applied Linguistics* 22, 1–22.

Wen, Z. (2012b) Foreign language aptitude. *ELT Journal* 66 (2), 233–235.

Wen, Z. (2014) Theorizing and measuring working memory in first and second language research. *Language Teaching* 47 (2), 173–190.

Wen, Z. (2016, manuscript under review) Working Memory and Second Language Learning: An Integrated Approach. Multilingual Matters.

Wen, Z. and Skehan, P. (2011) A new perspective on foreign language aptitude: Building and supporting a case for "working memory as language aptitude". *Ilha Do Desterro: A Journal of English Language, Literatures and Cultural Studies* 60, 15–44.

Wen, Z., Mota, M. and McNeill, A. (2013) Working memory and SLA: Towards an integrated theory. *Asian Journal of English Language Teaching* 23, 1–103.

Wen, Z., Biedron, A. and Skehan, P. (2016, forthcoming) Foreign language aptitude theory: Yesterday, today and tomorrow. *Language Teaching*.

Williams, J.N. (2012) Working memory and SLA. In S. Gass and A. Mackey (eds) *Handbook of Second Language Acquisition* (pp. 427–441). Oxford: Routledge/Taylor & Francis.

Williams, J.N. and Lovatt, P. (2003) Phonological memory and rule learning. *Language Learning* 53, 67–121.

4 Working Memory and Interpreting: A Commentary on Theoretical Models

Yanping Dong and Rendong Cai

Introduction

Interpreting, especially simultaneous interpreting (SI), is probably one of the most demanding language processing tasks (Frauenfelder & Schriefer, 1997). Its success is thus thought to depend on working memory (WM), as was recognised as early as the report on aptitude testing for interpreters by Keiser (1965) in the AIIC Paris Colloque. However, WM has seldom been included in screening tests for potential interpreting students (for a detailed review of aptitude testing, see Russo [2011]). This discrepancy is a reflection of the controversial views about the role of WM in interpreting and in interpreter training.

The role of WM in interpreting has been examined in empirical studies and speculated in theoretical models, which will be introduced in the following part of this chapter. In terms of the empirical studies, there are three main lines of research: studies testing whether expert interpreters have an advantage in WM compared to novice interpreters and non-interpreters, studies investigating the relationship between WM and interpreter training and studies probing into the issue of how WM as one sub-skill contributes to the complex skill of interpreting together with other interpreting-related sub-skills. Among these three lines of research, the first line is most widely studied but the findings are mixed. The remaining two lines are less studied and call for further systematic research. As for the theoretical models, they attempt to provide a comprehensive picture of how WM operates in conjunction with other processes in the service of interpreting. These models still await more empirical evidence.

Interpreter Advantage in WM

Evidence supporting an interpreter advantage in WM

Padilla *et al.* (1995) conducted one of the first studies reporting an interpreter advantage in WM. They used free recall with and without articulatory suppression, digit span and reading span to test the memory skills of four groups of participants: 10 interpreters, 10 non-interpreter controls, 10 student interpreters who had finished their training programme in translation but had not yet received any SI training and 10 student interpreters who had received some SI training. The *digit span test* in Padilla *et al.* (1995) required recalling a series of digits in their exact same presentation order. The task started with a set of three sequences of four digits, with the number of digits increasing gradually until participants were unable to recall them correctly. The design of the *reading span task* followed the first viable WM span task developed by Daneman and Carpenter (1980). The participants were asked to read sets of sentences and then recall the last word of each sentence. The number of sentences in a set increased from set to set and the participants were required to produce perfect recall of the final words. The third task, *free recall*, was conducted in two conditions – with or without articulatory suppression. In the non-articulatory suppression condition, participants were visually presented with 3 lists of 16 words. They were instructed to read and remember the presented words, and then to report verbally as many words as possible on completion of the presentation of each list. In the articulatory suppression condition, participants were required to repeat the syllable 'bla' while reading and memorising the words presented, and then recall the words. The result was that the group of interpreters outperformed the other groups in digit span, reading span and free recall with articulatory suppression (but not free recall without articulatory suppression), suggesting that interpreters have a memory advantage and are less disturbed by phonological interference compared with the other groups. This pattern was replicated by Padilla *et al.* (2005) with a similar design and participants of similar background.

An interpreter memory advantage was also observed in word span, speaking span and reading span tasks by Christoffels *et al.* (2006). The authors compared 13 professional Dutch–English interpreters with (1) 39 unbalanced Dutch–English bilingual students with a mean age of 21.1 years, and (2) 15 Dutch–English teachers matched in age (48.5 vs 43.5 years old), educational background and professional experience (15.7 vs 18.8 years). All the memory tasks were administered in both Dutch and English and the critical words in each task were matched in frequency and length across languages. For the *word span task*, the participants were presented with 3 successive sets of 4–10 words, and were then asked to recall the words in exactly the same presentation order. When the participant failed to correctly recall one out of the three series of a given number of words, the test was terminated. The number of correctly recalled sets was calculated as the participant's word span. The *reading span task* was also adapted from Daneman and Carpenter (1980). Forty-two sentences were randomly divided into three lists, each with successive sets of two, three, four and five sentences. The sentences were presented to the participants in increasing set sizes and the participants were asked to verbally recall the final word of each sentence on completion of each set. The reading span of each participant was the total number of words recalled correctly. There was no order restriction on recall. For the *speaking span task*, 42 words were selected to make up three successive sets of two, three, four and five words. Participants were asked to read and remember the words presented. After the presentation of a complete set, the participant was asked to verbally produce a grammatically correct sentence for each of the words in the set. The total number of proper sentences containing the correctly memorised words was the participant's speaking span. Again, there was no order restriction on recall.

An interpreter advantage was further reported for listening span, free recall with articulatory suppression and category probe by Köpke and Nespoulous (2006). The participants in this study included 21 professional interpreters, 18 second-year interpreting students and two control groups (20 multilinguals and 20 students). All three span tasks in Köpke and Nespoulous (2006) – word span, digit span and listening span – required serial recall, that is, the participants were required to recall the items in the exact same presentation order. In the *category probe task*, participants were instructed to listen to lists of between 4 and 12 items. At the end of each list, they saw a phonological or semantic probe word, and were then asked to judge whether the probe word rhymed with or belonged to one of the words in the list by saying 'yes' or 'no'. The result was that an interpreter advantage was found in listening span, free recall and category probe, but not in digit span and word span.

It should be noted that the significant group effects observed in free recall with articulatory suppression, in category probe and in listening span in Köpke and Nespoulous (2006) were mainly shown for by novice interpreters rather than expert interpreters. In other words, it was novice interpreters rather than expert interpreters who performed best. To explain these results, Köpke and Signorelli (2012) suggested that memory skills might be more developed in novice interpreters because novice interpreters frequently encounter cognitive overload, whereas interpreting experts, with extensive practice and rich experience, may have developed specific strategies or schemas (e.g. Norman & Shallice, 1986) that are less reliant on WM.

In addition to the aforementioned studies, an interpreter advantage in WM was also observed in Tzou *et al.* (2012) and in Signorelli *et al.* (2012). Both studies will be reviewed in detail in the section 'Possible confounding factors leading to the mixed results'.

Data failing to support an interpreter advantage in WM

Although an interpreter advantage in WM has been observed in many tasks and in various research settings, some studies have failed to support this advantage. For example, no advantage for interpreters was found for digit span in a study conducted by Chincotta and Underwood (1998). The participants for this study included 12 interpreting students with about 100 hours of interpreting practice and 12 bilingual students majoring in English. Both groups were asked to recall lists of digits presented visually and the test stopped when the participant made two incorrect responses. The digit span task was administered in two languages, Finnish and English, and with or without articulatory suppression. The result was that no group effect was found for digit span in any conditions. Similarly, no interpreter advantage was observed for digit span or word span in Köpke and Nespoulous (2006).

Another study that failed to support an interpreter advantage in WM was conducted by Liu et al. (2004). The authors recruited three groups of participants: 11 professional interpreters, 11 advanced student interpreters at the end of their second year (final year) of training and 11 beginning student interpreters at the end of their first year of training. The authors measured participants' memory capacity with a listening span task. Listening span tasks are similar to reading span tasks in that both tap the storage-plus-processing function of WM, by asking participants to recall the last word in each of a set of sentences while simultaneously attempting to comprehend these sentences. The result of Liu et al. (2004) was that significant group effects for SI performance were observed but the difference in WM capacity between the three groups of participants failed to reach significance. The authors attributed the difference in SI performance, at least in part, to the development of specific interpreting skills rather than to WM capacity.

Possible confounding factors leading to the mixed results

The review above illustrates that the evidence for an interpreter advantage in WM is mixed, with a majority of studies supporting such an advantage. The mixed findings are probably a result of the different research designs adopted.

First of all, participant selection may be responsible for the mixed findings. In most of the empirical studies, participant size was relatively small, for example being 10 participants per group in Padilla et al. (1995), 11 in Liu et al. (2004), 12 in Chincotta and Underwood (1998) and less than 13 in Signorelli et al. (2012). Because of these studies' small participant sizes, their null results may reflect a lack of statistical power for detecting an effect (Signorelli, 2008).

More importantly, there have been some qualitative differences between participants across these studies. One such qualitative difference is professional experience. As pointed out by Köpke and Signorelli (2012), different studies have different definitions of interpreters, especially professional interpreters. For example, in Padilla et al. (1995), 5 of the 10 professional interpreters were students who had just passed the final exam of an interpreting training programme. Such participants would have been considered novices rather than expert interpreters in Köpke and Nespoulous (2006). In other words, in terms of professional experience, the professional interpreters in Padilla *et al.* (1995) were more like novice interpreters in Köpke and Nespoulous (2006). Therefore, the contradictory results across the studies might be more apparent than real. The findings seem to support the specific development of memory skills in novice interpreters who often encounter cognitive overload but not in interpreting experts who may not depend as heavily on WM due to strategies developed from experience and practice.

Another factor that may account for the mixed results concerning a WM advantage in interpreters is age. The studies on a WM advantage in interpreters have often involved the comparison between professional interpreters and novice and/or bilingual students. Professional interpreters are generally older than novice or student interpreters in age. Research on individual differences in WM show that WM capacity is closely related to age: WM capacity declines as a function of age (Caplan *et al.*, 2011; Carpenter *et al.*, 1994; Charlton *et al.*, 2010). Therefore, it is possible that the older age of professional interpreters has contributed to their lack of a WM advantage when compared with younger novice interpreters and untrained bilinguals. This consequence of confounding age and interpreter experience was confirmed recently by Signorelli *et al.* (2012). The participants in their studies included 12 younger interpreters (8 female) ranging in age from 30 to 40 years with a mean age of 34.5 (SD=3.5); 11 younger non-interpreters (6 female) ranging in age from 26 to 41 years with a mean age of 31.8 (SD=5.0); 13 older interpreters (9 female) ranging in age from 46 to 67 with a mean age of 56.2 (SD=7.3); and 11 older non-interpreters (6 female) ranging in age from 48 to 81 with a mean age of 63.6 (SD=11.6). The tasks were non-word repetition, cued recall and reading span tasks. The result was that younger interpreters were marginally better in non-word recognition and cued recall than older interpreters, suggesting age may have contributed to an interpreter advantage in WM.

Another potential confounding factor is the L2 proficiency of interpreters. Research from WM studies has indicated that language proficiency plays a role in the capacity differences between L1 and L2 WM span (Chincotta & Underwood, 1998; Service *et al.*, 2002). In the field of interpreting, evidence from a study by Tzou *et al.* (2012) sheds some light on this issue. They used digit and reading span tasks to compare memory performance in three groups of participants: student interpreters with one year of formal training (*n*=11), student interpreters with two years of formal training (*n*=9) and Mandarin–English bilingual controls (*n*=16). They observed that participants with higher L2 proficiency had larger WM spans than participants with lower L2 proficiency, suggesting that L2 proficiency contributes to an interpreter advantage in WM.

Lastly, some methodological factors of the tasks used in measuring participants' WM capacity may have also contributed to the contradictory results bearing on whether an interpreter advantage in WM exists. There are mainly two types of memory span tasks: (1) simple span tasks, such as digit span, word span or non-word repetition tasks, that mainly tap the storage component of WM or short-term memory (STM), and (2) complex span tasks, such as speaking span or reading span tasks, that tap the storage-plus-processing function of WM. Research from WM studies indicates that STM and WM function differently in language processes, such as reading comprehension (Daneman & Merikle, 1996). This may explain why a significant advantage was observed in interpreters using complex WM span tasks but no such advantage was found using simple span tasks in the same study (e.g. Kopke & Nespoulous, 2006). Even with the same type of tasks that measure the storage-plus-processing function of WM, some features of the task, such as the number of trials or the scoring method, may result in the observed difference in cognitive ability. For example, Köpke and Signorelli (2012) pointed out that variable recall constraints (serial recall vs free recall) may be related to inconsistencies in results from reading or listening span tasks across studies probing for a WM advantage in interpreters.

In short, future studies testing for an interpreter advantage in interpreting may need to pay more attention to research design, which is crucial to the validity of research conclusions. Possible factors in the research design that may have affected the results include participant selection (e.g. age, language learning history and proficiency, interpreting training history and interpreting practice history) and other methodological details like scoring methods.

WM and Interpreting Training

Initial findings

Studies testing for an interpreter advantage in WM could provide many insights into the relationship between WM and interpreting. However, there is a theoretical limitation to this line of research: Even if we could establish an interpreter advantage in WM over non-interpreters, we would still not be in a position to claim that extensive practice in interpreting leads to the development of WM capacity. An alternative explanation for this finding would be that it simply reflects a pre-training trait in interpreters, which led them to pursue that particular career path (Christoffels *et al.*, 2006). One way to solve this problem is to conduct a longitudinal study to see if WM improves with interpreting training, and as far as we know, only one study has been published.

Zhang (2008) collected longitudinal data about the memory performances of three groups of Chinese–English participants in China: 35 beginning interpreting students (university students in their first year of training), 35 advanced interpreting students (university students in their second year of training) and 13 professional interpreters with 5 or more years of professional experience. Data were first collected on reading span (in Chinese) and on participants' ability to coordinate in situations of encountering difficulty. Six months later the same tests were readministered. The results indicated that the six months of interpreting training and practice improved the first group's reading span (beginning interpreting students) and the second group's (advanced interpreting students) coordination ability. Prolonged interpreting training and practice thus seem to improve WM capacity, although there may be a ceiling effect for advanced interpreting students and for professional interpreters.

Our own lab has also been engaged in an effort to test WM improvement in interpreting training. The participants for our project included two groups of Chinese–English student interpreters at a university in China: 120 beginning student interpreters and 20 advanced student interpreters. Students in each group were comparable in age and language learning history. A battery of WM tasks were used to test participants' WM capacity in both groups on two separate occasions at the beginning and end of the academic year. By statistically controlling for participants' initial WM capacities measured at pre-test, we could determine whether WM capacities had developed after one year's training in interpreting. Major findings were that participants' WM improved on some measures like listening span but not on others like digit span.

Just as interpreting training may improve WM, so too may the size of WM capacity contribute to the development of interpreting performance. We have made an initial attempt to test this by collecting longitudinal data from a group of student interpreters on a series of tests of WM capacity (English/Chinese listening/speaking span, digit span), English proficiency and interpreting performance (Cai et al., forthcoming). The tests were conducted twice, at the beginning and end of a 10-month academic year throughout which the student interpreters received interpreting training. By statistically controlling for the starting point of interpreting skills, we can determine whether the gains in interpreting skills are different for participants with different WM capacity. Major results are that only general language proficiency made a significant contribution to the variance in consecutive interpreting (CI) performance after removing the effects of prior CI skills for these beginning interpreting students. In other words, the magnitude of the students' progress in interpreting performance was not related to their difference in WM capacity.

The factor of WM tasks at work

There are too few empirical studies to date for us to make many comments about the mechanism of WM in interpreting. But the three attempts reviewed above seem to indicate that when we interpret experimental results about WM, we have to take into consideration what kinds of WM span tasks are used to measure WM. Zhang (2008) found that for beginning interpreting students, six months' interpreting training improved reading span in L1, which has been replicated by our lab. However, we conducted more tests of WM span and found that although listening span in both L1 and L2 improved, digit span did not. The conclusion about the issue of WM improvement in interpreting training is, therefore, dependent on the type of WM task used. The name of the WM task itself has to be included in the conclusion.

The highly complex nature of WM span tasks is highlighted by the hierarchical view of WM, according to which WM span tasks may tap both domain-general (controlled attention or central executive) and domain-specific components (Engle et al., 1999a). There are no pure WM tasks because individual differences in the performance of any WM task reflect not only domain-general components but also domain-specific components, such as coding, grouping, rehearsal strategies and familiarity with the specific type of stimuli used (Engle et al., 1999b). In short, the hierarchical view suggests that, when compared to digit and spatial spans, language spans like reading span are more closely related to language processes like reading comprehension.

To explore the relationship between different measurements of WM span, Cai and Dong (2012) asked 68 Chinese–English bilingual students to complete 8 WM span tasks (testing Chinese and English listening/speaking/reading spans, digit span and spatial span). The result from cluster analysis is displayed in Figure 4.1. The factors that may account for the differences in various WM tests differ in their distinguishing power: from relatively strong (information type: verbal or non-verbal), to medium (encoding modality: listening, reading or speaking), to relatively weak (encoding language: L1 or L2). This result provides additional evidence for the domain specificity of WM, which implies that WM is closely connected with other cognitive skills such as language skills and spatial processing skills.

Role of WM in Interpreting in Relation to Other Relevant Sub-Skills

Initial findings

This section discusses the third line of research, which aims to examine the role of WM in interpreting performance in relation to other relevant

* * * * * * H I E R A R C H I C A L   C L U S T E R   A N A L Y S I S * * * * * *

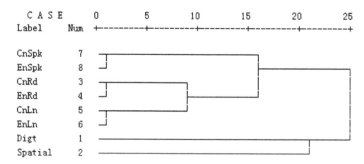

Dendrogram using Average Linkage (Between Groups)

Rescaled Distance Cluster Combine

```
    C A S E       0       5      10      15      20      25
    Label     Num  +---------+---------+---------+---------+---------+

    CnSpk      7
    EnSpk      8
    CnRd       3
    EnRd       4
    CnLn       5
    EnLn       6
    Digt       1
    Spatial    2
```

Figure 4.1 The relationship between different measures of WM span (CnSpk: Chinese speaking span, EnSpk: English speaking span; CnRd: Chinese reading span; EnRd: English reading span; CnLn: Chinese listening span; EnLn: English listening span; Digit: digit span; Spatial: spatial span) (Cai & Dong, 2012)

sub-skills. So far, to our knowledge, there have only been two studies on this issue, one by Christoffels *et al.* (2003) and the other by our lab (Dong *et al.*, 2013).

Christoffels *et al.* (2003) focused on the roles of memory and lexical retrieval in B-to-A SI (English–Dutch SI) for untrained bilinguals. Memory capacity was measured in a reading span task in both languages and a verbal digit span task in Dutch, while lexical retrieval efficiency (i.e. response time) was measured in a picture naming task in both languages and a word translation task in both directions (from Dutch to English and from English to Dutch). Based on the data collected, the authors constructed a graphic model (see Figure 4.2). In this model, L2 reading span and L1–L2 word translation were the most relevant to SI because they had a direct effect on interpreting performance. Any influence of the other variables was mediated by these two variables. Christoffels *et al.* (2003) concluded that WM and word translation efficiency form independent sub-skills of SI performance in untrained bilinguals.

Unlike the 24 untrained bilinguals in Christoffels *et al.* (2003), the participants in our study (Dong *et al.*, 2013) were 52 Chinese–English student interpreters who had just completed two semesters of interpreting training. Altogether, 19 tests were administered, including CI in two directions, tests of language skills (English proficiency, source language comprehension and source language summarising skills in the writing modality), different measures of WM span (listening, reading and speaking

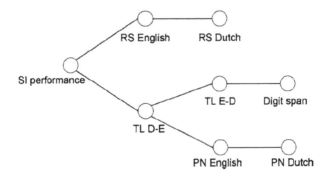

Figure 4.2 Graphical model on the relation between performance on simultaneous interpreting and other tasks (RS=reading span, TL=word translation, E=English, D=Dutch, PN=picture naming task) (Christoffels *et al.*, 2003: 207)

spans in both languages, and digit and spatial spans), cognitive control tasks (a number Stroop task and a flanker task) and an interpreter anxiety test. Based on the analysis of correlations between the interpreting scores and the other test scores, a valid structural equation model was established for English–Chinese CI (see Figure 4.3). The results indicate that, for student interpreters, although language skills are important to English–Chinese interpreting performance, these skills mostly function through the mediation of psychological competence, which includes interpreter anxiety, English listening span and Chinese speaking span. The general conclusion is that interpreting training is perhaps a process of learning to coordinate one's relevant capabilities during the demanding task of interpreting.

More research needed

It is clear that the role of WM in interpreting in relation to other relevant sub-skills is under-explored. Interpreting strategies, important to interpreters, are not touched on yet in this line of research. The two studies reviewed above are far from enough. Christoffels *et al.* (2003) only studied the role of WM (reading span and digit span) in SI in relation to lexical retrieval efficiency (efficiency in word translation and picture naming). Dong *et al.* (2013) tested more variables in CI but there are still other variables not included such as interpreting strategies used by the participants. It will be very interesting to see how the relative contribution of WM changes as bilingual students gradually grow to be novice and then professional interpreters.

What is more, according to our understanding, studying the role of WM in CI rather than in SI may be a better way to study the role of WM in interpreting, especially when interpreting performance needs to be tested as in Christoffels *et al.* (2007) and Dong *et al.* (2013). Up until now, almost

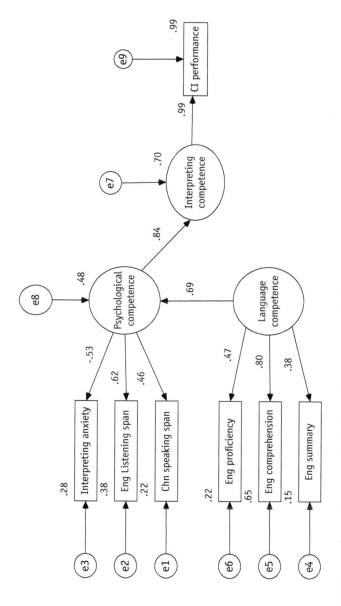

Figure 4.3 Structural equation model for English–Chinese consecutive interpreting (Dong et al., 2013)

all the studies regarding WM in interpreting have focused on SI, probably because SI is considered more demanding than CI. SI is demanding in that interpreters have to coordinate the two tasks of comprehension and production simultaneously. Coordination and suppression are therefore more important than WM capacity for this feature of multitasking and are perhaps better research topics for SI. On the contrary, the task of CI is demanding in that interpreters have to first comprehend the coming input while trying to remember as much as possible and to then produce coherent messages from what has been remembered, which matches closely the storage-plus-processing definition of WM. Studying the role of WM capacity in CI is therefore more promising than studying its role in SI.

Models for Relation Between WM and Interpreting

The effort models

Gile (1997/2002) proposed the effort models to describe the non-automatic cognitive operations involved in interpreting. In this general conceptual framework, efforts for interpreting are not strictly separate from each other and sometimes the operation of one effort needs support from the operation of another.

The effort models for SI and CI differ to some extent because of the different task demands in the two forms of interpreting. The effort model for SI is represented as

$$SI = L + P + M + C$$

In this equation, the L ('listening and analysis') effort refers to the operations of decoding the source language (SL) to obtain the conveyed meaning. The P ('production') effort includes operations starting from the generation of the intended message to target language (TL) articulation. The M ('memory') effort contributes to the processing of L and P and to strategies used to guarantee successful interpreting (e.g. dealing with errors in SL speech). The C ('coordination') effort refers to the management of all the other efforts.

As for CI, the efforts involved are analysed separately in the input phase (e.g. listening to SL speech) and in the output phase (e.g. reformulating the message into the TL), which are shown as follows:

$$CI \text{ (listening)} = L + M + N + C$$
$$CI \text{ (reformulation)} = Rem + Read + P$$

In the equation of 'CI (listening)', the L and C efforts are the same as those in the SI equation discussed above. The N ('note-taking') effort is a distinguishing feature in this model. It includes operations for deciding what information should be written and operations for recording notes. The M ('memory') effort sustains the L and C efforts, as in the SI model, and also supports the efforts related to note-taking. In the equation of 'CI (reformulation)', the Rem ('remembering') effort refers to retrieving the to-be-conveyed meaning from memory and from the notes; the Read ('note-reading') effort comes from reading the notes; and the P effort is the production operation as in the SI model. Taken together, in the effort models for CI, efforts related to note-taking and note-reading play an important role, and they require support from an interpreter's memory (especially at the reformulation stage).

The gist of the effort models is that for an interpretation to be successful, the total processing capacity *available* should exceed or at least be equal to the processing capacity *required*; otherwise, inferior performance may occur, such as errors and omissions. Gile (1999), in a test of the 'tightrope hypothesis', found errors and omissions affecting source language segments that present no intrinsic difficulty and that were more a result of processing capacity deficits, as predicted by the effort models.

In all the effort models, the M ('memory') effort is supposed to support much of the other efforts. Although the term 'working memory' is not used here, this M effort can be roughly considered as the functioning of WM. Furthermore, the notion that various efforts or operations involved in interpreting need support from an interpreter's finite cognitive resources matches the key feature of the function of WM. In a word, the essential role of WM in interpreting is recognised in the effort models. But as was mentioned, this model is largely a conceptual framework whose significance mainly lies in its contribution to interpreting training.

The process models

The two most recent models that are applied to account for the process of interpreting are the multi-component model of WM proposed by Baddeley (2000) and Baddeley and Hitch (1974) and the embedded-processes model of memory proposed by Cowan (1988, 1995, 2005). In the classical model by Baddeley and Hitch (1974), there are three components: two domain-specific storage subsystems (the phonological loop and the visuospatial sketchpad) and the central executive control that acts as an attention-control structure and coordinator for the two storage components. A fourth component, the episodic buffer, was subsequently added to this tripartite model by Baddeley (2000).

Based on the original tripartite model and on findings about long-term memory, Darò and Fabbro (1994) proposed their influential process model for SI. The model mainly illustrates how WM and long-term memory function together in the process of SI. It should be noted that one of the storage subsystems in WM, the visuospatial sketchpad, is not included in the model because it is seldom involved in SI. More details are devoted to the phonological loop, which consists of a 'phonological store' and 'subvocal rehearsal'.

Contrasting with Baddeley and Hitch's multi-component models (Baddeley, 2000; Baddeley & Hitch, 1974), Cowan proposes that human memory is a single storage system composed of elements at various levels of activation (see Figure 4.4 for the embedded-processes model). This system can be conceived of as long-term memory, in which most of the elements are relatively inactive. Within long-term memory, some elements are above the threshold of activation. This information is thought to be in STM and outside of conscious awareness but nevertheless affects online processing such as semantic priming. Among the pieces of information in STM, some elements are in an even higher state of activation because they fall into the focus of attention (FOA). The information in the FOA is in a hyper-activated state and maintained or manipulated with conscious effort.

In Cowan's (1995: 100) embedded-processes model, 'WM is a more complex construct than STM, defined as the set of activated memory elements; there is no doubt that WM is based on that activated information along with central executive processes'. Because of the proposal of differential activation levels for the memory system, which seems to be more consistent with language processing, attempts have been made to adapt the model for the demanding task of interpreting. In fact, Cowan (2000) himself suggests that the embedded-processes model can be applied to explain the process of interpreting.

On the basis of Cowan's embedded processes model, Mizuno (2005) proposed his enlarged embedded-processes model for SI. This model is valuable in that it emphasises the interaction between the memory system and the language system. As illustrated in Figure 4.5, the central executive and long-term memory overlap with the language comprehension system and the language production system. The

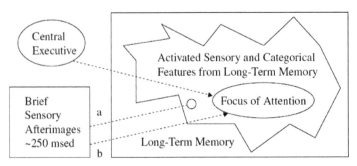

Figure 4.4 The embedded-processes model of memory (Cowan, 1988, 1995, 2005)

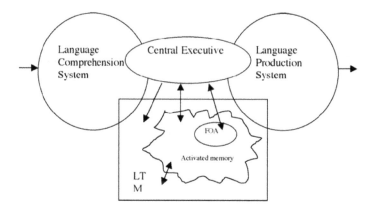

Figure 4.5 The process model of WM and interpreting by Mizuno (2005: 744)

separation of the comprehension system and the production system represents the two stages of SI and the direction of the arrows indicates how information is processed at each stage. However, just as Mizuno (2005: 744) said, the model 'may seem indistinguishable from the normal language processing system'.

More empirical research needed

The above-introduced theoretical models depicting the role of WM in the process of interpreting work well as conceptual frameworks. But more work is apparently needed to test the claims and to specify exactly how different components work together in different stages of the interpreting process. For example, for the process models, are the connections between boxes and the direction of each connection empirically verified? Are these models of interpreting essentially different from models of general language processing? If not empirically tested, the models will remain largely speculative, which will limit their theoretical power.

Models, like the one by Darò and Fabbro (1994) and the one by Mizuno (2005), may look quite different as they are based on different WM models and are intended to emphasise different aspects of how WM functions in the process of interpreting. It is no use trying to combine them together so as to include all their merits in a single model before more empirical evidence is available to justify this move. But attempts may be made first to simplify the models because simple models are frequently more powerful and parsimonious. For example, the two interpreting directions depicted by Darò and Fabbro (1994) seem unnecessary. The model would be more economical while remaining every bit as powerful if the two boxes for interpreting directions were replaced by a single box.

Future Directions

As mentioned at the very beginning of the chapter, the important role of WM in interpreting was recognised half a century ago but WM is seldom taken as part of screening tests (see Russo, 2011). Underlying this paradox are at least three issues. First, empirical studies on the role of WM in interpreting have not always reached the same conclusion as reviewed in the second section. Second, language proficiency and interpreting strategies are generally considered more important than WM for interpreting. Third, it is not easy to select some specific WM task as part of screening tests since WM itself is a very complex concept. To address these issues is the task for future studies. Although it is not necessary to aim at taking WM as part of screening tests at the present stage, investigating the above paradox may lead to a more systematic study of the role of WM in interpreting.

Some of the topics for future research have already been suggested in the relevant sections, but what we need most at present is perhaps for psychologists of WM and practitioners of interpreting to cooperate in clarifying the issue of WM in interpreting. First, WM is a complex concept and it is always an issue how to test WM capacity. We may find dozens of tasks to measure WM span, but do they all measure the same thing? Evidence from WM studies indicates that WM may not be a unitary construct and different WM span tasks may tap different pools of cognitive resources (Daneman & Carpenter, 1980; Daneman & Tardif, 1987; Just & Carpenter, 1992; MacDonald & Christiansen, 2002). What's more, each span task measures not only the core part of WM but also domain-specific skills like language processing skills and spatial processing skills (see Engle *et al.*, 1999b). Therefore, future studies have to take all this into consideration so that different studies can be compared with each other.

Second, executive control is an essential part of WM, which is true not only in the multi-component models of Baddeley and Hitch (Baddeley, 2000; Baddeley & Hitch, 1974) but also in the embedded-processes model of Cowan (1988, 1995, 2005). What exactly is the relation between executive control and different measurements of WM span? And what is the relationship between WM span tasks and tasks testing cognitive control such as the Stroop task and the flanker task? These questions are apparently related to the issue of WM in interpreting. Dong *et al.* (2013) employed both the Stroop task and the flanker task but they were not correlated to CI performance and therefore could not be put in the structural equation model (Figure 4.3). More studies are therefore needed to test the relationship between different measures of WM and cognitive control in different stages of interpreting training.

Acknowledgements

We would like to thank Dr Zhisheng Wen, Dr Jiexun Lin and Dr Kalim Gonzales for their insightful suggestions and detailed edits of previous versions of this chapter. The writing of this chapter was supported by grants from the Chinese Ministry of Education (2009JJD740007), the National Social Science Foundation of China (10BYY010) and the New Century Talents Program by the Chinese Ministry of Education.

References

Baddeley, A.D. (2000) The episodic buffer: A new component of working memory? *Trends in Cognitive Sciences* 4 (11), 417–423.

Baddeley, A.D. and Hitch, G.J. (1974) Working memory. In G.H. Bower (ed.) *The Psychology of Learning and Motivation* (Vol. 8; pp. 47–89). New York: Academic Press.

Cai, R. and Dong, Y. (2012) Effects of information type, encoding modality, and encoding language on working memory span: Evidence for the hierarchical view (in Chinese). *Foreign Language Teaching and Research* 44 (3), 376–388.

Cai, R., Dong, Y., Zhao, N. and Lin, J. (forthcoming) Factors contributing to individual differences in the development of consecutive interpreting competence for beginning student interpreters. *Interpreter and Translator Trainer*.

Caplan, D., DeDe, G., Waters, G.S., Michaud, J. and Tripodis, Y. (2011) Effects of age, speed of processing, and working memory on comprehension of sentences with relative clauses. *Psychology and Aging* 26 (2), 439–450.

Carpenter, P.A., Miyake, A. and Just, M.A. (1994) Working memory constraints in comprehension: Evidence from individual differences, aphasia, and aging. In M.A. Gernsbacher (ed.) *Handbook of Psycholinguistics* (pp. 1075–1122). San Diego, CA: Academic Press.

Charlton, R.A., Schiavone, F., Barrick, T.R., Morris, R.G. and Markus, H.S. (2010) Diffusion tensor imaging detects age related white matter change over a 2-year follow-up which is associated with working memory decline. *Journal of Neurology, Neurosurgery & Psychiatry* 81 (1), 13–19. doi: 10.1136/jnnp.2008.167288

Chincotta, D. and Underwood, G. (1998) Simultaneous interpreters and the effect of concurrent articulation on immediate memory: A bilingual digit span study. *Interpreting* 3 (1), 1–20.

Christoffels, I.K., de Groot, A.M.B. and Waldorp, L.J. (2003) Basic skills in a complex task: A graphical model relating memory and lexical retrieval to simultaneous interpreting. *Bilingualism: Language and Cognition* 6 (3), 201–211.

Christoffels, I.K., de Groot, A.M.B. and Kroll, J.F. (2006) Memory and language skills in simultaneous interpreters: The role of expertise and language proficiency. *Journal of Memory and Language* 54 (3), 324–345.

Cowan, N. (1988) Evolving conceptions of memory storage, selective attention, and their mutual constraints within the human information processing system. *Psychological Bulletin* 104 (2), 163–191.

Cowan, N. (1995) *Attention and Memory: An Integrated Framework*. Oxford: Oxford University Press.

Cowan, N. (2000) Processing limits of selective attention and working memory: Potential implications for interpreting. *Interpreting* 5 (2), 117–146.

Cowan, N. (2005) *Working Memory Capacity*. New York & Hove: Psychology Press.

Daneman, M. and Carpenter, P.A. (1980) Individual differences in working memory and reading. *Journal of Verbal Learning and Verbal Behavior* 19, 450–466.

Daneman, M. and Tardif, T. (1987) Working memory and reading skill re-examined. In M. Coltheart (ed.) *Attention and Performance XII* (pp. 491–508). London: Erlbaum.

Daneman, M. and Merikle, P.M. (1996) Working memory and language comprehension: A meta-analysis. *Psychonomic Bulletin and Review* 3 (4), 422–433.

Darò, V. and Fabbro, F. (1994) Verbal memory during simultaneous interpretation: Effects of phonological interference. *Applied Linguistics* 15 (4), 365–381.

Dong, Y., Cai, R., Zhao, N. and Lin, J. (2013) An empirical study on interpreting competence structures in student interpreters (In Chinese). *Foreign Languages* 36 (4), 76–86.

Engle, R.W., Kane, M.J. and Tuholski, S.W. (1999a) Individual differences in working memory capacity and what they tell us about controlled attention, general fluid intelligence, and functions of the prefrontal cortex. In A. Miyake and P. Shah (eds) *Models of Working Memory: Mechanisms of Active Maintenance and Executive Control* (pp. 102–134). New York: Cambridge University Press.

Engle, R.W., Tuholski, S.W., Laughlin, J.E. and Conway, A.R.A. (1999b) Working memory, short-term memory, and general fluid intelligence: A latent-variable approach. *Journal of Experimental Psychology: General* 128 (3), 309–331.

Frauenfelder, U.H. and Schriefer, H. (1997) A psycholinguistic perspective on simultaneous interpretation. *Interpreting* 2, 55–89.

Gile, D. (1997/2002) Conference interpreting as a cognitive management problem. In F. Pöchhacker and M. Shlesinger (eds) *The Interpreting Studies Reader* (pp. 162–176). London: Routledge.

Gile, D. (1999) Testing the effort models' tightrope hypothesis in simultaneous interpreting – A contribution. *Hermes* 23, 153–172.

Just, M.A. and Carpenter, P.A. (1992) A capacity theory of comprehension: Individual differences in working memory. *Psychological Review* 99 (1), 122–149.

Keiser, W. (1965) Admission dans les écoles d'interprétation. Paper presented at the AIIC, Colloque sur l'enseignement de l'interprétation, 18–19 December, Paris.

Köpke, B. and Nespoulous, J.-L. (2006) Working memory performance in expert and novice interpreters. *Interpreting* 8 (1), 1–23.

Köpke, B. and Signorelli, T.M. (2012) Methodological aspects of working memory assessment in simultaneous interpreters. *International Journal of Bilingualism* 16 (2), 183–197. doi: 10.1177/1367006911402981

Liu, M., Schallert, D.L. and Carroll, P.J. (2004) Working memory and expertise in simultaneous interpreting. *Interpreting* 6 (1), 19–42.

MacDonald, M.C. and Christiansen, M.H. (2002) Reassessing working memory: Comment on Just and Carpenter (1992) and Waters and Caplan (1996). *Psychological Review* 109 (1), 35–54.

Mizuno, A. (2005) Process model for simultaneous interpreting and working memory. *Méta* 50 (2), 739–752.

Norman, D. and Shallice, T. (1986) Attention to action: Willed and automatic control of behaviour. In R.J. Davidson, G.E. Schwarts and D. Shapiro (eds) *Consciousness and Self-regulation* (Vol. 4; pp. 1–18). New York: Plenum Press.

Padilla, P., Bajo, M.T., Canas, J.J. and Padilla, F. (1995) Cognitive processes of memory in simultaneous interpretation. In J. Tommola (ed.) *Topics in Interpreting Research* (pp. 61–72). Turku: University of Turku.

Padilla, F., Bajo, M.T. and Macizo, P. (2005) Articulatory suppression in language interpretation: Working memory capacity, dual tasking and word knowledge. *Bilingualism: Language and Cognition* 8 (3), 207–219.

Russo, M. (2011) Aptitude testing over the years. *Interpreting* 13 (1), 5–30.

Service, E., Simola, M., Metsaenheimo, O. and Maury, S. (2002) Bilingual working memory span is affected by language skill. *European Journal of Cognitive Psychology* 14 (3), 383–407.

Signorelli, T.M. (2008) *Working Memory in Simultaneous Interpreters*. PhD dissertation. The City University of New York.

Signorelli, T.M., Haarmann, H.J. and Obler, L.K. (2012) Working memory in simultaneous interpreters: Effects of task and age. *International Journal of Bilingualism* 16 (2), 198–212.

Tzou, Y.-Z., Eslami, Z.R., Chen, H.C. and Vaid, J. (2012) Effect of language proficiency and degree of formal training in simultaneous interpreting on working memory and interpreting performance: Evidence from Mandarin–English speakers. *International Journal of Bilingualism* 16 (2), 213–227.

Zhang, W. (2008) A study of the effect of simultaneous interpreting on working memory's growth potential (in Chinese). *Modern Foreign Languages* 31 (4), 423–430.

Part 2

Working Memory in L2 Processing

5 Working Memory in L2 Character Processing: The Case of Learning to Read Chinese

Sun-A Kim, Kiel Christianson and Jerome Packard

Introduction

Working memory (WM) is 'a dedicated system to maintain and store information in the short term' (Baddeley, 2003: 829). According to the best-known view of WM (Baddeley & Hitch, 1974), WM comprises three components: a higher-level control system with limited capacity of attention called the central executive, and two storage subsystems called the phonological loop and the visuospatial sketchpad. The central executive plays a role in coordinating and supervising information taken in through the phonological loop and the visuospatial sketchpad. The phonological loop temporarily maintains verbal information including sound and language, while the visuospatial sketchpad temporarily holds visual and spatial information. In other words, the WM system has two memory components in the verbal and the visuospatial domains and one attention-control component, which coordinates and regulates these two memory domains.

Various measures have been used to assess individual WM, grouped into short-term memory (STM) span tasks and WM span tasks based on the complexity of the tasks. STM span tasks are simpler than WM tasks, because STM tasks require participants to maintain target items in memory (the storage component). In contrast, WM span tasks require participants to remember targets while performing another task (Miyake et al., 2001). In short, STM tasks consist of the storage requirement, whereas WM tasks have both storage and processing requirements. Digit span tasks and non-word span tasks are examples of verbal STM tasks, in that participants try to remember and recall as many digits or non-words as possible. On the other hand, reading span tasks are examples of verbal WM tasks, in that participants read aloud sentences and judge the plausibility of sentences (the processing component) while attempting to remember the word or letter at the end of each sentence (the storage component) for later recall.

Previous studies suggest that the components of WM reflected by STM and WM span tasks differ in the verbal and visuospatial domains. In the verbal domain, simple STM tasks reflect the storage component (i.e. the phonological loop) and complex WM tasks reflect both storage and central executive components (Engle *et al.*, 1999). In the visuospatial domain, on the other hand, both STM and WM tasks are posited to involve the central executive component, but their degree of involvement in the central executive has not yet been clearly established (Miyake *et al.*, 2001; Shah & Miyake, 1996). In general, maintaining visual images is more challenging than memorising a sequence of verbal stimulus, because in the visuospatial domain a rehearsal mechanism – such as the phonological loop in the verbal domain – does not seem to exist (Miyake *et al.*, 2001).

It has been documented that WM plays an important role in learning new words in another language (Cheung, 1996; Martin & Ellis, 2012; Service, 1992). However, most of these studies have been done in languages with alphabetic writing systems using verbal STM tasks and have focused on the role of verbal WM in learning new words. Verbal WM tasks have been used more for second language (L2) learning experiments requiring 'higher cognitive resources', such as grammar learning, reading comprehension and reasoning, and tend not to be used for L2 experiments requiring vocabulary learning and reading. Even when WM is occasionally included in L2 word learning, only the verbal domain of WM is examined (Cheung, 1996; Service, 1992).

To our knowledge, no empirical research in L2 acquisition has examined how the two domains of WM (i.e. verbal WM and visuospatial WM) influence learning L2 words. If one wants to investigate how visuospatial WM contributes to learning new L2 words, Chinese reading is an ideal candidate. Chinese script is visually more complex than alphabetic writing systems, because many strokes are condensed into the space occupied by a character (e.g. 繁 'complex' and 懿 'beautiful'), and a difference even in the slant or length of a stroke will sometimes distinguish two characters (e.g. 千 'thousand' vs 干 'shield'; 天 'heaven' vs 夫 'husband'). Also, written Chinese is phonologically opaque, with pronunciation not explicitly revealed in the script. Therefore, the Chinese writing system is an ideal candidate for examining the role of verbal WM and visuospatial WM in L2 word learning due to its visual complexity and phonological opacity. If visuospatial WM plays a role in L2 word learning, then it is reasonable to expect that it would be manifested more clearly in learning to read a language like Chinese.

Although the results of research on the use of visual skills in reading Chinese are still not conclusive (e.g. McBride-Chang, 2004), it has been reported that first language (L1) Chinese readers tend to use visual strategies longer in the beginning stage of literacy and have better visual skills than native readers of alphabetic writing systems, ostensibly due to the Chinese readers' experience with visually complex characters. Four-year-old L1 Chinese children who are able to read 15 characters on average are found to still use visual strategies, although L1 English readers of an equivalent age who read about four words on average are reported not to use visual reading strategies but do use phonology-based strategies (Chen, 2004). This is further supported by another study in which five-year-old L1 Chinese children outperformed their Western counterparts in a visual task (McBride-Chang *et al.*, 2011).

The current study aimed to examine the influence of individual visuospatial WM and verbal WM on adult L2 learners' reading of simple Chinese characters with different visual features. Specifically, this study attempts to answer two questions. First, how do the visual features of characters affect learning to read? It has been reported that a visually enhanced feature in a word or a character helps less experienced readers read better (Chen, 2004; Ehri & Wilce, 1985). To examine how visual properties of characters influence reading characters by adult beginning L2 Chinese learners, visual features of simple characters were varied in three levels: distinctive, normal and similar sets. In the distinctive set, one stroke of each character was artificially enhanced to make the characters visually distinctive. The normal set consisted of normal characters, and the similar set consisted of character pairs whose members were visually similar to each other. The second question is whether both visuospatial and verbal WM play a role in learning to read Chinese, and if so, whether they predict distinct learning behaviours. Individual differences in ability to process visual-orthographic information measured by visuospatial WM is thought to be important in learning to read Chinese because of the visual complexity of the Chinese script, and verbal WM may be necessary to hold phonological forms in memory while setting up a lexical entry.

Methods

Participants

Seventy students (28 females; 18–27 years old; mean age: 20 years old) enrolled in Chinese language classes at the University of Illinois participated and received monetary compensation for their participation. Forty-five students were native speakers of English, and 25 were not native speakers of English, but their L2 was in all cases English. There were 14 Korean, 2 Thai, 1 Spanish, 1 German, 1 Russian and 6 Chinese dialect (Taishanese, Cantonese and Fuzhouese) speakers. Forty-three students were enrolled in first-semester (beginning) Chinese classes and 27 in third-semester (intermediate) classes. At the time of participation in the experiment, the beginning learners had completed in-class instruction for 6 weeks (around 30 hours of in-class instruction) and learned approximately 60 characters in class, while most of the intermediate learners had completed 32 weeks (around 160 hours of instruction) of a two-semester beginning Chinese course which used a textbook containing 840 words and 745 characters.

Individual differences measures

WM tasks

Both a letter rotation task and a reading span task were used to assess individual participants' visuospatial and verbal WM capacity, respectively. Since both tasks measure WM, which involves not only information storage but also concurrent processing of additional information, the tasks consisted of two components: the presentation of to-be-remembered target stimuli, such as the spatial orientation of the top of a letter or a letter at the end of the sentence, and the completion of a secondary processing task, such as answering whether an image was normal or mirrored or judging the semantic plausibility of a sentence.

The letter rotation and reading span tasks had the same overall structure. Each task consisted of 42 items divided into 12 sets with a single set consisting of 2, 3, 4 or 5 items. Each set size appeared three times in each WM task. Each participant viewed the same items in the same predetermined single random order. WM tasks assess individual participants' differences in WM capacity, so the tasks needed to be implemented for each participant under the exact same conditions and order. In each WM task, participants were told to answer a question about an item while simultaneously retaining another piece of information about the item in memory, and were then asked to write down the remembered information on an answer sheet.

Letter rotation task

The letter rotation task used in the current study was modified from the task of the same name by Miyake *et al.* (2001) and was implemented using E-Prime software by the first author. The capital letters of F, J, L, P or R were used as items in this task. Two manipulations were made of the position of the letters. In the first manipulation, the letters either remained as normal or were flipped along their vertical axis, making them either normal or mirror images. In the second manipulation, both normal and mirror images of each letter were rotated at multiples of 45 degrees, yielding the 8 possible positions of 45, 90, 135, 180, 225, 270, 315 and 360 degrees of rotation. These two manipulations required participants to identify both flipped and rotated orientations of letter images. Each letter had 16 possible normal or mirror-image orientations in total, yielding 80 possible images for all 5 letters. This task contained 42 random items among 80 possibilities, assigned to 1 of 12 sets. Each set contained sizes of two, three, four or five items and appeared three times in the entire task. The set started with the two-item presentation, with the same number of items presented three times. Then the number of letters per set was increased stepwise to 3, 4 and then to 5 letters per set, which yielded 12 sets in total.

Participants were instructed to say aloud 'Regular' for normal letters or 'Flipped' for mirrored letters immediately after seeing each letter on the computer screen and to remember the spatial orientation of the letter (i.e. where the top of the letter was pointing) simultaneously. After each set of items, participants were asked to report the orientation of each letter's top surface in the correct serial order of presentation by writing numbers on an answer sheet containing a grid representing the eight possible positions of the letter's top surface. Figure 5.1 displays the procedure of a set size of two. Participants started with a practice trial with three sets of two items and continued the practice trials until they became comfortable with the task. The task was designed to be fast paced moving to the next item as soon as participants answered or reached the maximum time interval of three seconds between items. However, after each set when participants reported the orientation of the letters, they were given as much time as they wanted. This took 10–15 minutes, including instruction, practice and the main task.

Scoring the letter rotation task data followed the methods used by Gupta (2003), Miyake *et al.* (2001) and Shah and Miyake (1996). The memory portion of the test consisted of participants' recalled report of the letter's top surface orientation. Participants' vocal judgements on normal or mirrored images were recorded by the experimenter but were not included in the data analysis. In the WM tasks, the processing performance (in our case, image report) usually serves to ensure that participants paid attention to the secondary task and correlates positively

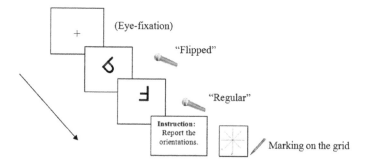

Figure 5.1 Example of a letter rotation task with a two-item set

with the performance on the storage component, which indicates there is no trade-off between processing and recall accuracy (Conway *et al.*, 2005; Kane *et al.*, 2004; Shah & Miyake, 1996).

Individual written reports on the orientation of the top of the letter were collected, scored by the experimenter and included in the data analysis as a measure of participants' visuospatial WM capacity. Items that were correctly recalled in the correct serial position were counted as correct and given one point. The maximum score was 42 points.

Reading span task

The reading span task required participants to memorise the letter at the end of each sentence while judging the semantic plausibility of the sentence. Inefficient comprehension of sentences can influence holding the memorised letters in the correct order, so conducting the reading span task in the participant's native language is the ideal. Among the total of 70 participants, because the majority of participants were native speakers of English and Korean (64.3% and 20%, respectively), the reading span task was conducted in those two languages. For the participants whose native language was not Korean, the English version was used.

The English version of the task used in this study was the task taken from Kane *et al.* (2004) developed by the study authors. The Korean version of the task was from Kim (2008) based on the original Kane *et al.* (2004) task. For the English version, each sentence consisted of 10–15 English words and was either semantically plausible or implausible. The total number of sentences in the task was 42. Out of 42 sentences, 19 sentences were semantically plausible and the other 23 were implausible. At the end of each sentence, an alphabetic letter was presented. A sentence and a letter comprised a single item for the task, and a set consisted of two, three, four or five items. Each set size occurred three times in the entire task, which yielded 12 trials in total. The set size did not progressively increase but was randomly assigned to prevent the participants from strategically focusing on the to-be-remembered final letters.

The Korean version was created by matching the total number of items, the number of items in each set and the order of the 12 sets appearing in the task. The sentences and recall-syllable at the end of the items were presented in Korean, and were not direct translations of the English version but were matched with the English version for the order and number of 'yes' and 'no' answers to the semantic plausibility judgement subtask. The Korean task was shown to be comparable with the English version by Kim (2008), who conducted both the English and Korean reading span tasks on 32 Korean–English late bilinguals, yielding a significant correlation of 0.71 ($p<0.01$).

Participants required 10–15 minutes to complete the reading span task. They were required to read aloud the presented sentence, answer

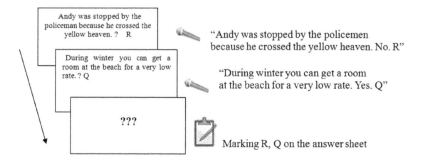

Figure 5.2 Example of the reading span task with a set size of two

'yes' or 'no' prompted by a single question mark (?) regarding whether the sentence was semantically plausible, say aloud the letter after the question mark and remember the letters until they were told to write them down. Immediately after a set of two to five items ended, three question marks (???) appeared, which signalled the participant to write the letters down in serial order on the answer sheet. After that, participants moved to the next set by pressing the spacebar. Figure 5.2 displays the procedure of a set size of two.

The reading span task was scored using 'All-or-nothing Unit Scoring' (Conway *et al.*, 2005). Each item of the set received one point if all the items of the set were correct and in the correct serial order. If any item of the set was incorrect, then no credit was given. The maximum score for the reading span task was 42.

Chinese character test

This test was created by the lead author based on the Chinese textbooks used at the research site. The test consisted of 60 Chinese words, and required participants to write the pronunciation (*pinyin*) and meaning (English) of each word. Twenty words were selected from the first semester, another 20 from the second semester and the last 20 were drawn from the third and fourth semesters. Of the 60 words, 34 were one syllable and 26 were two syllable, totalling 86 characters altogether. Partial points were given for the *pinyin* portion of the test, with 0.3 point given, respectively, for the correct initial, final and tone. However, no partial point was given for the meaning portion. The maximum score on the character test was 146.

Questionnaires

At the beginning and the end of the experimental session, participants were asked to fill out two questionnaires, a Language Background

Questionnaire and a Post-experiment Questionnaire. The Language Background Questionnaire obtained a detailed linguistic profile of the participants, such as their native language, foreign languages and the length and the setting of their Chinese language learning. The Post-experiment Questionnaire confirmed that it was the first time for the participants to learn the characters provided in the experimental session, with no participant reporting that there was a previously known character in the study.

Character learning experiment

Materials

Eighteen characters were used as stimuli in the experiment. Only structurally simple characters without any phonetic component were selected to test for visual strategies. Also, all characters were ancient or extremely uncommon in order to ensure that even though all were real characters, none of the participants would have had any prior experience with them, as was confirmed by the Post-experiment Questionnaire. All character stimuli were selected from the *Comprehensive Chinese Character Dictionary* (漢語大字典, 1993), and had identical forms in the traditional and simplified character types. The complete stimulus set for the experiment appears in Appendix A. Character pronunciations were recorded by a female native speaker of Chinese.

The 18 stimuli consisted of 3 character-type sets with 6 characters in each set. The three types were visually distinctive, normal and similar. The mean number of character strokes in each type was 4.8, 4.8 and 5, respectively. The distinctive set contained characters with a visually enhanced feature, created by exaggerating the width or length of one stroke of a normal character (Chen, 2004). This is similar to methods used in previous studies on English orthography, in which the height and width of alphabetic components within an English word were varied (Ehri & Wilce, 1985). As an example of a distinctive character, a stroke in the centre of the character 夈 was exaggerated to form the character 夅. The normal set consisted of six regular (albeit ancient or uncommon) Chinese characters without enhancement, e.g. 㐅. The similar type consisted of three pairs of characters that were visually similar to each other, differing only in one or two character components, e.g. 无 vs 旡. The characters used in the distinctive and normal types were counterbalanced by participant by constructing two lists. For the similar set, counterbalancing was not applied. Each participant was randomly assigned to one of two lists.

Procedure

Participants were tested individually, seated in front of a laptop computer and wearing a headset in a quiet lab. Participants were instructed that they would first learn 18 novel Chinese characters one at a time and then be asked to name the learned characters. The experimenter sat behind the participant to monitor, record and score performance.

Each character appeared individually on the computer screen with its pronunciation simultaneously presented over the headset. The entire set of 18 characters was presented in random order by E-Prime software, starting with a fixation point displayed for 700 ms. After the fixation point, each character was presented for 5000 ms with its pronunciation played twice over the headphones. As soon as participants heard the pronunciation, they repeated aloud what they heard two times for each character. Immediately after learning the characters, all 18 were presented randomly one at a time on the computer screen, and participants were asked to name them. The learning and test phases were repeated three times.

Results

Descriptive statistics and correlations

Descriptive statistics for individual differences measures are presented in Table 5.1. Figure 5.3 shows the mean proportion correct in naming accuracy for character types by trial. There was a significant effect of trial from a mixed logit analysis (listed in Table 5.3), with a significantly higher naming accuracy rate in Trial 2 and Trial 3 than in Trial 1, which indicates that participants were gradually able to learn to read the characters over three trials. Although the average proportion correct is not high even in Trial 3, there was a substantial amount of learning within less than 20 minutes.

Correlations among individual differences measures, i.e. letter rotation, reading span and character test are listed in Table 5.2. A significant correlation was found between letter rotation and reading span ($r=0.31$, $p<0.05$) but other measures did not correlate. This suggests that the two WM measures share some cognitive resources, but they are independent of the Chinese reading proficiency measure, i.e. the character test.

Table 5.1 Descriptive statistics for the individual differences measures

Variable	M	SD	Min	Max
Letter rotation	19.86	6.85	6	33
Reading span	18.24	9.66	2	42
Character test	60.92	9.66	24.50	129
Age	20.14	1.82	18	27

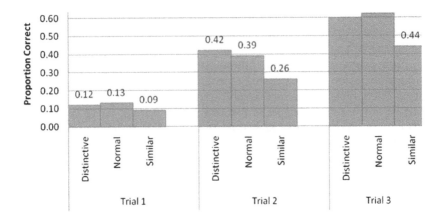

Figure 5.3 Proportion correct in naming accuracy for character types by trial

Table 5.2 Correlations among individual differences measures

Variable	Letter rotation	Reading span	Character test
Letter rotation	–	–	–
Reading span	0.31*	–	–
Character test	0.12	0.12	–

*$p<0.05$.

Mixed logit analysis

A character was scored as *correct* if participants named an entire syllable (excluding tone) correctly, and as *incorrect* otherwise. If participants produced two or more syllables, the last syllable was taken as their final answer. Because character naming results from the experiment were dichotomous data, statistical analyses were carried out using a mixed logit model (Jaeger, 2008) in R (R Development Core Team, 2009).[1] Naming accuracy was the dependent variable, with discrete predictors (trial, character type, list and participants' L1) and continuous predictors (character test scores, reading span task scores and letter rotation task scores) as fixed-effect factors, and participants and items as random-effect factors. To obtain the most parsimonious model with the best fit using the minimum number of predictors, all predictors and all possible interactions were first entered into the model, with the least contributing predictors eliminated one by one using likelihood ratio tests. In what follows, the coefficients and significance levels for those predictors remaining in the minimal, best-fitted model will be presented in the tables.

No significant effects were found for list, character knowledge or participants' L1. There was a significant effect of trial, with significantly

Table 5.3 Naming accuracy on all three character types in all three naming trials

Predictor	Estimate	SE	z-value	Pr(>|z|)
(Intercept)	−3.155	0.319	−9.889	<0.001***
Trial 2	1.798	0.119	15.050	<0.001***
Trial 3	2.848	0.122	23.302	<0.001***
Reading span	0.032	0.013	2.497	0.013*

*p<0.05; ***p<0.001.

higher naming accuracy rates in the second and the third trials than in the first trial, which indicates that participants gradually progressed in learning to read characters over the learning trials. Table 5.3 displays naming performance on all three character types combined over all three trials, and naming performance is seen as a coefficient (log-odds estimate) whose positive value indicates performance over a set baseline. In the predictor column, the naming accuracy of the first trial of learning (Trial 1) serves as the intercept and therefore the baseline for the other predictors, shown as the differences from the Trial 1 (intercept) baseline. The positive estimate and significance values for Trial 2 and Trial 3 mean that naming was more accurate in Trial 2 and Trial 3 than in Trial 1, indicating that participants improved in learning to read characters trial by trial, following our general expectation. The estimate for reading span is also positive and significant, meaning that participants whose reading span test scores were higher performed better in learning to read characters over all trials.

Table 5.4 shows the results of naming accuracy by trial. The row for Trial 1 shows no significant predictor, meaning that no variable significantly predicted participants' ability to learn characters in the first trial. The column for Trial 2 lists three predictors, and only similar character type and reading span were statistically significant. Since character type is a categorical and not a numerical variable, the intercept represents the naming accuracy for the default level of the character type, which here

Table 5.4 Naming accuracy in each naming trial

Trial	Predictor	Estimate	SE	z-value	Pr(>|z|)
1	(Intercept)	−2.416	0.219	−11.01	<0.001***
2	(Intercept)	−1.002	0.317	−3.166	0.002**
	Normal	−0.114	0.151	−0.755	0.450
	Similar	−0.866	0.389	−2.228	0.026*
	Reading span	0.032	0.011	2.900	0.004**
3	(Intercept)	−0.408	0.336	−1.216	0.224
	Reading span	0.038	0.013	3.061	0.002**

*p<0.05; **p<0.01; ***p<0.001.

is the distinctive character type. The negative coefficient value for the 'similar' type indicates that naming performance for the similar character type was worse than the baseline (distinctive) type by an estimate (log-odds) of −0.866. The positive coefficient for reading span indicates that participants with higher reading span scores performed significantly better than those with lower reading span scores. In Trial 3, only reading span scores were significant, indicating that participants with higher reading span scores learned to read characters significantly better than those with lower reading span scores. Taken together, these results indicate that individual WM capacity contributed to participants' character learning more than the character types, because the reading span effect was found in Trial 2 and Trial 3, but the character type effect was only found for the similar type in Trial 2.

Table 5.5 shows the results of separate analysis of each character type by each trial. In Trial 1, no variable contributed significantly to naming performance for any character type. From Trial 2, however, significant contributors to learning started to emerge. Letter rotation scores significantly predicted participants' accuracy in reading distinctive characters, while reading span scores significantly predicted accuracy in reading normal characters. This pattern for distinctive and normal types was also observed in Trial 3. For similar characters, no predictor was found in Trial 2, but reading span score was a significant predictor in Trial 3. The similar type showed these effects later than the distinctive and the normal types, possibly because in Trial 2 the accuracy rate for the similar type was

Table 5.5 Naming accuracy on each character type in each trial of the training phase

Trial	Character type	Predictors	Estimate	SE	z-value	Pr(>|z|)
1	Distinctive	(Intercept)	−2.128	0.198	−10.770	<0.001***
	Normal	(Intercept)	−2.281	0.270	−8.448	<0.001***
	Similar	(Intercept)	−2.786	0.429	−6.490	<0.001***
2	Distinctive	(Intercept)	−1.747	0.515	−3.391	<0.001***
		Letter rotation	0.066	0.023	2.822	0.005**
	Normal	(Intercept)	−1.068	0.329	−3.250	0.001**
		Reading span	0.031	0.011	2.674	0.007**
	Similar	(Intercept)	−1.434	0.260	−5.505	<0.001***
		Reading span	0.013	0.022	0.592	0.554
3	Distinctive	(Intercept)	−0.757	0.571	−1.325	0.185
		Letter rotation	0.066	0.025	2.615	0.009**
	Normal	(Intercept)	−0.039	0.385	−0.101	0.920
		Reading span	0.037	0.015	2.488	0.013*
	Similar	(Intercept)	−0.889	0.408	−2.178	0.029*
		Reading span	0.033	0.014	2.432	0.015*

*p<0.05; **p<0.01; ***p<0.001

too low to show any significance compared to the normal type. In Trial 3, however, when the similar type reached a sufficiently high level of naming accuracy, verbal WM emerged as a significant factor. It is notable that there was no interaction between letter rotation and reading span scores. The absence of an interaction suggests that visuospatial WM and verbal WM resources are independent.

The results can be summarised as follows. First, participants significantly improved in learning characters from one trial to the next. Second, different levels of visual distinctiveness did not affect participants' learning to read characters, as seen in Table 5.4. Third, higher levels of individual WM resources increased participants' ability to read characters. Specifically, visuospatial WM as measured by the letter rotation task and verbal WM as measured by the reading span task contributed differently to learning different types of characters. Stronger visuospatial WM helped participants learn visually distinctive characters, whereas stronger verbal WM helped in learning regular characters. This interesting finding may be related to the nature of the different types of WM, to be further discussed below. Finally, in the first trial when participants were exposed to the characters for the first time, not only was their learning performance not good, but their individual differences in WM also had no effect. However, the effects of WM resources started to become noticeable as early as the second trial resulting in better learning, which then continued to the third trial.

Discussion

The present study of WM in learning to read L2 Chinese characters had two research questions. The first question was how different visual features of characters might interact with WM and affect the learning of those characters. The second question was whether visuospatial WM or verbal WM would play a more important role in learning Chinese characters. For the first question, the results indicate that higher levels of individual WM resources increased participants' ability to learn simple Chinese characters, and that visuospatial properties represented by an exaggerated stroke in a character taxed participants' visuospatial WM, while regular characters taxed their verbal WM. In particular, visuospatial WM as measured by the letter rotation task and verbal WM as measured by the reading span task contributed to learning different types of characters. Participants who had higher visuospatial WM capacity were better able to learn visually enhanced characters, whereas participants with higher verbal WM capacities performed better in learning regular Chinese characters belonging to the normal and the similar sets. It is intriguing that visuospatial WM facilitated learning visually enhanced characters, whereas verbal WM was helpful in learning regular Chinese characters.

For the second question, the results suggest that verbal WM plays a more important role than visuospatial WM even in learning to read ordinary Chinese characters. Although visuospatial WM effects were found in reading visually distinctive characters, the visually distinctive characters were artificially created, and not ordinary characters.

The fact that visuospatial WM was implicated in learning the visually distinctive characters implies that participants used the bold strokes as cues for recall. In other words, participants linked the position of the bold stroke to the rest of the character, and the visually exaggerated stroke was not recognised as being a linguistic cue even by novices. Using the position of the visually enhanced stroke to recall a character is obviously a visuospatial task, which is what the letter rotation task measures and predicts.

Altogether, this result suggests that learning ordinary Chinese characters is essentially a linguistic task for L2 character learners, as shown in the reading span effect (i.e. verbal WM) on performance for the normal and similar types. On the other hand, the manipulation of providing a distinctive, exaggerated bold stroke in a character may be considered non-linguistic, so the visuospatial WM factor only correlated with this distinctive type with its visual manipulation, and not with any of the other types.

Visuospatial and verbal working memory in learning to read Chinese

Although the conditions of the experiment were devised with three degrees of visual distinctiveness of the characters, the results may be seen as applying to the two domains of WM. Visuospatial WM was linked to the characters with a visually distinctive stroke (distinctive type), whereas verbal WM was related to normal, conventional characters (normal and similar types) regardless of whether there were visually similar characters in the pool of the characters to be learned. It is important to note that a visually salient stroke was artificially made for the experiment and is not typical in the modern Chinese script. The results suggest that L2 learners relied more heavily on visuospatial WM while processing characters with atypical, exaggerated strokes, and on verbal WM when processing regular and conventional Chinese characters.

The results raise two further questions. One involves what beginning L2 Chinese readers are aware of in learning to read Chinese, and the other involves visual processing in learning to read Chinese. First, it seems that even novice adult L2 Chinese readers are aware that an exaggerated stroke in a character makes no distinction in the Chinese writing system, and that they consider characters with a salient stroke as non-distinctive. This is congruent with previous studies showing that adult L2 learners learn very quickly which visual features and configurations are allowed in written

Chinese (e.g. Liu *et al.*, 2007; Wang *et al.*, 2003), suggesting that sensitivity to conventional and legal forms of Chinese is developed quite early in L2 Chinese reading. Compared to the awareness of which form or position is allowed in the Chinese writing system, knowledge that stroke thickness does not make a character different is easier and more obvious. Thus, it is likely that the participants in this study who had learned approximately 60–750 characters perceived that a visually salient stroke in the distinctive type characters is extraordinary and unusual when they were learning 18 new characters in this experiment.

Why was the visuospatial WM measure not related to learning to read conventional characters in this study, but related to characters with a visually distinctive stroke? We suggest two possibilities. One possibility is that the naming task used in the character learning experiment could have demanded more verbal WM than visuospatial WM. In the experiment, participants learned to read characters by hearing and repeating the pronunciations, and learning was measured by the correct naming of the characters. Since the learning procedure is more closely related to the verbal domain of WM – especially the function of the phonological loop and rehearsal – than the visuospatial sketchpad, verbal WM may have been more activated and involved. A silent reading procedure in the character learning experiment could have made visuospatial WM more relevant, but we cannot be certain how much more visuospatial WM would be involved in a silent reading procedure because previous studies suggest that phonological recoding occurs even in silent reading (Rayner & Pollasek, 1989), and phonological involvement is thought to be inevitable in reading regardless of how transparent or opaque a writing system is (Perfetti, 2003).

Another possible reason why visuospatial WM effects were not found in reading regular characters in this study is that the letter rotation task – the visuospatial WM measure used in this study – may not be a sensitive measure for reading ordinary Chinese characters. A recent empirical study based on L1 Chinese kindergarteners and Grade 1–2 elementary students revealed that a traditional visual skill measure using geometric figures (geometric-figure processing task) only predicted Chinese reading among kindergarteners, but that a visual judgement measure using real and pseudo Chinese characters (character-configuration processing task) was a stronger predictor of character reading for both kindergartners and early elementary students (Luo *et al.*, 2013). It is possible that a Chinese character-related visuospatial task may have been a more appropriate task, and that visuospatial WM effects were not found for regular characters in this study because the letter rotation task used five Roman alphabet letters (F, J, L, P and R) not related to the character configuration of Chinese. In future examinations of visuospatial WM in reading Chinese, this issue needs to be considered.

Implications for learning to read Chinese characters

The results of this study suggest that better verbal WM is significantly helpful for students learning simple characters that do not contain a pronunciation cue, regardless of character knowledge. However, the situation changes once they start learning the majority of Chinese characters called 'phonetic compound characters' containing a pronunciation cue, which represent more than 80% of modern Chinese characters. When the same participants of this study learned another set of 18 characters in a separate study in which simple and phonetic compound characters were mixed and the simple characters served as the pronunciation part of the phonetic compounds, WM effects were not seen while character knowledge significantly helped the participants learn phonetic compounds whose pronunciation cues were consistent (Kim, 2010). Since frequent characters are usually simpler in form and are taught in the earlier stage of Chinese education than less frequent ones (Shu et al., 2003), higher verbal WM capacity would presumably have benefits in the very beginning stage of learning to read Chinese. However, once learners have learned a number of phonetic compound characters and developed an awareness of how phonetics play a role in characters containing them, character knowledge becomes a more significant contributor to reading and character learning. This implies that learning simple characters that do not contain any pronunciation cue depends on mnemonic techniques that vary among individual readers, whereas learning to read phonetic compound characters is based on finding and utilising the systematic principles underlying the phonetic components of characters which are inherent in the Chinese writing system.

Hierarchical view of working memory

This study also has implications for the general WM system. Researchers disagree whether WM is a unitary system (i.e. domain general) or consists of multiple separate subunits (i.e. domain specific), and what kind of subsystems constitute WM if it is not unitary (see Shah & Miyake [1996] for a review). The domain-general and domain-specific views recently seem to agree that the complex nature of WM tasks yields results consistent with both domain specificity and domain generality, which can be summarised in the hierarchical view of WM suggested by Engle et al. (1999; Miyake, 2001). According to Engle et al., WM consists of a storage component and a controlled attention component. The storage component is the same as the traditional concept of STM and is domain specific, whereas controlled attention is the ability to maintain relevant task information in the midst of distraction or interference, inhibit irrelevant information for the task and switch attention between these, which is related to higher-order cognition and is domain general. For example, memorising the last letter presented after the sentence in a reading span task or the direction of the top of the letter in a letter rotation task are tests of the storage component, while judging whether the read sentence is semantically valid in a reading span task or whether the letter on the screen is a normal or a mirrored image are examples of the controlled attention component. This hierarchical view incorporates both the domain-general and the domain-specific views by considering WM as a 'hierarchical structure with a general domain-free factor overarching several subordinate domain-specific factors' (Engle *et al.*, 1999: 125). In other words, both domain-specific and domain-general systems exist, and the domain-general system is hierarchically above the domain-specific systems.

The findings from the two WM tasks in the current study support the hierarchical view containing a domain-general as well as a domain-specific effect. A significant correlation ($r=0.31$, $p<0.05$) was found only between the letter rotation and the reading span tasks, and not with any other variables.[2] This moderate correlation implies that the visuospatial and the phonological domains of the WM share some cognitive resources. At the same time, the results from the mixed logit analysis found that letter rotation scores significantly predicted participants' performance in learning visually distinctive characters and reading span scores significantly predicted better learning of regular characters without any artificial visual enhancement. Yet, there were no interaction effects between the two measures. This pattern suggests that the visuospatial and the verbal domains are separate from each other. Taken together, these results imply that there are domain-general and domain-specific components in the WM system, consistent with the hierarchical view of WM (Engle *et al.*, 1999).

Acknowledgements

The manuscript was supported by a research grant from The Hong Kong Polytechnic University (G-U950) to the first author. The experiment reported here is a portion of the first author's doctoral dissertation which was funded in part by a Jiede Empirical Research Grant from the Chinese Language Teachers Association.

Notes

(1) Mixed logit models are a generalisation of logistic regression for binomially distributed outcomes which accounts for random subject and item effects in a single analysis. Analysis of variance (ANOVA) is inappropriate to analyse dichotomous data (Dixon, 2008; Jaeger, 2008).
(2) In other studies, correlation effects between the letter rotation and the reading span scores are mixed. Friedman and Miyake (2000) found a significant correlation between them in their first experiment, but not in their second experiment using a reduced version of the reading span task. Shah and Miyake (1996) did not find correlation effects when they used the same measures as the first experiment of Friedman and Miyake (2000).

References

Baddeley, A. (2003) Working memory: Looking back and looking forward. *Nature Reviews Neuroscience* 4 (10), 829–839.

Baddeley, A.D. and Hitch, G. (1974) Working memory. In G.H. Bower (ed.) *The Psychology of Learning and Motivation* (Vol. 8; pp. 47–89). New York: Academic Press.

Chen, X. (2004) *Developmental stages in learning to read Chinese characters.* Doctoral dissertation, University of Illinois at Urbana-Champaign.

Cheung, H. (1996) Nonword span as a unique predictor of second-language vocabulary learning. *Developmental Psychology* 32 (5), 867–873.

Comprehensive Chinese Character Dictionary [漢語大字典] (1993) Chengdu: Sichuan Dictionary Publisher/Hubei Dictionary Publisher.

Conway, A.R.A., Kane, M.J., Bunting, M.F., Hambrick, D.Z., Wilhelm, O. and Engle, R.W. (2005) Working memory span tasks: A methodological review and user's guide. *Psychonomic Bulletin & Review* 12, 769–786.

Dixon, P. (2008) Models of accuracy in repeated-measures designs. *Journal of Memory and Language* 59, 447–456.

Ehri, L.C. and Wilce, L.S. (1985) Movement into reading: Is the first stage of printed word learning visual or phonetic? *Reading Research Quarterly* 20, 163–179.

Engle, R., Tuholski, S.W., Laughlin, J.E. and Conway, A.R.A. (1999) Working memory, short-term memory and general fluid intelligence: A latent variable approach. *Journal of Experimental Psychology: General* 128 (3), 309–331.

Friedman, N.P. and Miyake, A. (2000) Differential roles for visuospatial and verbal working memory in situation model construction. *Journal of Experimental Psychology: General* 129, 61–83.

Gupta, P. (2003) Examining the relationship between word learning, nonword repetition, immediate serial recall in adults. *Quarterly Journal of Experimental Psychology* 56A, 1213–1236.

Jaeger, T.F. (2008) Categorical data analysis: Away from ANOVAs (transformation or not) and towards logit mixed models. *Journal of Memory and Language* 59, 434–446.

Kane, M.J., Hambrick, D.Z., Tuholski, S.W., Wilhelm, O., Payne, T.W. and Engle, R.W. (2004) The generality of working memory capacity: A latent-variable approach to verbal and visuospatial memory span and reasoning. *Journal of Experimental Psychology: General* 133 (2), 189–217.

Kim, J. (2008) Working memory effects on bilingual sentence processing. Doctoral dissertation, University of Illinois at Urbana-Champaign.

Kim, S. (2010) Developmental stages in reading Chinese as a second language. Doctoral dissertation, University of Illinois at Urbana-Champaign.

Liu, Y., Wang, M. and Perfetti, C.A. (2007) Threshold-style processing of Chinese characters for adult second-language learners. *Memory & Cognition* 35 (3), 471–480.

Luo, Y.C., Chen, X., Deacon, S.H., Zhang, J. and Yin, L. (2013) The role of visual processing in learning to read Chinese characters. *Scientific Studies of Reading* 17 (1), 22–40.

Martin, K.I. and Ellis, N.C. (2012) The roles of phonological STM and working memory in L2 grammar and vocabulary learning. *Studies in Second Language Acquisition* 34 (3), 379–413.

McBride-Chang, C. (2004) *Children's Literacy Development.* London: Arnold.

McBride-Chang, C., Zhou, Y., Cho, J., Aram, D., Levin, I. and Tolchinsky, L. (2011) Visual spatial skill: A consequence of learning to read? *Journal of Experimental Child Psychology* 109 (2), 256–262.

Miyake, A. (2001) Individual differences in working memory: Introduction to the special section. *Journal of Experimental Psychology: General* 130 (2), 163–168.

Miyake, A., Friedman, N.P., Rettinger, D.A., Shah, P. and Hegarty, M. (2001) How are visuospatial working memory, executive functioning, and spatial abilities related? A latent-variable analysis. *Journal of Experimental Psychology: General* 130 (4), 621–640.

Perfetti, C.A. (2003) The universal grammar of reading. *Scientific Studies of Reading* 7, 3–24.

R Development Core Team (2009) *R: A Language and Environment for Statistical Computing.* Vienna: R Foundation for Statistical Computing. See http://www.R-project.org.

Rayner, K. and Pollatsek, A. (1989) *The Psychology of Reading.* Hillsdale, NJ: Lawrence Erlbaum.

Service, E. (1992) Phonology, working memory and foreign-language learning. *Quarterly Journal of Experimental Psychology* 45A (1), 21–50.

Shah, P. and Miyake, A. (1996) The separability of working memory resources for spatial thinking and language processing: An individual differences approach. *Journal of Experimental Psychology: General* 125 (1), 4–27.

Shu, H., Chen, X., Anderson, R.C., Wu, N. and Xuan, Y. (2003) Properties of school Chinese: Implications for learning to read. *Child Development* 74 (1), 27–47.

Wang, M., Perfetti, C.A. and Liu, Y. (2003) Alphabetic readers quickly acquire orthographic structure in learning to read Chinese. *Scientific Studies of Reading* 7 (2), 183–208.

Appendix A

Materials for Experiment

List	Character Type					
	Distinctive		Normal		Similar	
List 1	乵 bai3	叵 fang4	玉 fa2	斥 ju2	先 zan1	旡 ji4
	昼 liang2	伞 qin4	乎 kua4	众 pin3	兆 gu3	那 mao3
	仓 shi1	弓 tan2	甶 zai1	夫 zhang3	忄 kuang4	北 qiu1
List 2	玉 fa2	斥 ju2	乵 bai3	叵 fang4	先 zan1	旡 ji4
	乎 kua4	众 pin3	昼 liang2	伞 qin4	兆 gu3	那 mao3
	甶 zai1	夫 zhang3	仓 shi1	弓 tan2	忄 kuang4	北 qiu1

6 Working Memory in L2 Sentence Processing: The Case with Relative Clause Attachment

Yuncai Dai

Introduction

Previous studies of second language acquisition (SLA) focused more on the structure and function of learners' linguistic knowledge as well as the role of linguistic and environmental factors in second language (L2) development; on the other hand, there is a dearth of studies on processing research in real time by L2 learners. This line of research is primarily concerned with understanding the mental processes responsible for language as a dynamic, real-time entity, so it is an indispensable element in a complete theory of SLA (Juffs, 2001). The study of how to process language input online by learners can provide information about the variation of learners' L2 language and the constraints of processing, thereby helping researchers to cognise the developmental process of an L2. According to Gregg (2001), the theory of SLA can be divided into two categories: property theory and transition theory. Traditional studies of SLA pay more attention to learners' static linguistic knowledge, which places emphasis on the representation of the language, and is less concerned with the process of learning. While studying sentence processing online, researchers can find out the processing strategies, constraints and individual differences. This line of research can try to account for the mechanisms of variation of the language system of L2 learners, thus providing valuable data for transition theory.

It has long been established that there exists a fundamental difference between first language (L1) and L2 acquisition. L1 learners can successfully acquire a native language despite degenerated input, while, in contrast, adult L2 learners rarely achieve total success. Some researchers (Fernandez, 1999; Juffs, 2001) have argued that parsing deficits rather than competence deficiencies might help to explain the differences between the two. In another way, we might conclude that the reason why L2 learners are unable to reach native speakers' language proficiency is due to processing strategies, but not language competence, for L2 learners are capable of acquiring L2 grammar to comprehend L2 sentences. There is an asymmetry between their language competence and processing ability, which leads to a situation in which they cannot represent L2 grammar correctly. In this connection, the study of relative clause (RC) attachment disambiguation, a potentially valuable line for examining this difference, can shed light on the underlying processing mechanism and the sources of the asymmetry.

When processing L2 sentences, L1 processing strategies might be transferred to the L2, so a study of this area can help to verify whether this hypothesis is correct. Moreover, by comparing L1 and L2 sentence processing, we can discover the differences and similarities between them. This area of research has resulted in advances in our understanding of L2 processing and can be expected to yield further insights into the processes involved in L2 learning. On account of the fact that Chinese and English belong to typologically different language families, the investigation of Chinese learners' processing of L2 English sentences can provide more evidence as to whether there is processing transfer. It is hoped that this research can complement the studies of learners of the same linguistic typology, and thus contribute to a re-evaluation of processing principles.

RC attachment in English and Chinese

The RC, which possesses some universal characteristics, exists in most world languages including Chinese (Keenan & Comrie, 1977; Lee, 1992; Li & Thompson, 1989), so the processing principles of the RC can be compared in different languages (Cuetos *et al.*, 1996). In studies that compare RC processing in Chinese and English, it needs to be recognised that while, on the one hand, there are RC structures in both English and Chinese, on the other hand, the two languages are typologically different in that the Chinese RC is prenominal, while the English RC is postnominal, indicating that the Chinese RC, a left branching sentence structure, is in contrast with the English RC in this respect. Sentences (1) and (2) illustrate this difference.

(1) Someone shot [the servant]$_{NP1}$ of [the actress]$_{NP2}$ [who was standing on the balcony].
(2) Youren sheji le [zhan zai yangtai shang de] nage [nv yanyuan]$_{NP1}$ de [puren]$_{NP2}$
     Someone shoot (tense mark) [standing on the balcony (RC mark)] that [female actress]$_{NP1}$ (attributive mark) [servant]$_{NP2}$.

In fact, both the Chinese RC and the English RC are ambiguous because the RC *who was standing on the balcony* can be attached either to the first noun *the servant* at the high position or to the second noun *the actress* at the low position. To resolve the ambiguity in English RC attachment, grammatical features, especially agreement, are frequently used. The following examples can explicate this.

(3) Someone shot [the servant]$_{NP1}$ of [the actresses]$_{NP2}$ [who was standing on the balcony].

For Sentence (3), according to the rule of agreement, the RC can only be attached to noun phrase 1 (NP1) *the servant*. But in Chinese, there is no subject and predicate agreement, so animacy is often used to resolve the problem.

(4) Zhuren xihuan [daizhe xianliang de]mishu de weijing.
     Director like [wear necklace (tense mark)] secretary (attributive mark) scarf.
     'The director likes the scarf of the secretary that is wearing a necklace'.
(5) Tom guihuan le guazai qiangshang de yudongyuan de yudongfu.
     Tom returned (tense mark) hang on the wall (RC mark) athlete (attributive mark) sportswear.
     'Tom returned the sportswear of the athlete that was hung on the wall'.

Role of Working Memory in RC Attachment

In both L1 and L2 acquisition, learners have to process the form and meaning of language input and make form-meaning connections (VanPatten, 2004). Therefore, if learners have a larger capacity of working memory (WM), they possess more attention resources, which can facilitate their language learning because their stronger memory enables them to process form and meaning at the same time. Besides, learners with a larger capacity of WM can make full use of pragmatic information to process multiple factors simultaneously (MacDonald *et al.*, 1992; Waters & Caplan, 1996).

However, there are also some discrepancies in this area of study. For example, Juffs (2004, 2006) examined whether WM capacity could explain individual differences in L2 learners' reading speed in structures imposing a very high processing cost. The results show that, in most cases, no reliable evidence of the role of WM as measured by a reading span task was found. However, reliable effects of L1 were identified in L2 processing (see also Juffs & Harrington, 2011). Rodriguez (2008) also investigated the relationship between WM and three structures that imposed a high processing load, including long-distance RC resolution, on high-proficient Spanish-speaking and Chinese learners of English. He did not find a marked effect of WM on reading times at key regions in the sentence. Nor was any effect found in the study by Felser and Roberts (2007), who examined the role of WM in explaining differences in a complex cross-modal task of processing complex RCs by Greek learners of English.

Although the research results by Havik *et al.* (2009) indicated that high-span non-native speakers were able to use their WM to come close to the behaviour of low-span native speakers, WM span had no effect on the L2 learners' real-time processing when only structural information was available to guide parsing decisions. These findings support the assumption that WM cannot compensate for processing purely structural difficulties in L2 tasks using a self-paced reading methodology.

On the other hand, Williams (1999) concluded that a measure of phonological memory was related to rule learning, and the more typologically distant the language to be learned is from the learners' L1, the more effective the WM is. Dussias and Pinar's (2010) research showed that English L2 participants in the higher-span group resembled English native readers in their ability to exploit plausibility information to recover from mis-parses They thus concluded that the individual cognitive resources of the learner were an important factor in determining the extent to which sentence processing might be qualitatively similar or different in an L1 and an L2. Swets *et al.* (2007) found that readers with low WM spans were less likely to use recency strategies for disambiguation than were readers with high spans.

In summary, WM plays a different role in L1 and L2 processing. In L1 processing, high WM readers have an advantage in that they can integrate post-structural information such as semantic and pragmatic information to resolve ambiguity or allow multiple parallel syntactic analyses for purely syntactic ambiguity, while in L2 processing, L1 plays a more important role than WM capacity. It is therefore concluded that learners from different native language backgrounds could attach the RC differently. In this respect, the causes may be native language transfer or cognitive capacities. Although many studies have been reported in this area of research, the results are far from conclusive (Fernandez, 2002; Papadopoulou, 2005). Furthermore, although some studies have involved Chinese-speaking learners of English, few in-depth studies are based on Chinese-speaking learners in the Chinese context and the transfer of Chinese L1 processing strategies to English L2.

The Present Study

The present study builds on previous findings on ambiguity resolution with RC attachment and aims to further investigate (a) whether low-intermediate Chinese L2 English learners use the same semantic information and interpretative principles to process L1 and L2 ambiguity in RC attachment, or whether they transfer the processing principles from their L1 when parsing the L2; (b) whether WM capacity plays a significant role in L2 ambiguous sentence processing; and (c) whether there exists a difference between processing strategies in online sentence parsing and that in offline questionnaires.

Three experiments are reported in this chapter. Experiment 1 examines the disambiguation strategies in L2 RC attachment by Chinese learners of English as an L2 by using an online reaction time technique; additionally, the role of participants' WM capacity, which is measured by a Chinese reading span test, is also examined in relation to the ambiguity resolution. Experiment 2 investigates the ambiguity resolution strategies in L1 RC attachment together with the role of WM by the same group of participants. In Experiment 3, an English and a Chinese questionnaire on RC attachment preferences are administered to determine whether there is any difference between online sentence processing and offline questionnaire results, in order to investigate the possible effects of post-structural information in the disambiguation of RC attachment.

Experiment 1

Method

Participants

The participants of the study consisted of an entire class of first-year college students ($n=30$, mean age 19, range 18–20, 20 female) who had just entered a Chinese non-key university. All the participants had six years' experience of learning English as an L2 in their high schools, and none of them had learned English in a target language country. In addition, the students were all regarded as high performers and well motivated, having been selected from 3500 freshmen of the university to form a fast-track class based on their English score and total score in the Chinese matriculation test. Even so, their L2 proficiency was considered to be at low-intermediate level, because Chinese high school graduates are only required to master basic language skills and key grammatical knowledge as well as around 2200 English words according to their English course curriculum.

Reaction time test materials

The materials in this experiment consist of 80 sentences in total, including 8 practice sentences and 48 experimental sentences, of which 24 are forced to high attachment, 24 are low attachment and the remaining 24 are filler sentences. All the experimental sentences have the same structure and are temporarily ambiguous, containing an RC which modifies either NP1 or NP2 of the complex object NP in the matrix clause. To be more specific, the structure of each stimulus sentence can be formalised as

NP+VP+[NP1 of NP2]+RC, where the verb phrase (VP) is the matrix verb. Additionally, all the stimuli possess the same number of nodes with a similar number of words. Considering that the animacy of the subjects of matrix clauses may play a role in the processing of materials, an animate noun is always used as the subject of each matrix clause. Disambiguation is forced by the semantic agreement between the noun modified and the predicate of an RC, yielding two experimental conditions, as illustrated by Examples (6) and (7).

Condition 1
(6) Tom returned the sportswear of the athlete that was hung on the wall.
Condition 2
(7) The secretary posted the mail of the manager that was reading the report.

In Sentence (7), the RC *that was reading the report* can be structurally attached to either *the mail* or *the manager*, causing a temporary ambiguity, but as the verb *was reading* appears, the ambiguity can be resolved (Condition 2); because the verb requires an animate head noun, and *the mail* in the complex noun is non-animate, while the manager is, the RC is forced to be attached to the low noun *the manager*. On the other hand, in Sentence (6), the verb of the RC *was hung* has to be attached to a non-animate noun, leading to high attachment (Condition 1). By controlling the animacy of the head NP, the RC is forced to be attached to either one of the complex NPs so as to resolve the ambiguity. In the sequencing of the stimulus sentences, all the test items are pseudorandomised and mixed with fillers.

To ensure that the participants made an active effort to complete the task, all the stimulus sentences were followed by an A/B choice question which the participants responded to by pressing the A or B button on the keyboard. Participants were instructed to answer the questions by choosing one of the two choices before proceeding to the next sentence. A sample of each sentence type with its corresponding question is as follows:

Condition 1
(6) Tom returned the sportswear of the athlete that was hung on the wall.
Question: Who returned the sportswear?
Answer: (a) Tom; (b) the athlete
Condition 2
(7) The secretary posted the mail of the manager that was reading the report.
Question: Who posted the mail?
Answer: (a) the secretary; (b) the manager

Working memory test

In order to obtain a measure of the participants' WM capacity, they were requested to complete a computerised Chinese reading span test (CCRST) adapted from one originally produced by Cui and Chen (1996) based on Daneman and Carpenter's (1980) reading span test, in which participants have to finish two tasks simultaneously. One is to recall the final word of each stimulus sentence shown on the screen; the other is to assess the truth of a judgement sentence according to the sentence they read on the screen. The CCRST was composed of 75 Chinese complex sentences, each of which consisted of 26–28 Chinese words, and it was arranged in five sets each of one, two, three, four and five sentences. Of the 75 judgement sentences, half were true, while the other half were false. An example of the CCRST is given as follows:

Stimulus sentence: 中国印章有三千多年的历史, 然而没人知道它的发明者和发明过程
Zhongguo yinzhang you sanqian duo nian de lishi, raner meiyou ren zhidao tade faming zhe he faming guocheng.
'Chinese seal has a history of more than three thousand years, but nobody knows its inventor and inventing process'.
Judgement sentence: 中国印章的发明者和发明过程广为人知
zhongguo yingzhang de famingzhe he faming guocheng guanweirenzhi. (false)
'The inventor and inventing processes of Chinese seal is well-known to most people'.
Last word: 过程/guocheng, 'process'

Procedure

First, to obtain an online record of the unfolding parse, a self-paced reading task was generated by using E-Prime software. In this task, participants read a sentence in a segment-by-segment fashion by pressing a pacing button to continue the test. The basic rationale underlying the self-paced reading technique is that an increased reading time on a particular segment reveals a relatively higher processing load at this point during the parsing. Thus, the reaction time to the disambiguating segment should be higher for those conditions that force the dis-preferred attachment. Before the experiment began, participants were told that they were engaging in a study of reading comprehension and were presented with an instruction on the screen that explained the procedure and emphasised the importance of both speed and accuracy in responding to the questions. To put it differently, they were asked to read the sentences at their normal speed of reading.

In order to detect reaction time differences in processing the critical region for high and low attachment, each sentence was divided into five segments, in which the critical region was always the fourth segment as illustrated in Sentence (6).

(6) Tom returned/the sportswear of the athlete/that/was hung/on the wall.

The experiment lasted approximately 20–30 minutes in total and was preceded by eight practice sentences. After the practice session, a reminder appeared on the screen indicating that participants could seek help if they wanted to or start the test by pushing the 'Enter' button. When the experiment was completed, the reaction times for each segment of all stimulus sentences together with the answer to each question were recorded by the software.

One week later, the participants took part in the CCRST, which was also operationalised on a personal computer (PC) through a pre-designed software package using E-Prime. The experiment was preceded by three sets of practice sentences from one sentence to a three-sentence set. In the real test, the participants were presented with increasingly longer sets of sentences from two-sentence sets to five-sentence sets. The maximum set size at which a participant was correct on three out of five sets was taken as a measure of his/her reading span, which was scaled into five levels from one to five.

Results

Both the participants' answer accuracy and reaction time results were examined. As the aim of the experiment was to investigate the participants' online disambiguation preferences, statistical analyses were performed only on the reaction time data. The accuracy data were used to judge whether a participant carried out the test seriously. The overall accuracy rate was good, with the participants correctly answering 80.5% of the questions related to all the stimulus sentences, indicating that they were paying attention to the task. Since the first three segments and the fifth segment did not reveal any statistical significance, only the reading time data from the critical (fourth) segment were included in the analysis. Prior to the analysis of the reaction time data, two participants' data were removed because their response accuracy rates were close to chance (58.5% and 42.3% correct, respectively). In addition, two items in the test were also excluded from the analysis for reaction times as the critical region for the two were abnormal. To eliminate individual outliers, we further excluded reading times above or below 2 SD from the group mean for each condition, leading to the exclusion of three more participants' data (affecting 10.7% of the remaining total data). The remaining data from 25 participants were included in the final statistical analysis. Table 6.1 provides an overview of the participants' raw reading times for critical regions from the two conditions. In Table 6.1 and the following tables, all reaction times are given in milliseconds.

Table 6.1 Mean reading times by conditions for Segment 4 (English)

Condition	Mean	n	SD	SE
NP1 attachment	963.03	25	271.75	54.35
NP2 attachment	901.13	25	234.03	46.81

Paired samples t-tests showed that the reading time at the critical region for NP1 attachment was significantly higher than that for NP2 attachment ($t(24)=2.33$, $p=0.03$). The relatively higher standard deviation indicates that there was considerable variation within this condition.

In order to identify the role of WM capacity in the processing of RC attachment as well as its interactional role with conditions, a 2×2 repeated measures analysis of variance (ANOVA) with condition as the within-subjects variable and WM (half the participants as high WM ones, the other half as low WM ones) as the between-subjects variable was performed on the reaction time results for the fourth segment. The descriptive statistics for the analysis are shown in Table 6.2.

NP1 attachment of Condition 1 elicited substantially longer reaction times than did NP2 attachment of Condition 2 (963 vs 901 ms). The ANOVA revealed that the difference observed between the reading times for the two conditions was statistically significant ($F(1, 23)=5.18$, $p=0.03$). In addition, the ANOVA also showed a significant main effect for WM capacity, higher WM elicited longer reading times (1046 vs 809 ms) and pairwise comparisons showed a reliable difference between two levels of WM in reaction times ($F(1, 23)=7.37$, $p=0.01$). Moreover, there was no interactive effect between WM and condition in the reaction times ($F(1, 23)=0.61$, $p=0.45$). To further determine the effect of WM on processing, Pearson's correlations were performed, and the results did not show significant correlations between WM and the reading times either in Condition 1 ($r=0.23$, $p=0.27$) or in Condition 2 ($r=0.20$, $p=0.34$). These results indicate that Chinese-speaking learners of English at a low-intermediate language proficiency level showed a preference for NP2 attachment in online processing, and learners of higher WM capacity required significantly longer time to process the ambiguity. In

Table 6.2 Mean reading times by conditions and WM for Segment 4

Condition	WM	Mean	SD	n
NP1 attachment	1.00	1086.54	248.66	13
	2.00	829.22	236.87	12
	Total	963.03	271.75	25
NP2 attachment	1.00	1004.62	226.47	13
	2.00	789.03	192.82	12
	Total	901.13	234.03	25

addition, WM does not interact with condition to affect the ambiguity resolution.

Experiment 2

Method

Participants

The 25 participants with effective data for analyses in Experiment 1 also took part in Experiment 2.

Materials

Chinese RCs are positioned before the complex NPs which they modify, while in English, RCs are placed after the head noun. Owing to this difference, an RC attached to a high noun or a low noun may bring about varied processing difficulty in the two languages. In order to make a marked contrast, the Chinese online test materials were translated from English materials in Experiment 1, so they also included 72 Chinese sentences, of which 24 were forced to high attachment, 24 were low attachment and the remaining 24 were fillers. Since Chinese has no subject–verb agreement, using animacy to disambiguate RC attachment in Chinese sentences is an appropriate strategy. And considering that Chinese is a pro-drop language and its RC is placed before the complex NP, all the stimulus Chinese sentences were divided into five segments different from English ones. Two examples of Chinese stimulus sentences (Sentences (8) and (9)) are provided as follows:

(8) 秘书寄出了/正在看/报告的/经理的/邮件
Mishu jichu le/ zhengzai kan/ baogao de /jingli de /youjian.
Secretary borrow (tense mark)/[(tense mark) read/report (RC mark)]/ manager (attributive mark)/mail.
'The secretary posted/the mail of the manager/that/was reading/the report'.
(9) 汤姆借走了/挂/在墙上的/运动员的/运动服
Tom jiezou le/ gua/zaiqiangshang de/ yundongyuan de/ yudongfu.
Tom borrow (tense mark)/[hang/on the wall (RC mark)]/athlete (attributive mark)/sportswear.
'Tom borrowed/the sportswear of the athlete/that/was hung/on the wall'.

Based on the animacy requirement, the Chinese RC in Sentence (8) has to cling to the high noun *jingli* (*manager*), while in Sentence (9), the RC is forced to stick to the low noun *yundongfu* (*sportwear*).

Table 6.3 Mean reading times by conditions for Segment 4 (Chinese)

Condition	Mean	n	SD	SE
NP1 attachment	501.71	25	130.89	26.18
NP2 attachment	510.74	25	166.45	33.29

Procedure

The procedure of this experiment was identical to that of Experiment 1.

Results

The results were treated in exactly the same way as those of Experiment 1. The overall accuracy rate of the questions to all the stimulus sentences was 93.5%, and no participant's response accuracy rate was close to chance, nor was any subject's reading time above or below 2 SD from the group mean for each condition. Thus, the same 25 participants' data were included in the statistical analysis. Table 6.3 provides an overview of the participants' mean reading times at critical regions for each condition.

As in the analysis of reading times data for English RC attachment, paired samples t-tests were carried out first, and the results showed that there was no significant difference between the reading times at the critical region for NP1 and NP2 attachment ($t(24)=-0.44$, $p=0.66$). In order to determine whether WM plays a role in L1 ambiguity resolution, a 2×2 ANOVA with repeated measures for the factors WM capacity and attachment condition (NP1 vs NP2) was computed on the reaction time results. The mean reading times and standard deviation at the critical region for participants of two WM levels are shown in Table 6.4.

The ANOVA results for reading times at Segment 4 showed no significant main effect of condition ($F(1, 23)=0.36$, $p=0.56$). In addition, the main effect of WM did not approach a significant level ($F(1, 23)=2.86$, $p=0.10$). However, an interaction of WM capacity by condition appeared significant, which suggests that high and low WM participants differ in their method of processing RC attachment ($F(1.23)=6.79$, $p=0.02$).

Table 6.4 Mean reading times by conditions and WM for Segment 4 (Chinese)

Condition	WM	Mean	SD	n
NP1 attachment	1.00	480.50	132.75	13
	2.00	524.69	130.57	12
	Total	501.71	130.89	25
NP2 attachment	1.00	443.80	114.88	13
	2.00	583.27	187.13	12
	Total	510.74	166.45	25

Independent samples t-tests indicated that the difference of the reading times between the two WM levels was statistically reliable for NP2 attachment ($t=-2.27$, $p=0.03$), but not for NP1 attachment ($t=-0.84$, $p=0.41$).

These results showed that Chinese-speaking learners of English had different disambiguation preferences between L2 and L1 RC attachment. When processing English as an L2, the participants significantly preferred NP2 over NP1 disambiguation, and higher WM elicited significantly longer time in both NP1 and NP2 attachment, but there was no correlation between WM capacity and attachment preference. While processing Chinese as an L1, they did not reveal a bias towards NP1 or NP2 attachment, and WM did not demonstrate a main effect in the disambiguation, but further examination indicated that high WM caused a substantial effect on the reading times for NP2 attachment.

Experiment 3

Method

Participants

The 25 participants with effective data for analyses in Experiment 1 also took part in Experiment 3.

Materials

To gain a deeper insight into the processing strategies of the participants, two questionnaires were constructed, one in English and one in Chinese. The Chinese questionnaire was a word-for-word translation of the English questionnaire. Each questionnaire comprised 20 ambiguous sentences, which had the same form as those in Experiment 1 (NP+VP+[NP1 of NP2]+RC), where the RC can be attached either to NP1 or NP2 of the complex NP which they modify.

The major difference between online and offline test sentences lies in the former's use of a semantic feature [+human] to resolve ambiguity, while the latter preserves ambiguity there, that is, both NP1 and NP2 of the complex NP had human referents, linked by the preposition *of* in English or by the attributive mark *de* in Chinese, and a subject RC that could be a plausible modifier of NP1 or NP2 immediately followed the complex NP of all experimental sentences. Furthermore, each ambiguous sentence was followed by a question together with an A/B choice answer. Example (1) from the English questionnaire illustrates this principle.

(1) Someone shot [the servant] $_{NP1}$ of [the actress] $_{NP2}$ [who was standing on the balcony].
Question: Who was standing on the balcony?
Answer: (a) the servant; (b) the actress

When processing the above sentence, participants could attach the RC *who was standing on the balcony* either to the servant or the actress. In this way, this task allowed us to find out learners' preference in deciding RC attachment. Compared with the online test, which mainly dealt with the structural processing, the offline test was adopted to measure the role of post-structural information in the processing because participants could change their choices after they finished reading the whole sentence and may have been affected by semantic or pragmatic information.

Procedure

Participants were told that they were taking part in a study on memory and the comprehension of sentences. They were instructed to read the sentence printed on the questionnaire silently and to answer the question following it by ticking the choice that they thought was more appropriate. The materials were counterbalanced so that for half of the sentences, NP1 in the complex NP took the first-choice position in the answer, and in the remaining half, NP2 occupied the first-choice position in the answer. The participants were also instructed to make their choices as spontaneously as possible.

Results

The raw data were the number of selections made for NP1 or NP2 options. Because the two sentences might have caused misunderstanding, they were removed from the analysis. Table 6.5 compares the number of two attachment responses in L1 and L2 disambiguation.

Table 6.5 reveals that, for L1 processing, the mean high attachment was 10.6 out of 18. This indicates that approximately 59% of the participants selected NP1 rather than NP2 as the correct answer. For the L2 ambiguity resolution, the pattern of the results was quite different. On average, 65% of the participants (12.92 out of 20) selected NP1 responses. These numbers indicate that the participants had a preference for high attachment either in L1 or L2 RC attachment to some extent. The data were then submitted to paired samples *t*-tests, which revealed a significant difference between the number of high attachment and low

Table 6.5 Attachment preferences in L1 and L2 disambiguation

Language	Condition	Mean	n	SD	SE
L2 disambiguation	NP1 attachment	12.92	25	4.17	0.83
	NP2 attachment	7.12	25	4.14	0.83
L1 disambiguation	NP1 attachment	10.60	25	6.26	1.25
	NP2 attachment	7.40	25	6.26	1.20

attachment responses in the L2 questionnaire ($t(24)=3.49$, $p<0.01$). This finding contradicts the online ambiguity resolution, which showed a bias towards NP2 attachment. On the other hand, no reliable difference was found between the two conditions of RC attachment in the L1 questionnaire ($t(24)=1.28$, $p=0.21$). This result replicates the report in online L1 disambiguation.

Discussion

Our main results can be summarised as follows:

- Low-intermediate Chinese L2 English learners showed a strong preference for NP2 over NP1 disambiguation in self-paced reading tasks.
- Different from L2 RC ambiguity resolution, Chinese native speakers did not reveal a bias towards NP1 or NP2 attachment in L1 self-paced reading tasks; this indicated that Chinese-speaking learners of English had different L2 and L1 RC disambiguation strategies.
- WM played a substantial role in L2 RC attachment with higher WM eliciting a longer reading time in both NP1 and NP2 attachment; it did not show a main effect in L1 RC disambiguation, but further examination indicated that high WM caused a substantial effect on the reading times for NP2 attachment.
- In offline questionnaire tasks, those learners revealed a strong attachment preference towards NP1 in the L2 questionnaire, which was at variance with the results from the online tasks, but no preference was shown in the L1 questionnaire, which replicated the findings from the self-paced reading tasks.

In the following section, we discuss the implications of our research findings for theories of L2 processing.

Use of universal strategies in L2 parsing

Experiment 1 showed that low-intermediate Chinese learners of English exhibited a strong preference for NP2 over NP1 disambiguation in self-paced L2 reading tasks. The results of this study confirmed previous findings that recency took precedence over predicate proximity for ambiguous RC attachment in English (see Dussias, 2003; Fernandez, 2002). Thus, our findings support the universal parsing principles such as recency and late closure. A possible explanation may lie in the cognitive demands on the bilingual language processor. The storage and integration cost linked with managing two linguistic systems might decrease the amount of information that the parser can effectively process. NP2 attachment allows readers to immediately integrate incoming materials with prior materials and minimises memory load of the sentence processing mechanism. In order to process more information effectively and minimise delays in processing time coming about from housing two languages, the bilingual parser will default to those operations such as late closure that results in the simplest and most quickly derived analysis. This interpretation may explain why Chinese L2 learners comply with late closure in processing L2 English attachment. Another possibility that needs to be considered is L2 learners' incomplete knowledge of the target language in our experiment. Although the participants had studied English as an L2 for 6.5 years and had acquired the rules of RC structure as well as fundamental linguistic knowledge of English, they were much less proficient than L1 English speakers, as a result of which they may be less efficient in representing L2 lexical and syntactic information that could affect their ability to parse this kind of sentence in a different way; at the same time, their limited language competence may have restricted them from making full use of all the information, leading them to select the simplest operation principles such as late closure in online processing. The third possible explanation might be that Chinese learners are taught to attach an RC to the noun that is processed most recently.

Transfer and experience-based parsing

According to experience-based parsing models such as the Tuning Hypothesis (see Dussias & Sagarra, 2007; Mitchell et al., 1995), RC attachment preference in the learners' L1 directly influences their L2 performance, especially at the early stage of L2 development, because learners at this stage are still more exposed to their L1. Correspondingly, the low-intermediate Chinese learners of English in our study might be expected to transfer their L1 processing strategies to the L2. However, our research findings showed that there was no particular attachment preference in their L1 processing, contrary to the bias to NP2 attachment in L2 processing. This indicated that Chinese-speaking learners of English had different L2 and L1 RC disambiguation preferences, thus the research findings did not confirm the prediction of L1 transfer. A number of previous studies (Felser et al., 2003; Fernandez, 1999; Papadopoulou & Clahsen, 2003) echoed these results. A major possibility might be that L2 learners postpone associating an ambiguous RC with either of the two potential host NPs until other cues to interpretation become available, rather than transferring the structure-based predicate proximity (or recency) strategy from their native language to the L2. If other information, such as pragmatic or contextual information, is involved, it might help learners to resolve RC attachment ambiguities (see also Felser et al., 2003). Papadopoulou and Clahsen (2003) conducted a thorough study of different L1 groups of learners of Greek, and they ruled out the possibility that the lack of L1 transfer was due to linguistic differences between the particular languages involved.

Another explanation is related to the method of English language instruction in China. To be more specific, there are numerous contrastive analyses and accompanied practice in and out of language learning classes in China in order to cope with standardised language proficiency tests; these lead to the avoidance of the transfer of L1 processing strategies into the L2. Furthermore, language-particular differences between English and Chinese might preclude the use of L1 transfer. Since Chinese is typologically distant from English, the participants may use different cues, particularly the semantic or pragmatic cues, when processing Chinese as an L1, because lexical-semantic information usually preponderates structural information in sentence processing in the Chinese language. The marked divergence between the two languages makes it less possible for Chinese learners of English to transfer L1 strategies into the L2.

Role of WM in L2 parsing

Our study indicated that WM played a substantial role in L2 RC attachment with higher WM eliciting a longer reading time in both NP1 and NP2 attachment; it did not show a main effect in L1 RC disambiguation, but further examination indicated that high WM caused a substantial effect on the reading times for NP2 attachment. The results are contradictory to most previous research findings in the area in that past findings that exhibited higher WM capacity either facilitated RC attachment ambiguity resolution or had no effect. Three possibilities might explain our research results. First, the disambiguation tasks in L1 Chinese RC attachment as a whole were not highly demanding, so the role of WM might not have been detectable; on the other hand, during the processing of NP2 attachment in Chinese, which posed a greater processing load, WM played a substantial role. Secondly, in the process of RC disambiguation, various variables including linguistic variables and learner variables come into effect (Dussias, 2009).

As one of the variables, WM, which may interact with other variables to influence the results, especially at a lower level of language proficiency, could not determine the results of the processing. Thirdly, the effects of individual WM differences are not fixed, but task dependent, and the advantage of high WM in individuals lies in its ability to facilitate learners' rapid use of pragmatic information, but not in purely syntactic parsing. Havik et al.'s (2009) finding also indicated that WM could not compensate for processing purely structural difficulties presented by an L2 in the self-paced reading methodology. Only Carpenter and Keller (1996) argue that in purely syntactic parsing cases, high WM individuals are able to maintain all parses active in parallel, and hence take longer to process them. However, they are more accurate with comprehension probes, whereas low WM capacity individuals are faster, because low WM individuals allow the parse to crash, and therefore read more quickly. All the above explanations taken together might then account for the longer reading times by higher WM participants in L2 RC attachment processing compared to low WM participants.

Processing strategies in L2 parsing

Our online self-paced reading tasks and offline questionnaires clearly indicated that L2 parsing is influenced not only by structural information but also by semantic and other information, such as world knowledge, and language learning experience. So the structurally based principles, though partly confirmed by the present study and some previous studies, need to be supplemented with other parsing models to adequately explain RC attachment preferences. As Papadopoulou and Clahsen (2003) argued, attachment preferences by native speakers are influenced by both structurally based parsing strategies and lexical or thematic biases, whereas L2 learners' RC attachment preferences are mainly guided by lexical cues. In the same vein, Clahsen and Felser's (2006) Shallow Structure Hypothesis claims that adult L2 learners are guided by lexical-semantic cues during parsing in the same way as native speakers, but less so by syntactic information.

Additionally, L2 learners might have more difficulty in integrating different sources of information during L2 parsing. For example, Felser et al. (2003) observed that L2 processing was qualitatively different from L1 processing. Their results suggested that L2 learners did not rely on phrase structure information to the same extent that both young and mature native speakers did when processing input from the target language, and instead attempted more direct form-function mappings. More specifically, the L2 sentence processing mechanism did not necessarily integrate incoming ambiguous words or phrases immediately into the current syntactic analysis during online processing; rather, it delayed their integration under certain conditions until sufficient information had been received on which to base the attachment decision. Furthermore, in the offline questionnaires, in which the speed pressure was not so high, L2 learners were more likely to use post-structural cues. This tendency was partly verified by our offline English questionnaire data, which appeared to contradict the results of the online tasks. L2 learners disambiguated RC attachment not only by structural information but also by other cues, which were then integrated with structural information to perform a reanalysis.

Conclusion

The research reported in this chapter addresses the question of L2 sentence processing by low-intermediate Chinese L2 English learners. It was found that Chinese L2 learners demonstrated universal processing strategies in L2 parsing, and there was no L1 transfer in the disambiguation of L2 English RC attachment. Although our findings suggested that WM played a significant role in RC attachment with higher WM L2 learners eliciting more time processing temporally ambiguous RCs, the effects of WM on the L1 and L2 sentence processing were different. In line with some previous studies, we argued that the processing of L2 sentences such as RC disambiguation involved a variety of factors including both structural information and contextual cues, and they interacted with each other to influence the decision of RC ambiguity resolution. As Roberts (2012: 183) concluded, 'future research would greatly benefit from the unpacking of factors such as working memory capacity, processing speed/efficiency and general proficiency to better assess their impact, both individually and combined, on real-time comprehension and this will push forwards our understanding of the nature of sentence processing in both the L1 and the L2'.

Due to the small sample size and the participants' L2 proficiency, caution needs to be taken before generalising the findings of the present study to other contexts. The following directions might be worth probing. First, the effects of L2 proficiency on the processing of L2 sentences. Fernandez (1999: 232) suggested that L2 processing strategies different from the learners' L1 were harder to learn after puberty, and they were dependent on the L2 proficiency of the speakers. This line of research might help to find the variation in the strategies used as learners improve their proficiency, and a longitudinal study with dense data would be very conducive. Secondly, combined methods might be employed to investigate some subtle variations in L2 parsing. The self-paced reading tasks might not be sensitive enough to capture the attachment preference, and the investigation of L2 ambiguity resolution should use a variety of experimental techniques before any firm conclusion is drawn with respect to the L2 processing strategies. Thus, more sophisticated techniques, such as the eye-tracking technique, might be used in future studies. Thirdly, due to the typological distance between the Chinese language and Romance languages, the study of RC attachment by learners of Chinese as an L2 will be a promising direction. This focus might allow linguistic influences to be exhibited more clearly. Moreover, a comparative study of the ambiguity resolution by Chinese-speaking learners of English and English-speaking learners of Chinese will prove to be even more insightful in discovering the processing strategies and psychological mechanism of L2 learners.

References

Clahsen, H. and Felser, C. (2006) Grammatical processing in language learners. *Applied Psycholinguistics* 27, 3–42.

Cuetos, F., Mitchell, D.C. and Corley, M.B. (1996) Parsing in different languages. In M. Carreiras, J.E. Garcia-Albea and N. Sebastian-Galles (eds) *Language Processing in Spanish* (pp. 145–187). Mahwah, NJ: Lawrence Erlbaum Associates.

Dussias, P.E. (2003) Syntactic ambiguity resolution in L2 learners: Some effects of bilinguality on L1 and L2 processing strategies. *Studies in Second Language Acquisition* 25, 529–557.

Dussias, P.E. and Sagarra, N. (2007) The effect of exposure on syntactic parsing in Spanish-English L2 speakers. *Bilingualism: Language and Cognition* 10, 101–116.

Dussias, P.E. and Pinar, P. (2009) Sentence parsing in L2 learners: Linguistic and experience-based factors. In W. Ritchie and T. Bhatia (eds) *Handbook of Second Language Acquisition* (pp. 295–317). London: Academic Press.

Dussias, P.E. and Pinar, P. (2010) Effects of reading span and plausibility in the reanalysis of wh-gaps by Chinese–English second language speakers. *Second Language Research* 26, 443–472.

Felser, C., Roberts, L., Marinis, T. and Gross, R. (2003) The processing of ambiguous sentences by first and second language learners of English. *Applied Psycholinguistics* 24, 453–489.

Felser, C. and Roberts, L. (2007) Processing wh-dependencies in a second language: A cross-modal priming study. *Second Language Research* 23, 9–36.

Fernandez, E.M. (1999) Processing strategies in second language acquisition. In E. Klein (ed.) *The Development of Second Language Grammars: A Generative Approach* (pp. 217–240). Philadelphia, PA: John Benjamins.

Fernandez, E.M. (2002) *Bilingual Sentence Processing: Relative Clause Attachment in English and Spanish*. Amsterdam: John Benjamins.

Gregg, K. (2001) Learnability and second language acquisition theory. In P. Robinson (ed.) *Cognition and Second Language Acquisition* (pp. 152–180). Cambridge: Cambridge University Press.

Havik, E., Roberts, L., van Hout, R., Schreuder, R. and Haverkort, M. (2009) Processing subject-object ambiguities in the L2: A self-paced reading study with German L2 learners of Dutch. *Language Learning* 59, 73–112.

Hopp, H. (2006) Syntactic features and reanalysis in near-native processing. *Second Language Research* 22, 369–397.

Juffs, A. (2001) Psycholinguistically oriented second language research. *Annual Review of Applied Linguistics* 21, 207–220.

Juffs, A. (2004) Representation, processing and working memory in a second language. *Transactions of the Philological Society* 102, 199–225.

Juffs, A. (2006) Processing reduced relative vs. main verb ambiguity in English as a second language: A replication study with working memory. In R. Slabakova, S. Montrul and P. Prevost (eds), *Inquiries in Linguistic Development in Honor of Lydia White* (pp. 213–232). Amsterdam: John Benjamins.

Juffs, A. and Harrington, M. (2011) Aspects of working memory in L2 learning. *Language Teaching* 44, 137–166.

Keenan, E.L. and Comrie, B. (1977) Noun phrase accessibility and universal grammar. *Linguistic Inquiry* 8, 63–99.

Lee, T. (1992) The inadequacy of processing heuristics evidence from relative clause acquisition in Mandarin Chinese. In T. Lee (ed.) *Research on Chinese Linguistics in Hong Kong* (pp. 47–85). Hong Kong: The Linguistic Society of Hong Kong.

Li, C. and Thompson, S. (1989) *Mandarin Chinese: A Functional Reference Grammar*. Berkeley, CA: University of California Press.

MacDonald, M.C., Just, M.A. and Carpenter, P.A. (1992) Working memory constraints on the processing of syntactic ambiguity. *Cognitive Psychology* 24, 55–98.

Mitchell, D., Cuetos, F., Corley, M. and Brysbaert, M. (1995) Exposure-based models of human parsing: Evidence for the use of coarse-grained (nonlexical) statistical records. *Journal of Psycholinguistic Research* 24, 469–488.

Papadopoulou, D. (2005) Reading time studies of second language ambiguity resolution. *Second Language Research* 21, 98–120.

Papadopoulou, D. (2006) *Cross-linguistic Variation in Sentence Processing: Evidence from RC Attachment Preferences in Greek*. Amsterdam: Springer.

Papadopoulou, D. and Clahsen, H. (2003) Parsing strategies in L1 and L2 sentence processing: A study of relative clause attachment in Greek. *Studies in Second Language Acquisition* 25, 501–528.

Roberts, L. (2012) Individual differences in second language sentence processing. *Language Learning* 62 (S2), 172–188.

Rodriguez, G.A. (2008) Second language sentence processing: Is it fundamentally different? Unpublished PhD dissertation, University of Pittsburgh.

Swets, B., Desmet, T., Hambrick, D.Z. and Ferreira, F. (2007) The role of working memory in syntactic ambiguity resolution: A psychonometric approach. *Journal of Experimental Psychology: General* 136, 64–81.

VanPatten, B., Williams, J., Rott, S. and Overstreet, M. (2004) *Form-Meaning Connections in Second Language Acquisition*. Mahwah, NJ: Lawrence Erlbaum Associates.

Waters, G.S. and Caplan, D. (1996) The measurement of verbal working memory capacity and its relation to reading comprehension. *Quarterly Journal of Experimental Psychology* 49A, 51–79.

Williams, J. (1999) Memory, attention, and inductive learning. *Studies in Second Language Acquisition* 21, 1–48.

7 Working Memory and Sentence Processing: A Commentary

Alan Juffs

Introduction

In this volume, many chapters address the question of how working memory (WM) affects a wide range of phenomena in a second language (L2). This overview considers some of the main concerns of this field of inquiry where syntax is concerned. This topic is important to second language acquisition (SLA) researchers for at least two reasons. First, if L2 sentence processing proceeds in the same way that first language (L1) processing does, as some researchers maintain, WM effects could provide additional evidence for this claim at key points in the sentence. The reasoning is that if individual WM differences have an impact under the same conditions in L2 processing as they do in L1, it suggests similar pressure on computational resources to those found in L1 processing. Hence, research in this area addresses a fundamental concern of theoretical SLA. Second, finding and describing WM effects in L2 processing may help understand individual differences in reading comprehension in general, and so the confirmation of WM effects may have practical pedagogical and testing implications.

Since the publication of Daneman and Carpenter's (1980) seminal article, SLA researchers have focused more on sentence-level WM effects in syntactic processing. The chapter therefore begins by considering some of the sentence-level structures that have been deemed to permit the tracking of WM effects. It then moves on to review some of the key findings relating WM effects with these structures. The chapter concludes by considering some pilot data from a study that investigates the effect of relative clauses on pronoun–antecedent links in paragraph-length texts.

Structures Used to Investigate WM

A fundamental assumption in sentence processing is that the human processor begins to build an appropriate syntactic structure for each single word in the incoming string of words (either read or heard) immediately; it does not wait for several words before deciding on a structure. However, disagreements remain as to the precise timing of the kind of information the parser uses to build and revise these rapidly formed structures. Some researchers have proposed that only purely syntactic considerations are made in the initial parse and such models assume a serial parsing architecture in which only one possible structure is created at a time. This model is known as the Garden Path (GP) model of processing (Frazier, 1987; Frazier & Clifton, 1996). Such proposals differ fundamentally from 'constraint-based' models of processing that assume that many parallel possible parses are created at the same time; they are ranked using not only syntactic but also pragmatic and frequency information (MacDonald et al., 1994; MacDonald & Seidenberg, 2006). This overview is not the place to determine which model may be the 'right' one, but the structures we discuss below have in part been chosen to try to distinguish between the two models.

Generally speaking, the processing of simple, unambiguous sentences in a clear discourse context does not tax WM because an interpretation can immediately be created from a straightforward parse. Hence, in order to study WM effects, pressure must be applied to the parser to create computational complexity. This complexity usually involves choosing among several competing interpretations of a sentence or partial clause (global or temporary ambiguity). For example, the sentence in (1) is temporarily ambiguous because the verb in the preposed adjunct permits both a transitive and intransitive reading; the noun phrase (NP) 'the baby' needs to be integrated into the structure as soon as possible so it is attached as the object of the verb 'washed'. However, once the second verb 'began' is encountered, the parse has to be revised because the second verb requires a subject.

(1) While the woman [$_1$ washed [$_2$ the baby]$_1$ began]$_2$ to cry.

This reanalysis may be costly for the processor, because the NP 'the baby' must be reassigned a grammatical function (object to subject) and a theta role (theme to agent) in an entirely new clause. Pritchett (1992) provides a broad taxonomy of such structures and their processing costs.

Processing pressure can also involve tracking the relationship between displaced constituents and their original place in a clause, with the number of intervening referents playing a role in increasing the pressure on storage (Gibson, 2000). For example, in sentences (2) and (3), the gap between the referent of the relative pronoun 'who' is separated by words in (2) but not in (3). As a consequence, Gibson and others have proposed various reasons why participants in experiments find (2) harder to process (they are slower and answer comprehension questions less accurately) than (3).

(2) The ranger who t the branch crushed t knew the hunter was aiming at the turkey.

(3) The ranger who t t crushed the branch knew the hunter was aiming at the turkey.

In other types of sentences that contain wh-movement, it is the subject extraction that seems to pose greater problems for the processor. This may be for the same reason that GP sentences are challenging, because an object NP must be reanalysed as a subject NP in (4) but not in (5), even though in both cases the parse could terminate at the verb 'know' (Juffs, 2005; Juffs & Harrington, 1995).

(4) Who $_i$ does the ranger know t $_i$ saw a poacher in the woods?

(5) Who $_i$ does the ranger know the hunter saw t $_i$ in the woods?

Next, sentences that contain reduced relative clauses may be either very easy to process or very hard. For example, in (6) the reduced relative clause is entirely unambiguous due to the morphology of the part participle 'chosen'.

(6) The athletes chosen to represent their country are usually the most outstanding competitors.

However, as is well known, such morphological cues are not always available. Hence, a sentence such as (7) is temporarily ambiguous between a main clause, a reduced relative clause reading and an intransitive reading.

(7) The fat pigeon watched almost every second remained unaware of the falcon in the tree.

The full correct parse is not really available until the end of the adverbial 'second', because 'almost every' could introduce an object NP which is the complement of the verb 'watched'; for example, 'the fat pigeon watched almost every person eating a sandwich in the park'. For such sentences, MacDonald and colleagues have suggested that all three possible parses are created at the verb; evaluation may then take place of the various possible structures as the parse unfolds, depending on the cues available: the morphology of the verb, the valency of the verb, the frequency with which the verb has been encountered in the various sentence frames and the usefulness of the post-verbal adverbial phrase.

In addition to purely structural cues, it has been proposed that pragmatics also plays a role in the parsing of sentences. For example, in well-known sentences such as (8), animacy cues and real-world knowledge play an important role.

(8) (a) The wound examined by the doctor was severely swollen.

(b) The doctor examined by the nurse was severely swollen.

(c) The patient examined by the doctor was severely swollen.

In (8a), the parser may immediately be alert to the fact that a reduced relative might follow because 'wound' is inanimate and unlikely to be the agent of the verb. In (8b), the doctor is animate, but given real-world knowledge is more likely to be the agent, even though this turns out not to be the case. In (8c), the 'patient' may be more likely to be the object of examining than (8b), but perhaps less likely than (8a). Hence, the parser may be sensitive to animacy, a facet of language that is grammaticised in some languages; for example, in Japanese, inanimate subjects cannot be syntactic subjects (Harrington, 1987).

However, such cues as 'the doctor' versus 'the patient' being the subject of 'examine' come down to real-world knowledge and thus straightforward plausibility. Hence, in the past decade, researchers have started to look at the issue of plausibility with a view to considering whether L2 learners make more, and potentially exclusive, use of semantics and pragmatics to the exclusion of purely structural analysis (Clahsen & Felser, 2006). For example, in a recent paper that uses eye-tracking data, Felser and colleagues considered such sentences as those in (9). In a first experiment, Felser *et al.* (2012) showed that learners do not posit gaps in relative clause islands and also that L2 learners are highly sensitive to the plausibility and possibility of a gap. The authors wished to determine whether L2 learners are also sensitive to structural gaps or not, independently of plausibility. To this end, they developed a set of stimuli as in (9).

(9) There are all sorts of magazines on the market.

(a) Everyone liked the magazine $_i$ [that $_i$ [the hairdresser read t$_i$ quickly and extremely thoroughly about t$_i$] before going to the beauty salon. (Plausible gap at 'read', but later shown to be an *incorrect* gap due to 'about'.)

(b) Everyone liked the magazine $_i$ [that $_i$ [the hairdresser read *articles* with such strong conclusions about t$_i$] before going to the beauty salon. (Filled gap 'articles' at 'read' – hence surprise predicted at 'read' if a gap is posited before 'read' in anticipation of a gap, no matter what its plausibility is.)

(c) Everyone liked the magazine $_i$ [that [the hairdresser [who read *t$_i$ quickly and yet extremely thoroughly] bought **t**$_i$ before going to the beauty salon. (Illicit gap at 'read'.)

(d) Everyone liked the magazine $_i$ [that $_i$ [the hairdresser [who read articles with such strong conclusions] bought t$_i$ before going to the salon. (Constraint *and* filled gap at 'read'.)

In this experiment, important differences between a German L2 English group and native English speakers were revealed. Both groups answered the comprehension questions with similar accuracy (both over 90%), showing that the results of parsing are similar. However, during processing, the native speakers' eye-tracking data showed an interaction between the gap and the syntactic constraint at the first pass reading times, with the filled gap condition producing higher reading times in the non-relative clause conditions. On the other hand, the German-speaking English as a second language (ESL) learners revealed no interaction in the first pass or other regression reading times, but they did show an interaction when rereading the critical region. That is, an effect occurred much later in the eye-tracking data than the native speakers' initial reaction. The native speakers also had a major interaction on rereading and this seems to have been greater than at the regression path portion. Therefore, Felser and colleagues suggested that where filled gaps are concerned, the German speakers evinced a *delayed* use of syntactic gaps. In their analysis of these results, the authors propose that the best interpretation of these data is that L2 *structural* grammar knowledge is not immediately used in first pass parsing, but only at later stages. Hence, for L2 learners the shallow parsing route may dominate in processing because it can operate faster than the full parsing route.

Working memory effects

Juffs and Harrington (2011) and Wen (2016 manuscript under review) provide extensive reviews of WM in SLA. In *online* sentence processing, the WM measure that is used most often is based on the reading span task of Daneman and Carpenter (1980) or an adaptation of Waters and Caplan's (1996) tasks, rather than the word span tasks (e.g. Baddeley, 2000). Reading span tasks require participants to carry out a processing activity, such as reading aloud or making a plausibility judgement, and then recall a word at the end of the sentence that is read aloud or judged. Early research had students read from 4×6 cards, but research has now become much more sophisticated in its use of computers and the scoring procedures have also been adjusted (see Conway *et al.* [2005] for details).

L1 processing and working memory

In studies on the structures discussed in 'Structures Used to Investigate WM' above, WM effects as measured by the reading span task have been found quite reliably in L1 sentence processing. Interestingly, the effects were not always the same. An interesting facet of WM capacity in this model is that the effects of individual memory differences are not immutable, but may in fact depend on the type of linguistic properties of the sentences being processed (Just *et al.*, 1996; Miyake & Friedman, 1998). For example, an individual with a high memory capacity will be more accurate in comprehension and resolve an ambiguity at crucial points in reading a sentence such as (10) more quickly than a low capacity individual.

(10) The evidence *examined* by the lawyer convinced the jury.

As discussed for example (7), the verb 'examined' in (10) is *temporarily* ambiguous between a main verb and a reduced relative clause structure. As we have already seen, pragmatic information rapidly assists the parser to correctly assume that a reduced relative clause is present because 'evidence' is inanimate and unlikely to be the agent of any 'examining'. High WM capacity readers are able to resolve this ambiguity more quickly than low WM capacity readers. According to Just and colleagues, this is because high capacity readers are able to combine pragmatic and syntactic information in parsing more efficiently than low-span readers. On the other hand, in a sentence such as (11), while high capacity readers are more accurate in comprehension, they take *more time* to resolve the parse. As previously mentioned, the concerns in this sentence with a reduced relative clause are related to the argument structure of the verb, the morphology and the type of cue following the verb.

(11) The soldiers *warned* during the midnight raid attacked after midnight.

In contrast to (10), in (11) the ambiguity of 'warned' sets up three *purely syntactic* possible parses: a main verb reading, an intransitive verb reading and a reduced relative reading. MacDonald *et al.* (1994) argue that high WM individuals in this case are able to maintain all three parses active in parallel processing, and hence take *longer* to process them. Ultimately, however, they are more accurate with comprehension probes. In contrast, low WM capacity participants read more quickly, but have less comprehension. The explanation for this trade-off is that low WM individuals allow the parse to crash, and therefore read more quickly. However, the cost is that they reject these sentences as implausible or fail to understand the relationships among the NPs.

Working memory and L2 sentence processing

In L2 sentence processing, researchers have wanted to investigate WM effects due to the large within-group variation in sentence processing. That is to say, when investigating sentence processing in L2 speakers, individual members of different language groups vary quite considerably as to the speed with which they process sentences. Researchers have been interested in whether such variation is due to general cognitive capacity differences, as measured by WM, or other factors such as speed of lexical access, proficiency, frequency and so on. For example, Hopp (2013) and Miller (2013) have recently suggested that task demands, e.g. lexical access, mean that research in sentence processing in the L2 needs to ensure that issues of proficiency and lexical access are accounted for. We will not address these important recent developments in this overview, but review the questions regarding WM, including effects in longer discourse.

Early research in L2 sentence processing considered WM effects in sentences which contained subject extraction from an embedded clause; e.g. 'Who does the nurse know saw the doctor in the hospital?'. Processing such sentences is challenging because of the high processing load at the embedded verb as described in (1) and (4). Just as processing research is able to infer how the parser works from processing breakdown, so WM effects among individuals are only really evident when pressure is put on the parser. Hence, WM effects and processing breakdown should occur together because processing breakdown provides the context in which memory is taxed.

Early research on this topic used both L1 and L2 measures of WM to avoid a confound between WM score and L2 proficiency. Such cautions remain advisable despite the fact that L1 and L2 WM scores usually correlate. Juffs (2004, 2005, 2006) used the manual file card methodology with several groups of learners of English as their L2. These three studies, which included the same learners with different structures, sought to find WM effects in GP sentences, long-distance wh-movement and reduced relative clauses as illustrated in (1), (4) and (7). No robust WM effects were found – possibly due to the manual nature of the task or possibly because the L1 effects were too strong. Using computerised methodology advocated by Conway et al. (2005), Rodriguez looked for WM effects with GP sentences but also found no WM effects. Similarly, Felser and Roberts (2007) found no WM effects in their study of wh-traces. Naturally, null effects are not necessarily definitive evidence that they cannot be found.

Indeed, not all researchers have failed to find WM effects. These effects are most often found when learner groups are split into groups of high WM and low WM.[1] Havik et al. (2009) investigated relative clause processing in Dutch by native speakers of German and found that where pragmatic cues could be used, the language learners who scored high on WM measures resembled the low WM capacity native speakers. Dussias and Pinar (2010) similarly found effects with wh-extraction structures in (4) and (5) with high-level Chinese-speaking learners of English. Finally, Sagarra and Herschensohn (2010) found WM effects in their intermediate group when investigating agreement phenomena in Spanish adjective agreement in NPs, but not with advanced learners. The intermediate level is 'the one that shows the emerging ability to compute gender concord— is also the bellwether for WM. At this intermediate level, WM can be a significant factor whereas it is essentially irrelevant at ceiling' (Sagarra & Herschensohn, 2010: 2035). Hence, it seems that there is a proficiency level by structure interaction when it comes to finding WM effects. The questions that remain are in which structures and how does WM mediate development and parsing in very advanced learners who may be said to have 'completed' acquisition.

Working memory effects in discourse: A pilot study and call for further research

Most research in L2 sentence processing has focused on sentence-level phenomena and processing breakdown. Almost no research has addressed the interaction of sentence-level processing and longer texts. However, in their original article, Daneman and Carpenter (1980) extended WM effects to many aspects, including the distance between a pronoun and its referent. High-span readers (4 and above on the old scale of silent reading WM span) comprehended pronoun–antecedent relationships 100% of the time even when there were six or seven sentences between the pronoun and the referent, whereas low-span readers achieved a comprehension rate of only about 10% (Daneman & Carpenter, 1980: 461, Figure 2). This discourse tracking aspect of WM has not been extensively addressed in the L2 sentence processing literature.

If psycholinguistic research is going to be relevant to L2 instruction, as indeed it should be (Juffs & Harrington, 2011), the implications of this important aspect of WM should be further explored for assessing the difficulty of texts for the assessment of reading comprehension. With this goal in mind, Juffs and Rodríguez (2014) reported on a pilot study that combines sentence-level processing with discourse referent recovery. It is well established in the literature that subject relative clauses are easier to process than object relative clauses (e.g. King & Just, 1991) and that discourse effects can be found even at the sentence level (e.g. Gibson *et al.*, 2005). Hence, (12) is processed faster and comprehended more accurately than (13).

(12) The student who _ visited his friend completed the homework on time.

(13) The student who his friend visited __ completed the homework on time.

In a previously unpublished study, Juffs and Rodríguez (2014) report on whether such processing asymmetry, when inserted into a longer text, would impact comprehension in pronoun relationships. For example, in (14) the correct antecedent of the italicised pronoun 'she' is 'Jane'. However, between the antecedent and the pronoun is a sentence containing an object relative clause. The comprehension question in (15) tests that relationship.

(14) *Jane* is going to be 17 years old in one week. Her best friend Anna is planning a surprise birthday party for her. **All of the people *who Anna invited* have promised to keep the party a secret**. Anna feels sure that *she* will be surprised. All the work will be worth it when she sees her friend's face!

(15) Probe: Anna will be surprised. TRUE or **FALSE**?

In other versions of the story, the object relative clause was replaced either by a sentence with a subject relative clause, e.g. 'All of the people *that answered the invitation* have promised to keep the party a secret', or a sentence containing no relative clause at all, e.g. 'All the invited people have promised to keep it a secret until the day of the party'.

For the very advanced Spanish-speaking learners and native speakers who participated in the study, results confirmed that stories with subject relative clauses were reliably easier to process for both Spanish-speaking and native English readers (91.67% vs 92.26% correct, respectively, comprehension in the TRUE/FALSE task) than the object relatives (85.83% vs 80.35%) and the no relative clause conditions (80.0% vs 79.15%), which did not differ. There were no differences in clause type in the time it took to answer the comprehension question. The WM task that was used was computer based and required the learners to assess the grammaticality of the sentence and to store the final words. Scoring followed the partial credit unit scoring procedure suggested by Conway et al. (2005). (The maximum score for this method is 25.) Although the native speakers showed no WM effects, the storage component (i.e. how many words were remembered on a Spanish WM task) correlated positively with accuracy on the passages without relative clauses for the Spanish speakers ($r=0.55$, $p=0.012$), and a negative correlation was found with latency ($r=-0.48$, $p=0.031$) in the time it took to answer the no relative clause condition. These results are of course inconclusive, but they do suggest that in the passages where there was the most variation (and the lowest accuracy), WM effects were found in the formation of pronoun–antecedent references.

Conclusion

The study of sentence processing in SLA has focused mainly on sentence-level phenomena. Early research developed processing explanations for effects that had been found in grammaticality judgement tasks, but recent research has deployed the full rigor of psycholinguistic methodology in exploring L2 sentence processing (e.g. Felser et al., 2012). Because WM effects are indicative of (structural or semantic) parsing, finding such effects could be an important indicator that the cognitive resources used in L2 processing are comparable if not identical to native speaker processing. Such evidence has been found in some cases. More research is needed for cases in which WM effects may be evident beyond the level of the sentence, and in texts that are more consistent with real-world processing and comprehension challenges.

Acknowledgements

Some research discussed in this chapter was supported by grants from the University of Pittsburgh Central Research Development Fund and the Pittsburgh Science of Learning Center to Alan Juffs. The Pittsburgh Science of Learning Center is funded by the National Science Foundation (NSF) award no. SBE-0836012. Previously, it was funded by the NSF award no. SBE-0354420.

Note

(1) Usually, it is hard to find reliable correlations between WM scores and reading times on specific words in sentences. Although some variance is lost by putting learners into groups based on their WM score, it is here that effects are most often observed.

References

Baddeley, A. (2000) Short-term and working memory. In E. Tulving and F. Craik (eds) *The Oxford Handbook of Memory* (pp. 77–92). New York: Oxford University Press.

Clahsen, H. and Felser, C. (2006) Grammatical processing in language learners. *Applied Psycholinguistics* 27, 3–42.

Conway, A.R.A., Kane, M.J., Bunting, M.F., Hambrick, D.Z., Wilhelm, O. and Engle, R.E. (2005) Working memory span tasks: A methodological review and user's guide. *Psychonomic Bulletin and Review* 12, 769–786.

Daneman, M. and Carpenter, P. (1980) Individual differences in working memory and reading. *Journal of Verbal Learning and Verbal Behavior* 19, 450–466.

Felser, C. and Roberts, L. (2007) Processing wh-dependencies in a second language: A cross-modal priming study. *Second Language Research* 23, 9–36.

Felser, C., Cunnings, I., Batterham, C. and Clahsen, H. (2012) The timing of island effects in nonnative sentence processing. *Studies in Second Language Acquisition* 34, 67–98.

Frazier, L. (1987) Theories of sentence processing. In J.L. Garfield (ed.) *Modularity in Knowledge Representation and Natural Language Understanding* (pp. 291–307). Cambridge, MA: MIT Press.

Frazier, L. and Clifton, C. (1996) *Construal.* Cambridge, MA: MIT Press.

Gibson, E. (2000) The dependency locality theory: A distance based theory of linguistic complexity. In Y. Miyashita, A. Marantz and W. O'Neil (eds) *Image, Language, Brain* (pp. 95–126). Cambridge, MA: MIT Press.

Gibson, E., Desmet, T., Grodner, D., Watson, D. and Ko, K. (2005) Reading relative clauses in English. *Cognitive Linguistics* 16, 313–353.

Harrington, M. (1987) Processing transfer: Language-specific processing strategies as a source of interlanguage variation. *Applied Psycholinguistics* 8, 351–377.

Havik, E., Roberts, L., Schreuder, R., van Hout, R. and Haverkort, M. (2009) Processing subject-object ambiguities in the L2: A self-paced reading study with German L2 learners of Dutch. *Language Learning* 59 (1), 73–112.

Hopp, H. (2013) Individual differences in the second language processing of object-subject ambiguities. *Applied Psycholinguistics* 1–45; first view: doi:10.1017/S0142716413000180.

Juffs, A. (2004) Representation, processing and working memory in a second language. *Transactions of the Philological Society* 102, 199–226.

Juffs, A. (2005) The influence of first language on the processing of wh-movement in English as a second language. *Second Language Research* 21, 121–151.

Juffs, A. (2006) Processing reduced relative vs. main verb ambiguity in English as a second language: A replication study with working memory. In R. Slabakova, S. Montrul and P. Prevost (eds) *Inquiries in Linguistic Development in Honor of Lydia White* (pp. 213–232). Amsterdam: John Benjamins.

Juffs, A. and Harrington, M.W. (1995) Parsing effects in L2 sentence processing: Subject and object asymmetries in *wh*-extraction. *Studies in Second Language Acquisition* 17 (4), 483–516.

Juffs, A. and Harrington, M.W. (2011) Aspects of working memory in L2. *Language Teaching* 44 (2), 137–166.

Juffs, A. and Rodríguez, G.A. (2014) *Second Language Sentence Processing*. New York: Routledge.

Just, M.A., Carpenter, P. and Keller, T. (1996) The capacity theory of comprehension: New frontiers of evidence and arguments. *The Psychological Review* 103, 773–780.

King, J. and Just, M.A. (1991) Individual differences in syntactic processing: The role of working memory. *Journal of Memory and Language* 30, 580–602.

MacDonald, M.C., Pearlmutter, N.J. and Seidenberg, M.S. (1994) The lexical nature of syntactic ambiguity resolution. *Psychological Review* 101 (4), 676–703.

MacDonald, M.C. and Seidenberg, M.S. (2006) Constraint satisfaction accounts of lexical and sentence comprehension. In M. Traxler and M.A. Gernsbacher (eds) *Handbook of Psycholinguistics* (pp. 581–611). New York: Academic Press.

Miller, A.K. (2013) Second language processing of filler-gap dependencies: Evidence for the role of lexical access. In E. Voss, S.-J.D. Tai and Z. Li (eds) *Selected Proceedings of the 2011 Second Language Research Forum: Converging Theory and Practice* (pp. 82–94). Somerville, MA: Cascadilla Proceedings Project.

Pritchett, B.L. (1992) *Grammatical Competence and Parsing Performance*. Chicago, IL: Chicago University Press.

Roberts, L. and Felser, C. (2011) Plausibility and recovery from garden paths in second language processing. *Applied Psycholinguistics* 32 (2), 299–331.

Rodriguez, G. A. (2007) Second language sentence processing, is it fundamentally different? Doctoral Dissertation, University of Pittsburgh.

Sagarra, N. and Herschensohn, J. (2010) The role of proficiency and working memory in gender and number agreement processing in L1 and L2 Spanish. *Lingua* 120, 2022–2039.

Waters, G.S. and Caplan, D. (1996) The measurement of verbal working memory capacity and its relation to reading comprehension. *Quarterly Journal of Experimental Psychology: Human Experimental Psychology* 49A, 51–79.

Wen, Z. (2016, manuscript under review) Working Memory and Second Language Learning: Towards an Integrated Approach. Multilingual Matters.

Part 3

Working Memory in L2 Interaction and Performance

8 Working Memory, Language Analytical Ability and L2 Recasts

Shaofeng Li

Introduction

According to the Interaction Hypothesis (Gass, 2003; Long, 2007), second language (L2) interaction leads to interlanguage development by providing opportunities for modified input, pushed output and corrective feedback. Corrective feedback has become an important theme in recent second language acquisition (SLA) research not only because its role is theoretically justifiable but also because it is a useful pedagogical tool for language teachers. Synthetic reviews (Li, 2010; Lyster & Saito, 2010) have unequivocally shown that feedback was indeed facilitative of L2 development; however, they also demonstrated that the effects of feedback were moderated by various learner-internal and learner-external factors (e.g. instructional setting and age). Therefore, it is necessary to view the effects of feedback as situated and relative and ascertain how feedback interacts with other variables in affecting L2 learning. This study explores whether the effectiveness of one type of feedback (recasts) is constrained by two components of language aptitude, namely working memory and language analytic ability, in different ways when the feedback is provided to learners at different proficiency levels. To date, there has been no research on the relationship between language aptitude and proficiency. Thus, this study also constitutes a valuable endeavour to fill a gap in aptitude research.

Review of the Literature

The literature review section of almost all feedback studies starts with Lyster's seminal work based on Canadian French immersion classes (e.g. Lyster, 1998; Lyster & Ranta, 1997). It is Lyster who provided a clear taxonomy of corrective feedback that has enabled subsequent researchers to carry out descriptive and experimental studies regarding the occurrence and effectiveness of different types of feedback in various instructional contexts. Lyster identified six types of feedback, which according to Ellis (2010) fall into two broad categories – input providing and output prompting. Recasts and explicit correction are input providing in that they contain the correct form; the other four feedback types (elicitation, metalinguistic clue, repetition and clarification request) are output prompting because they withhold the correct form and encourage self-repair. Another way to categorise feedback strategies is to label them as implicit or explicit depending on whether there is a device that draws the learner's attention to errors. It is generally agreed that recasts stand at the implicit end and explicit correction and metalinguistic clue at the explicit end. With some basic concepts in place about the typology of feedback and where recasts stand in different taxonomies, the following review will focus exclusively on recasts and how they relate to learners' individual differences in working memory and language analytic ability.

Previous research on recasts

A recast refers to the reformulation of a wrong utterance without changing its central meaning and with the primary focus on 'meaning, not language as object' (Long, 2007: 77). In Long's view, recasts are provided to solve communication problems, and this type of recast can be called conversational recasts (Ellis & Sheen, 2006). In language classes and most empirical studies investigating the effectiveness of recasts, however, recasts are provided to achieve pedagogical purposes, and in most cases, there are no communication problems because of the shared knowledge about the task procedure and information to be exchanged between interlocutors and the predictable turn-taking patterns and sequence organisation of classroom discourse. The recasts that are embedded in conversational exchanges but not in response to communication problems can be called corrective or form-focused recasts. The attempt to distinguish the two types of recasts is not intended to solve any controversy but to dispel a myth, that is, the types of recasts feedback that researchers investigate are not the recasts that Long advocated, although this line of research has been cast in the theoretical framework of his Interaction Hypothesis.

The study of recasts has revolved around three themes: occurrence, noticing and effectiveness. With regard to occurrence, recasts have been found to be the most frequent feedback type in L2 classes across instructional settings (e.g. Choi & Li, 2012; Sheen, 2004), and they are also the most studied feedback among all identified feedback types. Recasts are favoured by teachers because of their advantages compared with other feedback types, such as the availability of both positive and negative evidence, non-intrusiveness, immediate juxtaposition of the wrong and correct forms and their non-threatening nature. Such characteristics cater to the widely accepted practice in L2 pedagogy of embedding focus on form in meaning-oriented tasks.

The noticing of recasts has been investigated through verbal report in stimulated recall and uptake – learner responses after recasts. Studies based on retrospective verbal reports showed that recasts were more likely to be recognised when they followed phonological and lexical errors than errors relating to morphosyntax (Kim & Han, 2007; Mackey *et al.*, 2000). Studies investigating uptake demonstrated that the uptake level after recasts *per se* and in relation to other feedback types varied considerably across instructional contexts. In general, recasts were followed by less uptake in meaning-oriented classes than form-oriented contexts (Lyster & Mori, 2006; Sheen, 2004). However, research also showed that uptake after recasts was not indicative of L2 development and therefore may instead be only mechanical repetition of preceding utterances (Loewen & Philp, 2006; Mackey & Philp, 1997).

In terms of the extent to which recasts facilitate L2 development, it has been found that the effects of this type of feedback were constrained by multiple factors. Recasts were less effective than prompts and more explicit feedback types in classroom settings (Lyster, 2004; Sheen, 2007) but they were equally effective as prompts (Lyster & Izquierdo, 2009) and more effective than negotiation (confirmation check and clarification request) (Iwashita, 2003) in laboratory settings. Also, recasts were less effective for beginners but as effective as prompts (Ammar & Spada, 2006) and explicit feedback for advanced learners (Li, 2009). Furthermore, learners were able to benefit from recasts when learning salient linguistic targets such as English possessive *his/her* in Ammar and Spada (2006), but not opaque or redundant linguistic structures such as English articles in Sheen (2007) or English regular past in Yang and Lyster (2010).

Clearly, the effects of recasts are mediated by various contextual and learner factors. To date, however, there has been little research on the interface between recasts and individual difference variables and no research on whether different cognitive aptitudes are implicated when recasts are provided to learners at different stages of L2 development. The next section justifies why such research is needed.

Language aptitude

Language aptitude refers to a set of cognitive abilities that are predictive of ultimate L2 attainment and that interface with different learning contexts. L2 aptitude research commenced with the publication of the modern language aptitude test (MLAT; Carroll & Sapon, 1959), validated based on the test results contributed by 5000 learners from high school and university language classes and government-funded intensive training programmes in the U.S. The MLAT is composed of five subtests tapping the three basic components of aptitude: phonemic coding, language analytic ability and rote memory.

There have been two venues of aptitude research in SLA: predictive and interactional. Early aptitude research was mostly predictive and investigated the relationships between aptitude and L2 achievements reflected via end-of-semester course grades or scores on standardised proficiency tests (e.g. Bialystok & Frohlich, 1978; Ehrman, 1998; Horwitz, 1980). Interactional research probes into how aptitude or different aptitude components mediate the effects of instructional treatments (e.g. de Graaff, 1997; Erlam, 2005; VanPatten & Borst, 2012). Interactional studies take a dynamic and situated approach to the role of aptitude, and their findings are more revealing about the mechanism and processes of SLA than those of predictive studies, which to some extent thwarted the advancement of aptitude research. What is appealing about the notion of aptitude–treatment interaction is that learners with different profiles may benefit from different instructional approaches, which set different processing demands on learners' cognitive abilities (Robinson, 2005). This study aimed to show whether two aptitude components – working memory and language analytic ability – played differential roles in mediating the effects of recasts.

Working memory and feedback

The term 'working memory' was developed to reflect the dual function of information storage and processing of short-term memory. Working memory has been operationalised as phonological short-term memory (alternatively called 'phonological memory'), which essentially refers to the storage component, or as complex working memory (also called 'executive working memory'), which consists of both the storage and processing components (see Wen, this volume, for a discussion on the confusion over the two types of working memory). Phonological short-term memory is typically measured via digit span or non-word recall tests, and complex working memory through reading or listening span tests. Phonological short-term memory has been found to be related to L2 vocabulary (Cheung, 1996; Speciale et al., 2004) and grammar (Ellis et al., 1999; French & O'Brien, 2008) learning; complex working memory is predictive of listening and reading comprehension (Berquist, 1997) and grammar learning (Harrington & Sawyer, 1992).

In aptitude research, there has been a call to replace the traditional rote memory component with working memory (Miyake & Friedman, 1998; Robinson, 2005). It has been argued that rote memory, tapped through the paired associates subtest of the MLAT, is only sensitive to traditional audiolingual contexts that emphasise decontextualised, discrete item (rote) learning, not to current instructional contexts where more emphasis is placed on exposure to authentic language use and incidental learning.

Conversely, working memory is a more dynamic and viable construct that is central to activating previously stored data and attending to, processing and internalising new linguistic input in meaning-oriented tasks. Therefore, working memory has the potential to become the most important aptitude component.

A few studies have investigated the relationship between working memory and the effectiveness of recasts (Goo, 2012; Mackey *et al.*, 2002; Révész, 2012; Sagarra, 2007; Trofimovich *et al.*, 2007). These studies seemed to demonstrate that working memory was beneficial when learners tried to assimilate the positive and/or negative evidence contained in corrective feedback provided by an interlocutor or a computer. Mackey *et al.* reported that learners with high working memory capacities were better at noticing recasts. Goo's results provided further support for the noticing function of working memory in that it was only correlated with the effects of recasts, not those of metalinguistic feedback, the explicit nature of which, as Goo argued, neutralised the learners' individual differences in their ability to notice the linguistic target. Both Sagarra and Trofimovich *et al.* investigated computerised recasts, but the effects of recasts were found to relate to working memory only in the former but not the latter study. In discussing the conflicting results of the two studies, Goo pointed out that this was due to the letter-string test used in Trofimovich *et al.*, which did not tap the processing component of working memory.

One limitation of the above studies is that learners' working memory scores were only based on the recall component of the tests and did not include reaction time and veracity judgement – important indicators of the processing components of working memory. However, previous studies found that there was a trade-off effect between the different elements of a working memory test, that is, testees tended to sacrifice one element for a better performance on the other. For instance, they may focus more on the part to be recalled than the parts involving semantic processing (as when making a judgement about the truthfulness of the meaning of a sentence in a reading or listening span test) or mental calculation (as when solving math problems in an operation span test) (Leeser, 2007). This limitation, along with the other gaps identified, is to be addressed in this study.

Language analytic ability and feedback

Language analytic ability refers to learners' ability to extrapolate and generalise linguistic rules. It is measured through the words in sentences subtest of the MLAT and the linguistic analysis subtest of the *Professional and Linguistic Assessments Board* (PLAB). Predictive studies that investigated the relationship between aptitude and ultimate L2 outcome showed that language analytic ability is predictive of general proficiency (Gordon,

1980; Sparks et al., 1999), less so for grammar learning (DeKeyser, 1993; Gardner & Lambert, 1965), reading (Hummel, 2009), speaking (Grenena & Long, 2012) and least for listening (Yoshizawa, 2002) and writing (Harley & Hart, 2002; Kormos & Trebit, 2012). Studies investigating aptitude–instruction interaction showed that language analytic ability was more likely to be drawn upon when metalinguistic information was unavailable (Erlam, 2005; Hwu & Sun, 2012; Robinson, 1997).

The studies relating to corrective feedback indicated that the role of language analytic ability had to do with the implicit/explicit nature of the feedback. Sheen (2007) examined the interface between language analytic ability and the effects of metalinguistic correction and recasts in the learning of two uses of English indefinite and definite articles: *a* as first mention and *the* as anaphoric reference. Sheen found that language analytic ability was only correlated with the effects of metalinguistic correction but not those of recasts. The results conflicted with those of Trofimovich et al.'s study (2007) which detected a significant connection between this aptitude component and recasts in the learning of possessive *his/her* in English. A plausible explanation for the disparity between these two studies may be sought by recourse to the different levels of saliency of the feedback in the two studies. The classroom setting, the implicit nature of recasts and the opaque, redundant nature of the English articles in Sheen's study may have made it very difficult for the learners to notice the feedback. In Trofimovich et al., in contrast, the treatment was delivered via a computer targeting a relatively easy and transparent linguistic structure, and the feedback was thus easily recognised by the learners. In both studies, as can be seen, proficiency was not a variable, so it is unclear if different levels of learners used their analytic ability in different ways.

Aptitude and proficiency

One area of aptitude research that is nearly unexplored concerns the roles of aptitude and different aptitude components in different stages of L2 development. Carroll (1981: 86) stated that aptitude as measured by conventional aptitude tests such as the MLAT represents 'an individual's initial state of readiness and capacity for learning a foreign language'. Carroll (1990: 24) also admitted that most of his research related to the rate of learning a language 'from scratch' and it remained to be seen how aptitude correlated with advanced learning. Other theorists of language aptitude (Robinson, 2005; Skehan, 2012) also posited that different clusters of cognitive abilities might be involved at different stages of SLA. There has been some empirical evidence to back up this postulation, although to date there has been no systematic investigation of the impact of proficiency on the role of aptitude.

Winke (2005) administered the MLAT and a working memory test to beginning learners enrolled in a first-semester Chinese course at

Georgetown University and advanced Chinese learners at the Defence Language Institute. For the beginners, both their MLAT and working memory scores were correlated with their proficiency scores; for advanced learners, however, significant correlations were only found for working memory. Curtin *et al.* (1983) reported that beginning high school foreign language learners' aptitude scores (on the PLAB test) were substantially more correlated with their course grades than advanced learners. Furthermore, Hummel (2009) investigated the relationship between L2 proficiency, phonological short-term memory (PWM) and language aptitude among a group of very advanced English as a second language (ESL) learners. Proficiency was measured by the Michigan Test of English Language Proficiency, phonological short-term memory by a non-word repetition test and aptitude by the short version of the MLAT. It was found that proficiency, phonological short-term memory and aptitude loaded on separate factors and that aptitude was not a significant predictor.

These findings afford empirical support for the foregoing theoretical claims that (1) aptitude measured via traditional aptitude tests tends to relate to initial L2 learning, and (2) different aptitude components are drawn on by learners at different proficiency levels. However, the three studies are all predictive without systematic variable manipulation. In both Winke and Curtin *et al.*, for example, proficiency was operationalised as enrolment status rather than on the basis of results on a proficiency test, the measures for the criterion/response variable (e.g. course grades) were different for the two groups and the type of instruction they received was not controlled. This study overcomes these limitations by operationalising proficiency via a standardised proficiency test, using the same measures for the criterion variable and implementing the same instructional treatment.

The following research questions were formulated to explore the possible differential role of two aptitude components in mediating the effects of recasts on beginning and advanced L2 Chinese learners:

(1) Are recasts effective in facilitating beginning and advanced L2 Chinese learners in their learning of Chinese classifiers?
(2) Are working memory and language analytic ability drawn on differently by learners at the two proficiency levels?

Method

Participants

The participants were 28 learners of Chinese from two large US universities. The mean age of these learners was 20.82, and they were enrolled in the fourth, sixth and eighth semesters of their Chinese study.

Table 8.1 Group statistics

Group	n	Median	SD
Beginning	17	26.29	5.06
Advanced	11	35.36	7.49

The learners were divided into two proficiency levels based on their enrolment status: the fourth-semester students were called beginners and the sixth- and eighth-semester students were labelled as advanced learners. To ensure that the two groups of learners were different in their Chinese proficiency, a revised Chinese proficiency test (details of which will be provided in the 'testing' section) was administered, and the descriptive statistics appear in Table 8.1. An independent samples t-test was performed and the results showed a significant difference between the two proficiency groups ($t(26)=-3.8$, $p<0.01$).

Target structure

The linguistic structure that corrective feedback targeted was Chinese classifiers. A Chinese classifier is used between a determiner (which is often a quantifier but can also be a demonstrative) and a noun (e.g. y also be a demonstrative) and a noun (e.g. yī gè rén, one CLASSIFIER person). A classifier is used to categorise and quantify a set of objects with the same or similar physical properties or characteristics. For instance, the classifier *tiáo* is used with objects that are long and curvilinear such as 'snake', 'string', etc. Classifiers are different from English measure words because the former are used with both countable and uncountable nouns, and the latter only with uncountable nouns. The Chinese classifier is a difficult structure for L1 English speakers because it is not part of the English language and because in Chinese there is a general classifier (*gè*) in Chinese that can in many cases replace special classifiers.

However, in order to establish the obligatory contexts for classifier use, that is, selecting the classifier–noun combinations where the general and special classifiers do not stand in free variation, a survey was administered to 45 native speakers of Chinese in the local community, who were provided with 40 sentences and were asked to determine what classifier should be used and if the classifier can be replaced by the general classifier. A classifier use must reach an 80% agreement rate to be included in the treatment tasks. Based on the survey results, 15 contexts for classifier use were obtained.

Treatment tasks

Two tasks were used where obligatory contexts for classifier use were available. During both tasks, the learners received recasts on their wrong classifier use. The first task is called picture description, where the learner was asked to describe 7 pictures that contained 15 cases of classifier use. The pictures had different numbers of various objects (such as two trees, a river, three horses, etc.) so that the learner would have to use classifiers when he/she described the objects and reported how many of them there were. Distracter objects were included in addition to the objects related to the use of the selected classifiers. A vocabulary list (with Chinese characters, the Pinyin, and their English equivalents) was provided in each picture that contained the nouns that accompany the classifiers the learner was expected to produce. The purpose was to increase the learner's chances of using classifiers and to facilitate the flow of communication, especially for less advanced learners who may not have sufficient linguistic resources to draw on. Also, the learner was allowed to ask the native speaker researcher vocabulary questions but not grammar questions. The sequence of the pictures was randomised so that each learner described them in a different order.

The second task is called spot the difference, where there were three sets of pictures. Each set had two pictures that contained more or less the same items but the two pictures were different in a number of aspects. The native speaker and the learner each held a picture, and the learner asked questions to find out what the differences were. Completion of the task required the use of the same 15 selected classifiers as appeared in Task 1. As in Task 1, the learner was provided a vocabulary list for each picture and was allowed to ask vocabulary-related questions. The sequence of the three picture sets was randomised for each learner.

Recasts

As in other feedback studies, a recast is operationalised as a corrective device that reformulates an erroneous utterance while maintaining its central meaning. The recasts in this study were relatively salient because they were provided in a laboratory setting in dyadic interaction and they targeted a single linguistic structure. Besides the utterances containing the target structure, utterances that contained errors relating to other structures were also responded to with recasts as well as other feedback types when the errors caused communication breakdown or misinterpretation. Attending to forms other than the target forms helped maintain the flow of communication and mask the linguistic foci. The following example illustrates how a recast was provided:

NNS: zhàopiàn	yǒu	liǎng	gè	zhū
照片	有	两	个	猪。
Photo	has	two-*CL* [wrong]		pig

This photo has two pigs.

NS: liǎng   tóu   zhū

　　　两头　　　猪。

　　　Two-CL　　pig

　　　Two pigs.

As can be seen, the non-native speaker used a wrong classifier for 'pigs', and the native speaker researcher reformulated the noun phrase containing the error by replacing the wrong classifier *gè* with *tóu*.

Testing

Proficiency

A revised HSK (*hànyǔ shuǐpíng kǎoshì*, which means Chinese proficiency test) test was used to measure the learners' Chinese proficiency. The HSK is required for non-Chinese-speaking students who intend to obtain an academic degree at a Chinese university. The test has high degrees of validity and reliability (Nie, 2006). The revised HSK has 60 items, 30 of which relate to listening comprehension, 20 to grammar and 10 to reading comprehension. The possible score for this test is 60, with 1 point assigned to each item.

Treatment effects

The effectiveness of recasts was measured via a grammaticality judgement test (GJT) and an elicited imitation (EI) test. The GJT was intended as a measure of explicit knowledge and the EI test as a measure of implicit knowledge (Ellis *et al.*, 2009). During the GJT, each learner was asked to judge whether a given item was grammatical, and if it was ungrammatical, to find the error and correct it. The GJT was untimed to allow time for the learners to access their explicit knowledge about the linguistic target. During the EI test, the learner listened to some audio-recorded sentences, decide whether they were true or not true and indicate whether he/she was not sure, and repeat them in correct Chinese. The purpose of the EI test was to tap the learners' ability to produce the linguistic structure spontaneously using their automatised, unconscious knowledge about the target structure.

Both the GJT and EI tests had 15 target items and 8 distracters. Among the target items, eight were ungrammatical and seven grammatical. Both had three versions – a pre-test, an immediate post-test and a delayed post-test. The target items of the three versions were the same, but the distracting items were different. The test items were randomised so that the sequence in which they appeared in each test was different. The total score for each test was 15.

Working memory

Working memory was measured by means of a listening span test. The test consists of 72 sentences, which are divided into 4 sets at span sizes 3, 4, 5 and 6 (a span size refers to the number of sentences). The sentences are syntactically varied, and half of them were semantically reasonable and half were not. All were created and validated by Waters and Caplan (1996). The test was developed using DMDX, free software used in psycholinguistic studies to measure reaction time when visual and auditory stimuli are responded to. During the test, the learner was asked to listen to each item, decide whether the sentence made sense or not, and at the end of each set (when the program paused) recall the final word of each sentence in that set. All three components of the test were scored – reaction time, veracity judgement and sentence-final word recall. The three scores generated by the test were transformed into z scores, and the averaged z scores were used for statistical analysis.

Language analytic ability

The learners' language analytic ability was measured by using the words in sentences subtest of the MLAT. The test consists of 45 items which must be completed within 15 minutes. Each item contains a key sentence where a linguistic unit is underlined, and below the key sentence there are one or two sentences with five underlined linguistic parts. The learners were asked to choose one from the five that matches the function of the underlined part in the key sentence. One point is assigned for each item, so the total score of this test is 45.

Procedure

All participants partook in three sessions to complete the study. In session one, they took the proficiency test and the GJT pre-test. In session 2, they took the EI pre-test, followed by the treatment task, which lasted about 40 minutes. At the end of the treatment session, the learners took the GJT and EI immediate post-tests. One week after the treatment session, the learners attended the final session in which they took the working memory test, the language analytic ability test and the delayed GJT and EI post-tests.

Results

To answer research question 1, that is, whether recasts were effective in facilitating the learning of Chinese classifiers, mixed design repeated measure analyses of variance (ANOVAs) were performed for the pre-test and post-test scores of the two proficiency groups, with timing (pre-test, immediate post-test and delayed post-test) as a within-group variable and proficiency (beginning vs advanced) as a between-group variable. Follow-up pairwise comparisons were conducted using *t*-tests with Bonferroni corrections.

To answer research question 2, that is, whether the effects of recasts were mediated by working memory and language analytic ability in different ways depending on the learners' proficiency, correlation analyses were performed on the scores of the two aptitude components and the post-test scores after the treatment. To obtain a comprehensive picture of the relationship under investigation, correlation analyses were complemented with multiple regression analyses and *t*-tests, and gain scores were analysed as well as post-test scores. All analyses were conducted for each proficiency level separately.

The effects of recasts

The descriptive statistics of the raw scores of the two proficiency groups are displayed in Table 8.2, including the means and standard deviations of the GJT and EI scores on the pre-tests, immediate post-tests and delayed post-tests. The descriptive statistics of the gain scores on the immediate and delayed post-tests are shown in Table 8.3. The results showed that both groups made substantial improvements after the treatment, as reflected by their higher post-test scores in comparison with their pre-test scores and by the positive gain scores. Overall, the learners improved more in their EI scores than their GJT scores.

A repeated measure ANOVA on the GJT raw scores showed a significant main effect for timing ($F(2, 52)=49.46$, $p<0.01$), which means that overall the two groups performed differently at the three time points. *Post hoc* analyses showed that their immediate and delayed post-test scores were significantly higher than their pre-test scores, but there was no significant difference between the two post-test scores. Furthermore, there was no

Table 8.2 Descriptive statistics of raw scores

		Pre-test		Immediate post-test		Delayed post-test	
Level	n	Mean	SD	Mean	SD	Mean	SD
GJT							
Beginning	17	5.92	1.27	8.85	2.22	8.55	2.15
Advanced	11	6.13	0.97	9.81	2.63	10.18	2.79
EI							
Beginning	17	2.32	1.72	7.02	3.35	6.08	2.81
Advanced	11	4.41	1.94	8.90	1.42	9.00	2.39

Note: GJT=grammaticality judgement test; EI=elicited imitation; SD=standard deviation.

Table 8.3 Descriptive statistics of gain scores

Level	n	Immediate gains		Delayed gains	
		Mean	SD	Mean	SD
GJT					
Beginning	17	2.94	2.00	2.64	1.73
Advanced	11	3.08	2.44	4.04	2.76
EI					
Beginning	17	4.70	2.55	3.76	2.51
Advanced	11	4.50	2.11	4.59	2.54

Note: GJT=grammaticality judgement test; EI=elicited imitation; SD=standard deviation.

significant effect for proficiency, which indicates that the effects of recasts were similar for both levels of learners. The interaction between timing and proficiency was also non-significant.

The analysis of the EI test scores showed a significant effect for timing ($F(2, 52)=56.13$, $p<0.01$). *Post hoc* comparisons showed that the learners scored significantly higher on the two post-tests than the pre-test, but they performed similarly on the two post-tests. A significant main effect was also found for proficiency ($F(1, 26)=8.83$, $p<0.01$). *Post hoc* analyses revealed that the advanced learners scored significantly higher than the beginning learners on the delayed post-test, but they also outperformed the beginners on the pre-test. Further analyses based on gain scores failed to show significant difference between the two groups, indicating that after the difference in their pre-test scores was controlled, the advanced learners did not benefit more from recasts than the beginners.

To summarise the results relating to research question 1, both beginning and advanced learners made significant improvements in their learning of Chinese classifiers after receiving a quantity of recasts, the effects were sustained and neither group benefited more from recasts than the other.

The aptitude–proficiency interaction

Table 8.4 shows the descriptive and inferential statistics of the two groups' working memory and language analytic ability scores. The advanced learners seemed to have higher working memory capacities but lower analytic ability than the beginners. However, the differences were statistically negligible: $t(26)=-0.47$, $p=0.64$ for working memory and $t(26)=1.31$, $p=0.20$ for language analytic ability.

Beginners

Table 8.5 shows the correlation coefficients regarding the relationships between the two aptitude components and the effects of recasts at the

Table 8.4 Working memory and language analytic ability of the two proficiency groups

Level	n	Mean	SD	t	p
Working memory				−0.47	0.64
Beginning	17	0.12	0.84		
Advanced	11	0.25	0.59		
Language analytic ability				1.31	0.20
Beginning	17	26.29	8.17		
Advanced	11	22.64	5.32		

lower proficiency level. The results reveal that working memory was significantly correlated with the learners' performance on the delayed post-test; language analytic ability was significantly correlated with the delayed GJT gains (both post-test and gain scores) and with the delayed EI post-test scores. However, the results also showed a strong significant correlation between the beginning learners' working memory capacities and language analytic ability ($r=0.69$, $p<0.05$), suggesting a need to tease out the roles of the two aptitude components.

In order to show the unique contribution of each of the two variables, three multiple stepwise regression analyses were performed. For each regression analysis, working memory and language analytic ability served as predictor variables and the delayed GJT post-test scores, delayed GJT gain scores and delayed EI post-test scores as response variables, respectively. The results showed that in all three analyses, language analytic ability was the only significant predictor, explaining 32% of the variance of the delayed GJT post-test scores (adjusted $R^2=0.32$, $\beta=0.16$, $p<0.05$), 42% of the delayed gain scores (adjusted $R^2=0.42$, $\beta=0.14$, $p<0.01$) and 27% of the delayed EI test scores (adjusted $R^2=0.27$, $\beta=0.19$, $p<0.05$).

To explore the causal effects of the two aptitude components on the learners' performance after the treatment, the (beginning) learners were divided into high and low working memory groups, and high and low language analytic ability groups, using the medians as the cut-off points.

Table 8.5 Correlation results for beginners

	Grammaticality judgement test					Elicited imitation test				
	Pre	Post 1	Post 2	Gain 1	Gain 2	Pre	Post 1	Post 2	Gain 1	Gain 2
WM	0.45	0.31	0.57*	0.06	0.38	0.21	0.36	0.41	0.33	0.31
LAA	0.09	0.38	0.61*	0.36	0.68*	0.33	0.43	0.56*	0.34	0.40

Note: $n=17$; Pre=pre-test; Post 1=immediate post-test; Post 2=delayed post-test; Gain 1=immediate gains; Gain 2=delayed gains; WM=working memory; LAA=language analytic ability. *$p<0.05$.

Independent samples *t*-tests showed that the high language analytic group performed significantly better than the low language analytic group on the delayed GJT post-test in terms of both post-test scores ($t(15)=-2.29$, $p<0.05$) and gain scores ($t(15)=-2.77$, $p<0.05$). However, the high and low working memory groups did not show significant differences on any of the post-tests.

The above results demonstrated via different statistical analyses that the low-level learners drew on their language analytic ability, but not working memory, in their learning of the linguistic target.

Advanced learners

The results for the advanced learners appear in Table 8.6. As shown, a strong correlation was found between working memory and the delayed EI post-test scores ($r=0.70$, $p<0.05$). Language analytic ability was not correlated with any post-test scores after the treatment. Note that among the advanced group, the correlation between working memory and language analytic ability was nearly zero ($r=0.003$, $p=0.99$). Therefore, the possibility can be obviated that a portion of the variance of the criterion variable – the delayed EI post-test scores – was accounted for by the shared variance of the two aptitude components. Accordingly, a regression analysis was not performed to show the unique variance explained by the two variables. Also, due to the relatively small sample ($n=11$), the advanced learners were not split into high and low working memory groups to explore the causal effect via a *t*-test.

Discussion

This study investigated the interactions between the effectiveness of recasts and two cognitive variables – working memory and language analytic ability. To achieve the goal, the study sought to answer two research questions: (1) Do L2 Chinese learners benefit from recasts in their learning of classifiers? and (2) Do beginners and advanced learners draw on different cognitive abilities? With regard to the first question, it was found that the learners did make significant improvements after

Table 8.6 Correlation results for advanced learners

| | Grammaticality judgement test | | | | | Elicited imitation test | | | |
| | | Post 1 | Post 2 | Gain 1 | Gain 2 | | Post 1 | Post 2 | Gain 1 | Gain 2 |
	Pre					Pre				
WM	−0.29	0.40	0.37	0.55	0.48	0.49	0.08	0.70*	−0.40	0.28
LAA	−0.13	0.33	0.46	0.41	0.52	0.53	0.58	0.45	−0.09	0.02

Note: $n=11$; Pre=pre-test; Post 1=immediate post-test; Post 2=delayed post-test; Gain 1=immediate gains; Gain 2=delayed gains; WM=working memory; LAA=language analytic ability. *$p<0.05$.

receiving recasts, and the effects were sustained. Also, learners at the two proficiency levels seemed to benefit equally from the feedback. With regard to the second question, the results demonstrated that the beginners were more likely to draw on their language analytic ability whereas the advanced learners seemed more likely to take advantage of their working memory.

The finding that recasts facilitated the learning of Chinese classifiers was in line with Li (2009). However, one disparity between this study and Li (2009) is that the advanced learners in this study did not benefit more from recasts than the beginners. The disparity is possibly attributable to the fact that in Li (2009) the learners were in their second and fourth year of study and in this study, the high-level participants (8 out of 11) were mostly in their third year of Chinese study. In other words, the advanced learners may not have been 'advanced' enough to have an advantage over their low-level peers. It must also be pointed that in Li (2009) the number of participants in each treatment group ($n=5$ or 6) was very small, and the effects of the treatment were measured via a test that required the learners to produce discrete noun phrases containing classifiers. These methodological differences may have contributed to the different results.

Previous research (Ammar & Spada, 2006; Mackey & Philp, 1998) also found that learners who were developmentally ready benefited more from recasts. Developmental readiness was operationalised as previous knowledge about the target structure. However, in this study, the two proficiency groups did not differ significantly in their pre-test GJT scores, and although their pre-test EI scores were different, they did not show significant differences in their gains after the treatment. However, this should not be taken as counter-evidence against the role of developmental readiness, and it is speculated that learners' difference in their pre-test scores within each proficiency group may affect their post-test performance.

To pursue this possibility further, correlation analyses were conducted on each group's pre-test and post-test scores. The results showed an interaction between general L2 proficiency and developmental readiness (i.e. whether pre-test scores were correlated with post-test scores). It was found that at the low proficiency level, the GJT pre-test scores were significantly correlated with the delayed GJT post-test scores ($r=0.59$, $p<0.05$) and the delayed EI scores ($r=0.57$, $p<0.05$). There were also significant correlations between the EI pre-test scores and the GJT immediate post-test scores ($r=0.50$, $p<0.05$) and the EI immediate post-test scores ($r=0.66$, $p<0.05$). However, at the high proficiency level, the pre-test scores were not related to any post-test scores. It would seem that developmental readiness is more important to beginners than to advanced learners. The finding suggests a need to consider the role of general proficiency in mediating the effect of L2 learners' developmental readiness on the acquisition of a particular target structure.

How can we account for the interactions between language aptitude and proficiency, that is, the beginners drew more on analytic ability and the advanced learners more on working memory? An explanation can be sought with recourse to the target structure. The acquisition of a Chinese classifier requires two steps: (1) understanding the rule that a classifier must be used between a determiner (e.g. a numeral) and a noun, and (2) acquiring a lexical item (the classifier) that semantically matches the physical properties of the object the noun signifies. It is possible that for beginning learners, especially speakers of a non-classifier language (in this case, English), the initial step of extrapolating the rule about classifier use from the input available through recasts posed heavy processing demands on their ability to identify linguistic regularities. This does not obviate the learners' need to use their working memory to manipulate and store the incoming linguistic data; rather the ability to extract the related rule may be more important and therefore eclipse the role of memory at this stage. The advanced learners, however, drew more on their memory abilities to store the correct classifiers contained in the aural input because they had been exposed to the rule at the beginning stages of their study. For them, the ability to retrieve or reactivate the previously learned rule stored in their long-term memory and store the incoming new linguistic items seemed more important.

The above account for an aptitude–proficiency interaction relates to the nature of the linguistic structure that corrective feedback targeted; it constitutes a micro perspective. An explanation can also be sought from a macro perspective by drawing on Skehan's (2012) theoretical postulation about the cognitive activities learners engage in at different phases of SLA. Skehan posited that L2 development involves six stages, i.e. input processing and noticing, pattern identification, complexification/restructuring/integration, error avoidance, repertoire and salience creation, and automatisation/lexicalisation. The first three relate more to rule learning and the second set of three stages 'are concerned much more with control and access to material already in long-term memory' (Skehan, 2012: 387). A corollary of these arguments is that language analytic ability is more relevant to the initial stages of SLA because they involve more rule learning. It can be further argued that working memory is more implicated at higher stages of SLA because a central function of working memory is the activation of information stored in long-term memory (Cowan, 1999). Thus, in this case, for the advanced learners the ability to activate the syntactic information about classifiers and hold it in an accessible state for subsequent processing of new linguistic information is integral to the genesis of learning in spontaneous communication.

A caveat that potentially sabotages the above explanations is the fact that the two proficiency groups differed, albeit non-significantly, in language analytic ability and working memory. The beginners happened to have higher analytic ability, and the advanced group larger working memory capacities. One may argue that the coincidence may have made it more likely for the beginners to utilise their analytic ability and the advanced learners to take advantage of their working memory. However, the non-statistical difference in the two aptitude components makes this unfortunate coincidence less of a concern than it appears.

Conclusion and Implications

This study constitutes the first attempt to investigate the impact of the interaction between proficiency and aptitude components on the effectiveness of corrective feedback. It demonstrates that the effectiveness of corrective feedback must be viewed *in situ*, that is, it is constrained by cognitive factors such as language analytic ability and working memory. The results afford further evidence against an eclectic approach to language teaching/learning (Carroll, 1966) and underscore the importance of tailoring instruction to cater to learners at different stages of L2 development. For instance, since the initial stages of SLA impose heavy processing demands on learners' ability to extrapolate linguistic rules, it is perhaps a better idea for instructors to adopt more explicit approaches coupled with metalinguistic explanation to alleviate learners' processing burden, especially those with limited language analytic ability. By the same token, assuming that higher levels of L2 learning set heavier demands on working memory that involve the retrieval and application of previously acquired information to process new linguistic information or proceduralise previous information, it may be necessary to design tasks that help learners utilise their memory strategically.

In terms of aptitude research, this study shows that it is time to reconsider the construct of aptitude and reorient the research. First, it seems that working memory is a viable aptitude component because it is this cognitive factor, not language analytic ability, that is sensitive to advanced L2. However, more research is in order to map the relationship between working memory and the traditional aptitude components such as those measured by the MLAT. Second, the study demonstrates the value of a process-oriented approach to aptitude research, which is revealing about how different cognitive variables interface with environmental factors. It stands in stark contrast with the traditional, product-oriented approach which concerns the relationship between aptitude and ultimate L2 outcome and ignores 'the process'.

Notwithstanding the contributions of this study, it has several limitations. First, it has a small sample size, which is especially true of the advanced group. Therefore, it is premature to generalise the obtained findings to other contexts. Second, due to logistic constraints, the researcher was unable to recruit participants from only Levels 2 (fourth semester) and 4 (eighth semester) and was accordingly unable to better manipulate the variable of proficiency. Including students from Level 3 (sixth semester) may have confounded the results, although the two resultant treatment groups did differ significantly in terms of their scores on the proficiency test.

References

Ammar, A. and Spada, N. (2006) One size fits all? Recasts, prompts, and L2 learning. *Studies in Second Language Acquisition* 28, 543–574.

Berquist, B. (1997) Memory models applied to L2 comprehension: A search for common ground. In G. Taillefer and A.K. Pugh (eds) *Lectire à l'Université: Langues maternelle, seconde et étrangère. Reading in the University: First, Second and Foreign Languages* (pp. 29–44). Toulouse: Presses de l'Université des Sciences Sociales de Toulouse.

Bialystok, E. and Fröhlich, M. (1978) Variables of classroom achievement in second language learning. *The Modern Language Journal* 62, 327–336.

Carroll, J.B. (1981) Twenty-five years of research on foreign language aptitude. In K.C. Diller (ed.) *Individual Differences and Universals in Language Learning Aptitude* (pp. 83–118). Rowley, MA: Newbury House.

Carroll, J.B. (1990) Cognitive abilities in foreign language aptitude: Then and now. In T.S. Parry and C.W. Stansfield (eds) *Language Aptitude Reconsidered* (pp. 11–29). Englewood Cliffs, NJ: Prentice Hall.

Carroll, J. and Sapon, S. (1959) *Modern Language Aptitude Test*. New York: The Psychological Corporation/Harcourt Brace Jovanovich.

Cheung, H. (1996) Nonword span as a unique predictor of second-language vocabulary learning. *Developmental Psychology* 32 (5), 867–873.

Choi, S. and Li, S. (2012) Corrective feedback and learner uptake in a child ESOL classroom. *The RELC Journal* 43, 331–351.

Cowan, N. (1999) An embedded-process model of working memory. In A. Miyake and P. Shah (eds) *Models of Working Memory* (pp. 62–101). Cambridge: Cambridge University Press.

Curtin, C., Avner, A. and Smith, L.A. (1983) The Pimsleur Battery as a predictor of student performance. *The Modern Language Journal* 67 (1), 33–40.

DeKeyser, R. (1993) The effect of error correction on L2 grammar knowledge and oral proficiency. *The Modern Language Journal* 77, 501–514.

Ehrman, M. (1998) The Modern Language Aptitude Test for predicting learning success and advising students. *Applied Language Learning* 9, 31–70.

Ellis, N.C., Lee, M.W. and Reber, A.R. (1999) Phonological working memory in artificial language acquisition. Unpublished manuscript, University of Wales.

Ellis, R. (2010) Epilog: A framework for investigating oral and written corrective feedback. *Studies in Second Language Acquisition* 32, 335–349.

Ellis, R. and Sheen, Y. (2006) Reexamining the role of recasts in second language acquisition. *Studies in Second Language Acquisition* 28, 575–600.

Erlam, R. (2005) Language aptitude and its relationship to instructional effectiveness in second language acquisition. *Language Teaching Research* 9, 147–171.

French, L.M. and O'Brien, I. (2008) Phonological memory and children's second language grammar learning. *Applied Psycholinguistics* 29, 463–487.

Gardner, R.C. and Lambert, W.E. (1965) Language aptitude, intelligence, and second-language achievement. *Journal of Educational Psychology* 56, 191–199.

Gass, S. (2003) Input and interaction. In C.J. Doughty and M.H. Long (eds) *The Handbook of Second Language Acquisition* (pp. 224–255). Malden, MA: Blackwell.

Goo, J. (2012) Corrective feedback and working memory capacity in interaction-driven L2 learning. *Studies in Second Language Acquisition* 34, 445–474.

Gordan, M. (1980) Attitudes and motivation in second-language achievement: A study of primary school students learning English in Belize, Central America. PhD dissertation, University of Toronto.

Granena, G. and Long, M.H. (2012) Age of onset, length of residence, language aptitude, and ultimate L2 attainment in three linguistic domains. *Second Language Research* 29, 1–33.

Harley, B. and Hart, D. (2002) Age, aptitude and second language learning on a bilingual exchange. In P. Robinson (ed.) *Individual Differences and Instructed Language Learning* (pp. 301–330). Amsterdam/Philadelphia, PA: John Benjamins.

Harrington, M. and Sawyer, M. (1992) L2 working memory capacity and L2 reading skill. *Studies in Second Language Acquisition* 14, 25–38.

Horwitz, E. (1980) The relationship of conceptual level to the development of communicative competence. PhD dissertation, The University of Illinois at Urbana-Champaign.

Hummel, K. (2009) Aptitude, phonological memory, and second language proficiency in nonnovice adult learners. *Applied Psycholinguistics* 30, 225–249.

Hwu, F. and Sun, S. (2012) The aptitude-treatment interaction effects on the learning of grammar rules. *System* 40, 505–521.

Iwashita, N. (2003) Positive and negative input in task-based interaction: Differential effects on L2 development. *Studies in Second Language Acquisition* 25, 1–36.

Kim, J. and Han, Z. (2007) Recasts in communicative EFL classes: Do teacher intent and learner interpretation overlap? In A. Mackey (ed.) *Conversational Interaction in Second Language Acquisition* (pp. 269–297). Oxford: Oxford University Press.

Kormos, J. and Trebits, A. (2012) The role of task complexity, modality, and aptitude in narrative task performance. *Language Learning* 62, 439–472.

Leeser, M. (2007) Learner-based factors in L2 reading comprehension and processing grammatical form: Topic familiarity and working memory. *Language Learning* 57, 229–270.

Li, S. (2009) The differential effects of implicit and explicit feedback on L2 learners of different proficiency levels. *Applied Language Learning* 19, 53–79.

Li, S. (2010) The effectiveness of corrective feedback in SLA: A meta-analysis. *Language Learning* 60, 309–365.

Loewen, S. and Philp, J. (2006) Recasts in the adult English L2 classroom: Characteristics, explicitness, and effectiveness. *The Modern Language Journal* 90, 536–556.

Long, M.H. (2007) *Problems in SLA*. Mahwah, NJ: Erlbaum.

Lyster, R. (1998) Negotiation of form, recasts, and explicit correction in relation to error types and learner repair in immersion classrooms. *Language Learning* 48, 183–218.

Lyster, R. (2004) Different effects of prompts and effects in form-focused instruction. *Studies in Second Language Acquisition* 26, 399–432.

Lyster, R. and Ranta, L. (1997) Corrective feedback and learner uptake. *Studies in Second Language Acquisition* 19, 37–66.

Lyster, R. and Mori, H. (2006) Interactional feedback and instructional counterbalance. *Studies in Second Language Acquisition* 28, 269–300.

Lyster, R. and Izquierdo, J. (2009) Prompts versus recasts in dyadic interaction. *Studies in Second Language Acquisition* 59, 453–498.

Lyster, R. and Saito, K. (2010) Oral feedback in classroom SLA: A meta-analysis. *Studies in Second Language Acquisition* 32, 265–302.

Mackey, A. and Philp, J. (1998) Conversational interaction and second language development: Recasts, responses, and red herrings? *The Modern Language Journal* 82, 338–356.

Mackey, A., Gass, S. and McDonough, K. (2000) How do learners perceive international feedback? *Studies in Second Language Acquisition* 22, 471–497.

Mackey, A., Philp, J., Egi, T., Fujii, A. and Tatsumi, T. (2002) Individual differences in working memory, noticing of interactional feedback, and L2 development. In P. Robinson (ed.) *Individual Differences and Instructed Language Learning* (pp. 181–209). Philadelphia, PA: John Benjamins.

Miyake, A. and Friedman, N. (1998) Individual differences in second language proficiency: Working memory as language aptitude. In A. Healy and L. Bourne (eds) *Foreign Language Learning: Psycholinguistic Studies on Training and Retention* (pp. 339–364). Mahwah, NJ: Erlbaum.

Révész, A. (2012) Working memory and the observed effectiveness of recasts on different L2 outcome measures. *Language Learning* 62, 93–132.

Robinson, P. (1997) Individual differences and fundamental similarity of implicit and explicit adult second language learning. *Language Learning* 47, 45–99.

Robinson, P. (2005) Aptitude and second language acquisition. *Annual Review of Applied Linguistics* 25, 46–73.

Sagarra, N. (2007) From CALL to face-to-face interaction: The effect of computer-delivered recasts and working memory on L2 development. In A. Mackey (ed.) *Conversational Interaction in Second Language Acquisition* (pp. 229–248). New York: Oxford University Press.

Sheen, Y. (2004) Corrective feedback and leaner uptake in communicative classrooms across instructional settings. *Language Teaching Research* 8, 263–300.

Sheen, Y. (2007) The effects of corrective feedback, language aptitude, and learner attitudes on the acquisition of English articles. In A. Mackey (ed.) *Conversational Interaction in Second Language Acquisition* (pp. 301–322). New York: Oxford University Press.

Skehan, P. (2012) Language aptitude. In S. Gass and A. Mackey (eds) *The Routledge Handbook of Second Language Acquisition* (pp. 381–395). London/New York: Routledge.

Sparks, R., Ganschow, L. and Patton, J. (1995) Prediction of performance in first-year foreign language courses: Connections between native and foreign language learning. *Journal of Educational Psychology* 87, 638–655.

Speciale, G., Ellis, N.C. and Bywater, T. (2004) Phonological sequence learning and short-term store capacity determine second language vocabulary acquisition. *Applied Psycholinguistic* 25, 293–321.

Trofimovich, P., Ammar, A. and Gatbonton, E. (2007) How effective are recasts? The role of attention, memory, and analytical ability. In A. Mackey (ed.) *Conversational interaction in second language acquisition* (pp. 171–195). New York: Oxford University Press.

VanPatten, B. and Borst, S. (2012) The roles of explicit information and grammatical sensitivity in processing instruction: Nominative-accusative case marking and word order in German L2. *Foreign Language Annals* 45, 92–109.

Winke, P. (2005) Individual differences in adult Chinese language acquisition: The relationships among aptitude, memory, and strategies for learning. PhD dissertation, Georgetown University.

Yang, Y. and Lyster, R. (2010) Effects of form-focused practice and feedback on Chinese EFL learners' acquisition of regular and irregular past tense forms. *Studies in Second Language Acquisition* 32, 235–263.

Yoshizawa, K. (2002) Relationships among strategy use, foreign language aptitude, and second language proficiency: A structural equation modelling approach. PhD dissertation, Temple University.

9 Working Memory, Online Planning and L2 Self-Repair Behaviour

Mohammad Javad Ahmadian

Introduction

In 1957, Lee Cronbach called for a unification of what he labelled 'the two disciplines of scientific psychology', arguing that it is only through the synergy of experimental (which focuses on the universal features of human behaviour) and differential psychology (which studies the role of inter-individual variations) that we can depict a comprehensive picture of human behaviour. This chapter aims to link three areas of research: individual differences in working memory capacity (WMC), task-based language teaching/learning and second language (L2) speech production processes.

Although a number of studies have examined the universalistic aspects of planning and its effects on complexity, accuracy, fluency and lexis (see Ahmadian, 2012a; Ahmadian & Tavakoli, 2011, 2014; Yuan & Ellis, 2003), a review of the current literature reveals that there are two interrelated issues which are worth further exploration: (a) the interactions among ID factors (e.g. WM) and L2 oral performance under various planning conditions (see Ahmadian, 2012b; Guará-Tavares, 2008); and (b) the relationship between ID factors and the underlying mechanisms of speech production (e.g. self-monitoring) under different planning conditions. This chapter sets out to focus on the latter issue and reports on a study which attempted to investigate the relationship between WMC and self-monitoring under online planning condition. In this chapter, I will first provide an overview of the theoretical and empirical discussions regarding WM, online planning and self-repair behaviour. I will then report on the results of the study and, finally, the results will be discussed in light of the related theoretical and empirical issues.

Working Memory

WM is a flexible and capacity-limited cognitive system with domain-specific stores for the storage, processing and manipulation of information that is thought to be essential for a wide range of complex cognitive activities such as reading, speaking, reasoning, writing and performing arithmetic calculations (Baddeley, 2003; Engle, 2010; Kane *et al.*, 2005). The most widely used and accepted WM model is that proposed by Baddeley and Hitch (1974) in which WM was assumed to be comprised of three subsystems: a central executive component and two short-term storage slave systems (phonological loop and visuospatial sketchpad). A brief description of these components follows (see Baddeley [2012] for a comprehensive account of the model).

The *phonological loop* – originally labelled the 'articulatory loop' – is essentially a 'subvocal rehearsal system' which both maintains information and registers visual information if the items can be named (Baddeley, 2003: 191). By virtue of its tractability, this component has turned out to be the most researched compared to the other two systems (Baddeley, 2012; Juffs & Harrington, 2011). The findings of previous research indicate that the phonological loop could serve various functions such as facilitating comprehension (Vallar & Baddeley, 1987), promoting the acquisition of (both native and second) language and learning new words (Baddeley *et al.*, 1988; Service, 1992). The second slave system, the *visuospatial sketchpad*, integrates and unifies spatial, visual and kinaesthetic information which could be temporarily stored and processed (Baddeley, 2003). This component, too, has been shown to be implicated in language comprehension.

The *central executive* is responsible for focusing attention, dividing attention between two important stimuli and switching attention from one task to another (Baddeley, 2012). According to Daneman and Carpenter (1980), executive processes are perhaps one of the principal variables which determine individual differences in WM. More recently, the *episodic buffer*, as a fourth component, has been added to Baddeley and Hitch's tripartite model. This component, Baddeley (2012: 15) states, 'is assumed to hold integrated episodes or chunks in a multidimensional code [and] [i]n doing so, it acts as a buffer store, not only between the components of WM, but also linking WM to perception and LTM'. Research on the episodic buffer is scarce and more theoretical and empirical work has yet to be carried out (Baddeley, this volume).

By and large, research findings in the area of second language acquisition (SLA) point to the facilitative role of the WM system in both language learning and use (see Juffs & Harrington [2011] and Wen [2012] for comprehensive reviews). The underlying assumption in most of these studies has been that if WM plays a central role in higher-level cognitive functions, then individual differences in terms of WMC could result in significant differences in fulfilling these functions. One of the earliest studies on WMC and L2 speech production (measured in terms of fluency) is that of Fortkamp (1999) who found that, overall, WMC aids L2 fluency. In another study, Fortkamp (2003) found that WMC correlates positively with fluency, accuracy and complexity but negatively with lexical diversity. These positive results notwithstanding, the relationship between WMC and the underlying mechanisms of speech production under different planning/performance conditions is an under-researched realm of investigation. In the next section, online planning and its link to WM will be discussed.

Online Planning

In the parlance of cognitive psychology, the term 'planning' applies to many different aspects of cognition and cognitive control where a 'blueprint' for achieving a particular goal is required (Ward & Morris, 2005). In the context of task-based language teaching and learning, planning is conceptually characterised as 'the process by which speakers attend carefully to the formulation stage during speech planning and engage in pre-production and post-production monitoring of their speech acts' (Yuan & Ellis, 2003: 6). Based on this conceptual definition, Ahmadian (2012b) operationally defined online planning as providing learners with ample time to do mental work on their utterances *conceptually* and/or *formally* while performing a task. Virtually all conceptual and operational definitions of planning (be it online or pre-task) draw on Levelt's (1984) speech production model. According to this model, speakers are assumed to be *'complex information processors'* capable of translating conceived communicative intentions, thoughts and feelings into articulated speech.

For Levelt, speaking is *the* most complex cognitive–motor activity, which involves three overlapping stages, each stage being performed via a particular autonomous processing component (Levelt, 1999). The first stage, *conceptualisation*, 'involves conceiving of an intention, selecting the relevant information to be expressed for the realization of this purpose, ordering this information for expression, keeping track of what was said before' (Levelt, 1989: 9). During this stage, the speaker determines and plans what message or intention is to be communicated and marshals the appropriate information and means with which to realise the intended message. These activities require the speakers' focal attention. The product of the conceptualisation stage is what Levelt (1989) labels the *preverbal message*, which is essentially a conceptual, non-linguistic structure and is the input to the second processing stage: *formulation*. During this second stage, as a result of grammatical encoding of the message, the preverbal message translates into a linguistic structure in the form of a phonetic plan or *internal speech*. In the third stage, *articulation*, the speaker acts upon the internal speech, executes the phonetic plan and produces *overt speech*, i.e. actual words.

Another important processing component of Levelt's model which is of great relevance and significance to planning studies and is operative against the backdrop of the three aforementioned stages is the *monitoring* component. This component is responsible for monitoring, *inter alia*, the speaker's *internal speech* as represented in their *WM* (Levelt, 1989). It is clear, then, that WMC could play a crucial role in if/how the speaker monitors his/her speech. Also, it is possible to posit that the more time speakers have for task performance (i.e. online planning time) the more successful they will be in drawing on their WMC to do the required pre- and post-articulatory monitoring and self-repairs. The issue of monitoring and self-repair will be taken up in the next section.

To date, as of writing this chapter, the vast majority of the studies conducted on online planning have focused on complexity, accuracy and fluency (the CAF triad) and, except for one study (Ahmadian, 2012b), no published work has explored the possible correlations between WMC and L2 speech production under online planning condition. Overall, the results of online planning and CAF studies point to the positive effects for this task-based implementation variable on the CAF triad with some trade-offs being reported (see Ahmadian, 2012a; Ahmadian & Tavakoli, 2011, 2014; Ahmadian *et al.*, 2013; Yuan & Ellis, 2003).

In Ahmadian (2012b), I investigated the way that WMC correlates with the CAF triad under the task-based online planning condition. The results of this study showed that WMC correlates with accuracy and fluency under online planning condition. However, the relationship between WMC and complexity under online planning condition did not reach the level of significance. This latter finding was attributed to the fact that complexity pertains to learners' tendency to take risks and use their cutting-edge grammatical knowledge; thus, viewed from this perspective, this aspect of performance has little (if nothing) to do with WMC.

In order to shed more light on the relationship among WM, online planning and speech production, it is worthwhile focusing on self-repair behaviour (rather than the CAF triad) which could be conceived of as the observable and quantifiable manifestation of the underlying speech production processes.

Self-Repair Behaviour

As the foregoing indicates, within Levelt's model, self-monitoring is a *sine qua non* for speech production (de Bot, 1992; Levelt, 1987). However, not unlike other mental constructs, self-monitoring processes and mechanisms are not amenable to direct observation and therefore the standard practice in the speech production literature has been to capitalise on the self-repair phenomenon as a means of making inferences regarding the speakers' underlying monitoring mechanisms (Ahmadian & Tavakoli, 2014; Ahmadian *et al.*, 2012; Kormos, 1999, 2000, 2006; Levelt, 1989; Mojavezi & Ahmadian, 2014). Levelt (1989) argues that speakers are capable of monitoring virtually all aspects of speech; nevertheless, by virtue of the selective, limited and fluctuating nature of their attentional resources, speakers cannot attend to all aspects of their speech simultaneously. Since attention control is among the primary functions of WM and some researchers even consider attentional control as equal to WM (Kane & Engle, 2002), one could argue that how speakers monitor their speech is, at least in part, a function of their WMC. Online planning involves, among other things, engagement in pre- and post-articulatory monitoring; therefore, the provision of ample time for planning speech on the fly in conjunction with instructing speakers how to make use of this planning time could be consequential in this regard.

Levelt (1989) assumes three loops for *self-monitoring*: (a) the conceptual loop, in which the preverbal message is checked against the original communicative intentions; (b) the pre-articulatory loop, in which encoding errors are detected prior to articulation; and (c) the external loop of monitoring, in which the speaker self-monitors the overt speech in terms of communicative appropriacy and grammatical well-formedness. A self-repair takes place when the speaker realises that the output entails an erroneous or infelicitous stretch of language, interrupts the speech flow and finally effectuates a repair (Kormos, 2006; Levelt, 1989).

Building on the work of Levelt (1983, 1989), Kormos (1998) has provided a comprehensive taxonomy of self-repair behaviour in L2 speech which will be used in the present study. Succinctly put, the taxonomy includes (examples are excerpted from the data obtained for a series of studies on self-repair behaviour and the stimulated recall comments (SRCs) have been translated into English):

- *Error (E-) repair*, which happens at the formulation stage and includes lexical repair, syntactic repair and phonological repair.
  (5) They started escape and they **run away** [filled pause] **ran away**
  SRC: Here I realised that I was narrating the story in the past tense and I committed a grammatical mistake, so I corrected it.
- *Appropriacy (A-) repair*, which is usually used when the speaker decides to produce the originally intended content but in a modified way for reasons of inaccuracy, ambiguity, incoherence and/or pragmatic inappropriacy.
  (4) … so asked him to throw away **the drinks** [pause] **the wine**
  SRC: Here I tried to be as precise as possible in narrating the story; I thought wine was more accurate.
- *Different information (D-) repair*, where the speaker decides to encode new information at the conceptualisation stage.

(3) … **he wanted** [filled pause] **because the light was off he turned on the light**
SRC: I wanted to say 'he wanted to sleep' then I realised that what I was saying differed from what happened in the video so I paused and tried to recall what exactly happened in the video.

There are two recent empirical studies in the area of SLA which have drawn on this taxonomy and are relevant to this study. To begin with, Ahmadian *et al.* (2012) investigated how the degree of task difficulty, operationalised as the existence of a loose or tight storyline structure, affects self-repair behaviour in L2 oral speech. Results of the analyses revealed that there was a relationship between task difficulty and self-repair behaviour such that with the difficult task, participants mostly made appropriacy and different-information repairs. However, participants who performed the less difficult task were predominantly concerned with rectifying their ungrammatical or lexically inappropriate utterances and therefore executed error repairs more frequently. We interpreted these results in light of the theories of attention and put forth what we labelled the 'Extended Trade-off Hypothesis' (ETH) according to which trade-offs are conceivable not only among the three dimensions of L2 speech (complexity, accuracy and fluency), as suggested by Skehan (1998), but also among the three different loops of monitoring (conceptual, pre-articulatory and external). The ETH also predicts that trade-off involves the amount of attentional resources which is allocated for effectuating E-repairs on the one hand and D- and A-repairs on the other.

In the second study, Mojavezi and Ahmadian (2014) explored the relationship between WMC and self-repair behaviour in first language (L1) and L2 oral production. The results of the study pointed to positive correlations between WMC and self-repair in the L2 but not in the L1. Also, the results revealed that whereas in the case of L1 the participants made different-information and appropriacy repairs more than error repairs, in the case of L2 more error repairs were made.

Using Levelt's (1983, 1989) self-repair taxonomy, Oomen and Postma (2001) investigated the effects of time pressure on mechanisms of L1 speech production and self-monitoring. They found that L1 speech becomes more erroneous under pressured conditions. However, given that Oomen and Postma's (2001) study concerns L1 speech, it is not clear to what extent their results are applicable for L2 learners. Ahmadian and Tavakoli (2014) attempted to cover this gap by investigating the effects of (pressured and careful) online planning condition on self-repair behaviour. The results showed that the careful online planning condition induces learners to execute more error repairs and fewer appropriacy and different-information repairs compared to the pressured online planning condition.

As the above review reveals, the relationship between WMC and self-repair behaviour under online planning condition could provide insights into three areas of research: WM, task-based language teaching and learning, and speech production processes.

The Study

The study reported in this chapter used a correlational design and sought to address the following research question:

- In there any relationship between WMC and self-repair behaviour under online planning condition?
  As I discussed in the previous section, self-repair behaviour is normally classified into three types, and thus the study aimed to see if there is any relationship between WMC and the number of;
- error repairs;
- different-information repairs;
- appropriacy repairs under careful online planning condition.

The whole study was carried out in four separate sessions for each participant. In the first session, a proficiency (placement) test was administered to all participants. In the second session, participants' WM was measured via a computerised listening span test. In the third session, participants were asked to perform an oral narrative task under online planning condition and in the final session they were invited one by one to help classify the repairs they had made in their narrations.

Methodology

Participants

The participants of this study involved 53[1] Iranian intermediate English as a foreign language (EFL) learners (23 males and 30 females). All participants had Farsi as their mother tongue and had been studying English for 1–1.5 years in private language centres; their ages were between 18 and 21 years. They were told that the overall purpose of the study was to enhance the quality of instruction in language classrooms and to contribute to researchers and teachers' understanding of learning and teaching processes. All participants signed the informed consent form and were told that they were free to withdraw from the study at any time. Although the participants were randomly selected from among intermediate language learners studying in a private language centre and they had all taken placement tests before being assigned to intermediate level, I used the test of English as a foreign language internet-based test's (TOEFL iBT) independent and integrated speaking tests to make sure they were almost equal in terms of language proficiency. Two experienced language teachers were requested to rate students' speaking ability on a scale of 0–30. Participants obtained scores of between 13 and 17 (mean=14.717; SD=1.230). All participants then took a WM test in a separate session and then performed the oral narrative task under online planning condition.

Working memory test

WM span tasks, otherwise known as complex span tasks, are assumed to tap both the storage and the processing functions of WM; therefore, these tasks have come to prominence in such fields as (cognitive) psychology and SLA (Conway et al., 2005; Daneman & Carpenter, 1980; Juffs & Harrington, 2011). In the present study, following Ahmadian (2012b), Mackey et al. (2002) and Mojavezi and Ahmadian (2014), a listening span test was employed. Thirty-six Farsi sentences were taken from a high school Farsi textbook (the participants' L1). The lengths of the sentences ranged from 9 to 13 words. By rearranging some content words, half of the sentences were designed to be syntactically possible but semantically implausible. According to Conway et al. (2005), administering the WM test to more than one participant at a time introduces greater risk of measurement error. Therefore, a computerised test was utilised and participants took the test individually. During the session, each participant was presented with prerecorded sets of sentences read at normal speed by a native speaker of Farsi. A set comprised three, four or five sentences and each sentence span level consisted of three sentences with a two-second interval in between. The participants were required to react to each sentence by pressing the 'ACCEPTABLE' or 'NOT ACCEPTABLE' button on the computer screen. A 'ding-dong' sound was emitted at the end of each set and the participants were then required to write down the final word of each sentence within that set. An attempt was made to ensure that the recalled words were not highly abstract nor were they semantically related. The partial-credit method was used for scoring the answers (see Conway et al., 2005) such that for each correct recall, participants were assigned 1 point and therefore the participants' WMC scores could range between 0 and 36.

The oral narrative task and the operationalisation of planning conditions

Following previous online planning studies (e.g. Ahmadian, 2012b; Yuan & Ellis, 2003), in the present study online planning was operationalised experimentally in a two-pronged way: (a) by providing participants with ample time for task completion; and (b) by requiring all participants to start task performance straightaway to avoid them engaging in pre-task planning. All participants watched a seven-minute silent video cartoon and were then asked to narrate the story of the video in English (i.e. their L2) under careful online planning condition.[2] The standard procedure in online planning studies is to use silent videos to preclude learners from taking advantage of the immediate exposure to authentic language. Further, the monologic nature of the task was assumed to induce learners to produce stretches of language which were not contaminated by interactional variables (Yuan & Ellis, 2003) and to make sure that their L2 oral performance was being investigated 'as an individual attribute' (De Jong *et al.*, 2012). All narrations were audio-recorded for further analysis.

Stimulated recall

Although it is possible to categorise self-repairs and assign them to one of the above-mentioned categories (E-, A-, D-repair) according to where they occur, using SRCs considerably enhances the precision of this undertaking. In a stimulated recall session, the researcher uses some sort of support (e.g. showing a videotape, playing the participants' voices) so that they can watch or hear themselves doing an activity while they are asked to vocalise their thoughts at the time of the original activity (Gass & Mackey, 2000). According to Ericsson and Simon (1993), however, the validity of the data obtained via this technique is contingent on the time intervening between the occurrence of the thought (task performance) and its verbal report in a stimulated recall session; therefore, in the present study the participants' task performance was immediately followed by stimulated recall interviews conducted in the participants' native language (with a 10- to 15-minute time interval which was used for delivering instructions to the participants).

During the 10–15 minutes which were allocated to instructing the participants, following Gass and Mackey's (2000) recommendations, participants were told what I was interested to know, namely, why they repaired their speech (all instructions were in Farsi – the L1 of the participants). My colleague and I would pause the audio tracks especially when we noticed self-repairs in the participants' speech and request them to recall what they were thinking about at that particular moment, or why they hesitated to produce the rest of the sentence in the first place. The stimulated recall interview for each participant took about 12 minutes. All interviews were audio-recorded for further coding and analysis.

Analysis

Online planning

In online planning studies, the time spent on performing the task assumes paramount importance. In the present study, I calculated the overall time (seconds) used by each participant for task completion to see whether all participants had taken almost equal time for narrating the story (mean=185.20 seconds, min=180, max=210). As in Ahmadian (2012b), prior to the study, I decided to exclude the outliers (defined as one or more than one standard deviation [SD] above or below the mean) from the analysis. The rationale behind this decision was to ensure that careful online planning had been operationalised homogeneously in the sample. Therefore, the time consumed by each participant was converted to z score. Six cases were excluded from the analyses by virtue of being more than 1 SD above or below the mean (z scores for the excluded cases: −4.01; −1.44; 1.67; 1.55; 3.50; and 1.36). As a result, only 47 participants were included in the analysis. Considering that online planning has been operationalised homogeneously in the sample, I will now address the research questions and will discuss each in turn.

Self-repair behaviour

SRCs were used to classify the different self-repairs that each participant produced. In order to enhance the comparability of the results, we decided that the criteria for the identification of self-repairs be similar to those employed in previous studies, such that in order to be identified as self-repair the utterance should entail a clear *reparandum*, which could be an erroneous or inappropriate stretch of language, and a *reparatum*, which replaces the *reparandum* (Ahmadian et al., 2012; Ahmadian & Tavakoli, 2014; Kormos, 1998; Mojavezi & Ahmadian, 2014; van Hest, 1996). Overall, we randomly selected 20 instances of self-repair from the beginning (eight instances), middle (four instances) and end (eight instances) of each participant's performance. Then, taking into account participants' retrospective comments and in light of the context of the self-repair, each self-repair was coded as one of three categories: *different-information repair*, *appropriacy repair* and *error repair*. The instances of self-repair which we coded were double-checked by an independent expert colleague to see whether they had been assigned to the appropriate category. Also, 10% of the data, which included self-repair instances, was analysed and coded by the independent colleague; thereby, we achieved inter-coder reliability of more than 89% for all of the above-mentioned analytical and coding procedures. Pearson's correlation coefficient was used to perform the statistical analyses.

Results and Discussion

The data were first checked in terms of normality of distribution. All kurtosis and skewness values were between −2 and +2 which point to a reasonably normal distribution. As the minimum and maximum values illustrated in Table 9.1 indicate, the WM scores range from 21 to 29 (out of 36);

Table 9.1 Descriptive statistics

Variables	n	Minimum	Maximum	Mean	SD
Working memory	47	21.00	29.00	25.574	2.092
Error repair	47	4.00	12.00	8.212	2.413
Different information repair	47	2.00	12.00	6.617	2.541
Appropriacy repair	47	4.00	10.00	5.191	1.262

this shows that participants have not been closely grouped in terms of WMC. The means and SDs are also shown in Table 9.1. The mean scores clearly indicate that, compared to the other two types of self-repair, participants have made more error repairs (E-repair) (mean=8.212) in their speech and the smallest mean value pertains to the number of appropriacy repairs (A-repair) (mean=5.191).

As pointed out in the previous section, E-repairs include lexical repair, syntactic repair and phonological repair. Levelt (1989) argues that a large portion of the speaker's attentional resources (WMC) is devoted to the conceptualisation phase of speech production as most formulation and articulation operations run automatically. This being the case, more D- and A-repairs are expected to be made. This account, however, is germane to the L1 speaker and it might turn out to be somewhat different for L2 speakers (see de Bot, 1992). One major differentiating factor is that, unlike L1 users, L2 speakers do not possess large repertoires of prefabricated chunks and therefore they need to allocate a large part of their attentional resources to the formulation and articulation processes (Ahmadian, 2012a; Skehan, 2009). Thus, under online planning condition – that is, when there is no time pressure for task completion – L2 speakers produce more E-repairs compared to A- and D-repairs. This observation and argument fits well with the findings of Ahmadian and Tavakoli (2014) that whereas under careful online conditions participants produce more E-repairs, under pressured online planning condition they produce more A- and D-repairs. I will now turn to the results of Pearson's correlation coefficient for each type of self-repair and will discuss the results in light of related theoretical frameworks and empirical findings.

As for E-repairs, Table 9.2 reveals that there is a statistically significant positive relationship between WMC scores and the number of E-repairs ($r=0.531$, $p<0.000$). According to Cohen's (1992) criteria for interpreting effect size, r values greater than 0.50 are considered as large effect size magnitudes and therefore we can claim that the association between WMC and E-repair is relatively strong. It is crucial to note that for each participant, only 20 instances of self-repair were randomly selected and analysed. Therefore, if a given participant with larger WMC has made more E-repairs, say 12 E-repairs, there are only 8 remaining repairs which could either be A- or D-repairs. The upshot of this finding is that individual differences in WMC could play a pivotal role in the way that participants

Table 9.2 Pearson's correlation coefficient

Working memory	Error repair	Different-information repair	Appropriacy repair
Pearson's correlation	0.531**	−0.644**	0.303*
Sig. (two-tailed)	0.000	0.038	0.000
n	47	47	47

*p<0.05; **p<0.001

allocate their attentional resources to different aspects of L2 speech; such that speakers with larger WMC devote more processing resources to the pre-articulatory and external loops of monitoring and consequently effectuate more E-repairs compared to their low-WMC counterparts. This finding is, in a way, consistent with the results of Ahmadian (2012b) that under careful online planning condition, speakers with larger WMC produce more accurate language. The observed accuracy, one could deduce, might have been preceded by successful covert and overt (syntactic and lexical) error repairs. It also provides further empirical support for the ETH (Ahmadian *et al.*, 2012), whereby trade-offs are conceivable not only among the three dimensions of L2 speech (complexity, accuracy and fluency), as suggested by Skehan (1998), but also among the three different loops of monitoring (conceptual, pre-articulatory and external).

The results for A-repairs are most interesting. As shown in Tables 9.1 and 9.2, although, compared to E- and D-repairs (mean=8.212 and mean=6.617, respectively), participants have overall produced less A-repairs (mean=5.191), the relationship between WMC and A-repairs is positive and statistically significant (r=0.303, p<0.000). Considering Cohen's (1992) criteria, the strength of this relationship could be considered as *moderate.* As discussed earlier, A-repairs are used when the speaker decides to produce the originally intended content but in a modified way for reasons of inaccuracy, ambiguity, incoherence and/or pragmatic inappropriacy. This finding, too, could be interpreted in light of the limited-capacity nature of the WM system. Participants with larger WMC are more successful in not only paying attention to the appropriacy-related aspects of their speech but also in maintaining the inappropriate word(s) active in their WM and at the same time searching for and retrieving its appropriate replacement. It is also reasonable to suggest that for lower-WMC participants, communicating the message, i.e. the story of the video, and choosing grammatically and lexically sound forms to match the intended meaning is of a higher priority than polishing their language in terms of coherence and pragmatic appropriacy.

The pattern of results for D-repairs, however, is totally different. As illustrated in Tables 9.1 and 9.2, although the number of D-repairs (mean=6.617) that the participants have made in their speech is greater than that of A-repairs (mean=5.191), there exist a statistically significant negative relationship between WMC and the number of D-repairs ($r=-0.644$; $p=0.038$). This could be taken to mean that participants with larger WMC tend to produce less D-repairs in their speech and the relatively large magnitude of effect size (-0.644) testifies to this claim. In a recent study, Mojavezi and Ahmadian (2014) found that WMC correlates negatively with D-repairs ($r=-0.812$). The discrepancy between the effect sizes found in Mojavezi and Ahmadian (2014) and the present study could be attributable to the pedagogically oriented nature of this study. Language learners' orientation towards tasks has been shown to be quite sensitive to the way that they are instructed to perform the task (see Ahmadian & Tavakoli, 2014; Batstone, 2005). Levelt, too, argues that monitoring is 'context sensitive', and that the 'context of discourse' is among the prime factors which determine and regulate the amount of attentional capacity to be devoted to monitoring each aspect of speech. In the present study, participants were, indirectly, directed towards form and as a result they produced more E-repairs. This differential orientation is perhaps regulated via the WM system and it follows to postulate that if the communicative aspect of a given task is highlighted in the rubric, WM allocates more attentional resources to the conceptualiser which will result in making more D-repairs. Alternatively, if the formal, linguistic or systemic dimensions of task performance are emphasised in the rubric (e.g. under online planning condition), WM appropriates and channels more processing and attentional resources to the formulator and perhaps the articulator which will give rise to the production of more E-repairs in L2 speech. These interpretations are in line with the tenets of the ETH which was described above.

Conclusions

This study attempted to link three areas of research, namely, WM, task-based language teaching and learning and speech production processes. The findings revealed that under online planning condition there are significant relationships between WMC and L2 self-repair behaviour: participants with larger WMC produced more E- and A-repairs but less D-repair. As regards WM, these findings provide empirical evidence in support of the central role of WMC in channelling attentional capacity to different dimensions of L2 speech. Regarding speech production processes, the results showed that trade-offs involve different aspects of L2 speech production such that if one aspect of L2 comes to prominence (e.g. formulation and articulation), the other areas (e.g. conceptualisation) suffer. As for task-based language teaching and learning, a comparison between the results of the present study and those of Mojavezi and Ahmadian (2014) reveals that online planning condition induce speakers to allocate more attentional resources to the formulation and articulation stages of speech production. There is a need for further studies to examine the relationship between WMC and L2 self-repair behaviour under different performance conditions (e.g. pre-task planning) and using various task types.

Acknowledgements

The study reported in this chapter was first presented at the Language Learning International Roundtable on Working Memory and Second Language Learning in 2012. I would like to thank Zhisheng (Edward) Wen, Mailce Mota and Arthur McNeill for inviting me to this roundtable.

Notes

(1) It is important to point out that as a result of the statistical decisions described in the analysis ('Online Planning' section), only 47 participants were included in the final analyses.
(2) The Instructions for Performing the Task under Online Planning Condition (all instructions were originally in Farsi): You will now watch a silent video. This video has a story. Please retell this story in English immediately after watching the video. In the meantime, imagine that you are retelling this story to someone who is very eager to know all the details of the story. Therefore, please be as detailed as possible in narrating the story. Feel free to take as much time as you need for task completion. Many thanks for your cooperation.

References

Ahmadian, M.J. (2012a) The effects of guided careful online planning on complexity, accuracy, and fluency in intermediate EFL learners' oral production: The case of English articles. *Language Teaching Research* 16, 129–149.

Ahmadian, M.J. (2012b) The relationship between working memory capacity and oral L2 performance under task-based careful online planning condition. *TESOL Quarterly.* doi: 10.1002/tesq.8.

Ahmadian, M.J. and Tavakoli, M. (2011) The effects of simultaneous use of careful online planning and task repetition on accuracy, fluency, and complexity of EFL learners' oral production. *Language Teaching Research* 15, 35–59.

Ahmadian, M.J., Abdolrezapour, P. and Ketabi, S. (2012) Task difficulty and self-repair behavior in second language oral production. *International Journal of Applied Linguistics* 22, 310–330.

Ahmadian, M.J. and Tavakoli, M. (2014) Investigating what second language learners do and monitor under careful online planning condition. *Canadian Modern Language Review* 70(1), 50–75.

Baddeley, A.D. (2000) The episodic buffer: A new component of working memory? *Trends in Cognitive Sciences* 4, 417–423.

Baddeley, A. (2001) Is working memory still working? *American Psychologist* 56, 851–864.

Baddeley, A. (2003) Working memory and language: An overview. *Journal of Communication Disorders* 36, 189–208.

Baddeley, A.D. (2012) Working memory: Theories, models and controversies. *Annual Review of Psychology* 63, 1–30.

Cohen, J. (1988) *Statistical Power Analysis for the Behavioral Sciences.* Newbury Park, CA: Sage.

Cronbach, L.J. (1957) The two disciplines of scientific psychology. *American Psychologist* 12, 671–684.

Conway, A., Kane, M., Bunting, M., Hambrick, D., Wilhelm, O. and Engel, R. (2005) Working memory span tasks: A methodological review and user's guide. *Psychonomic Bulletin & Review* 12, 769–786.

Conway, A.R.A., Jarrold, C., Kane, M.J., Miyake, A. and Towse, J.N. (eds) (2007) *Variation in Working Memory*. New York: Oxford University Press.

Daneman, M. and Carpenter, P.A. (1980) Individual differences in working memory and reading. *Journal of Verbal Learning and Verbal Behavior* 19, 450–466.

de Bot, K. (1992) A bilingual production model: Levelt's 'speaking' model adapted. *Applied Linguistics* 13, 1–24.

De Jong, N.H., Steinel, M.P., Florijn, A.F., Schoonen, R. and Hulstijn, J.H. (2012) Facets of speaking proficiency. *Studies in Second Language Acquisition* 34 (1), 5–35.

Ellis, R. (2005) Planning and task-based research: Theory and research. In R. Ellis (ed.) *Planning and Task-Performance in a Second Language* (pp. 3–34). Amsterdam: John Benjamins.

Ericsson, K. and Simon, H. (1993) *Protocol Analysis: Verbal Reports as Data* (2nd edn). Boston, MA: MIT Press.

Fortkamp, M.B.M. (1999) Working memory capacity and aspects of L2 speech production. *Communication and Cognition* 32, 259–296.

Fortkamp, M.B.M. (2003) Working memory capacity and fluency, accuracy, complexity and lexical density in L2 speech production. *Fragmentos* 24, 69–104.

Gass, S.M. and Mackey, A. (2000) *Stimulated Recall Methodology in Second Language Research*. Mahwah, NJ: Lawrence Erlbaum.

Guara-Tavares, M.G. (2008) Pre-task planning, working memory capacity and L2 speech performance. Unpublished doctoral thesis, Universidade Federal de Santa Catarina.

Juffs, A. and Harrington, M.W. (2011) Aspects of working memory in L2 learning. *Language Teaching: Reviews and Studies* 44, 137–166.

Kane, M.J. and Engle, R.W. (2002) The role of prefrontal cortex in working-memory capacity, executive attention, and general fluid intelligence: An individual-differences perspective. *Psychonomic Bulletin & Review* 9, 637–671.

Kormos, J. (1998) Self-repairs in the speech of Hungarian learners of English. Unpublished doctoral dissertation, Eotvos University.

Kormos, J. (1999) Monitoring and self-repair in L2. *Language Learning* 49, 303–342.

Kormos, J. (2006) *Speech Production and Second Language Acquisition*. New York: Lawrence Erlbaum.

Levelt, W.J.M. (1983) Monitoring and self-repair in speech. *Cognition* 33, 41–103.

Levelt, W. (1989) *Speaking: From Intention to Articulation*. The MIT Press.

Mackey, A., Philp, J., Egi, T. and Fujii, A. (2002) Individual differences in working memory, noticing of interactional feedback and L2 development. In P. Robinson (ed.) *Individual Differences and Instructed Language Learning* (pp. 181–209). Amsterdam: John Benjamins Publishing.

Mojavezi, A. and Ahmadian, M.J. (2014) Working memory capacity and self-repair behavior in L1 and L2 speech production. *Journal of Psycholinguistic Research* 43 (3), 289–297.

Service, E. (1992) Phonology, working memory and foreign-language learning. *Quarterly Journal of Experimental Psychology* 45A (1), 21–50.

Van Hest, E. (1996) *Self-Repair in L1 and L2 Production*. Tilburg: Tilburg University Press.

Ward, G. and Morris, R. (2005) Introduction to the psychology of planning. In R. Morris and G. Ward (eds) *The Cognitive Psychology of Planning* (pp. 1–34). Hove: Psychology Press.

Yuan, F. and Ellis, R. (2003) The effect of pre-task planning and online planning on fluency, complexity, and accuracy in L2 oral production. *Applied Linguistics* 24, 1–27.

10 Working Memory, Cognitive Resources and L2 Writing Performance

Yanbin Lu

Introduction

Since the introduction of the concept of working memory (WM) into the study of second language acquisition (SLA), a number of studies have investigated the role of WM in various aspects of second language (L2) learning and use (e.g. N. Ellis, 1996, 2002; Harrington & Sawyer, 1992; Mackey *et al.*, 2002; Miyake & Friedman, 1998; Osaka & Osaka, 1992; Service, 1992; Service *et al.*, 2002; Van den Noort *et al.*, 2006; Williams, 1999; and see various chapters in this volume). Research has suggested that WM plays a significant role in SLA in aspects such as reading comprehension (e.g. Harrington & Sawyer, 1992), grammar learning (e.g. McDonald, 2006), sentence parsing (e.g. Juffs, 2004, 2005) and oral production (O'Brien *et al.*, 2006). However, there are relatively few empirical studies examining the relationship between WM capacity and L2 writing.

The role of WM in writing has been highlighted in both Hayes' (1996) and Kellogg's (1996) models of writing. According to Hayes (1996), WM plays a central role in the activity of text generation and occupies the central position in his model of writing. Within this model, WM serves as a maintaining and processing interface of different kinds of knowledge involved in the writing process. Such a central role of WM is also demonstrated in Kellogg's (1996) model of WM in writing, who argued that all three components of Baddeley's (1986) WM model were in use during the composing process of writing.

There is consensus in the field of cognitive psychology that WM has a limited capacity. Drawing on this notion, McCutchen (1996) proposed a capacity theory of writing and posited that due to overall resource limitations within the WM system, fewer resources will be available for storage when more resources are devoted to processing and vice versa. Therefore, if either processing or storage functions are compromised, overall writing performance will suffer. It seems logical to assume, then, that for language learners, when they are writing in their L2, they must use part of their cognitive resources to focus on the language so that other functions, such as higher-order functions for organisation and discourse, cannot be engaged at full capacity.

Weigle (2005) extended this notion to L2 writing and postulated that for many L2 writers, particularly those with lower L2 proficiency, their access to L2 lexical and syntactic resources is not yet automatic, so they need to pay conscious attention while retrieving such information in the writing process. With a limited WM capacity, this consumption of attention in turn hinders their access to higher-level strategies and knowledge bases that might be available to them when writing in their first language (L1). It is possible that more attention to language will result in less attention to more global writing functions. Therefore, their written performance might be undermined.

Despite the conception of the role of WM in L2 writing, there are only a few empirical studies on the relationship between WM capacity and L2 writing (e.g. Abu-Rabia, 2003; Bergsleithner, 2010). Therefore, this study attempts to fill in this gap by exploring the role of WM capacity on L2 writing performance.

Writing in one's native language (L1) is a complex cognitive activity. Writing in a second/foreign language (L2) is even more demanding, more difficult and less effective, due to the additional constraints arising from the writer's L2 proficiency (Silva, 1993). Hence, L2 proficiency is an indispensable factor in the investigation of L2 writing. More importantly, L2 proficiency has also been found to be related to one's WM capacity (e.g. Gass & Lee, 2011; Van den Noort *et al.*, 2006). Therefore, this study intends to investigate the relationship between WM capacity, L2 proficiency and L2 writing performance. More specifically, the research questions to be investigated in this study are as follows:

(1) What is the relationship between Chinese English as a foreign language (EFL) learners' L2 written performance, their WM capacity in L1 and L2 and their L2 language knowledge? Is there an interaction between learners' L2 proficiency and WM capacity and L2 written performance?
(2) What is the relationship between Chinese EFL learners' WM capacity in L1 and L2? Is there any difference between learners' L1 WM capacity and L2 WM capacity?

The Study

The data for this study come from a larger study in which a battery of tests was used to measure various factors that may contribute to L2 writing performance. In this chapter, only those that are relevant to the focus of this study will be reported, specifically, timed essay writing in L2 for written performance, vocabulary tests for L2 language knowledge and WM span tasks in L1 and L2 for WM capacity. In this section, the demographics of the participants will first be presented; then the instruments for each variable will be introduced and the rationale for their choice explained, followed by their respective scoring methods.

Participants

Data collection took place in a key university in Beijing, China, in the fall semester of 2009. Participants were recruited from both undergraduate and graduate students from various disciplines. A total of 136 students participated in this study, with 104 undergraduates and 32 graduates. Among this sample group, 78 were male and 58 were female. Their age varied from 16 to 30 years old, with a mean of 20 years and both a median and a mode of 19 years. The mean for years of English learning was 9.4, with a majority of the participants (89.7%) studying English for 6–12 years; 70.6% of the participants started learning English at the age of 10–13 years.

Instruments

Operation span tasks for WM capacity

Operation span tasks were used as a measure of participants' WM capacity in L1 (Chinese) and L2 (English). The operation span task for English was modified from the one developed by Unsworth et al. (2005). It has been used as an established test for WM capacity in the field of psychology. The operations used in the task are simple arithmetic operations involving addition, subtraction, multiplication and division (e.g. $(10 \times 1) - 7 = 3$). The English words for recall are all high-frequency words with only one syllable and four to six letters. To measure WM capacity in L1, the researcher, who is a native speaker of Chinese, compiled a list of Chinese words, and three other native speakers of Chinese were consulted to make sure that the target words were high-frequency words in Chinese.

The operation span task was chosen over other span tasks on the basis of the following reasons:

- First, a complex span task was considered over a simple span task because the former is supposed to tap into both the storage and processing capacity of the WM.
- Second, the commonly used reading span task was not employed in order to avoid the confounding relationship between reading span and language proficiency. A number of studies (e.g. Service et al., 2002; Van den Noort et al., 2006) have shown that WM capacity as measured by the

reading span task interacts with language proficiency. According to Service *et al.* (2002), significant differences in reading span were reported between a native speaker group versus a foreign language group as well as more proficient versus less proficient foreign language groups. The results of Van den Noort *et al.*'s (2006) study confirmed that participants' WM capacity as measured by reading span tasks was highly correlated with their language proficiency.

• Third, the operation span task was chosen because, according to Turner and Engle (1989) and La Pointe and Engle (1990), WM capacity is independent of tasks and operation span tasks can measure WM capacity equally well as reading span tasks and can serve as a powerful predictor of reading comprehension. Unsworth *et al.* (2005) demonstrated that the operation span task correlated well with other measures of WM capacity (including the reading span task) and that it had good internal consistency and test-retest reliability. They claimed that the operation span task was a reliable and valid indicator of WM capacity. The reliability and validity of the operation span task have also been attested in the comprehensive review of WM span tasks by Conway *et al.* (2005).

Timed essay writing in L2 for written performance

Written performance in L2 was measured by a timed essay writing task. Participants were instructed to complete an essay in English within 30 minutes on a given prompt. The prompt was:

> Some people choose their major field of study based on their personal interests, while others are more concerned about future employment possibilities. What position do you support? Use specific reasons and examples to support your answer.

The rationale for choosing this type of task and this specific prompt was as follows:

• First, the mode of timed essay writing was adopted because essay writing is the most efficient and reliable way to assess writing ability. Although it has to be acknowledged that a timed impromptu writing test has its limitations (e.g. one's writing ability is judged based on a single sample which is written in a limited time frame on a given prompt), the use of timed impromptu writing tasks is a widely accepted common practice in large-scale English proficiency tests, such as the test of English as a foreign language (TOEFL) and the international English language testing system (IELTS) for international students who intend to apply for American or UK universities, and the College English Test (CET; Band-4 and Band-6) for non-English major college students in China. The time allowance of 30 minutes was decided on the basis of common practice as well as the research done by Jacobs *et al.* (1981) which found that this amount of time probably gave most students enough time to produce an adequate sample of their writing ability.

• Second, the genre of argumentative essay was employed because it is believed that the ability to generate and organise ideas with examples or evidence for this type of writing involves complex cognitive functions (Hale *et al.*, 1996). Moreover, argumentative essay writing is one of the common essay genres that college students may encounter across their curriculum. It is also typical of large-scale writing tests.

• Third, the specific prompt was designed because the topic was believed to be closely related to the participants' life as college students; therefore, it was hoped that the participants would find it relatively easy to write about this topic. Specifically, the prompt required the participants to write about the most important factor(s) they considered while choosing their major field of study. They had thought this question over in their real lives (just recently for freshmen and a little earlier for other students); therefore, this topic was relevant, familiar, potentially interesting and accessible to all the participants (this was confirmed by informal chats with some of the participants after the written test).

L2 language knowledge

Vocabulary is an indispensible component in any model of language competence, and vocabulary size is generally believed to be a good indicator of a learner's linguistic knowledge. As Read (2000) has pointed out, adequate knowledge of vocabulary is a prerequisite for effective language use. Receptive vocabulary knowledge is important for comprehension such as listening and reading, whereas productive vocabulary is important for language production such as speaking and writing. In the current study, both receptive and productive vocabulary knowledge were tested. Two vocabulary size tests developed by Nation and colleagues were used to measure participants' vocabulary size. The test in Nation and Gu (2007) was used for receptive vocabulary knowledge, and the test developed by Laufer and Nation (1999) was used for productive ability in vocabulary use.

The receptive vocabulary test consisted of 13 sets of questions, with 10 multiple-choice items within each set (a total of 130 items). The first 10 items tested the first thousand word level, the second 10 items tested the second thousand word level and so on, with increasing difficulty for later items. For each item, the target word was given first, followed by a sentence with the target word in brackets. Then, four choices were listed. The participants were supposed to choose the best meaning for each word. The test was printed on a 10-page, double-sided test booklet with a separate answer sheet for the participants to record their answers on.

The controlled-production vocabulary test consisted of 5 sets of 18 incomplete sentences (a total of 90 items). There was a blank in each sentence. On the blank, the first two to five letters of the expected answer were given. The participants were supposed to complete each sentence with an appropriate word starting with the given letters. The test was printed on three pages and a separate answer sheet was also attached to the test booklet for the participants to record their answers on.

Scoring

WM capacity in L1 and L2

WM capacity in L1 and L2 was measured by an operation span task in L1 (Chinese) and another in L2 (English), respectively, with 60 items in each task. The total words scoring method was used in calculating the participant's WM capacity score, that is, the total number of target words correctly recalled by a participant on each WM task was recorded as his/her WM capacity score for L1 and L2, respectively.

Traditionally, the span score is calculated as the maximum number of words that a participant recalls within a set.[1] However, this way of scoring one's reading span, a 'quasi-absolute span score' in Conway et al.'s (2005) nomenclature, has serious drawbacks in terms of its reliability and distribution due to data loss/discarding (Conway et al., 2005; Friedman & Miyake, 2005). After comparing four scoring methods for the reading span test, Friedman and Miyake (2005) highly recommended the total words scoring method because it yielded normal distributions and good reliability. The total words scoring method was also used by Van den Noort et al. (2008) in their validation of a computerised reading span test which they developed in four different languages.

For this study, the total number of correctly recalled target words was recorded as the score for a participant's WM span. The order of the target words within a set was ignored. That is, the target words could be recalled in any order within the set they were shown. However, any target word that was recalled in a different set other than the set in which it appeared was counted as wrong (sometimes participants would recall and write down a target word that appeared in an earlier set). Any change in a letter of an English word or a stroke of a Chinese word was also counted as wrong. The maximum score for WM span in Chinese (WMC) and that in English (WME) was 60 points each.

Written performance in L2

For this study, the rating scales and scoring rubrics for English essays were developed on the basis of several sources, including TOEFL iBT independent writing rubrics (ETS, 2008), Jacobs et al.'s (1981) scoring profile and the Tsinghua English Proficiency Test (TEPT-I) scoring guide for writing (Tsinghua University, 2009).

An analytic rating scale was adopted for the essay rating. Compared with holistic scoring, analytic scoring is believed to be able to provide more detailed information about a test taker's performance in different aspects of writing. It is more suitable than holistic scoring especially for L2 learners who may have a disproportionate development in their L2 writing ability – they might be better at content and organisation but poorer in terms of vocabulary and language use (Weigle, 2002).

Two categories were included in the rubrics: Content and Organisation and Language Use. Each essay was rated by two experienced raters on the two categories Content and Language with a scale of 1–15. The average of the scores assigned by the two raters in each category was computed as the final score for each essay. Therefore, each essay has a content score (EC) and a language score (EL) with a maximum of 15 points each.

L2 Language Knowledge

Two vocabulary scores were recorded according to the number of correct items the participant obtained in the vocabulary size tests – one for the receptive vocabulary test (VOC1) and the other for the controlled-production vocabulary test (VOC2). The receptive vocabulary score was totally objective, because all the items were multiple-choice questions. The productive vocabulary score was mostly objective, but for some of the answers, 0.5 was given if the word was correct but not the form (e.g. tense for verbs or plural for nouns). The total score for the receptive vocabulary test was 130 and that for the productive test was 90.

Results

In this section, the results of statistical analyses, in particular, the descriptive and reliability statistics for each measure as well as the inferential statistics including correlation coefficients and stepwise regression among the variables will be presented. All the statistical analyses were performed using SPSS (version 17.0).

Table 10.1 presents the descriptive statistics of the observed variables: WM capacity in Chinese (WMC), WM capacity in English (WME), English content (EC), English language (EL), receptive vocabulary score (VOC1) and productive vocabulary score (VOC2). The means and standard deviations vary considerably among these variables because different measures have different total scores.

Cronbach's alphas were calculated as estimates of internal consistency for WM capacity tests and vocabulary tests. The reliability measures for WMC, WME, VOC1 and VOC2 were 0.824, 0.783, 0.916 and 0.913, respectively, showing acceptable to fairly high reliability. Inter-rater reliability was calculated to measure the consistency of the raters

Table 10.1 Descriptive statistics of the observed variables

Measure	Minimum	Maximum	Possible maximum score	Mean	SD
Working memory Chinese (WMC)	34.0	60.0	60	55.60	4.46
Working memory English (WME)	36.0	60.0	60	51.47	5.32
English content (EC)	5.0	14.5	15	9.57	1.99
English language (EL)	5.5	14.5	15	9.03	1.78
Receptive vocabulary (VOC1)	15.0	84.0	130	35.65	12.42
Productive vocabulary (VOC2)	11.0	67.5	90	30.82	10.40

for the English essays, respectively. The inter-rater reliability estimates were found to be sufficiently high, ranging from 0.854 for EC and 0.859 for EL.

Table 10.2 shows the correlations between variables for WM capacity in Chinese and English (WMC and WME), L2 receptive and productive language knowledge (VOC1 and VOC2) and L2 written performance in terms of content and language (EC and EL).

From Table 10.2, we can see that the two measures for WM capacity in the two languages correlate with each other moderately ($r=0.594$, $p<0.01$). Table 10.2 also shows that all the measures for L2 language knowledge (receptive and productive vocabulary) and for L2 written performance (English content and English language) are moderately or highly correlated. However, no correlation was found between the observed measures of WM capacity and L2 language knowledge or L2 writing performance, except for a slightly significant correlation between WME and VOC2 ($r=0.191$, $p<0.05$).

Table 10.2 Correlations between WM capacity, L2 language knowledge and L2 writing scores

Variable	WM capacity		Language knowledge		English writing	
	Chinese (WMC)	English (WME)	Receptive (VOC1)	Productive (VOC2)	Content (EC)	Language (EL)
WMC	–	0.594**	0.086	0.048	0.039	0.035
WME		–	0.164	0.191*	0.167	0.117
VOC1			–	0.670**	0.268**	0.269**
VOC2				–	0.424**	0.465**
EC					–	0.885**
EL						–

**Correlation is significant at the 0.01 level (two-tailed).
*Correlation is significant at the 0.05 level (two-tailed).

Stepwise regression was performed twice taking EC and EL as the dependent variables, respectively, and WMC, WME, VOC1 and VOC2 as the independent variables. In both regression results, only VOC2 was found to be a significant predictor for EC ($r=0.424$) and EL ($r=0.465$).

In order to determine if there is an interaction between participants' L2 proficiency and WM capacity and L2 written performance, participants were divided into two groups – high and low – according to their total score of VOC1 and VOC2. Correlation coefficients were calculated and stepwise regression was performed for both groups. However, similar patterns were seen for both groups, which were also similar to the results reported above for the whole group. In other words, only VOC2 was found to be a significant predictor of EC and EL for both proficiency groups and no correlations were seen between WM capacity and L2 writing performance for either proficiency group.

With regard to the second research question, that is, to determine if participants' WM capacity differs in their L1 and L2, a paired-samples t-test was conducted on the number of words recalled in Chinese and that in English. Results show that participants recalled significantly more words in Chinese than in English ($t=10.794$, $df=135$, $p=0.000$). Therefore, it can be concluded that the functional WM capacity of the participants was larger in their L1 compared to that in their L2.

Discussion

The results showed no correlation between WM capacity and written performance or vocabulary knowledge, which is not consistent with previous studies that investigated similar issues (e.g. McCutchen et al., 1994; Ransdell & Levy, 1996, 1999). One of the possible reasons for this discrepancy might be related to the different instruments that were used to measure WM capacity and writing ability. McCutchen et al. (1994) used short writing tasks for measuring writing ability – primary and secondary students were asked to write 12–15 minutes each on two essay topics in their regular classrooms. Therefore, the operationalisation of the construct of writing ability was different in their study from this study, which engaged the participants in a 30-minute academic essay writing task in L2 in test settings. More importantly, the measures for WM capacity were very different – McCutchen et al. (1994) employed reading and speaking span tasks for measuring WM capacity. However, it is self-evident that a person's reading ability is correlated with his/her writing ability (e.g. Carson et al. [1990] reported statistically significant correlations between reading and writing in L1 and L2). In order to avoid this confounding factor of reading ability, operation span tasks rather than reading span tasks were used in the current study to measure participants' WM capacity.

Nonetheless, no correlation was found between WM capacity and writing ability in the current study, which was contrary to what had been expected. This result led to the following questions: in terms of methodology, is WM capacity task dependent or task independent? Is it domain specific or domain general? That is, does an individual's WM capacity vary with different tasks? Is the operation span task measuring a different WM capacity from the use of a reading span task? Is it possible that different mechanisms are involved in performing operation span tasks and reading span tasks?

The choice of operation span tasks in this study was based on the literature which argued for the notion that WM capacity is domain general (Engle *et al.*, 1999; Kane *et al.*, 2004) and task independent (La Pointe & Engle, 1990; Turner & Engle, 1989). Engle and colleagues found in their studies that operation span tasks tap into the domain-general attention control and that WM capacity is task independent – operation span tasks are as effective as reading span tasks in measuring one's WM capacity. However, as Miyake and Shah (1999) have summarised, the limits of WM capacity reflect multiple factors rather than one single factor. They pointed out that one likely possibility, in terms of the type of tasks, is that 'the nature of WM constraints varies as a function of the novelty and/or complexity of the task' (Miyake & Shah, 1999: 456). Even though both Turner and Engle (1989) and La Pointe and Engle (1990) have argued that WM capacity is independent of the specific nature of the processing component of the span task and that WM capacity measured with operation span tasks as well as with reading span tasks can predict reading comprehension, it is not clear if the two types of tasks activate or tap into the same storage and processing functions of WM. Researchers have proposed different explanations as to what span tasks really measure. For example, Daneman and Carpenter (1980), who proposed the original measure of reading span tasks for WM capacity, posited that the performance on reading span tasks reflected the amount of resources remaining for storage after processing. However, Engle *et al.* (1999) proposed that WM span tasks measure the short-term storage memory capacity plus one's controlled attention ability, particularly the ability of the central executive to coordinate the processing and storage components.

As proposed by Wen (2012) in his integrated framework of WM for SLA, domain-specific complex memory span tasks should be adopted to measure the executive WM in studies targeting specific L2 sub-skills. Therefore, domain-specific writing span tasks, which are supposed to tax the participants' language processing in the event of a writing activity, should be constructed in the investigation of the relationship between WM capacity and written performance. In addition, more investigation is needed to find out if operation span tasks and other span tasks are measuring the same WM capacity. For instance, using both operation and reading span tasks for measuring WM capacity to replicate the current study (or part of it) with a similar group of Chinese EFL learners and investigating the processes or strategies the participants employ during the span tasks via verbal protocols such as think aloud, retrospective interview or stimulated recall may reveal if the two types of tasks are measuring the same WM construct.

Another possible explanation for the lack of correlation between WM capacity and written performance in the current study might be the inadequacy of the specific instrument used in this study. A closer look at the item statistics shows that even though the tasks for measuring WM capacity achieved acceptably high internal reliability ($\alpha=0.824$ for WMC and 0.783 for WME), the item mean was very high (mean=0.923 for WMC and 0.855 for WME) and the item variance was rather small (0.067 for WMC and 0.110 for WME). These items were probably too easy for the participants and thus not differentiating enough. In reality, 18 out of the 136 participants obtained a full score in WMC and five in WME. The score distribution was skewed rather than normal, especially for WMC. There might be a ceiling effect due to the easy span tasks. In fact, Turner and Engle (1989) reported that when the difficulty level of the reading or operation span tasks was moderate, the correlations between WM span and reading comprehension were higher in magnitude than when the secondary tasks were very simple or very difficult. One way to improve the instrument in future research is to redesign the operation span task and include more difficult items so as to increase the difficulty level of the instrument and in turn improve the statistics for normal distribution and variance of the measure. In addition, only one type of task (operation span task) was used in this study. According to Waters and Caplan (2003), memory span on the basis of a single measure tends to be highly inconsistent. Therefore, using more than one task to assess WM capacity might yield a more reliable measurement of memory spans.

In terms of the relationship between WM capacity, L2 written performance and L2 language knowledge, statistical results with correlation coefficients and stepwise regression showed productive vocabulary knowledge as the only predictor of L2 written performance in the current study. Apparently, writing, which is a productive skill, is highly associated with productive language knowledge. If we regard language knowledge as something that is stored in one's long-term memory, we may assume that in the process of writing, the writer taps into his/her long-term memory, activates relevant productive vocabulary and brings it in to complete the writing task.

Despite the unexpected results in regard to the relationship between WM capacity and written performance, the paired-samples t-test of WMC and WME did show a significant difference in the participants' WM capacity in Chinese as compared to that in English, which is consistent with the results from other studies that used other memory span tasks (such as reading span tasks) for measuring participants' WM capacity in native and foreign languages (e.g. Service *et al.*, 2003; van den Noort *et al.*, 2006). This result added to the evidence for the notion that the functional WM capacity in one's native language is larger than that in one's second or foreign language.

Conclusion

In conclusion, the current study investigated the relationship between WM capacity, L2 language knowledge and L2 written performance with operation span tasks as the measurement for WM capacity. WM capacity in L1 and L2 has been found to be highly correlated with each other, with a larger L1 capacity than that of L2. However, no correlation has been found between WM capacity and written performance or L2 language knowledge, which is not consistent with relevant theories proposed by McCutchen (1996, 2000) and Weigle (2005). This failure might be due to the choice of a domain-general rather than a domain-specific span task, or due to the construction of inadequate operation span tasks which seemed to be too easy for the participants. Therefore, more research should be carried out to further investigate the relationship between WM capacity and writing performance with more appropriate and more adequate measures of WM capacity.

Further research can also be directed towards different stages of writing which was not touched upon in this study. According to Kellogg (1996), all the components of WM are involved in different stages of writing. It would be interesting to find out how these components function and interact during the process of L2 writing.

Acknowledgements

Special thanks go to Dr Edward Zhisheng Wen for his insightful comments on drafts of this chapter as well as his invitation to me to the Language Learning Roundtable on Memory and Second Language Acquisition convened in Hong Kong University of Science and Technology in June 2012. I also wish to thank Professor Sara Weigle for her supervision of my doctoral thesis, of which this chapter was a part. I am also grateful to the TOEFL Grants and Awards Committee at Educational Testing Service and the Dissertation Grant Program at Georgia State University for providing grants to support the completion of my dissertation project.

Note

(1) According to Daneman and Carpenter (1980), the reading span test contained three sets of items, each with two to six sentences. The participants were presented with sets of increasingly more items until they failed all the three sets at a particular level. The level at which a participant recalled the target words correctly in two out of three sets was taken as a measure of his/her reading span.

References

Abu-Rabia, S. (2003) The influence of working memory on reading and creative writing processes in a second language. *Educational Psychology* 23 (2), 209–222.

Baddeley, A.D. (1986) *Working Memory*. Oxford: Oxford University Press.

Baddeley, A.D. (2003) Working memory and language: An overview. *Journal of Communication Disorders* 36, 189–208.

Bergsleithner, J.M. (2010) Working memory capacity and L2 writing performance. *Ciências & Cognição* 12 (2), 2–20.

Carson, J., Carrell, P., Silberstein, S., Kroll, B. and Kuehn, P. (1990) Reading–writing relationships in first and second language. *TESOL Quarterly* 24, 245–266.

Conway, A.R.A., Kane, M.J., Bunting, M.F., Hambrick, D.Z., Wilhelm, O. and Engle, R.W. (2005) Working memory span tasks: A methodological review and user's guide. *Psychonomic Bulletin & Review* 12 (5), 769–786.

Daneman, M. and Carpenter, P.A. (1980) Individual differences in working memory and reading. *Journal of Verbal Learning and Verbal Behavior* 19, 450–466.

Ellis, N.C., (1996). Sequencing in SLA: phonological memory, chunking and points of order. *Studies in Second Language Acquisition* 18, 91–126.

Ellis, N. C. (2002). Frequency effects in language acquisition: A review with implications for theories of implicit and explicit language acquisition. *Studies in Second Language Acquisition* 24, 143–188.

Engle, R.W., Tuholski, S.W., Laughlin, J.E. and Conway, A.R.A. (1999) Working memory, short-term memory and general fluid intelligence: A latent variable approach. *Journal of Experimental Psychology: General* 128 (3), 309–331.

ETS (Educational Testing Service) (2008) TOEFL iBT Test Independent Writing Rubrics (Scoring Standards). See http://www.ets.org/Media/Tests/TOEFL/pdf/Independent_Writing_Rubrics_2008.pdf (accessed 28 September 2009).

Flower, L. and Hayes, J. (1980) The dynamics of composing: Making plans and juggling constraints. In L. Gregg and E. Steinberg (eds) *Cognitive Processes in Writing* (pp. 31–50). Hillsdale, NJ: Lawrence Erlbaum Associates.

Freedman, A., Pringle, I. and Yalden, J. (1983) *Learning to Write: First Language/Second Language*. New York: Longman.

Friedman, N.P. and Miyake, A. (2005) Comparison of four scoring methods for the reading span test. *Behavior Research Methods* 37 (4), 581–590.

Hale, G., Taylor, G., Bridgeman, B., Carson, J., Kroll, B. and Kantor, R. (1996) *A Study of Writing Tasks Assigned in Academic Degree Programs*. (TOEFL Research Report No. 54.) Princeton, NJ: Educational Testing Service.

Hayes, J.R. (1996) A new framework for understanding cognition and affect in writing. In C.M. Levy and S. Ransdell (eds) *The Science of Writing* (pp. 1–27). Mahwah, NJ: Lawrence Erlbaum Associates.

Jacobs, H.L., Zinkgraf, S.A., Wormuth, D.R., Hartfiel, V.F. and Hughey, J.B. (1981) *Testing ESL Composition: A Practical Approach*. Rowley, MA: Newbury House.

Kane, M.J., Hambrick, D.Z., Tuholski, S.W., Wilhelm, O., Payne, T.W. and Engle, R.W. (2004) The generality of working memory capacity: A latent-variable approach to verbal and visuospatial memory span and reasoning. *Journal of Experimental Psychology: General* 133 (2), 189–217.

Kellogg, R.T. (1996) A model of working memory in writing. In C.M. Levy and S. Ransdell (eds) *The Science of Writing: Theories, Methods, Individual Differences and Applications* (pp. 57–71). Mahwah, NJ: Lawrence Erlbaum Associates.

La Pointe, L.B. and Engle, R.W. (1990) Simple and complex word spans as measures of working memory capacity. *Journal of Experimental Psychology: Learning, Memory, and Cognition* 16 (6), 1118–1133.

McCutchen, D. (1994) The magical number of three, plus or minus two: Working memory in writing. In E.C. Butterfield (ed.) *Children's Writing: Toward a Process Theory of the Development of Skilled Writing* (pp. 1–30). Greenwich, CT: JAI.

McCutchen, D. (1996) A capacity theory of writing: Working memory in composition. *Educational Psychology Review* 8 (3), 299–325.

McCutchen, D. (2000) Knowledge, processing, and working memory: Implications for a theory of writing. *Educational Psychologist* 35 (1), 13–23.

McCutchen, D., Covill, A., Hoyne, S.H. and Mildes, K. (1994) Individual differences in writing: Implications of translating fluency. *Journal of Educational Psychology* 86, 256–266.

Ministry of Education in China (2009) *2009 Putong Gaodeng Xuexiao Zhaosheng Quanguo Tongyi Kaoshi Dagang (Syllabus for College Entrance Examinations for Matriculation of College Students in 2009)*. Beijing: Ministry of Education.

Miyake, A. and Shah, P. (1999) Toward unified theories of working memory: Emerging general consensus, unresolved theoretical issues, and future research directions. In A. Miyake and P. Shah (eds) *Models of Working Memory: Mechanisms of Active Maintenance and Executive Control* (pp. 442–481). Cambridge: Cambridge University Press.

Ransdell, S. and Levy, C.M. (1996) Working memory constraints on writing quality and fluency. In C.M. Levy and S. Ransdell (eds) *The Science of Writing: Theories, Methods, Individual Differences, and Applications* (pp. 93–105). Mahwah, NJ: Lawrence Erlbaum Associates.

Ransdell, S. and Levy, C.M. (1999) Writing, reading, and speaking memory spans and the importance of resource flexibility. In M. Torrance and G. Jeffrey (eds) *The Cognitive Demands of Writing: Processing Capacity and Working Memory in Text Production* (pp. 99–113). Amsterdam: Amsterdam University Press.

Scardamalia, M. (1981) How children cope with the cognitive demands of writing. In C.H. Frederiksen and J.F. Dominic (eds) *Writing: The Nature, Development, and Teaching of Written Communication, Vol. 2. Writing: Process, Development, and Communication* (pp. 81–103). Hillsdale, NJ: Lawrence Erlbaum Associates.

Service, E., Simola, M., Metsaenheimo, O. and Maury, S. (2002) Bilingual working memory span is affected by language skill. *European Journal of Cognitive Psychology* 14, 383–407.

Silva, T. (1993) Toward an understanding of the distinct nature of L2 writing. *TESOL Quarterly* 27, 657–677.

Tsinghua University (2009) Introduction to Tsinghua English Proficiency Test-I. See http://www.tsinghua.edu.cn/docsn/wyx/chinese/TEPT/tept1%20intro_for%20 on%20line.htm (accessed 28 September 2009).

Turner, M.L. and Engle, R.W. (1989) Is working memory capacity task-dependent? *Journal of Memory and Language* 28, 127–154.

Unsworth, N., Heitz, R.P., Schrock, J.C. and Engle, R.W. (2005) An automated version of the operation span task. *Behavior Research Methods* 37, 498–505.

Van den Noort, M., Bosch, P. and Hugdahl, K. (2006) Foreign language proficiency and working memory capacity. *European Psychologist* 11 (4), 289–296.

Van den Noort, M., Bosch, P., Haverkort, M. and Hugdahl, K. (2008) A standard computerized version of the reading span test in different languages. *European Journal of Psychological Assessment* 24 (1), 35–42.

Waters, G.S. and Caplan, D. (2003) The reliability and stability of verbal working memory measures. *Behavior Research Methods, Instruments, & Computers* 35 (4), 550–564.

Weigle, S.C. (2002) *Assessing Writing*. Cambridge: Cambridge University Press.

Weigle, S.C. (2005) Second language writing expertise. In K. Johnson (ed.) *Expertise in Second Language Learning and Teaching* (pp. 128–149). Basingstoke/New York: Palgrave Macmillan.

Wen, Z. (2012) Working memory and second language learning. *International Journal of Applied Linguistics* 22 (1), 1–22.

11 Working Memory and Second Language Performance: A Commentary

Peter Skehan

Introduction

Clear descriptions of working memory are contained elsewhere in this volume, so only the briefest account is needed here. I assume that working memory is limited in capacity, and that it is fractionated, in that it subsumes several components. In particular, there is a central executive and additional buffer systems – phonological and visual spatial for auditory and visual material, respectively (Wen, Chapter 3, this volume), and an episodic buffer (Baddeley, 2000) which links information across modalities and which has links to long-term memory. The central executive is then seen as marshalling these different resources, in the form of buffer systems, as well as itself, and as well as connections with long-term memory (Baddeley, this volume). In this way, it is central in processing input (of whatever sort), operating upon that input and then producing some sort of response or output.

If we relate this very general account to language specifically, it can be proposed that working memory is:

- A buffer for language input, while segmentation, analysis and meaning extraction take place.
- A buffer for output, while plans are made and lexis and syntax and articulatory plans are accessed and assembled.
- A workspace for the solution of problems which occur during input processing, output processing or general analysis and planning, when long-term memory is accessed and related to input or output, and even possibly modified.

The centrality this implies for all language operations suggests that working memory will have a major impact on language acquisition, on language processing, on discourse analysis and conversation analysis.

The latter two deal with language users' methods of circumventing the limitations of working memory (Chafe, 1994). Some models of grammar (O'Grady, 2005) are even designed to reflect working memory limitations.

This chapter will emphasise the significance of working memory for second language speech performance, drawing largely on a database of second language task-based performance (Skehan, 1998, 2011, 2014). To that end, it is useful to start with a model of speaking. For first language speaking, Levelt (1989; and see Kormos [2006] for second language speaking) proposes the three macro stages of conceptualisation, formulation and articulation. The first concerns the ideas to be expressed, and includes conceiving an intention to speak, determining what to say, selecting relevant information and a stance, and then finally producing a preverbal message. Formulation takes the preverbal message and translates it into linguistic form, first by embarking on a process of lemma retrieval and then syntax building. This leads into detailed phonetic and articulatory planning. The product of this stage is passed on to the articulator which handles the motor execution of these plans. These stages are accompanied by monitoring which may lead to modification of an utterance that is being produced, but only at certain points in the speech production process.

The key issue here is that Levelt proposes that these stages are modular (i.e. encapsulated) and function simultaneously. In other words, something like the following happens:

- Time 1: C_1
- Time 2: C_2>F (lexis)$_1$
- Time 3: C_3>F (lexis)$_2$>F (mor-syn)$_1$
- Time 4: C_4>F (lexis)$_3$>F (mor-syn)$_2$>A$_1$

(where C=conceptualiser, F=formulator and A=articulator, all with time period indicated) and so on. Simultaneously, at Time 3, for example, the conceptualiser is working on what might be termed 'Communication Chunk 3', while lemma retrieval is concerned in the formulator with the output of the conceptualiser from Time 2, while there is also activity to handle syntactic and morphological sentence building from the output of the formulator at Time 1. It is assumed that this merry-go-round continues while speaking is taking place, reflecting the modular, encapsulated parallel operation of the different stages in real time (Wang, 2014). This seemingly impossible task is discharged routinely by native speakers, and fluent speech results. A major point to make in this regard is that the seamlessness of the process is predicated upon the existence of an extensive, well-organised and deep mental lexicon where lemma information is readily accessible and elaborate. Ideas from the conceptualiser access rich lemmas which then drive the production system quickly and effortlessly, with communication and underpinning psycholinguistic processes operating below the level of consciousness. Of course, there may be times when a word resists access or when the thinking underlying speech is difficult. But mostly, things happen automatically, and as a result, working memory demands are not great and do not impact much on the speech production process.

Things may not be so smooth and effortless for second language speakers. At the heart of this problem is the smaller, less richly stocked, less organised and less accessible second language mental lexicon. Conceptualisation may proceed effectively, but the problems of access and the less rich information contained in lemmas which do exist mean that the formulation and articulation stages require more and conscious attention (Kormos, 2006). The result is that working memory resources are consumed and the process of speech production, ideally effortlessly parallel, becomes serial and difficult. What the normal range of working memory size can handle in first language speech becomes a considerable strain to working memory resources in a second language, because effort must be directed to making the best of any (limited) lemma retrieval that is taking place, and also to repairing the consequences of shortcomings in that retrieval. Lemma retrieval is more difficult; morphosyntax building is more time consuming or even impossible; and articulation based on a less-established syllabary is also likely to encounter problems. Working memory resources, as a result, are drained, and the capacity to simultaneously conceptualise is compromised by the need to allocate working memory resources elsewhere, to the formulator and the articulator.

There are, of course, enormous consequences that follow from limitations in working memory functioning for learning and for performance. Regarding the former, learning, many approaches argue that interaction alone contains a lot of what is needed to sustain development. The Interaction Hypothesis (Long, 1996), for example, sets great store in the usefulness of feedback during interaction to push second language development. But working memory limitations may mean that the insights from feedback might be ephemeral, as the demands of ongoing speaking compromise the possibility of registering such insights and linking them with long-term memory. For noticing and insight or the effects of feedback to have much impact, they need to make contact with long-term memory, and limited working memory capacity may make that less likely.

For the latter, performance, there are also major consequences. If attention is limited, the clear implication is that some aspects of performance may be prioritised at the expense of others, as attentional resources are consumed because of the priorities the speaker is following. This raises the question, of course, of what the likely performance features are that might be affected in this way, and of the conditions which are more likely to predispose attentional focus going one way or another.

The literature on performance on second language tasks would suggest that there is a contrast between a focus on meaning and a focus on form (Skehan, 1998). The former is more concerned with keeping up with real time as meanings are encoded and expressed, and so content-based fluency is the major goal. The latter is more concerned with producing language which is correct and which, perhaps, draws on more advanced and possibly less-established interlanguage. If this is the tension (and this will be discussed in more detail below) then the impact of working memory and attention limitations will be to emphasise one of these areas (meaning or form) at the expense of the other.

Working Memory Limitations and Second Language Task-Based Performance

Obviously, knowing about working memory–based limitations for performance in general is one thing. Understanding them in detail and predicting their effects is quite another, something which is particularly important when pedagogy and task performance are concerned. We now turn to exploring what is known about how to understand and mediate these tensions.

We will do this by considering a range of findings in relation to two main areas: task design, briefly, and task implementation conditions, in more detail. With the first, we will consider the issue of task structure. With the latter, we will look at planning, time conditions, repetition and posttask influences. All of these areas have been discussed extensively elsewhere (Foster & Skehan, 2014; Pang & Skehan, 2014; Wang, 2014; Wang & Skehan, 2014). What is different about the present discussion is that it is framed very much to illuminate the consequences for task performance of working memory limitations. In turn, though, there will be opportunities to theorise more clearly about the nature of second language task performance. In all cases, results from research studies are illuminated through the operation of working memory limitations and to the extent that these can be circumvented.

Task design

Research into second language task performance has shown that narrative tasks which are more structured lead to greater accuracy and sometimes complexity (Skehan & Foster, 1997, 1999; Skehan & Shum, 2014; Tavakoli & Foster, 2008). Skehan and Foster (1999) proposed that this is because the speaker with such tasks is 'sheltered' through a macrostructure which is known, and as a result, is required to do less conceptualiser work. In turn, this means more attention for formulator operations, and therefore lemma retrieval and consequent syntax building.

In the former case, there is more time to retrieve lemma information from a less extensive or organised lexicon, and with syntax building there may be more time to avoid error while syntactic frames are being built prior to articulation. More recently, Skehan (2014b) has proposed that such narrative tasks have the advantage that the structure they contain provides multiple restart points for someone who is experiencing difficulty in keeping up with real-time narration. If one assumes that second language speakers, at least some of the time, encounter difficulties which derail parallel performance and force them into a more serial mode of processing, they have to deal with the problem of how to re-establish the more desirable parallel performance and flow of speech. With unstructured tasks, this may be difficult to do, since there are no obvious points in a more loosely organised story at which fluency and parallel functioning can be regained. With structured tasks, in contrast, there will be intermediate points in the narrative where the harried speaker can relaunch, and then try to sustain parallel processing for as long as possible.

The heart of these findings is working memory. Narration, for second language speakers, is demanding, with lots of information in picture series or in video excerpts that have to be retold. What one can expect is that working memory capacity will be exceeded and then the major question is how second language speakers can get things back on track, and work within working memory constraints again after the point of trouble. The existence of a macrostructure first makes it slightly less likely that capacity limitations will be exceeded and then also eases the way that speakers can draw a line after previous difficulties, regain the structure of the story and restart anew. What they are doing is directly attributable to the limitations of working memory.

Task conditions

In this section, I will briefly describe four empirical studies involving task-based performance, and also offer an interpretation of the results which draws extensively on working memory operations. The first study illustrates how *general* working memory demands impact upon task performance. The second explores how demands on resources can be understood through the relationship between the different stages of speech production. The third suggests how working memory demands can be eased through task conditions and task design, and the fourth suggests that there are circumstances when second language speakers can be induced to direct their attention to particular performance dimensions, despite the limitations in working memory.

The first study to be discussed is Pang and Skehan (2014) who report a qualitative-quantitative study of planning. They used retrospective interviews to gather data on what planners said they did when given planning time before a narrative task. They were then able to code these reports and categorise them. Next, they related the codes to the actual performances which resulted when the narrative tellings took place, and at this stage interesting findings emerged. The planning literature, generally, supports the claim that planning has a beneficial impact on performance, especially for complexity and fluency, but less so for accuracy. However, Pang and Skehan's participants sometimes reported doing things in planning time which created difficulties for themselves and which were related to *lower* performance levels. What emerges from these findings is that 'good' planning should not lead speakers to overextend themselves, or to be too general. When learners did these things, performance suffered. It seems that (a) the transition from pre-task planning to actual performance may suffer from lack of transfer and recall; and (b) some things are easier to retain than others, e.g. less complicated and more specific planning. Getting the 'ambition' of planning wrong by trying to do too much, leads to *lower* levels of performance.

There are two connections between the Pang and Skehan (2014) study and working memory that are worth commenting on. First, it is clear that when working memory functions as a sort of transitional stage to what might be termed 'intermediate memory', this is central to the effectiveness of planning. Pang and Skehan (2014) argue that there are clear limitations on what can be retained by this means, and then activated during task performance. Second, it is clear that working memory operations while a task is running are demanding, and the speaker has to handle the consequences of ambitious planning, as well as remembering all the planning that has taken place. Speaking, by itself, is difficult and requires intensive working memory operations, and incorporating the result of planning adds to this difficulty. When the consequences of planning are to make a task more complex, the burden on working memory (accessing the fruits of this planning; keeping other aspects of what has been planned accessible; handling resources associated with speaking) becomes very considerable. The implication, in other words, is that planning itself, if misdirected, can overload what working memory can handle during performance. More direct applications of the fruits of planning (e.g. rehearsal, specific planning, organisation of ideas) can ease working memory operations, but it is also clear that planning is two-edged – it can just as easily make things more difficult to accomplish.

For the second study, the focus is on Wang (2014). Wang researched the impact of different types of planning on task performance, and she also explored the impact of participants repeating a task performance. The focus of her work was to isolate factors that are important in producing a higher level of accuracy, in the context of the contrast between strategic or pre-task planning, on the one hand, compared to online planning, on the other (Crookes, 1989; Ellis, 1987). With tight operationalisation of online planning through the use of a slowed video narrative-retelling task, she was able to show that online planning, in itself, did not lead to greater accuracy, but that if the online planning was preceded by some strategic planning opportunity, there was a clear increase in accuracy. In a separate experimental condition, she showed that immediately repeated performances were markedly better than the first performance, as measured through complexity, accuracy and fluency indices.

Obviously, any spoken language performance will draw upon the different stages outlined by Levelt (1989) in his model of first language speaking. This means conceptualisation (with a focus on the ideas, propositions to be expressed and the stance taken towards them), formulation (taking the preverbal message from the conceptualiser, and then engaging in lemma retrieval followed by syntactic structure building) and articulation (as sounds are attached to the output of the formulator). Effective communication therefore reflects a happy balance between conceptualiser, formulator and articulator operations. In Wang's (2014) study, an online condition eased the pressure on working memory operations, giving more time for preverbal messages to be expressed, and formulator operations to be carried out. Yet this was not enough to increase accuracy. Increased accuracy was found in an online planning condition only when there was also opportunity for pre-task planning. This seemed to enable the lower working memory demands in the online condition to produce higher accuracy. The pre-task planning probably implicated Conceptualiser operations. When this was done *and* there were eased conditions for the Formulator through online planning, sufficient attention available and guidance as to the ideas to be expressed, then higher levels of accuracy could be achieved. In other words, with online planning alone, formulation was eased but conceptualisation was not. With both eased, working memory could handle the demands placed upon it.

The other major condition from Wang's (2014) study was repetition. Clearly, the first narrative telling eased conceptualiser operations for the second performance. More important though is the functioning of the formulator. A major part of this stage in speech production is lemma retrieval (and then syntax building). The first performance appeared to prime actual lemmas and associated lexical material, thus easing memory demands on the second performance, so that fewer resources were required. In addition, the need to retrieve lemmas and activate features associated with them, such as syntax, seemed to lay down important traces which could then be built on during the second performance (Skehan, 2014b). This is in contrast to the (otherwise beneficial) effects of planning, where a more superficial level of lemma retrieval can suffice. So once again, working memory operations are 'scaffolded' so that they are less demanding of resources during the second performance. This is close to Cowan's (2005, this volume) view of working memory, where what happens is that aspects of long-term memory become more available, and accessible to working memory operations. The second performance then has more available material to work with, and so there is more attention available to focus on accuracy.

The third study to be interpreted through a working memory lens is Wang and Skehan (2014). They explored the competing claims of the Trade-off and Cognition Hypotheses, especially in cases where structural complexity and accuracy are jointly raised. Skehan (1998, 2011) proposes that limited attentional capacity means that these two performance areas are often in competition with one another: one being raised at the expense of the other being lowered. However, careful task and task conditions choices can mitigate this competition, and even produce raised performance in each simultaneously (Skehan, 2014b). Robinson (2011), in contrast, argues that attentional resources can expand if a task is more complex, with this task complexity driven by what he terms 'resource-directing factors' such as time perspective. More complex tasks cause learners to 'raise their game', as it were, and use more structurally complex language accordingly, while also speaking at higher accuracy levels to achieve precision to do justice to the more complex task. Wang and Skehan (2014) used a 2×2 design, contrasting a plus or minus structure and time perspective (here-and-now vs there-and-then) to explore these issues, based on video narrative retellings. Structure, as shown extensively in the task literature (Skehan & Shum, 2014), is associated with greater accuracy. But then they analysed time perspective differently to Robinson. He regards there-and-then conditions as more complex (with greater memory demands) compared to here-and-now conditions (which do not require so much use of long-term memory since stimuli are present while the participant is talking). Wang and Skehan (2014) regard the two conditions not as differing in task complexity, but simply as different. The latter condition benefits from visual presence, but suffers from (a) the quantity and rapidity of the input that is being received, factors which push working memory to the limit, because new input keeps arriving; and (b) the relative non-negotiability of this input, since under time pressure it is difficult for speakers to be selective on what they encode. On the other hand, there is the advantage that the visual input is actually there. The there-and-then condition obviously has the problem that the video which has been seen is no longer present, and so has to be remembered. So there are, as Robinson points out, memory implications, in this case requiring reference to something retained in long-term memory. But in contrast, there is no comparable input flood, and equally important, the speaker can 'shape' the story, choosing to highlight what he/she wants to highlight. The story, in other words, is negotiable. There may be memory problems in accessing the information from long-term memory, but there are far fewer memory problems in ongoing processing. Here, the speaking is more on the terms chosen by the participant.

This research design can, therefore, be revealing regarding the different working memory and long-term memory conditions. The results obtained suggested a clear superiority in performance for the there-and-then condition. They showed a significant advantage for this condition over the here-and-now condition (as Trade-off and Cognition would both predict here). But more interestingly, the *structured* there-and-then condition (in this 2×2 design) produced the highest levels of accuracy and complexity. In other words, there was an interaction between task and condition, as Trade-off would predict. What seemed to happen here was that the eased conditions through the speaker shaping the story, without ongoing remorseless input, allied to a structured task which enables easier transitions from general macrostructure to details of ongoing performance catalysed the higher levels of performance. In each case, the functioning and the constraints of working memory are crucial for this account of the results which were obtained.

The fourth study (Foster & Skehan, 2013) explored the impact on performance of giving learners a posttask to do in which they were given a recording of their performance while doing a task from which they were required to transcribe a short excerpt. This was done more than once, and the purpose of the study was to investigate the impact of this posttask transcription on the earlier task performance itself. In other words, the key influence here was the *anticipation* that what was being said during the task would be the input to the transcription which came later. We hypothesised that this anticipation and a concern that later they would not want to be transcribing their own errors would lead the participants on the task to prioritise accuracy selectively, causing this performance area to be raised, relative to a control group with no posttask activity. This prediction was fulfilled for narrative and decision-making tasks, and for the latter, there was an increase in complexity as well.

The central executive in working memory controls the focus of attention. Of course, within working memory operations there is the issue of quantity of material, but beyond that, the central executive may be able to prioritise. What is interesting from the Foster and Skehan (2013) study is that participants, even though pushed to communicate, seemed able to direct memory and attention resources to a particular performance domain. The natural emphasis might be towards getting the task done, but it appears there is scope to manipulate selective attention allocation if the conditions are right. The transcription condition seemed to achieve this. The broad constraint is working memory capacity, but the study showed that within this constraint, there is still potential to 'nudge' attention (Lynch, 2001) in particular directions, and in this case, towards a concern for form.

Working Memory and Task-Based Performance

So far, we have looked at each study separately. Now we turn to linking the studies to the Levelt model of speaking. In that model, as we have seen, the first stage is conceptualisation, followed by formulation: lexical and formulation: syntactic-morphological, with the third and final stage being articulation. In addition, monitoring is possible at various points. We will try to take these stages in turn.

Wang and Skehan (2014) illustrate several ways in which working memory operations can be pressured or, alternatively, eased. The pressuring is shown through their here-and-now condition, which overloads working memory resources and depresses performance, whether the task is structured or not. The overload washes out any potential advantage the structured task might have. Working memory is simply overextended in dealing with the quantity of input which is being received, and which is potential input to the details of the retelling which is taking place. The conceptualiser and formulator are deeply implicated and have too much to do. But then, in the there-and-then condition, immediate processing pressure is eased and the benefits of structure can reveal themselves. The existence of a macrostructure means that the speaker is more likely to know where he/she is in the storytelling, and so relating the detail to the big picture is much easier to do. As a result, central executive operations are eased because new links do not have to be made to relate the current focus of the narrative to the wider structure. More attention is therefore available. But in addition to that, if working memory is overloaded nonetheless, the structure of the narrative enables the disrupted story to be re-engaged with, and the general macroplan rejoined. At this point, fluency can be achieved once more, because once again, there is a good conceptualiser–formulator link, one which does not require so much working memory effort to re-establish.

Wang (2014) reported dramatic improvements in all measured aspects of performance in an immediate repetition condition. Engaging in deeper lemma retrieval motivated by the need to actually speak (in the first performance) provides a much more effective preparation than the shallower process associated with pre-task planning. Such planning may prepare aspects of lemmas for subsequent performance, but it still leaves a lot for the formulator to do, as the implications of making a particular lemma choice are confronted in the actual speaking task (e.g. syntactic frames and acceptable collocates). Repetition forces the speaker during the first performance to engage in such processes. In other words, working memory pressure during the repeated performance is eased considerably because of the more extensive work that was done earlier, work which, because it was deeper in processing, may also have been retained more. The formulator is more able to shape performance more effectively, and the whole system is more able to exploit monitoring opportunities because more free capacity is available. The heart of the operation, once again, is finding ways not to overload limited working memory resources.

One can look further at these advantages through one of Wang's other conditions in her research – her online planning condition. The base condition here, slowed performance conditions, did not have much effect on performance. The supported online condition, in contrast, did raise accuracy and complexity. A working memory perspective might have predicted that the base condition would, through slowing the visual input, sufficiently ease the pressure on limited working memory operations and storage so that improved performance would result. It didn't, whereas the supported condition, i.e. earlier planning then slowed processing, did. It seems that working memory needs input from the conceptualiser (arising from the strategic planning) and can then benefit from the eased processing conditions. This may partly be a (less deep) version of the claims from the previous paragraph – ideas can be more readily available, and associated lemmas primed so that what the formulator has to do is guided as well as eased (and the conceptualiser, during actual performance, makes fewer working memory demands). But it is also possible that the eased processing conditions have another benefit. Planning provides a basis for actual performance, but as we saw through Pang and Skehan (2014), what happens during planning may not convert into actual performance. Of course, this might be because it is planned and then completely forgotten. But it is also possible that the act of retrieval itself is demanding of resources, and that there may be times when the product of planning might be available, but performance conditions, i.e. working memory operations, are so demanding that this potential cannot be realised. What may have happened in Wang's (2014) repetition condition, therefore, is that the eased processing demands, and greater resource availability for working memory, may have enabled the product of planning to be retrieved and used where otherwise it would not be.

The final study has a different interpretation to the three already discussed. Their emphasis so far has been on the management and easing of resources so that 'good things might happen' in the shape of higher accuracy or complexity. But Foster and Skehan (2013) are not so concerned with making a limited amount of working memory resources work better. Rather, they are exploring how one can direct such limited resources. They show an effect on accuracy of anticipation of a subsequent posttask. This seems to lead the participants to direct attention, within limited working memory resources, towards particular aspects of form. The experimental conditions induce learners to do this simply because they connect ongoing performance with the subsequent posttask. Unless what is happening is that overall working memory resources are augmented (in a way which would please proponents of the Cognition Hypothesis; e.g. Robinson, 2011), then the effect can only be because the participants choose to focus attention towards form where otherwise they would not. In other words, attentional resources are diverted towards monitoring (Wen, this volume).

Conclusions

There are very many different ways one might explore the relevance of working memory for second language performance. I have chosen, in this chapter, to look at a small number of research studies. This is partly because each of them so naturally lends itself to interpretation in terms of limitations on attention which follow from working memory limitations (and structure). But it is also because the studies are firmly situated within the task literature and therefore relevant to the Trade-off–Cognition debate (Skehan, 2014b).

The Trade-off Hypothesis (Skehan, 1998, 2012) assumes working memory limitations and then explores how these limitations can be minimised or circumvented. It is also based on the assumption that we need a viable psycholinguistic model of speaking as a foundation. From this position, the studies show how the stages of speech production, and the associated process of monitoring, illuminate the results that have been summarised here. The functioning of the conceptualiser and the formulator, the balance between the two of them during speaking, the psycholinguistics of planning, as well as the directability of limited attention, all make sense only if one analyses them from the starting point of working memory resources and limited attention.

In contrast, the Cognition Hypothesis assumes that attention can expand to deal with the demands placed upon it, and Robinson (2011) claims that while working memory may have limitations in size, attention does not. The evidence reviewed here is more consistent with limited working memory resources leading to limited attentional resources. To sustain the claims of the Cognition Hypothesis, research evidence is needed consistent with the expandability of attention, and a freedom in performance from working memory limitations. So far, this has not been forthcoming.

References

Baddeley, A. (2000) The episodic buffer: A new component of working memory? *Trends in Cognitive Science* 4 (11), 417–423.

Chafe, W. (1994) *Discourse, Consciousness, and Time*. Chicago, IL: University of Chicago Press.

Cowan, N. (2005) *Working Memory Capacity*. New York and Hove: Psychology Press.

Crookes, G. (1989) Planning and interlanguage variation. *Studies in Second Language Acquisition* 11, 367–383.

Ellis, R. (1987) Interlanguage variability in narrative discourse: Style shifting in the use of the past tense. *Studies in Second Language Acquisition* 9, 12–20.

Foster, P. and Skehan, P. (2013) Anticipating a post-task activity: The effects on accuracy, complexity and fluency of L2 language performance. *Canadian Modern Language Review* 69 (3), 249–273.

Kormos, J. (2006) *Speech Production and Second Language Acquisition*. Mahwah, NJ: Lawrence Erlbaum.

Levelt, W.J. (1989) *Speaking: From Intention to Articulation*. Cambridge: Cambridge University Press.

Lynch, T. (2001) Seeing what they meant: Transcribing as a route to noticing. *ELT Journal* 55, 124–132.

O'Grady, W. (2005) *Syntactic Carpentry: An Emergentist Approach to Syntax*. London: Routledge.

Pang, F. and Skehan, P. (2014) Self-reported planning behaviour and second language performance in narrative retelling. In P. Skehan (ed.) *Processing Perspectives on Task Performance* (pp. 95–128). Amsterdam: John Benjamins.

Robinson, P. (2011) Second language task complexity, the Cognition Hypothesis, language learning, and performance. In P. Robinson (ed.) *Second Language Task Complexity: Researching the Cognition Hypothesis of Language Learning and Performance* (pp. 3–38). Amsterdam: John Benjamins.

Skehan, P. (1998) *A Cognitive Approach to Language Learning*. Oxford: Oxford University Press.

Skehan, P. (2012) *Researching Tasks: Performance, Assessment, Pedagogy*. Shanghai: Shanghai Foreign Language Education Press/Amsterdam: De Gruyter.

Skehan, P. (2014a) *Investigating a Processing Perspective on Task Performance*. Amsterdam: John Benjamins

Skehan, P. (2014b) Limited attentional capacity, second language performance, and task-based pedagogy. In P. Skehan (ed.) *Processing Perspectives on Task Performance* (pp. 211–260). Amsterdam: John Benjamins.

Skehan, P. and Foster, P. (1997) Task type and task processing conditions as influences on foreign language performance. *Language Teaching Research* 1 (3), 185–211.

Skehan, P. and Foster, P. (1999) The influence of task structure and processing conditions on narrative retellings. *Language Learning* 49 (1), 93–120.

Skehan, P. and Shum, S. (2014) Structure and processing condition in video-based narrative retelling. In P. Skehan (ed.) *Processing Perspectives on Task Performance* (pp. 187–210). Amsterdam: John Benjamins.

Tavakoli, P. and Foster, P. (2008) Task design and second language performance: The effect of narrative type on learner output. *Language Learning* 58 (2), 439–473.

Wang, Z. (2014) On-line time pressure manipulations: L2 speaking performance under five types of planning and repetition conditions. In P. Skehan (ed.) *Processing Perspectives on Task Performance* (pp. 27–62). Amsterdam: John Benjamins.

Wang, Z. and Skehan P. (2014) Structure, lexis, and time perspective: Influences on task performance. In P. Skehan (ed.) *Processing Perspectives on Task Performance* (pp. 155–186). Amsterdam: John Benjamins.

Part 4

Working Memory in L2 Instruction and Development

12 Working Memory in Processing Instruction: The Acquisition of L2 French Clitics

Kindra Santamaria and Gretchen Sunderman

Introduction

A common observance among language instructors is that not all students equally manifest the same language learning abilities. Some students excel on tests and written homework, but are unable to speak intelligibly in class. Other students may possess near native pronunciation yet struggle with grammatical accuracy and reading. It is clear that a wide range of individual differences affect second language (L2) learning. Indeed, individual differences consistently receive attention in the language acquisition literature (see Dörnyei & Skehan [2003] and Robinson [2002] for reviews).

Teachers and researchers have long acknowledged that individual differences in L2 learning exist. Indeed, even textbook publishers recognise this fact. Most textbooks do not cater to one specific learning style and are instead produced to address the largest possible audience. For example, *Vis-à-Vis* (Amon *et al.*, 2011) targets auditory and visual learners through its lessons. However, tailoring the lesson plan to different types of learners is still left to the language instructor. Unfortunately, few teachers have the background knowledge or time to accommodate all learners. Moreover, when teachers do attempt to make accommodations for different types of learners, they may be overlooking the cognitive processes one brings to language acquisition. It may not be enough to simply consider whether a student learns better visually or aurally. In fact, there may be underlying cognitive factors mediating any type of L2 learning.

In this chapter, we investigate the role of different cognitive resources in relation to L2 instruction, specifically the teaching of L2 French direct object pronouns. We operationalised cognitive resources as working memory (WM) capacity, measured by reading span (Waters & Caplan, 1996). Briefly, a reading span task measures participants' ability to simultaneously process and judge complex sentences and store the last word of each sentence in short-term memory. Low- and high-span learners of French received instruction targeting direct object pronouns through a specific type of instruction called processing instruction (PI; VanPatten & Cadierno, 1993).

PI is a teaching technique based on the theory of input processing (VanPatten, 1996, 2004, 2007), a theory that focuses on the creation of form-meaning connections during L2 acquisition. According to VanPatten (2005: 268), the principles of input processing specifically related to the processing of morphology are predicated on a limited capacity for processing information. In other words, learners can only absorb a certain amount of input before their WM resources are depleted. PI, unlike many other pedagogical interventions, is based on the psychological processes that occur during comprehension. A key aspect of this technique is that it attempts to alter learners' non-optimal processing strategies so that learners are more likely to make form-meaning connections.

Although VanPatten and colleagues have never explicitly made claims about individual differences and PI, in this chapter, we propose that certain cognitive factors can interact with this particular instructional intervention. We argue that by teaching learners to abandon inefficient strategies in favour of new strategies, specifically as they relate to sentence processing, PI can facilitate more accurate L2 parsing of sentences (i.e. determining who is doing what to whom). For example, PI includes explicit information to the learner that he/she may have a faulty processing strategy for determining who the subject of the sentence may be, and will then try to alter that faulty strategy. Because PI seeks to teach learners more efficient processing strategies, we believe it can be quite instrumental in permitting learners with lower WM to catch up with those of higher WM.

Given our assumption that PI will maximise learners' processing abilities, a critical and unanswered question remains: does PI differentially impact learners with varying cognitive capacities? Is it the case that those individuals with fewer cognitive resources greatly benefit from PI? Alternatively, are those with more cognitive capacities better able to take advantage of the strategies taught through PI than those with less cognitive capacities?

To be clear, this study does not compare PI with a more traditional instructional technique. PI's superiority is well established in the literature (Benati, 2001; Cheng, 2004; Farley, 2004; Sanz, 2004; Toth, 2006; VanPatten & Sanz, 1995; VanPatten et al., 2009; Wong, 2004) and according to Collentine (2004), comparisons between PI and traditional approaches to grammar instruction should be abandoned and instead the focus should remain on examining the underlying input processing mechanisms in L2 acquisition. This study hopes to further this objective by investigating the relationship between the cognitive resources individual learners bring to the acquisition process and the nature of the instruction they receive.

In the following sections, we first discuss general research findings on WM and L2 acquisition. Next, we explain French pronoun acquisition and why it is difficult for L2 learners. In this section, we outline the basis of PI and illustrate how PI attempts to alter inefficient processing strategies when acquiring clitics. Finally, we present our hypotheses about the role of WM in this instruction.

Research on Working Memory

WM is generally understood as a limited capacity system that a person uses for online processing before it is either forgotten or stored in long-term memory. Because adults use strategies and problem-solving abilities to learn an L2 that they did not necessarily need to use when acquiring their native language, WM plays a crucial role in learning the L2. In fact, Ardila (2003) reported that brain activation patterns during WM tasks are more complex when using the L2 than the first language (L1) because it is a more demanding task. In general, the effects of WM are more noticeable in the L2 than in the L1 because L2 processing and storing capacities are quickly compromised due to a high cognitive load (e.g. Harrington, 1992; Hulstijn & Bossers, 1992). It has been shown to play a role in a variety of L2 processes including parsing performance (Juffs, 2004, 2005) and comprehension (Chun & Payne, 2004; Harrington & Sawyer, 1992; Osaka & Osaka, 1992; Osaka et al., 1993).

Researchers interested in the relationship between WM and syntactical processing have found that cognitive capacity plays an important role in parsing complex sentences. Recent online studies include relative clause attachment ambiguities (e.g. Dussias, 2003; Papadopoulou & Clahsen, 2003), wh-movement (e.g. Jackson & Dussias, 2009; Juffs, 2005) and agent identification (e.g. Hopp, 2006; Jackson, 2008). These researchers found that those with high WM showed processing advantages when parsing syntactically complex strings. Individuals with high span were better able to retain information longer and process information more efficiently than those with low span. Fiebach et al. (2001) did an event-related potential (ERP) analysis that investigated German L1 wh-question processing. They found that left-anterior negativity appeared earlier for low WM participants than their high-span counterparts, and was stronger. Longer and stronger left-anterior negativity reflected how the low-span participants were coping with the increased processing demands. Overall, it is clear that WM plays an important role in syntactic processing. In the next section, we discuss a specific syntactic structure in French and discuss the processing difficulties associated with this structure.

French Clitics and Dislocation

It is undisputed today (Blanche-Beneviste, 1997) that spoken French differs quite substantially from what is commonly referred to as standard French. Lambrecht (1981) describes a number of grammatical features that differ between spoken and standard French. A few examples of the features of spoken French include dropping the *ne* in negative statements (e.g. *Je parle pas trop* rather than *Je ne parle pas trop* 'I do not speak too much'), increased use of analytic tenses (e.g. *Il va manger* rather than *Il mangera* 'He will eat') and dislocation (*Les moutons, je les ai déjà mis, moi* 'The sheep I them have already put me') (De Cat, 2007: 227).

Dislocation is a linguistic phenomenon that permits different word orders through syntactic redundancy. In this study, we focus on cases where both the pronoun and its antecedent are in the same sentence. French speakers use dislocation to differentiate between topic and comment, as in (1) from De Cat (2007: 221).

(1) *Tu   les   aimes bien, les colliers?*

You them like a lot the necklaces

'Do you like the necklaces?'

In this sentence, 'the necklaces' are the topic for the speaker even though they are not the subject. Dislocation permits the French language to borrow English stress without sacrificing intonation and rhythm.

One important goal in most post-secondary French programmes is to provide students with the skills to interact with native speakers. The spoken French described by Blanche-Beneviste and Lambrecht is heard frequently in francophone countries, and yet the French taught in many college classrooms is standard French. Recent beginning French textbooks, such as *Deux Mondes* (Terrell *et al.*, 2009) or *Vis-à-Vis* (Amon *et al.*, 2011) do introduce left dislocation as a way to emphasise the subject, but only stress pronouns are used, as in (2) from Amon *et al.* (2011: 328).

(2) *Et   lui, écrit-il   un roman?*

And him write he a novel

'What about him? Is he writing a novel?'

The authors of these textbooks neglect dislocation with unstressed pronouns and do not describe its pragmatic uses.

Thus, a typical student finds himself/herself poorly prepared to comprehend dislocation when he/she encounters it in the streets of the target culture. He/she must rely on the clitic (i.e. subject or object pronoun) to parse the sentence correctly. Although both English and French are subject–verb–object (SVO) languages, French is much more flexible with word order than is English. Trévise (1986) provides 30 examples of word orders permitted by French dislocation. This flexibility with word order forces French speakers to rely on clitics to determine which noun receives agent or subject status in sentences with direct object pronouns. In other words, a native French speaker pays attention to the direct object pronoun when determining who did the action to whom. Native English speakers, who are learning another language, including French, however, tend to assign agent status in relation to the verb rather than pay attention to other cues like animacy or clitics (Heilenman & McDonald, 1993; MacWhinney, 2005). Thus, English speakers prefer to interpret the noun before the verb as the subject and the noun after the verb as the object. They choose to pay attention to word order unless other cues in the sentence do not support the interpretation (i.e. a tree cannot climb a boy).[1]

For example, a beginning learner of French will interpret *Le professeur elle le croit l'étudiante* 'the student believes the professor' incorrectly as 'the professor believes the student' even though the clitics clearly name the student to be the subject and the professor to be the direct object. The student is relying more on word order than on the clitic to determine who is doing what to whom. For this reason, L2 learners of French may benefit from PI to help them overcome relying exclusively on word order for sentence interpretation.

If we now consider the relationship between WM and clitic acquisition, we can see that learners of French must store the clitic's referent until they come across the pronoun. Meanwhile, they must also distinguish the pronoun from definite articles and determine what type of pronoun it is (direct object, indirect object and stress pronouns all have certain words in common). At the same time, they must correctly parse the rest of the sentence. Daneman and Carpenter (1980) found these parsing decisions to be difficult for those with low WM.

Because spoken French deviates considerably from standard French, it is the French instructor's role, in effect, to teach two varieties of the same language. Instructors, however, generally rely on the textbook, which reflects standard French with a little spoken French vocabulary thrown in for good measure. The result, according to Katz and Blyth (2007: 146), is that learners are often taught a sort of hybrid language that is composed of both spoken and written elements.

As a consequence, when direct object pronouns are taught, students are only exposed to the standard French rules. When they encounter dialogues or transcripts that reflect spoken French they are unsure how to parse the sentences. Parsing a linguistic structure they do not encounter as often means that it will take longer for students to make form-meaning connections (McLaughlin, 1987, 1990). Low-span L2 learners begin with less capacity for storing and less efficient processing than do high-span L2 learners (Ardila, 2003). This reduced capacity and inefficiency compromise their ability to notice less meaningful items like clitics (VanPatten, 2005). In the sections below, we discuss how one would present dislocation to students through PI and discuss how PI attempts to alter the learners' form-meaning mappings.

Processing Instruction

PI is comprised of three components. First, learners are given information about a linguistic form. This explicit information occurs in the learner's L1 to ensure an understanding of the linguistic structure. Second, learners are presented with information that helps them to make correct form-meaning connections, usually in the form of specific strategies that guide them to make correct interpretations. Third, learners are given structured input activities. These activities differ from traditional drills because they require the learner to use the linguistic structure to comprehend rather than produce. The linguistic structure is situated in such a way that the learner must interpret it in order to complete the task. Through this combination of explicit information, strategies and activities, learners become proficient at parsing complex syntactical strings.

We argue that PI relieves processing demands because it teaches learners proper strategies to make form-meaning connections. By practicing these strategies through structured input activities, learners can parse complex sentences easier and more efficiently. French sentences with direct object clitics are difficult to parse. Through the processing strategies taught and applied through structured input activities, learners are able to parse clitics more quickly and accurately.

The current study

The purpose of the present study is to examine the interaction between WM and L2 direct object pronoun instruction. The studies described above indicate that high-span L2 learners are better able to understand and parse syntactically complex sentences, such as those with clitics, than are low-span learners. Low-span learners either misinterpret the clitic or they skip over it. Input processing asserts that individual differences in L2 learning are largely a result of learners being limited-capacity processors, and that PI can facilitate form-meaning connections by taking into account learners' processing capacities. Researchers have shown PI to be effective with direct object pronouns (VanPatten & Cadierno, 1993; VanPatten & Fernandez, 2004; VanPatten & Oikkenon, 1996; VanPatten & Sanz, 1995); however, proponents of this framework have yet to investigate whether PI differentially affects learners with varying cognitive capacities.[2] Is it the case that only participants with high span are able to take advantage of the strategies taught in PI? Or will both groups equally benefit from instruction? We hypothesise that all participants will benefit from instruction, but those with high span will score higher on the comprehension and production post-tests than those with low span. The comprehension test asks participants to listen to a French sentence and choose the best English translation. The production test asks participants to fill in the blanks with the correct direct object pronoun and verb conjugation.

Method

Participants

The participants came from second- and third-semester French classes and from three separate American universities.[3] There were 21 participants from the first university, 20 from the second and 21 from the third. Certain participants were excluded from the data pool for various reasons: their L1 was not English, they had studied in the target culture for more than three months, they scored above chance level on the pre-test, they were not present for the entire experiment, they spoke French with their parents or had attended a French immersion school, they scored less than 5 on the reading span test or they rated themselves advanced in Spanish or Italian. Those advanced in Spanish or Italian were excluded because both French and these languages have flexible word orders and advanced speakers are successful in processing complex syntax. There were 51 participants overall.

Materials

Instructional packets

An instructional packet was created that contained explicit instruction on dislocation. Direct objects in English and in French were introduced before dislocation was taught. In accordance with the guidelines in VanPatten and Cadierno (1993), participants received information on the incorrect processing strategy that English learners of French typically use: oftentimes they misinterpret or skip over the direct object pronoun. The structured input activities contained sentences that gave learners practice interpreting dislocated sentences. These activities follow the guidelines laid out in Lee and VanPatten (2003).[4] There were two referential activities and four affective activities that pushed students to interpret sentences by using the direct object pronouns. Referential activities have only one possible answer, whereas affective activities have more than one possible answer and push participants to use the content in the sentence or question to determine which answer best applies to it. Because object pronouns fall in the middle of the sentence, they are often overlooked. The affective activities were designed so that the pronoun was in a prominent position and participants would notice it when determining the meaning of the sentence.

Pre-test/post-test

The pre-test/post-test was created with a split-design in mind, so that one group's pre-test was another group's post-test. For the delayed post-test, participants received the same test they had seen for the pre-test. A split-design prevents participants from learning from the materials through repeated exposure. Each class took the same pre-test/post-test version, but distribution varied across classes within each level. Thus, in each level (second or third semester), half of the sections took the version A pre-test and half took the version B pre-test. The test had an interpretation section and a production section. Word order competed with agreement and case-marking on the interpretation task while it competed with agreement, animacy and case-marking on the production task. Animacy did not compete on the interpretation task because all subject and object pronouns referred to animate objects; this forced participants to pay attention to the clitic pronoun rather than context in order to parse the sentence.

In general, interpretation tasks require participants to comprehend and parse sentences correctly, whereas a production task asks them to write or say a grammatical structure. Unlike VanPatten and Cadierno (1993), the interpretation task in this study had no pictures. Students were forced to pay attention to the cues provided within the sentence. For example, if students were to hear *Il la critique la conductrice le piéton* and had the following two sentences to choose from: *The pedestrian criticises the driver* and *The driver criticises the pedestrian*, they would match each pronoun with its antecedent (*Il* and *le piéton* and *la* and *la conductrice*) in order to determine which English sentence best captures the meaning behind the French sentence. On the production section, learners read a dialogue or unrelated sentences that contained dislocated sentences, and wrote the appropriate direct object pronoun and conjugated the verb in each blank.[5,6]

The pre-test/post-test had 23 items: 15 sentences on the interpretation task and 8 sentences on the production task. The interpretation test contained three word orders: SVO, verb–object–subject (VOS) and object–verb–subject (OVS). Participants heard five sentences of each word order. The five SVO word order sentences were distractors given that it is the predominant word order in English. The remaining items on the interpretation task counted 1 point each, for a total of 10 points. The following example (3) contains VOS word order.

(3) *(Participants hear) Elle le saute le lapin la grenouille.*

$$It_{FEM-NOM} \; it_{MASC-ACC} \text{ jumps the rabbit the frog}$$

'The frog jumps over the rabbit'.

(They choose)   The rabbit jumps over the frog

or

The frog jumps over the rabbit.

Inserted in the production test were three verbs that require an indirect object rather than a direct object. The accompanying blanks elicited three distractors. The other items on the production task counted two points each: 1 point for the correct pronoun and 1 point for its correct placement, for a total of 10 points. The following example (4) comes from a dialogue between Paul and Christine as they clean out the attic.

(4) *Paul:*   *Tu vois cette lampe bleue?*

You see this lamp blue?

'Do you see this blue lamp?'

Christine: *Oh, cette lampe je _____ (détester)!*

'Oh, this lamp I _____ (to detest)!'

The production task used in this study is not a production test like those used in previous PI research, but is instead a discrete-point grammar test. We understand that our production test may bias towards explicit knowledge (see, e.g. Doughty [2003] and Long & Norris [2000] among others who caution against this type of assessment). We will return to this matter in our discussion and conclusion section. The interpretation and production tasks were analysed separately to evaluate the influence of WM on the different tasks.

Working memory test

The reading span test was based on Waters and Caplan (1996). In this task, participants were asked to judge the semantic plausibility of sentences and at the same time try to remember the last word of each sentence, thus requiring both processing and storage of information. The test was administered using PowerPoint presentation software. It was conducted in the participants' native language: English. It consisted of 80 test sentences with an additional 5 practice sentences. For example, the participants would see a sentence such as 'It was the story that told the librarian' and were asked to judge whether the sentence was plausible, and at the same time, remember the word librarian.

The test contained four sets of two, three, four, five and six sentences, half of which were plausible and half of which were not (as in the above example). The sentences were matched in terms of length and did not vary across plausible and implausible sentences or across the sentences in the different set sizes. Participants received a booklet in which to write their responses when asked to judge the semantic plausibility and recall the final words of each sentence. The test booklet contained plausibility and recall pages that contained eight y(es)/n(o) responses or blanks so that participants would not know how many sentences to expect in each set. There were 20 sets in total.

Procedure

The experiment lasted three days. The first day included the WM test and the direct object pre-test. On the reading span test, participants were instructed to read the sentence on the screen and judge its semantic plausibility. At the beginning of each set, participants saw a slide that appeared for two seconds with a fixation point. Next, an entire sentence appeared. The time that each sentence remained visible depended on the sentence word length: 4 seconds (9 words or less), 5 seconds (between 10 and 12 words) and 6 seconds (more than 12 words). The amount of time a sentence remained on a slide was determined through a pilot test. Then, a slide with a question mark appeared for four seconds. During this time, participants marked whether or not they thought the sentence was plausible. If the sentence made sense, they circled 'yes'. If it didn't make sense, they circled 'no'.

Afterwards, either another sentence or a slide with the word RECALL appeared. As soon as the RECALL screen appeared, they turned to the plausibility page as quickly as possible and recalled, in order, the last word of each sentence that they saw. If, for example, the set had five sentences, they should have written five words. RECALL slides were timed to allow participants enough time to write down all of the words from each set but not enough time to reason through their responses: 8 seconds (2 sentences), 9 seconds (3 sentences), 15 seconds (4 sentences), 20 seconds (5 sentences) and 25 seconds (6 sentences). Another set began after each RECALL slide. The PowerPoint presentation had 239 slides and lasted 22 minutes.

Participants were required to have both the plausibility judgement and the recall word correct in order to receive credit for their response. The total number of words correctly recalled was tallied for each participant. We then conducted a median split on the total words recalled with those in the lower-half qualifying as low span and those in the upper-half qualifying as high span. There were 30 low-span and 21 high-span learners on the interpretation and production tests. Participants were identified as having a high WM if they attained a mark above the median WM score of 55 and were identified as having a low WM if they were on or below that score. Similar scoring procedures for WM measures have been used by others in the field (e.g. Chun & Payne, 2004; Kroll *et al.*, 2002). On the second day, instructional treatment and the immediate post-test were given. We began the instructional treatment with explicit instruction and French processing strategies. Participants then spent the rest of the class period engaged in the structured input activities and took an immediate post-test. Two weeks later, the delayed post-test was administered.

Results

Table 12.1 presents the overall means for the learners with high and low WM on the pre-test, post-test and delayed post-test. We discuss the results for the interpretation data separate from the production data. We did not separate the second-semester data from the third-semester data because the results did not differ significantly both with interpretation ($F(2,49)=1.376, p=0.257$) and with production ($F(2,49)=0.463, p=0.631$).

Interpretation test

A repeated measures analysis of variance (ANOVA) was conducted on the interpretation data with one within-subject variable (time: pre-test,

Table 12.1 Means raw scores on interpretation and production tests for low- and high-span learners

Working memory	n	Pre-test M	Pre-test SD	Post-test M	Post-test SD	Delayed post-test M	Delayed post-test SD
Interpretation							
Low	30	3.10	1.72	6.27	2.00	5.27	1.80
High	21	2.71	1.90	7.00	1.76	5.48	2.18
Total	51	2.94	1.79	6.57	1.92	5.35	1.95
Production							
Low	30	0.93	1.70	5.73	3.62	4.40	4.01
High	21	0.52	1.29	7.76	2.88	6.57	3.87
Total	51	0.76	1.54	6.57	3.45	5.29	4.06

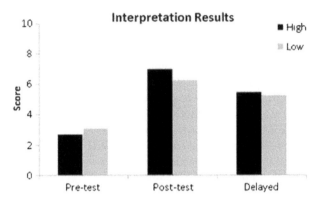

Figure 12.1 Interpretation scores as a function of working memory (WM) across test

post-test, delayed post-test) and one between-subjects variable (WM: high and low span). The ANOVA revealed a significant effect for time ($F(2,49)=61.407$, $p<0.001$) and no additional interactions. In other words, there were no differences between the high- and low-span learners; high- and low-span participants performed similarly on all tests. In reference to improvement over time, the low-span group improved from pre-test to post-test ($p<0.001$) and fell from post-test to delayed post-test ($p<0.05$). The high-span group also improved from pre-test to post-test ($p<0.001$) and fell from post-test to delayed post-test ($p<0.01$). Overall, both low- and high-span learners showed similar patterns of improvement on the immediate post-test, thus suggesting that in terms of the comprehension measure, the low-span learners were able to perform as well as the high-span learners. Figure 12.1 summarises these results.

Production test

A repeated measures ANOVA was conducted on the production data with one within-subject variable (time: pre-test, post-test, delayed post-test) and one between-subjects variable (WM: high and low span). The ANOVA revealed a significant effect for time ($F(2,49)=76.754$, $p<0.001$) and a significant interaction between time and WM ($F(2,49)=4.008$, $p<0.05$). Simple effect tests revealed that the high-span group outperformed the low-span group on both the post-test and delayed post-test. In other words, the high-span learners were more accurate in production compared to the low-span learners. In reference to improvement over time, the low-span group improved from pre-test to post-test ($p<0.001$) and fell from post-test to delayed post-test ($p<0.05$). The high-span group also improved from pre-test to post-test ($p<0.001$). However, there were no significant differences for the high-span group between the post-test and delayed post-test, revealing that the high-span group was able to

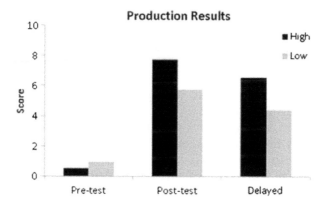

Figure 12.2 Production as a function of working memory (WM) across test

utilise their cognitive resources to recall the instructional treatment. Put differently, the high-span learners did not suffer the same decline from post-test to delayed post-test, suggesting that the additional cognitive resources may have provided an instructional boost for these individuals. Figure 12.2 summarises these results.

To summarise, both span groups performed similarly on the interpretation test, improving from pre-test to post-test and then falling from post-test to delayed post-test. On the production test, however, the high-span group was superior on both post-tests, and in particular, maintained their high level of performance in the delayed post-test. In the next section, we discuss the implications of these results.

Discussion

As a starting point and in response to the general question, do learners with certain cognitive resources respond differently to PI, the answer is that it depends on the modality. Although the interpretation data indicated no differential role for WM, the production data suggest an important role for WM.

With respect to our first hypothesis, namely that all participants would benefit from instruction, we find that this is supported, regardless of the modality of testing. On both the interpretation and production tests, both low-span and high-span participants improved from pre-test to post-test. Although both groups' scores dropped on the interpretation delayed post-test, only the low-span group's scores dropped on the production test. We discuss this result further below. Overall, however, all delayed post-test scores are significantly higher than pre-test scores, indicating a clear effect of instructional treatment.

The second and most important hypothesis related to the interaction between WM resources and PI. We argued that those individuals with high span would score higher on the post-test and delayed post-tests than those with low span. On the interpretation test, this idea was not supported by the data. There were no differences between the WM groups. On the production test, the high-span group did perform better on both post-tests.

Why did the findings show an influence for cognitive capacity on production but not interpretation? One alternative to consider is that the differences in WM become more evident on the more challenging task, production. On the production test, participants were required to determine the direct object noun from the dislocated sentences and write down the correct pronoun that agreed with it. They also had to remember to adjust the pronoun to an *l'* before a verb that began with a vowel. The task of parsing the sentence, deciding on an appropriate direct object pronoun and selecting its placement in relation to the verb proved a challenging task. For those individuals with greater WM resources, this task was not as challenging.

This result parallels recent evidence from Sunderman and Kroll (2009) who also found a significant role for WM in the production task, but not the interpretation task. Sunderman and Kroll were investigating the effects of the study abroad experience and WM on lexical comprehension and production. They found that without a certain threshold of cognitive resources (i.e. WM resources), a study abroad experience would be of little benefit in terms of L2 production. The researchers argue that being able to accurately select and produce a word in the L2 is by far the more difficult task compared to comprehension and thus any additional resources greatly benefit that process. The findings of the current study are in line with this proposal. Our high-span learners were better able to take advantage of the effects of PI and the benefits of such instruction were durable.

Another alternative that we must consider is related to the nature of the assessment used. Recall that the production test was a fill-in-the-blank task, or a discrete-point grammar test. The nature of this task may tap more explicit information and therefore could explain why the learners with more WM resources were more successful at the task.

Conclusion

This study was one of the first of its kind to look at the interaction between WM and PI. However, before any definitive conclusions can be drawn from the present study, we feel a replication of this experiment must be conducted in which several modifications are made. First, we inadvertently did not control for person-number and animacy issues in a few sentences, and thus learners could have relied on something other than the cues we wanted them to attend to in order to correctly provide responses during the treatment. Future research using PI as the treatment should control for these intervening variables. However, despite this limitation in the materials, there was still a clear effect of instruction. Second, the assessment used in the production task was not a traditional PI-type production task. Would we find an effect for WM if we altered the assessment task? While it is tempting to begin looking at the relationship between WM and various other instructional techniques, it would be prudent to first replicate the above findings with altered materials and assessment measures.

We do see a strong future for investigating the role of WM in L2 processing and instruction. For example, perhaps a question for future research on WM could arise from recent work by Fernandez (2008). Instead of a typical pre-test/post-test design, Fernandez conducted an online study using trials-to-criterion to evaluate the effects of explicit instruction with two linguistic structures: OVS word order with Spanish clitic pronouns and the Spanish subjunctive. She divided the participants for each study into two groups: a PI group with explicit instruction and a structured input group without explicit instruction. She found that explicit instruction made no difference with the clitic pronouns even though it had a significant effect with the Spanish subjunctive. More importantly, Fernandez found that even though the PI group may have started correctly processing the subjunctive earlier, the SI group eventually caught up. What this means in terms of our study is that perhaps the high-span learners initially outperformed the low-span learners, but with time these differences would not exist. Future research using the trials-to-criterion measure that Fernandez adopted would be a fruitful area of investigation with issues of WM.

In the end, we want to encourage other researchers to begin to address the role that individual differences may play with instruction. Although our study tentatively found a role for WM with PI and production, more research is clearly needed. Perhaps future research will continue to address the interplay of instruction and individual differences found in L2 classrooms.

Notes

(1) English has a relatively weak morphological structure. Its pronouns do not distinguish for case or gender (except with possession). French pronouns, however, distinguish for number, case and gender. Lexically, nouns carry all of the lexical information in English. Pronouns simply stand in for nouns to avoid redundancy. In French, instead of assuming that pronouns replace nouns, speakers assume that nouns are lexicalised representations of pronouns (Heilenman & McDonald, 1993: 544). Syntactically, English object pronouns follow the verb while French object pronouns precede it.

(2) An exception is Erlam (2005) who found a relationship between WM and the group that received structured input activities (processing instruction). While her study suggests that there is an interaction between WM and instruction type, her materials do not follow the guidelines for structured input activities. Thus, her findings are debatable and leave open the question of a role for WM within PI.

(3) Data were collected in 2006 at one university and then in 2008 at two additional universities.

(4) In classic PI research on word order and clitics in Spanish, person-number and animacy are controlled for so that the subject and the object are equally capable of performing the action. It was brought to the authors' attention by a reviewer that a few of the sentences in the structured input activities in the current study contained varying person-number and animacy information, thus undermining the full potential of what PI is supposed to do. We encourage readers to see Wong (2004) and Farley (2005) for current guidelines on designing SI activities.

(5) The pre-test/post-test and SI activities slightly varied in the 2006 and 2008 versions. The materials described above reflect the 2008 materials. Explicit instruction and scoring procedures remained the same. The 2006 pre-test/post-test had 10 items in the interpretation task while the 2008 assessment had 15 items. The same word orders were used and the same scoring procedure was used; the number of items was increased so as to give participants five samples of each word order. The 2006 production assessment had five unrelated sentences with a picture for each sentence. Participants filled in the blank with the correct direct object and conjugation of the verb. The 2008 version had a short story where participants filled in five blanks with the correct direct object and conjugation of the verb and three distractor blanks that required indirect objects rather than direct objects. We believe that these two versions evaluated the same type of knowledge and processing ability. In addition the participants who used the different versions had similar results.

(6) The production test here only evaluated written clitic production. It is possible that a test evaluating oral production would be a better measure. VanPatten and Sanz (1995) evaluated this possibility and found no significant differences between the written and oral measures for improvement from pre-test to post-tests. However, they found that both the treatment and no treatment groups scored significantly higher on written production than on oral production, demonstrating that they were more comfortable with the written measure.

References

Amon, E., Muyskens, J. and Omaggio Hadley, A. (2011) *Vis-à-Vis* (5th edn). New York: McGraw-Hill.

Ardila, A. (2003) Language representation and working memory with bilinguals. *Journal of Communication Disorders* 36, 233–240.

Benati, A. (2001) A comparative study of the effects of processing instruction and output-based instruction on the acquisition of the Italian future tense. *Language Teaching Research* 5, 95–127.

Blanche-Beneviste, C. (1997) *Approches de la langue parlée en français: L'essentiel français*. Paris: Ophrys.

Cheng, A. (2004) Processing instruction and Spanish *ser* and *estar*: Forms with semantic-aspectual values. In B. VanPatten (ed.) *Processing Instruction: Theory, Research, and Commentary* (pp. 119–141). Mahwah, NJ: Lawrence Erlbaum Associates.

Chun, D.M. and Payne, J.S. (2004) What makes students click: Working memory and look-up behavior. *System* 32, 481–503.

Collentine, J. (2004) Commentary: Where PI research has been and where it should be going. In B. Van Patten (ed.) *Processing Instruction: Theory, Research, and Commentary* (pp. 97–118). Mahwah, NJ: Lawrence Erlbaum Associates.

Daneman, M. and Carpenter, P.A. (1980) Individual differences in working memory and reading. *Journal of Verbal Learning and Verbal Behavior* 19, 450–466.

De Cat, C. (2007) *French Dislocation: Interpretation, Syntax, Acquisition*. Oxford: Oxford University Press.

Dörnyei, Z. and Skehan, P. (2003) Individual differences in second language learning. In C. Doughty and M. Long (eds) *The Handbook of Second Language Acquisition* (pp. 589–630). Oxford: Blackwell Publishing.

Doughty, C. (2003) Instructed SLA: Constraints, compensation, and enhancement. In C. Doughty and M. Long (eds) *The Handbook of Second Language Acquisition* (pp. 256–310). Oxford: Blackwell Publishing.

Dussias, P.E. (2003) Syntactic ambiguity resolution in second language learners: Some effects of binguality on L1 and L2 processing strategies. *Studies in Second Language Acquisition* 25, 529–557.

Erlam, R. (2005) Language aptitude and its relationship to instructional effectiveness in second language acquisition. *Language Teaching Research* 9, 147–171.

Farley, A. (2004) Processing instruction and the Spanish subjunctive: Is explicit information needed? In B. VanPatten (ed.) *Processing Instruction: Theory, Research, and Commentary* (pp. 227–239). Mahwah, NJ: Lawrence Erlbaum Associates.

Fernandez, C. (2008) Reexamining the role of explicit information in processing instruction. *Studies in Second Language Acquisition* 30, 277–305.

Fiebach, C., Schlesewsky, M. and Friederici, A. (2001) Syntactic working memory and the establishment of filler-gap dependencies: Insights from ERPs and fMRI. *Journal of Psycholinguistic Research* 30, 321–338.

Harrington, M. (1992) Working memory capacity as a constraint on L2 development. In R.J. Harris (ed.) *Cognitive Processing in Bilinguals* (pp. 123–135). Amsterdam: North Holland.

Harrington, M. and Sawyer, M. (1992) L2 working memory capacity and reading skill. *Studies in Second Language Acquisition* 14, 25–38.

Heilenman, L.K. and McDonald, J. (1993) Processing strategies in L2 learners of French: The role of transfer. *Language Learning* 43, 507–557.

Hopp, H. (2006) Syntactic features and reanalysis in near-native processing. *Second Language Research* 22, 369–397.

Hulstijn, J. and Bossers, B. (1992) Individual differences in L2 proficiency as a function of L1 proficiency. *European Journal of Cognitive Psychology* 4, 341–353.

Jackson, C.N. (2008) Processing strategies and the comprehension of sentence-level input by L2 learners of German. *System* 36, 388–406.

Jackson, C.N. and Dussias, P.E. (2009) Cross-linguistic differences and their impact on L2 sentence processing. *Bilingualism: Language and Cognition* 12, 65–82.

Juffs, A. (2004) Representation, processing and working memory in a second language. *Transactions of the Philological Society* 102, 199–225.

Juffs, A. (2005) The influence of first language on the processing of wh-movement in English as a second language. *Second Language Research* 21, 121–151.

Katz, S. and Blythe, C. (2007) *Teaching French Grammar in Context*. New Haven, CT: Yale University Press.

Kroll, J., Michael, E., Tokowicz, N. and Dufour, R. (2002) The development of lexical fluency in a second language. *Second Language Research* 18, 137–171.

Lambrecht, K. (1981) *Topic, Antitopic, and Verb-Agreement in Non-Standard French (Pragmatics and Beyond* vol. II: 6). Amsterdam: John Benjamins.

Lee, J. and VanPatten, B. (2003) *Making Communicative Language Teaching Happen*. New York: McGraw-Hill.

Long, M.H. and Norris, J.M. (2000) Task-based language teaching and assessment. In M. Byram (ed.) *Encyclopedia of Language Teaching* (pp. 597–603). London: Routledge.

MacWhinney, B. (2005) A unified model of language acquisition. In J.F. Kroll and A.M. DeGroot (eds) *Handbook of Bilingualism* (pp. 49–67). Oxford: Oxford University Press.

McLaughlin, B. (1987) *Theories of Second Language Learning*. London: Edward Arnold.

McLaughlin, B. (1990) Restructuring. *Applied Linguistics* 11, 113–128.

Osaka, M. and Osaka, N. (1992) Language-independent working memory as measured by Japanese and English reading span tests. *Bulletin of the Psychonomic Society* 30, 287–289.

Osaka, M., Osaka, N. and Groner, R. (1993) Language-independent working memory: Evidence from German and French reading span tests. *Bulletin of the Psychonomic Society* 31, 117–118.

Papadopoulou, D. and Clahsen, H. (2003) Parsing strategies in L1 and L2 sentence processing: A study of relative clause attachment in Greek. *Studies in Second Language Acquisition* 25, 501–528.

Robinson, P. (2002) *Individual Differences and Instructed Language Learning*. Philadelphia, PA: John Benjamins.

Sanz, C. (2004) Computer delivered implicit vs. explicit feedback in processing instruction. In B. VanPatten (ed.) *Processing Instruction: Theory, Research, and Commentary* (pp. 241–55). Mahwah, NJ: Lawrence Erlbaum Associates.

Sunderman, G. and Kroll, J.F. (2009) When study abroad experience fails to deliver: The internal resources threshold effect. *Applied Psycholinguistics* 30, 1–21.

Terrell, T., Rogers, M., Kerr, B. and Spielmann, G. (2009) *Deux Mondes: A Communicative Approach* (6th edn). New York: McGraw-Hill.

Toth, P. (2006) Processing instruction and a role for output in second language acquisition. *Language Learning* 56, 319–385.

Trévise, A. (1986) Is it transferable, topicalization? In E. Kellerman and M. Sharwood Smith (eds) *Crosslinguistic Influence in Second Language Acquisition* (pp. 186–206). New York: Pergamon Press.

VanPatten, B. (1996) *Input Processing and Grammar Instruction in Second Language Acquisition*. Norwood, NJ: Ablex Publishing Corporation.

VanPatten, B. (2004) Several reflections on why there is good reason to continue researching the effects of processing instruction. In B. VanPatten (ed.) *Processing Instruction: Theory, Research, and Commentary* (pp. 325–335). Mahwah, NJ: Lawrence Erlbaum Associates.

VanPatten, B. (2005) Processing instruction. In C. Sanz (ed.) *Mind & Context in Adult Second Language Acquisition* (pp. 267–281). Washington, DC: Georgetown University Press.

VanPatten, B. (2007) *Theories in Second Language Acquisition: An Introduction*. Mahwah, NJ: Lawrence Erlbaum Associates.

VanPatten, B. and Cadierno, T. (1993) Explicit instruction and input processing. *Studies in Second Language Acquisition* 15, 225–243.

VanPatten, B. and Sanz, C. (1995) From input to output: Processing instruction and communicative tasks. In F. Eckman, D. Highland, P. Lee, J. Mileham and R. Weber (eds) *Second Language Acquisition Theory and Pedagogy* (pp. 169–185). Mahwah, NJ: Lawrence Erlbaum Associates.

VanPatten, B. and Oikkenon, S. (1996) Explanation vs. structured input in processing instruction. *Studies in Second Language Acquisition* 15, 225–243.

VanPatten, B. and Fernandez, C. (2004) The long-term effects of processing instruction. In B. VanPatten (ed.) *Processing Instruction: Theory, Research, and Commentary* (pp. 273–289). Mahwah, NJ: Lawrence Erlbaum Associates.

VanPatten, B., Farmer, J.L. and Clardy, C.L. (2009) Processing instruction and meaning-based output instruction: A response to Keating and Farley (2008). *Hispania* 92, 116–126.

Waters, G. and Caplan, D. (1996) The measurement of verbal working memory capacity and its relation to reading comprehension. *The Quarterly Journal of Experimental Psychology* 49A, 51–79.

Wong, W. (2004) Processing instruction in French: The roles of explicit information and structured input. In B. VanPatten (ed.) *Processing Instruction: Theory, Research, and Commentary* (pp. 187–205). Mahwah, NJ: Lawrence Erlbaum Associates.

13 Working Memory, Learning Conditions and the Acquisition of L2 Syntax

Kaitlyn M. Tagarelli, Mailce Borges Mota and Patrick Rebuschat

Introduction

As this volume shows, working memory capacity (WMC) seems to play an important role in second language acquisition (SLA). However, there is some evidence that the role of WMC may change across different learning conditions, though the extent to which the predictive power of WMC is mediated by learning conditions remains unclear. Recently, research into individual differences and pedagogical approaches to SLA has merged because of the inextricable link between the two. As Robinson (2002: xi) claims, neither line of research on its own can account for differences in second language (L2) attainment; it is rather the 'interaction between learner characteristics, and learning contexts' that results in a range of success rates in L2 learners. Fundamental differences between learning contexts may be crucial in determining the type of knowledge a learner will acquire.

In cognitive psychology, and with increasing frequency in L2 research, implicit and explicit learning are understood to be distinct processes which allow for the acquisition of different types of knowledge (e.g. DeKeyser, 2003; Reber, 1989). Conditions designed to promote implicit or explicit learning are presumed to tap into separate processes, which may not be modulated by individual differences in the same way (Reber, 1993; Robinson, 2005a). Further research in this area should help determine how individual differences and learning conditions can interact most favourably to improve L2 attainment. The current study investigates the relationship between WMC and the acquisition of L2 syntax. In particular, this study seeks to understand whether WMC predicts L2 syntactic development in two conditions designed to promote either implicit or explicit learning.

Working Memory and Implicit and Explicit Processes in L2

The psychological literature suggests that differences in how aptitude influences performance in implicit and explicit learning conditions are based on the fact that these two systems are fundamentally distinct. Reber *et al.* (1991: 888) explain this distinction by evoking the idea of the 'primacy of the implicit' (see also Reber, 1989, 1990, 1993, 2003; Reber *et al.*, 1980). The basis of this primacy is that implicit processes have phylogenetically antique biological substrates, which vary little among 'corticated species' (Reber, 1989: 232), and even less so from human to human. Therefore, implicit processes should be more robust (i.e. less susceptible to neurological impairments) than explicit processes, unconscious functions should show tighter distributions among the population than conscious functions and individual differences should not contribute to variance in implicit processes, whereas they should in explicit processes. More recent evidence challenging Reber and colleagues, suggests that implicit learning is indeed an ability that varies across individuals (Kaufman *et al.*, 2010).

In SLA, there is some disagreement as to which types of learning conditions might be more susceptible to individual differences. Krashen (1981) suggested that aptitude should only predict learner success when emphasis is placed on formal accuracy and metalinguistic explanations, which may promote more explicit learning processes and the development of explicit knowledge. On the other hand, Skehan (2002) proposed that the controlled and structured nature of classroom environments makes aptitude less important in such contexts and more important in informal, and more demanding, environments where learners must rely on their own capacities. This seems to suggest that individual differences may be more important in an immersion-like setting, which may promote more implicit processes and the development of more implicit knowledge.

The findings to date are inconclusive. In a study comparing learning in implicit and explicit conditions to intelligence quotient (IQ), Reber *et al.* (1991) indeed found greater variance in performance on grammaticality judgement tasks (GJTs) between participants in the explicit condition than in the implicit condition, and a significant correlation between accuracy and IQ for the former group, but not for the latter. In an extended replication of this study, Robinson (2005b) also found that there was less variance in implicit than explicit learning. However, he found that learning in the implicit conditions was significantly negatively correlated with IQ, specifically the components of IQ that measure verbal abilities, whereas there were no correlations between explicit learning and IQ. An additional learning condition, incidental learning of Samoan, was not related to any aptitude measures. In a study using the artificial language eXperanto, de Graaff (1997) found that the explicit group outperformed the implicit group, but that there were positive correlations between aptitude, as measured by the words in sentences subtest of the Modern Language Aptitude Test (MLAT), and performance in both implicit and explicit conditions.

Erlam (2005) investigated the effects of aptitude on learning in three different conditions: deductive instruction (+rule-explanation, +production-practice, –input-based activities), inductive instruction (–rule-explanation, +production-practice, +input-based activities) and structured input (+rule-explanation, –production-practice, +input-based activities). There were few correlations for the deductive group, suggesting that 'instruction that provides students with explicit rule explanation and then gives them opportunities to engage in language production tends to benefit all language learners' (Erlam, 2005: 163). The words in sentences subtest correlated positively with performance in the inductive and structured input groups, analytic ability correlated negatively with performance in the inductive group and 'working memory capacity' (measured by a multisyllabic word test of the phonological loop that tested only storage, not processing) correlated with performance in the structured input group. Erlam concluded that students with higher WMC are better input processors, but it must be noted that this claim applies to phonological short-term memory (PSTM), rather than WM, because of the nature of the task used. Nevertheless, Erlam's results, and those of the other studies outlined above, demonstrate that cognitive abilities have differential effects on learning outcomes in different learning conditions.

Few studies have specifically looked at the interaction between WMC and instructional contexts. Considering the importance placed on the central executive in WM (Cowan, 1999; Engle, 2001; Engle et al., 1999), one might expect this component of aptitude to be a good predictor of language success in explicit rather than implicit learning conditions because explicit processes are closely related to attention, whereas implicit processes are not (DeKeyser, 2003; Schmidt, 2001). Robinson (2005b) measured WMC with a reading span task, and found that WMC was positively correlated with learning Samoan in an incidental learning condition, but was not correlated with implicit or explicit learning. Based on these findings, Robinson (2005a: 55) concludes that 'the ability to process for meaning while simultaneously switching attention to form during problems in semantic processing [is] an ability strongly related to working memory capacity', suggesting that incidental learning involves attention as well. In a study of Japanese fifth-grade students, Ando et al. (1992, as cited in Mackey et al., 2002) found an interesting interaction between WMC, as measured by complex span tasks, and L2 success. Children with high WMC benefited from an explicit teaching approach (namely, form-focused instruction), whereas children with low WMC benefited from an implicit teaching approach (communicatively oriented, meaning-focused instruction). The relationship between WMC and learning in explicit and implicit conditions appears to be a complicated one.

The Current Study

The study of the relationship between WMC and learning conditions is still in its infancy, and the results to date are inconclusive. With respect to implicit and explicit learning conditions, there is a lack of consensus on the operationalisation of these terms, and the type of instruction, learning and knowledge are often confounded, which makes findings even more difficult to interpret. This study aims to directly test the role of WM in implicit and explicit learning conditions, and to further explore this issue by assessing the degree to which these conditions result in implicit and explicit knowledge. There are two main research questions:

(1) Does WMC affect an individual's ability to learn L2 syntax?
(2) Does WMC have a differential effect on learning under incidental and intentional conditions?

A broader goal aims to answer the following question:
If WMC is predictive of L2 learning, which WM tasks best demonstrate this?

The learning conditions in this study are *incidental* and *intentional* conditions, which are designed to promote the acquisition of implicit and explicit knowledge, respectively. However, it is likely that learners will acquire both implicit and explicit knowledge in both conditions (Schmidt, 1994), so they are not simply named 'implicit' and 'explicit' learning conditions.

Method

Participants

The participants in this study were 62 native speakers of English (M_{age}=22.7, SD=6.0) with no background in German or any other verb-second (V2) language. Participants were randomly assigned to one of two experimental conditions: *incidental* and *intentional*. There were no significant differences between experimental groups across the variables age, gender, occupation (student vs non-student) and number of languages acquired (all $p > 0.05$). Participants received gift cards as compensation.

Table 13.1 Verb placement rules and stimulus creation in the semi-artificial language

Sentence type	Rule	Stimulus
V2	Finite verb placed in second phrasal position of main clauses that are not preceded by a subordinate clause.	In the evening *ate* Rose excellent dessert at a restaurant.
V2-VF	Finite verb placed in final position in all subordinate clauses.	George repeated today that the movers his furniture *scratched*.
VF-V1	Finite verb placed in first position in main clauses that are preceded by a subordinate clause.	Since his teacher criticism voiced, *put* Chris more effort into his homework.

Stimulus material

Semi-artificial language

A semi-artificial language consisting of English lexicon and German syntax was used to generate the stimuli for this experiment (see also Rebuschat, 2008; Rebuschat & Williams, 2006, 2009). There are two main advantages to using a semi-artificial grammar of this nature as opposed to the finite state grammars commonly used in artificial grammar learning paradigms: (i) the grammatical complexity of a natural language is maintained and (ii) semantic information is present. The sentences generated by the grammar followed three specific verb-order rules, as exemplified in Table 13.1.

A total of 150 sentences were generated by this grammar, in addition to 30 ungrammatical sentences. The training set consisted of 60 plausible and 60 implausible sentences, all of which were grammatical. The testing set consisted of 30 grammatical and 30 ungrammatical sentences, all of which were plausible (see Table 13.2). Plausibility and grammaticality were manipulated so that participants could judge each sentence based on one of these dimensions, depending on the task.

Ungrammatical sentences were similar to the grammatical ones, but the verb phrase (VP) position was incorrect (*V1, *V3, *V4, *VF, *VF-V2, *V1-VF; see Table 13.2). Plausible and implausible items were designed

Table 13.2 Distribution of sentence types across training and testing sets.

		Grammatical	Ungrammatical
Training set	Plausible	60	
	Implausible	60	
Testing set	Plausible	30	30
	Implausible		

so that the final word determined a sentence's plausibility, thus forcing participants to process the entire auditory string before judging its plausibility. Examples of plausible and implausible sentences are:

Plausible: Chris entertained today his colleagues with an interesting performance.

Implausible: Rose abandoned in the evening her cats on planet Venus.

All sentences were in the past tense. They were read aloud by a male native speaker of British English, digitally recorded on a Sony Mini-Disc player (MZ-R700) and edited to trim silence before and after each sentence using sound processing software (Audacity, version 1.2.4). Stimuli and experiment instructions were presented on a Macintosh computer using SuperLab, version 4.

The 120 sentences in the training set were evenly divided among verb placement rules (see Table 13.2). That is, 40 sentences followed the V2 sentence pattern, 40 followed the V2-VF pattern and another 40 the VF-V1 pattern. Half of all sentences for each verb placement rule were plausible and half were implausible. A frequency analysis of the training set showed that the average sentence length was 9.7 words per sentence in V2 constructions (9.9 for plausible items, 9.5 for implausible ones), 12.9 for VF-V1 constructions (13.2 plausible, 12.7 implausible) and 10.8 words per sentence for V2-VF constructions (10.6 plausible, 11 implausible).

The testing set consisted of 60 new sentences and was subdivided into 30 grammatical and 30 ungrammatical items, as described above. All sentences were new because this allowed us to test the transfer of grammatical rule knowledge. With the exception of a limited number of function words (e.g. articles, prepositions, etc.), no verbs or any other words were repeated from the training set. Table 13.2 illustrates the syntactic patterns that could occur in the testing phase.

A frequency analysis of the testing set indicated that the average sentence length was 11.1 words per sentence for grammatical items and 11.6 for ungrammatical items. There was no significant difference between grammatical and ungrammatical sentences with regard to sentence length ($F(1,193)=0.922$, $p>0.05$), so sentence length was not a reliable cue to grammaticality in the testing phase.

Working memory capacity measures

As mentioned above, complex span tasks have been shown to be more reliable predictors of language learning than simple span tasks. Therefore, we chose two complex span WM tasks. We also used non-verbal tasks (Daneman & Merikle, 1996; Linck *et al.*, 2014) because these have been shown to be strong predictors of language abilities (Daneman & Merikle, 1996; Linck *et al.*, 2014; Turner & Engle, 1989) but do not present a strong confound with first language (L1) ability that verbal tasks might.

Operation-word span task

The operation-word span task (OSpan) consists of solving simple math problems and remembering words simultaneously. This task was designed by Turner and Engle (1989), and it is meant to involve reading in a very broad sense. We used an L1 version of this task for several reasons. First, English was the only language common to all participants. Second, L1 abilities are less variable across individuals than L2 abilities, and thus performance on this task should not be substantially influenced by language-related ability. Finally, WM has been shown to be language independent; that is, its efficiency does not depend on the language of the task (Osaka & Osaka, 1992). In the OSpan task, participants saw an equation and word appear on a computer screen. They read the equation aloud, stated whether the answer provided was correct or not and then read the following word aloud. For example, if the participant saw 'IS $(6\times2)+1=10$? CAT', he/she would say 'Is six times two plus one equal to ten...no (because $(6'2)+1=13$, not 10)...cat'. Following instructions from Unsworth et al. (2005), they were asked to read all stimuli aloud to prevent rehearsal. Once the participant said the word, the researcher advanced to the next operation and word in the set. There was no time limit for responses. This allowed the participant ample time to process the information on the screen but reduced the amount of rehearsal time. However, it should be noted that this self-pacing potentially led to variability in the task due to factors such as mathematical ability and processing speed.

Each participant was presented with 12 sets overall, with 2–5 words in a set. At the end of each set, participants saw three question marks, which was their cue to write down all of the words that they could remember from that set on an answer sheet provided. The OSpan was based on a version created by Unsworth et al. (2005) and adapted to be presented on a Macintosh computer using SuperLab, version 4. Participants were awarded one point for every word remembered in the correct order, for a total possible score of 42 points. To ensure that both storage and processing components of memory were engaged during the task, participants had to reach the criterion of 85% accuracy on the math operations for their score to be counted. All participants reached this criterion, which was slightly stricter than Unsworth et al.'s (2005) criterion of 80%.

Letter-number ordering task

The letter-number ordering task (LNOT) is part of the WAIS-III Intelligence Scale (Wechsler, 1997). It is particularly useful in testing an individual's ability to process sequential information. For this experiment, the LNOT was taken from van den Noort et al. (2006, based on Wechsler, 2000) and translated into English. In this task, the researcher read aloud a series of letters and numbers, starting at two letters per series and going up to eight letters per series. The participant was asked to repeat the letters and numbers, but specifically to repeat the numbers in numerical order and then the letters in alphabetical order. For example, if the researcher read 'A-7' the participant would repeat '7-A'. If the researcher read 'W-1-K-5', the participant would repeat '1-5-K-W'. Participants received one point for every series repeated back correctly, for a maximum of 21 points. If a participant missed three series in a row, the researcher discontinued the task and counted the participant's score from all of the previous series.

Procedure

Participants attended two experimental sessions: an artificial language learning session and a WM test session. For each participant, the WM session occurred at least one day and no more than two weeks after the artificial grammar learning session. An overview of the procedure is shown in Figure 13.1.

Session 1: Artificial language learning

All participants participated in an artificial grammar learning session, which consisted of an exposure phase and testing. The testing session was the same for both groups but the exposure phase differed across groups.

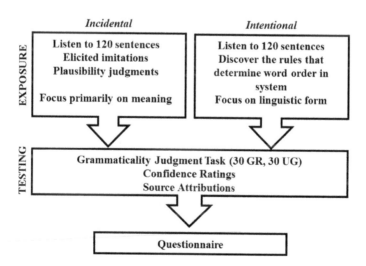

Figure 13.1 Procedure for Session 1: Artificial grammar learning paradigm

Exposure phase

The training sentences were presented to each participant in random order. The exposure phase began with a short practice session, which consisted of four practice trials which were not repeated in the actual testing set. The entire exposure phase took approximately 30–45 minutes.

Incidental group. Participants in the incidental group (n=31) were asked to listen to 120 sentences, repeat each sentence after a delayed prompt (1500 ms) and judge the plausibility of each sentence. They were told that they were being tested on their ability to understand the meaning of sentences with scrambled word order, but they were not told that they would be tested. The focus of their task was therefore primarily on meaning.

Intentional group. Participants in the intentional group (n=31) were asked to listen to the same 120 sentences as the incidental group, but they were told that there was a complex rule system that determined the word order of the sentences. They were asked to try to discover the rules by simply listening carefully to each sentence, and they were told that they would be tested on the rules later on in the session. The focus of their task was therefore primarily on form.

Testing

At the end of the training, participants in the incidental group were told and participants in the intentional group were reminded that the word order of the sentences presented during training followed a complex rule system. They then listened to 60 new sentences, 30 of which followed the grammar described above and 30 of which were ungrammatical. For each sentence, participants made a grammaticality judgement, rated their confidence (0=not confident, 5=somewhat confident, 9=very confident) and stated the basis for their judgement (guess, intuition, memory or rule knowledge). These judgements were collected to determine the extent to which the participants' judgement and structural knowledge were conscious or unconscious (Dienes, 2008; Dienes & Scott, 2005; see Rebuschat, 2013 for review).

In the case of the source attributions, participants were instructed to choose guess if they could have just as easily made a decision by flipping a coin. The intuition category indicated that the participant was confident in his/her decision but did not know why it was right. The memory category indicated that the judgement was based on the recollection of parts or entire sentences from the training phase. Finally, the rule knowledge category indicated that the participant based his/her decision on a rule that was acquired during the training phase and would be able to report the rule at the end of the experiment. The test sentences were presented to each participant in random order. The testing phase began with a short practice session, which consisted of four practice trials which were not repeated in the actual testing set. The entire testing phase took approximately 15 minutes.

The incidental and intentional groups in this study were compared to a group of 15 untrained control subjects from a previous study (Rebuschat, 2008, experiment 3). These subjects completed the exact same testing session as the intentional and incidental groups.

Questionnaire

All participants filled out a debriefing questionnaire, providing information on their levels of awareness with regard to the rule system. The questionnaire also included biographical data, such as age, gender, occupation, major field of study and language background.

Session 2: Complex working memory capacity tasks

On a separate day from Session 1, participants performed the OSpan and the LNOT. The first author was present during the entirety of Session 2 and personally administered both WM tests. The order of these tasks was counterbalanced across participants. The entire Session 2 lasted approximately 30 minutes.

Results

Performance on the GJT served as the measure of learning. Verbal reports, confidence ratings and source attributions were employed to determine the extent to which participants were aware of having acquired knowledge and whether the acquired knowledge was conscious or not. Performance on the OSpan and the LNOT served as measures of WMC. Of the 62 individuals who participated in this study, 7 were excluded because they did not follow directions correctly in the testing phase. We analysed the data of 29 participants from the incidental group, 26 participants from the intentional group and the 15 untrained controls from Rebuschat (2008, experiment 3).

Grammaticality judgements

An analysis of accuracy for each group shows that the incidental group made accurate grammaticality judgements for 58.9% (SD=8.6%, SE=1.6%) of trials, while the intentional group made accurate judgements for 71.2% (SD=15.5%, SE=3.0%) of trials. Accuracy for controls was 43.0% (SD=5.1%, SE=1.3%). A one-way analysis of variance (ANOVA) showed that the effect of group was significant ($F(2,69)=5.486$, $p<0.001$, $r=0.93$). Bonferroni corrected *post hoc* tests revealed that the difference between the experimental groups was significant ($p<0.001$), and that both experimental groups performed significantly above chance

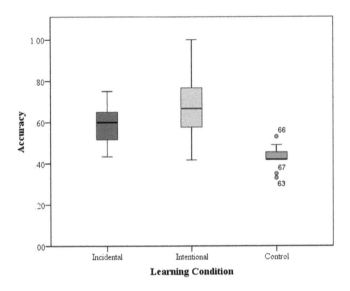

Figure 13.2 Accuracy on grammaticality judgement task. Accuracy is represented as the proportion of correct judgements. Asterisk indicates significantly greater than chance, *p*<0.05

and significantly better than controls (*p*<0.001). Controls performed significantly below chance (*p*<0.001). The training phase produced a clear learning effect in both experimental groups, and there seems to be a learning advantage for the rule search group. The results of the GJT are presented in Figure 13.2.

Endorsement rates

The intentional group endorsed 75.9% (SD=16.9%, SE=3.3%) of grammatical items and only 33.4% (SD=19.5%, SE=3.8%) of ungrammatical items. The incidental group endorsed 71.7% (SD=14.2%, SE=2.6%) of grammatical items and 54.0% (SD=19.1%, SE=3.5%) of ungrammatical items. Controls endorsed 36.5% (SD=30.4%, SE=7.8%) of grammatical items and 75.9% (SD=28.2%, SE=7.3%) of ungrammatical items. A 3×2 repeated measures ANOVA with learning condition as a between-groups factor and grammaticality as a within-groups factor revealed an interaction between grammaticality and group ($F(2,67)=6.293$, $p<0.05$, partial $\eta^2=0.158$). Bonferroni corrected *post hoc* tests show that both the intentional group and the incidental group endorsed more grammatical items than ungrammatical items, while the control group endorsed more ungrammatical than grammatical items ($p<0.001$) (see Figure 13.3).

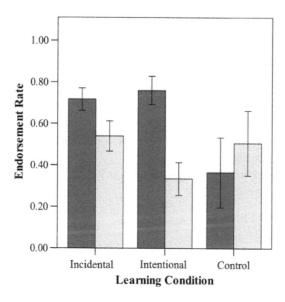

Figure 13.3 Endorsement rates on grammatical and ungrammatical items for the incidental, intentional and control groups. Endorsement of grammatical items is indicated by the dark grey bars, and endorsement of ungrammatical items is indicated by the light grey bars. Endorsement rates are expressed as proportions

Measures of implicit and explicit knowledge

Confidence ratings

Analyses of confidence ratings and source attributions are reported for the experimental groups only. The average confidence in the intentional group was 6.1 (SD=2.8) and the average confidence in the incidental group was 5.7 (SD=2.7). The intentional group reported significantly higher confidence than the incidental group ($t(3478)=4.369$, $p>0.001$). Proportionally, both the incidental and intentional groups indicated that they were somewhat confident most often. One-way ANOVAs show that for both groups, accuracy was not related to confidence, i.e. participant accuracy was not significantly different according to confidence rating (intentional: $F(2,1721)=2.133$, $p=0.119$; incidental: $F(2,1723)=1.220$, $p=0.295$). When the incidental group reported to be guessing, their accuracy was at chance, but when they reported being somewhat confident or very confident, their accuracy was above chance. The intentional group performed above chance for all confidence ratings. The guessing criterion for unconscious judgement knowledge was thus not satisfied for learners in the incidental group, but it was satisfied for learners in the intentional group; when participants in the intentional group reported that they were

Table 13.3 Ungrammatical patterns and example sentences from the testing set

Pattern	Example
*V1	Invited Emma after dinner some colleagues to her birthday party.
*V3	Some time ago John filled the bucket with apples.
*V4	Recently Susan much furniture imported for her new weekend retreat.
*VF	After dinner Susan an old car with her savings bought.
*VF–V2	Because his children recently a calculator required Jim called the electronics store.
*V1–VF	Stayed Jennifer at the hotel because her husband yesterday a boring conference attended.

guessing, they performed above chance. The results of the confidence rating analyses are summarised in Table 13.3.

The Chan difference score was computed in order to establish whether learning in the experimental group was implicit by the zero correlation criterion. For the incidental group, the average confidence for correct grammaticality decisions was 5.8 (SD=2.7) and the average confidence for incorrect decisions was 5.6 (SD=2.8). For the intentional group, the average confidence for correct decisions was 6.2 (SD=2.8) and the average confidence for incorrect decisions was 5.9 (SD=2.8). The difference between average confidence for correct and incorrect judgements was not significant for either the incidental group ($t(1724)=1.530$, $p=0.307$) or the intentional group ($t(1722)=1.748$, $p=0.173$). Experimental participants were not more confident in correct decisions than in incorrect ones. This indicates unconscious judgement knowledge according to the zero correlation criterion. Participants remained unaware of at least some of the knowledge they had acquired during the training phase.

Source attributions

Proportionally, the intentional group reported basing their grammaticality judgements most frequently on rule knowledge, followed by memory, guessing and finally, intuition. The incidental group reported basing their judgements equally on intuition and rule knowledge, followed by memory and then guessing. There were no differences in accuracy for either group based on which type of knowledge they reported using to make classification judgements. Both groups performed significantly above chance when basing their judgements on intuition, memory and rule, but only the intentional group performed above chance when basing their judgements on a guess. Above-chance accuracy when guessing for the intentional group and when using intuition for both

Table 13.4 Accuracy and proportions (%) across source attributions

		Guess	Intuition	Memory	Rule
Incidental	Accuracy	55	61**	58*	59**
	Proportion	16	32	21	31
Intentional	Accuracy	65**	62**	69**	75**
	Proportion	9	27	16	48

Significance from chance: *$p<0.005$, **$p<0.001$.

groups suggests that participants developed at least some unconscious structural knowledge of the grammar. Table 13.4 summarises the source attributions for both groups.

Working memory capacity

The average score of all participants in both experimental groups on the OSpan was 29.6 (SD=5.2, SE=0.7) out of a possible total of 42.[1] Participants in the incidental group scored an average of 29.6 (SD=5.5, SE=1.0) and participants in the intentional group scored an average of 29.6 (SD=5.0, SE=1.0). For the LNOT, the average score for all participants was 12.6 (SD=2.6, SE=0.4) out of 21. The average for the incidental group was 13.0 (SD=2.8, SE=0.5) and the average for the intentional group was 12.1 (SD=2.5, SE=0.5). The differences between groups was not significant on the OSpan ($t(53)=1.193$, $p=0.984$) or on the LNOT ($t(53)=1.193$, $p=0.238$). There was a moderate positive correlation between scores on the OSpan and scores on the LNOT ($r=0.327$, $p<0.05$). However, this correlation was driven by a higher correlation between the LNOT and the OSpan for participants in the incidental group ($r=0.509$, $p<0.01$). There was no correlation between the LNOT and the OSpan for participants in the intentional group ($r=0.089$, $p=0.664$).

There was no correlation between accuracy on the GJT and performance on either the OSpan ($r=0.117$, $p=0.394$) or the LNOT ($r=0.223$, $p=0.101$), when all participants were analysed together. Furthermore, there was no correlation between accuracy on the GJT and the OSpan ($r=0.168$, $p=0.384$) or the LNOT ($r=0.182$, $p=0.344$) for the incidental group. The accuracy scores of the intentional group did not correlate with scores on the OSpan ($r=0.117$, $p=0.570$). However, there was a moderate correlation between accuracy on the GJT and LNOT scores for the intentional group ($r=0.477$, $p<0.05$), suggesting that according to one of the WM measures, WMC predicts learning only in one learning condition. Correlations between WMC and accuracy for each test and learning condition are shown in Figure 13.4.

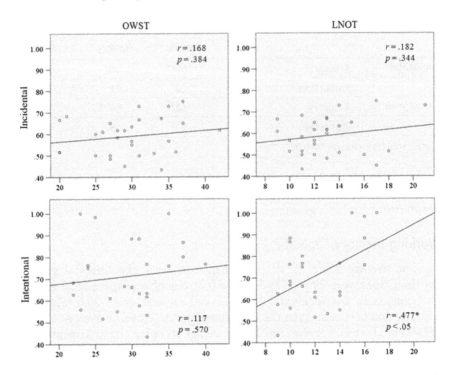

Figure 13.4 Correlations between WM tasks and accuracy on GJT for each experimental group. The y-axis represents percentage accuracy and the x-axis represents score on the WM task. Asterisk indicates a significant correlation, $p<0.05$

Debriefing questionnaires

In both the incidental and intentional groups, participants verbalised rules for the artificial grammar, but these rules were generally incorrect, mostly relating to the placement of time markers and adverbial phrases. Participants frequently mentioned that the verb could appear at the end of the sentence, but they did not seem to be aware that this was only possible in a subordinate clause. A few participants provided examples of one sentence type, but not the other two. There were, however, three participants in the rule search group who verbalised all three of the verb placement rules and provided examples of all three sentence types.

The three 'verbalisers' scored 98%, 100% and 100% accuracy on the GJT. Their scores on the LNOT were 16, 15 and 17, and their scores on the OSpan were 25, 35 and 23, respectively. All three were female, aged 26, 28 and 19, respectively, and none was raised speaking a language other than English.

Analyses without verbalisers

Because the three verbalisers seem to behave differently than the rest of the participants in the intentional group, further analyses were conducted without these participants.

Accuracy and endorsement rates without verbalisers

Without the verbalisers, the mean accuracy for the intentional group fell from 71.2% to 67.7% (SD=15.5%, SE=2.6%). This is still significantly greater than the mean accuracy for the incidental group ($t(50)=2.980$, $p<0.005$). Endorsement rates for grammatical items dropped slightly to 73% (SD=15.6%, SE=3.3%) and those for ungrammatical items increased to 37.8% (SD=16.1%, SE=3.4%), but all trends remain as reported above. Therefore, even without the verbalisers, participants in the intentional group seem to have a learning advantage that relies on their correct rejection of ungrammatical items.

Working memory analyses without verbalisers

When the relationship between WMC and accuracy was analysed with the verbalisers eliminated, the correlation between LNOT and accuracy disappeared ($r=0.156$, $p=0.476$) and the correlation between OSpan and accuracy remained non-significant ($r=0.309$, $p=0.152$). Graphs of the correlations between performance on the LNOT and accuracy with and without verbalisers are shown in Figure 13.5.

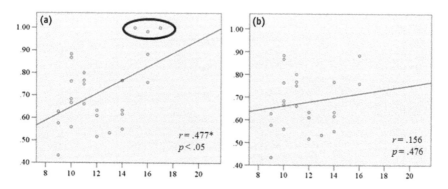

Figure 13.5 The effect of verbalisers on the correlation between LNOT and accuracy for the intentional group: (a) shows the correlation with verbalisers included and (b) shows the correlation without verbalisers. The y-axis is the proportion of accurate responses and the x-axis is the score on the LNOT. The three data points encircled in 6a represent the verbalisers. Asterisk indicates a significant correlation, $p<0.05$

Analysis by grammaticality

Because of the differential performance observed for grammatical and ungrammatical items, Pearson's correlations were run in order to determine whether there was a relationship between WMC and performance on different classes of items. These analyses revealed that there was a positive correlation between WMC and accuracy on grammatical items for participants in the intentional group only. This was true for both the LNOT ($r=0.424$, $p<0.05$; see Figure 13.6) and the OSpan ($r=0.542$, $p<0.05$; see Figure 13.7), and a t-statistic test comparing the correlations shows that they were not significantly different ($t<1$). There were no other significant correlations between WM task performance and accuracy for either group.

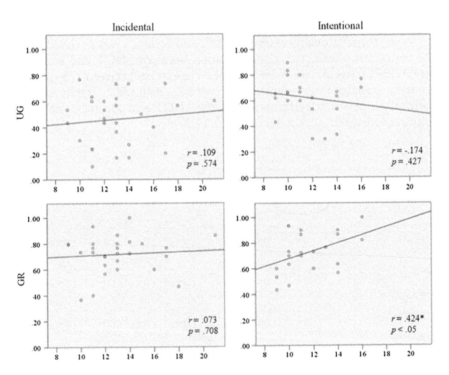

Figure 13.6 Relationship between LNOT scores and accuracy on grammatical and ungrammatical items on the GJT. The y-axis represents percentage accuracy and the x-axis represents the score on the LNOT. Asterisk indicates a significant correlation, $p<0.05$

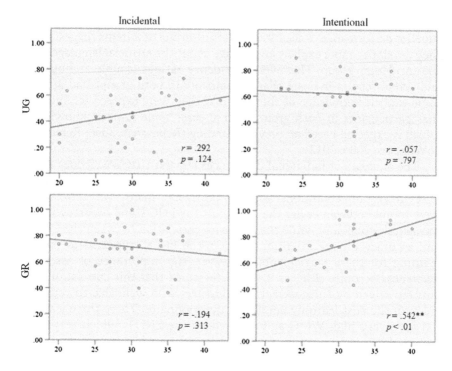

Figure 13.7 Relationship between OSpan scores and accuracy on grammatical and ungrammatical items on the GJT. The *y*-axis represents percentage accuracy and the *x*-axis represents the score on the OSpan task. Double asterisk indicates a significant correlation, *p*<0.01

Discussion

The analysis of accuracy and endorsement rates on the GJT produced similar results to those found previously for incidental and intentional conditions in this semi-artificial grammar (Rebuschat, 2008; Rebuschat & Williams, 2006, 2012). Both incidental and intentional groups performed significantly better than controls, and this observed learning effect appears to be driven by an ability to correctly endorse grammatical items. That is, both groups learned patterns from the training phase. Furthermore, the intentional group outperformed the incidental group by correctly rejecting a greater proportion of ungrammatical items. The incidental group performed at chance on ungrammatical items, whereas the intentional group classified three-quarters of the ungrammatical items correctly. The intentional condition therefore gave learners an advantage in distinguishing patterns they had learned from novel patterns. According to Ellis (2005), performance on ungrammatical items is driven by explicit knowledge; the superior performance of the intentional group on these items suggests that they developed more explicit knowledge about the artificial language than the incidental group. However, confidence ratings, source attributions and verbal reports indicate that participants in both groups had at least some explicit knowledge of the grammar they were exposed to, and also that participants in both groups had at least some implicit knowledge, which is expected based on previous finding (Rebuschat, 2008; Rebuschat & Williams, 2006, 2012).

The analyses of individual differences suggest that WMC does affect an individual's ability to learn L2 syntax, but this effect is apparent only in certain conditions and for particular items. No correlations were found between either the OSpan or the LNOT and accuracy in the incidental group, and while there was no correlation between the OSpan and accuracy for the intentional group, the LNOT appeared to predict learning for these participants. However, the importance of assessing awareness becomes clear, as it was determined that this correlation was entirely driven by three exceptional learners who were able to verbalise rules on the post-learning debriefing questionnaire. These three learners did have very high WMC as measured by the LNOT, which may have helped them discover rules. One of these learners also scored very high on the OSpan as well, but the other two actually scored quite low on this WM measure, which suggests that the LNOT may be a more reliable predictor of language learning abilities, or perhaps specifically of the ability to find explicit rules. However, there were other learners who also scored high on the LNOT but not on the GJT, suggesting that there are other variables at play.

Although correlations between WMC and overall learning outcomes were not maintained when the verbalisers were removed from the analyses, further analyses into the relationship between WMC and particular items revealed that in the intentional condition, WMC predicted performance on grammatical items only. Therefore, while WMC, as measured by the OSpan and the LNOT, does not appear to affect an individual's ability to learn L2 syntax in incidental learning conditions, it may play a role in helping learners in more explicit conditions incorporate positive evidence from a new language. In these follow-up analyses, the LNOT and OSpan were shown to predict language learning ability to a similar extent, though the findings pertaining to verbalisers, discussed above, may suggest an advantage for the LNOT, at least for some individuals.

The findings in this study suggest that individual differences influence learning in explicit, but not implicit conditions. However, the differential effect of WMC on grammatical and ungrammatical items suggests that this relationship is complex. Furthermore, while some claims can be made about the predictive value of WMC in language learning under implicit and explicit learning conditions, there are several limitations of this study that must be taken into account. First of all, untimed GJTs such as the one used in this study favour explicit processes, and there was not an adequate measure of implicit learning, such as elicited imitations or reaction times (Ellis, 2005). Additionally, WMC was the individual difference in question; it involves the *control* of attention and is therefore expected to be related to explicit learning, as this process involves attention as well, while implicit learning does so to a lesser extent (DeKeyser, 2003; Schmidt, 2001). Contrary to Reber's (1993) claims, recent evidence suggests that implicit learning is indeed an ability that varies across individuals (Kaufman *et al.*, 2010). However, as Kaufman and colleagues found, typical cognitive abilities, such as general intelligence, WM and associative learning, do not correlate with implicit learning outcomes, whereas verbal analogical reasoning, processing speed and personality traits, such as openness and intuition, are related to implicit learning. An exploration of the relationship between cognitive factors that might draw on some of the same processes as implicit learning might yield different results from those found in the current study. Finally, some studies have found that correlations become significant when comparing aptitude measures and *delayed* performance scores (e.g. Erlam, 2005; Mackey *et al.*, 2002; Robinson, 2005b), so it would be of interest to administer a delayed testing phase in this paradigm (Grey *et al.*, 2014, 2015).

Conclusions

In this study, a semi-artificial language was used as a model for the investigation of the relationship between WMC and L2 acquisition in conditions designed to promote implicit and explicit learning. While WMC did not predict overall learning for either group, it did predict accuracy on grammatical items for the intentional group only. This suggests that individuals with high WMC are more able to incorporate positive evidence when learning an L2 under conditions designed to promote explicit learning. These results support Reber's (1993) claim that individual difference measures, such as WMC, are only predictive of explicit learning. However, further research is needed to fully understand the validity of this theory for SLA.

Acknowledgements

The authors gratefully acknowledge the financial support of the Federal University of Santa Catarina and the Brazilian National Council for Scientific and Technological Development (CNPq), as well as Luke Amoroso, Phillip Hamrick, Katie Jeong-Eun Kim, Julie Lake and John Williams for their feedback.

Note

(1) The OSpan was coded two ways: traditionally (Turner & Engle, 1989), where points were only awarded for correct words in the correct placement, and in a way that allowed points for correct words in the correct order, but not necessarily in the correct place. These two methods of coding yielded highly correlated results ($r=0.930$, $p<0.01$), so only analyses on traditional scores are reported.

References

Ando, J., Fukunaga, N., Kurahashi, J., Suto, T., Nakano, T. and Kage, M. (1992) A comparative study of the two EFL teaching methods: The communicative and grammatical approach. *Japanese Journal of Educational Psychology* 40, 247–256.
Baddeley, A. (2000) The episodic buffer: A new component of working memory? *Trends in Cognitive Sciences* 4 (11), 417–423.
Baddeley, A.D. (2007) *Working Memory, Thought and Action*. Oxford: Oxford University Press.
Baddeley, A. (2010) Working memory. *Current Biology* 20 (4), R136–R140.
Baddeley, A.D. and Hitch, G. (1974) Working memory. In G.H. Bower (ed.) *The Psychology of Learning and Motivation* (pp. 47–90). New York: Academic Press.
Cain, K., Oakhill, J. and Bryant, P. (2004) Children's reading comprehension ability: Concurrent prediction by working memory, verbal ability, and component skills. *Journal of Educational Psychology* 96 (1), 31–42.
Carpenter, P.A., Miyake, A. and Just, M.A. (1994) Working memory constraints in comprehension: Evidence from individual differences, aphasia, and aging. In M.A. Gernsbacher (ed.) *Handbook of Psycholinguistics* (pp. 1075–1122). San Diego, CA: Academic Press.
Conway, A.R.A., Kane, M.J., Bunting, M.F., Hambrick, D.Z., Wilhelm, O. and Engle, R.W. (2005) Working memory span tasks: A methodological review and user's guide. *Psychonomic Bulletin & Review* 12, 769–786.
Conway, A.R.A., Jarrold, C., Kane, M.J., Miyake, A. and Towse, J. (2007) Variation in working memory: An introduction. In A.R.A. Conway, C. Jarrold, M.J. Kane, A. Miyake and J. Towse (eds) *Variation in Working Memory (pp. 3–17)*. New York: Oxford University Press.
Cowan, N. (1999) An embedded-processes model of working memory. In A. Miyake and P. Shah (eds) *Models of Working Memory: Mechanisms of Active Maintenance and Executive Control* (pp. 62–101). Cambridge: Cambridge University Press.
Cowan, N. (2005) *Working Memory Capacity*. New York: Psychology Press.
Daneman, M. (1991) Working memory as a predictor of verbal fluency. *Journal of Psycholinguistic Research* 20, 445–464.
Daneman, M. and Green, I. (1986) Individual differences in comprehending and producing words in context. *Journal of Memory and Language* 25, 1–18.
Daneman, M. and Merikle, P.M. (1996) Working memory and language comprehension: A meta-analysis. *Psychonomic Bulletin & Review* 3, 422–433.
de Graaff, R. (1997) The eXperanto experiment: Effects of explicit instruction on second language acquisition. *Studies in Second Language Acquisition* 19, 249–276.
DeKeyser, R. (2003) Implicit and explicit learning. In C.J. Doughty and M.H. Long (eds) *Handbook of Second Language Acquisition* (pp. 313–348). Oxford: Blackwell.
Dienes, Z. (2008) Subjective measures of unconscious knowledge. *Progress in Brain Research* 168, 49–64.

Dienes, Z. and Scott, R. (2005) Measuring unconscious knowledge: Distinguishing structural knowledge and judgment knowledge. *Psychological Research 69*, 338–351.

Ellis, R. (2005) Measuring implicit and explicit knowledge of a second language: A psychometric study. *Studies in Second Language Acquisition 27*, 141–172.

Engle, R.W. (2001) What is working-memory capacity? In H.L. Roediger III and J.S. Nairne (eds) *The Nature of Remembering: Essays in Honor of Robert G. Crowder* (pp. 297–314). Washington, DC: American Psychological Association.

Engle, R.W., Kane, M.J. and Tuholski, S.W. (1999) Individual differences in working memory capacity and what they tell us about controlled attention, general fluid intelligence, and functions of the prefrontal cortex. In A. Miyake and P. Shah (eds) *Models of Working Memory: Mechanisms of Active Maintenance and Executive Control* (pp. 102–134). Cambridge: Cambridge University Press.

Erlam, R. (2005) Language aptitude and its relationship to instructional effectiveness in second language acquisition. *Language Teaching Research 9* (2), 147–171.

Gebauer, G.F. and Mackintosh, N.J. (2007) Psychometric intelligence dissociates implicit and explicit learning. *Journal of Experimental Psychology: Learning, Memory, and Cognition 33* (1), 34–54.

Geva, E. and Ryan, E.B. (1993) Linguistic and cognitive correlates of academic skills in first and second languages. *Language Learning 43*, 5–42.

Grey, S., Williams, J. N., Rebuschat, P. (2015 in press) Individual differences in incidental language learning: Phonological working memory, learning styles, and personality. *Learning and Individual Differences*.

Grey, S., Williams, J. N., Rebuschat, P. (2014) Incidental learning and L3 learning of morphosyntax. Studies in *Second Language Acquisition, 36* (4), 611–645.

Harrington, M. (1991) Individual Differences in L2 Reading: Processing Capacity Versus Linguistic Knowledge. Paper presented at the Annual Meeting of the American Association of Applied Linguists, New York.

Harrington, M. and Sawyer, M. (1992) L2 working memory capacity and L2 reading skill. *Studies in Second Language Acquisition 14*, 25–38.

Havik, E., Roberts, L., van Hout, R., Schreuder, R. and Haverkort, M. (2009) Processing subject-object ambiguities in the L2: A self-paced reading study with German L2 learners of Dutch. *Language Learning 59* (1), 73–112.

Johnson, J. and Newport, E. (1989) Critical period effects in second language learning: The influence of maturational state on the acquisition of English as a second language. *Cognitive Psychology 21*, 60–99.

Just, M.A. and Carpenter, P.A. (1992) A capacity theory of comprehension: Individual differences in working memory. *Psychological Review 99*, 122–149.

Kane, M.J., Hambrick, D.Z. and Conway, A.R.A. (2005) Working memory capacity and fluid intelligence are strongly related constructs: Comment on Ackerman, Beier, and Boyle (2005). *Psychological Bulletin 131*, 66–71.

Kaufman, S.B., DeYoung, C.G., Gray, J.R., Jiménez, L., Brown, J. and Mackintosh, N. (2010) Implicit learning as an ability. *Cognition 116*, 321–340.

King, J. and Just, M.A. (1991) Individual differences in syntactic processing: The role of working memory. *Journal of Memory and Language 30*, 580–602.

Krashen, S. (1981) *Second Language Acquisition and Second Language Learning*. Oxford: Pergamon.

Linck, J.A., Osthus, P., Koeth, J.T. and Bunting, M.F. (2014) Working memory and second language comprehension and production: A meta-analysis. *Psychonomic Bulletin & Review 21*, 861–883.

Long, M.H. (1990) Maturational constraints on language development. *Studies in Second Language Acquisition 12*, 251–285.

Mackey, A., Philp, J., Egi, T., Fujii, A. and Tatsumi, T. (2002) Individual differences in working memory, noticing of interactional feedback, and L2 development. In P. Robinson (ed.) *Individual Differences and Instructed Language Learning* (pp. 181–209). Amsterdam: Benjamins.

Mackey, A., Adams, R., Stafford, C. and Winke, P. (2010) Exploring the relationship between modified output and working memory capacity. *Language Learning* 60, 501–533.

Miyake, A., Just, M.A. and Carpenter, P.A. (1994) Working memory constraints on the resolution of lexical ambiguity: Maintaining multiple interpretations in neutral context. *Journal of Memory and Language* 33, 175–202.

Miyake, A. and Friedman, N.P. (1998) Individual differences in second language proficiency: Working memory as language aptitude. In A. Healy and L. Bourne (eds) *Foreign Language Learning* (pp. 339–364). Mahwah, NJ: Lawrence Erlbaum.

Reber, A.S. (1989) Implicit learning and tacit knowledge. *Journal of Experimental Psychology: General* 118 (3), 219–235.

Reber, A.S. (1990) On the primacy of the implicit: Comment on Perruchet and Pacteau. *Journal of Experimental Psychology: General* 119 (3), 340–342.

Reber, A.S. (1993) *Implicit Learning and Tacit Knowledge: An Essay on the Cognitive Unconscious*. New York: Oxford University Press.

Reber, A.S. (2003) Implicit learning. In L. Nadel (ed.) *Encyclopedia of Cognitive Science* (Vol. 2; pp. 486–491). London: Macmillan.

Reber, A.S., Kassin, S.M., Lewis, S. and Cantor, G. (1980) On the relationship between implicit and explicit modes in the learning of complex rule structure. *Journal of Experimental Psychology: Learning, Memory, and Cognition* 6 (5), 492–502.

Reber, A.S., Walkenfeld, F.F. and Hernstadt, R. (1991) Implicit and explicit learning: Individual differences and IQ. *Journal of Experimental Psychology: Learning, Memory, and Cognition* 17 (5), 888–896.

Rebuschat, P. (2008) Implicit learning of natural language syntax. PhD thesis, Cambridge University.

Rebuschat, P. and Williams, J.N. (2006) Dissociating implicit and explicit learning of natural language syntax. In R. Sun and N. Miyake (eds) *Proceedings of the 28th Annual Conference of the Cognitive Science Society* (pp. 25–94). Mahwah, NJ: Lawrence Erlbaum.

Rebuschat, P. and Williams, J.N. (2009) Implicit learning of word order. In N.A. Taatgen and H. van Rijn (eds) *Proceedings of the 31st Annual Conference of the Cognitive Science Society* (pp. 425–430). Austin, TX: Cognitive Science Society.

Rebuschat, P. and Williams, J.N. (2012) Implicit and explicit knowledge in second language acquisition. *Applied Psycholinguistics* 33 (4), 829–856.

Roberts, L., Marinis, T., Felser, C. and Clahsen, H. (2007) Antecedent priming at trace positions in children's sentence processing. *Journal of Psycholinguistic Research* 36 (2), 175–188.

Robinson, P. (2001) Individual differences, cognitive abilities, aptitude complexes, and learning conditions in second-language acquisition. *Second Language Research* 17, 368–392.

Robinson, P. (2002) *Individual Differences and Instructed Language Learning*. Amsterdam: Benjamins.

Robinson, P. (2005a) Aptitude and second language acquisition. *Annual Review of Applied Linguistics* 25, 46–73.

Robinson, P. (2005b) Cognitive abilities, chunk-strength, and frequency effects in implicit artificial grammar and incidental L2 learning: Replications of Reber, Walkenfeld & Hernstadt (1991) and Knowlton & Squire (1996) and their relevance for SLA. *Studies in Second Language Acquisition* 27, 235–268.

Sagarra, N. (2007) From CALL to face-to-face interaction: The effect of computer delivered recasts and working memory on L2 development. In A. Mackey (ed.) *Conversational Interaction in Second Language Acquisition: A Series of Empirical Studies* (pp. 229–248). Oxford: Oxford University Press.

Sagarra, N. (2013) Working memory in second language acquisition. In C.A. Chapelle (ed.) *The Encyclopedia of Applied Linguistics*. Oxford: Wiley-Blackwell.

Sagarra, N. and Herschensohn, J. (2010) The role of proficiency and working memory in gender and number agreement processing in L1 and L2 Spanish. *Lingua* 120 (8), 2022–2039.

Schmidt, R. (1994) Implicit learning and the cognitive unconscious: Of artificial grammars and SLA. In N.C. Ellis (ed.) *Implicit and Explicit Learning of Languages* (pp. 165–210). San Diego, CA: Academic Press.

Schmidt, R. (2001) Attention. In P. Robinson (ed.) *Cognition and Second Language Instruction* (pp. 1–32). Cambridge: Cambridge University Press.

Seigneuric, A., Ehrlich, M-F., Oakhill, J.V. and Yuill, N.M. (2000) Working memory resources and children's reading comprehension. *Reading and Writing* 13 (1–2), 81–103.

Skehan, P. (1998) *A Cognitive Approach to Language Learning*. Oxford: Oxford University Press.

Skehan, P. (2002) Theorizing and updating aptitude. In P. Robinson (ed.) *Individual Differences and Instructed Language Learning* (pp. 69–93). Amsterdam: Benjamins.

Turner, M.L. and Engle, R.W. (1989) Is working memory capacity task dependent? *Journal of Memory and Language* 28, 127–154.

Unsworth, N., Heitz, R.P., Schrock, J.C. and Engle, R.W. (2005) An automated version of the operation span task. *Behavior Research Methods* 37, 498–505.

van den Noort, M.W.M.L., Bosch, P. and Hugdahl, K. (2006) Foreign language proficiency and working memory capacity. *European Psychologist* 11, 289–296.

Waters, G.S. and Caplan, D. (1996) The measurement of verbal working memory capacity and its relation to reading comprehension. *The Quarterly Journal of Experimental Psychology* 49A (1), 51–79.

Wechsler, D. (1997) *The Wechsler Adult Intelligence Scale: Revised*. New York: The Psychological Corporation.

Wechsler, D. (2000) *WAIS-III Nederlandstalige bewerking: Afname-en scoringshandleiding* [WAIS-III Dutch version: User manual]. Lisse: Swets & Zeitlinger.

Williams, J.N. (1999) Memory, attention, and inductive learning. *Studies in Second Language Acquisition* 21, 1–48.

14 Working Memory Capacity, Cognitive Complexity and L2 Recasts in Online Language Teaching

Melissa Baralt

Introduction

Language learners are able to notice and benefit from oral corrective feedback because of the cognitive system known as working memory capacity (WMC). As communicative tasks in the second language (L2) increase in cognitive complexity and approximate real-world tasks, working memory is theorized to increasingly moderate how well learners are able to perform (e.g. Robinson, 2010). Research in second language acquisition (SLA) is starting to show that learners with higher working memory are better at noticing feedback and at incorporating feedback by producing modified output (e.g. Mackey *et al.*, 2002, 2010). This has led researchers to question how practitioners might assist learners with lower working memory. Computer-mediated communication (CMC) is one environment for interaction practice that is posited to do so (e.g. Payne & Ross, 2005). The goal of this chapter is to bring together these lines of research on working memory, feedback during computerized interaction and communicative tasks of different levels of complexity. It tests the hypothesis that WMC moderates feedback efficacy online, and that the CMC environment can help learners with lower working memory, especially as tasks increase in complexity.

Theoretical background

It is important to understand the mechanisms of conversational interaction that support SLA, and where working memory fits in this model. There are several features of conversational interaction that are posited to be beneficial for L2 learning. First, learners have to *produce* the language. This forced output promotes syntactic processing and assists learners in recognizing those features of the language that they do not yet possess in their interlanguage (e.g. Swain, 2005). Recognizing these gaps may prompt learners to seek out input from the person with whom they are speaking. The interlocutor might also provide the learner with corrective feedback during the conversation, such as recasts. Recasts, or a reformulation of learners' own erroneous language production, are one of the most beneficial ways to provide learners with corrective feedback. This is because recasts convey information in a context in which both the learner and the interlocutor share a 'joint attentional focus' on the learner's own message content, which facilitates form-meaning mappings (Swain, 2005: 114). In addition, as Long (2007) highlights, recasts are typically juxtaposed immediately after the learner's error in the conversation. This contingency of recasts with the error helps the learner compare the two forms (the correct one with the deviant one), which occurs in his/her working memory (Long, 2007). The comparison of forms in working memory is crucial so that learners can notice and become aware of forms, which is necessary for language learning to take place (Schmidt, 1990).

WMC is thus the gateway for information to become long-term memory traces: traces that are based on actual neuronal growth, as opposed to temporary electrical activation (Baddeley, 2003). To provide a definition, WMC is a 'multicomponent system responsible for active maintenance of information in the face of ongoing processing and/or distraction' (Conway et al., 2005: 770). Extensive work by Baddeley suggests that there are different components of the multi-component system: the visuospatial sketchpad, the episodic buffer and the phonological loop. These three slave systems are subservient to the central executive, which is the controller (Baddeley, 2007). The central executive is what allows human beings to direct, divide and switch their attention to specific stimuli. This is obviously an important ability during conversational interaction, where learners might receive corrective feedback on the language they produce.

Research on working memory in face-to-face interaction

An incipient line of research indicates that learners with higher WMC may benefit more from face-to-face (FTF) interactional feedback. Mackey et al. (2002) explored working memory and how it impacts the way in which learners pay attention during L2 interaction. Thirty learners of English as a second language (ESL) participated in three dyadic task-based sessions during which they received recasts on their erroneous production of question formation in English. Learners also participated in a stimulated recall session to measure noticing, as well as pre- and post-tests to see how much they had improved in question formation from the sessions. Working memory was measured with a non-word repetition test and two listening span tests. The researchers reported that learners with higher working memory noticed and were better able to make use of interactional feedback that contained grammatical corrections, showing that learners with high WMC are more efficient at processing input. This was an important finding, because those learners who noticed more (due to their higher working memory) learned more.

Mackey *et al.* (2010) explored the relationship between working memory and learners' ability to modify their output after receiving corrective feedback. Forty-two learners of Spanish participated in four dyadic task-based sessions, during which they received corrective feedback on a variety of forms. Working memory was measured with a verbal span test. The researchers found that after feedback provision, learners with higher working memory modified their output more than those with lower WMC. These studies show that working memory mediates how well learners notice corrective feedback and incorporate feedback into their production during task-based interaction, two components of interaction that are essential for language development.

Cognition Hypothesis of task-based language teaching

The two studies by Mackey *et al.* (2002, 2010) employed tasks to engage participants in conversational interaction. This derives from one of the main tenets of task-based language teaching (TBLT): language learners can reap the benefits of conversational interaction (i.e. producing output, receiving feedback and incorporating that feedback by producing modified output) most effectively by performing meaningful tasks (e.g. Ellis, 2003; Mackey, 1999). Another premise of TBLT is that pedagogic tasks be sequenced in an order of simple to complex, so that they increasingly approximate target tasks, and eventually, real-world tasks for learners (e.g. Baralt *et al.*, 2014; Long, 2007; Robinson, 2010). A task's level of complexity refers to the 'attentional, memory, reasoning, and other information processing demands' that are asked of the learner when performing a task (Robinson, 2001b: 29). Robinson's Cognition Hypothesis of task-based language learning claims that there are two ways to manipulate a task's complexity. First, practitioners can implement resource-dispersing features into the task. Resource-dispersing variables place *performative* demands on the learner, such as giving a learner pre-planning time, and then not doing so, in order to make the task more complex. Second, practitioners can incorporate resource-directing features into the task. Resource-directing variables place *cognitive* demands on the learner, such as having a learner retell a sequence of events, and then, in addition, reflect on and express the reasons behind those events (i.e. causal or intentional reasoning). These variables have the capacity to make a learner aware of specific linguistic features needed in order to complete the task, and be more tuned in to feedback provided during the task that addresses those features.

Interestingly, there is evidence that the way in which tasks are designed can differentially mediate how well learners notice recasts (e.g. Baralt, 2013; Révész, 2009). This is important to take into account, because all of the tasks used so far in SLA research on WMC have been cognitively simple, according to Robinson's paradigm (e.g. Mackey *et al.*, 2002, 2010; Payne & Ross, 2005; Payne & Whitney, 2002). In fact, a key claim of the Cognition Hypothesis is that cognitive abilities – such as working memory – will increasingly affect task-based performance as tasks increase in cognitive complexity (Robinson, 2001a, 2001b, 2007, 2010, 2011; Robinson & Gilabert, 2007). Given that recent empirical work in SLA indicates that learners' WMC mediates how well they process oral corrective feedback (e.g. Mackey *et al.*, 2002, 2010), it is reasonable to assume that during more complex tasks, learners with lower working memory may not benefit from interactional feedback as much as learners with higher working memory.

Computer-mediated communication as a platform for interaction

How then might practitioners help low working memory learners, especially as language learning tasks increase in complexity? One interaction environment thought to assist language learners with such a profile is CMC. CMC is an online chat conversation that takes place over the internet and is in real time. A main theorized benefit assumed of CMC is that it alleviates constraints on working memory. In CMC, learners have extra processing time during which they can pre-plan, view and modify their output before sending their message to their partner. This is an affordance that is not available when interacting in person. The main difference in this mode is the written presence of language. While parsing and noticing feedback during FTF interaction is constrained by working memory (Long, 2007; Sauro, 2009), in CMC, forms are physically written out on the screen for learners. CMC permits learners to read forms, refer back to forms and take the time to reflect on forms – meta-activity that would not be natural in a FTF conversation. CMC does not require learners to hold forms in working memory. Corrective feedback in this mode may be especially effective then, and even more so for learners with limited WMC.

A study by Yilmaz and Yuksel (2011) provides empirical support for this hypothesis. Twenty-four learners of Turkish performed vocabulary learning tasks in both FTF mode and in CMC, during which they received corrective recasts. Those learners who received recasts in the CMC mode acquired vocabulary significantly better than those who received recasts in the oral mode. The researchers reported that the extra processing time, as well as the rereadability of the chat messages in CMC, may have facilitated the corrective intent of the recasts. They highlight the putative relief on working memory in this mode: 'Being able to view all the utterance-feedback pairs using the scrolling feature of the software program might have also decreased the burden on learners' working memory...' (Yilmaz & Yuksel, 2011: 470). These benefits of CMC for the processing of feedback are conjectural however, given that Yilmaz and Yuksel did not actually investigate WMC.

Working memory capacity and CMC

To date, a handful of studies have investigated how WMC moderates language practice, noticing of feedback and learning in the CMC environment. The findings so far are highly mixed. Payne and Whitney (2002) examined whether differences in working memory predict the rate of L2 proficiency development. Fifty-eight third-semester students of Spanish participated in the study. Half of the participants carried out tasks in the traditional mode (FTF), and half carried out tasks in both FTF mode and in CMC. WMC was measured using a reading span task (RSPAN) and a non-word repetition span task. Students' took the working memory tests online, and their scores from both spans were combined into one composite score. Oral proficiency was measured using the American Council on the Teaching of Foreign Languages (ACTFL) test. The researchers reported two main findings. First, learners in the hybrid group developed more oral proficiency than those who carried out tasks in only the traditional environment, implying that CMC chat can assist in language development. Second, the researchers did *not* find a relationship between oral proficiency scores and working memory. However, when they looked at the working memory span scores separately, a significant relationship was found between oral proficiency and the non-word repetition test. This led the researchers to claim that participating in CMC chat may assist learners with lower working memory, because it helps to automate language production processes.

Another study by Payne and Ross (2005) investigated how individual differences in WMC affect the frequency of repetition and other patterns of language use in chat room discourse. They analyzed 20 chat sessions for repetition, relexicalization and measures of language output. Working memory was measured with the same spans and method as Payne and Whitney (2002): an RSPAN and a non-word repetition span task that were delivered via a computer. Across time, the researchers found a significant increase in learners' repetition of words as well as relexicalization in CMC. These changes were not found to be related to working memory. A significant relationship was found, however, between working memory and learners' total output production. Specifically, lower phonological working memory learners produced significantly more output. Payne and Ross hypothesized that students with lower working memory were taking advantage of the reduced cognitive burden of CMC by producing more language that was more elaborate.

Lai *et al.* (2008) examined the predicting effects of working memory on accurate noticing of contingent versus non-contingent recasts in CMC (e.g. whether the recast is provided immediately after the error or a few turns after the error, which often occurs in CMC). Working memory was measured with a reverse digit span test, and noticing of feedback was determined with a stimulated recall methodology. The researchers found that learners noticed contingent recasts significantly more than non-contingent recasts. In addition, working memory was significantly correlated with noticing of *non-contingent* recasts. Lai *et al.* suggested that higher working memory may alleviate the problem of error-feedback non-contingency in CMC.

Sagarra (2007) was the first researcher to investigate feedback in the CMC mode and whether or not WMC moderates learning in this mode. Her study had one key difference from most CMC studies though: recasts were provided *orally* to students via a computer. Thirty-seven learners of Spanish participated in the study. All carried out vocabulary tasks on a computer, which targeted noun–adjective agreement. Half of the learners received recasts online, while the other half did not. Learning was measured with a written test and a FTF interaction task, and WMC was measured with an RSPAN. Sagarra also examined how learners modified their output, which was assessed with an information gap task. She found that the recast group developed significantly better on noun–adjective agreement than did the no feedback group, in both the written and oral tasks. Additionally, working memory was significantly related to the recast group's learning. Two months later, the recast group also modified their output on number and gender agreement forms significantly more than the non-recast group. Just as with Mackey *et al.*'s (2010) findings, participants' WMC predicted how much they modified their production in Sagarra's study, with higher working memory learners modifying more.

Sagarra and Abdul (2013) compared the effects of oral versus written feedback on learning in the computerized environment, and whether or not WMC was related to both. Two hundred and eighteen beginning-level learners of Spanish were assigned to one of the following groups: (1) the control group (no feedback), (2) written utterance rejection (i.e. 'Wrong. Move on to the next sentence'), (3) oral utterance rejection (i.e. same as written but delivered with an audio clip), (4) written recast, (5) oral recast, (6) typographically enhanced written recast (i.e. 'La silla es blancA') and (7) oral enhanced recast (same as typographically enhanced, but delivered with an audio clip). WMC was measured with a reading span test. All learners participated in one online treatment task, during which they received feedback on Spanish noun–adjective agreement forms (or no feedback, in the case of the control group). Learning was measured with three written post-tests as well as two oral FTF interactive tasks. The researchers also examined learners' ability to modify their output on one of the interactive post-tasks. Surprisingly, Sagarra and Abdul found that WMC significantly predicted learning for those who had received oral recasts online (both enhanced and unenhanced), but *not* those who had received written feedback. Working memory was also significantly related to modified output production, but only for those learners who had received oral feedback. In sum, WMC only mediated learning and modified output for learners in the oral feedback groups, not the written feedback groups. Sagarra and Abdul (2013: 211) speculated that processing demands may be the reason why no working memory effects were found for the written recast groups, saying that it may be that oral recasts consume more attentional resources than written ones. They suggest that tasks that require the processing of written input are cognitively easier than tasks that require oral input processing.

Sagarra and Abdul's (2013) findings suggest that WMC may only mediate the efficacy of recasts provided orally, regardless of whether the interlocutor is human or computerized. One characteristic of their study that limits generalizability is the type of task used. Learners simply typed sentences after being prompted to do so via a computer program, and did not engage in meaningful, task-based interaction. This certainly does not denigrate the benefit of automated computerized programs, as participants in Sagarra and Abdul's study learned. It is still an empirical question, however, whether or not WMC mediates feedback efficacy in the CMC mode alongside meaningful task-based interaction.

If it is the case that learners with lower WMC may benefit from interaction performed in the CMC mode (e.g. Payne & Whitney, 2002; Payne & Ross, 2005), CMC could be very beneficial to certain types of learners, especially as they perform more cognitively complex tasks (e.g. Robinson, 2010). However, there is little empirical work on task complexity and task design in the computerized environment, and no study to date on cognitive complexity and WMC in CMC. As far as the author knows, only one study has investigated the claims of the Cognition Hypothesis in traditional versus online environments (Baralt, 2013). Eighty-four learners of Spanish as an L2 completed two cognitive simple or complex tasks, in either the FTF or the CMC mode. They interacted one-on-one with the researcher and received recasts on erroneous uses of the past subjunctive. In the FTF mode, learners who received recasts alongside the cognitively complex tasks learned significantly better than those who had performed the cognitively simple tasks (operationalized as +/– intentional reasoning). Unexpectedly, in the CMC mode, the opposite effect was found. Those learners who performed the simple tasks in CMC, plus recasts, learned the most. The cognitively complex task in CMC proved to be ineffective. After analyzing screen recordings of the CMC interactions, Baralt found that cognitively complex tasks plus feedback did not work in the CMC mode because of dual processing inherent to cognitive complexity, as well as turn-taking problems which caused a lack of contingency of errors with feedback.

Baralt's results imply that the theoretical assumptions surrounding more cognitively complex tasks – such as their capacity to promote more noticing and incorporation of feedback – might only hold for the FTF mode. More research is needed on this topic, and especially on whether or not WMC moderates a learner's ability to profit from feedback alongside more cognitively complex tasks. This is relevant for the goals of TBLT: to prepare learners and set them up for maximal performance with real-world tasks in the L2. As language programs are increasingly offering courses online (Blake, 2011), research is needed on task types that best suit this environment and that can optimize opportunities for language learning.

The present study sought to fill this need by examining the effects of cognitive complexity in task design alongside feedback provision in the CMC mode, and whether the level of WMC makes a difference in being able to benefit from that feedback. In light of this, the following research questions guided the current study.

Research questions and hypotheses

(1) Does WMC moderate learners' ability to profit from feedback during cognitively simple versus cognitively complex tasks performed in the CMC environment?

(2) If so, are learning outcomes different for low working memory versus high working memory learners?

The Cognition Hypothesis (e.g. Robinson, 2010) predicts that WMC will increasingly moderate learners' ability to perform and learn from feedback provided during more cognitively complex tasks. Therefore, it was hypothesized that (1) working memory would affect learning in this study (feedback alongside meaningful interaction in CMC), and that (2) significant differences would be observed between high working memory learners and low working memory learners and their learning outcomes, particularly on the complex task.

Method

Participants

The participants in this study were 34 intermediate-level students of Spanish at a private, mid-Atlantic university. All were between the ages of 18 and 23. Twenty of the students were female and 14 were male. They had been studying Spanish for an average of about six years. Importantly, all participants had extensive experience in CMC activity, reporting an average of 3.4 hours per week chatting online (i.e. Gmail chat, Facebook, etc.).

Materials

Materials used in this study included two dyadic treatment tasks, three assessment tasks, three working memory span tests and two Mac OS X laptops for the CMC chat interaction. The laptops were equipped with iChat software version 4.0, as well as iShowU, a screen recording software that recorded all of the chat interactions.

Treatment tasks

The treatment tasks chosen for this experiment were interactive story retells. They were performed one-on-one with the researcher. After reading a story silently to themselves in English, participants had to retell that story in Spanish and in the past tense to the researcher. This was facilitated by a set of comic cards, and both the participant and the researcher had their own set of cards. The story was broken down into six short sections, or blurbs, to facilitate the participant being able to remember all of the events in the stories. Participants first read the first language (L1) blurb to themselves in English, and then moved on to the picture comic strip, which they used to assist in retelling the story. The first task was about a family living in Latin America who accuses their housekeeper of stealing some personal items. The second task was about two boys who get invited to play soccer for their city's team, but only one of them gets chosen to play at the end. The resource-directing variable +/– intentional reasoning was implemented in the task design in order to operationalize cognitive complexity. Two versions of both retell tasks were created: a simple version and a complex version. For the cognitively simple task version, learners were already provided with characters' intentional reasons behind their actions in both the L1 story blurbs and comic strip. Participants in the simple group thus only had to retell the story, relaying to the researcher the intentional reasoning information that was already provided to them. Their task input is illustrated in Figure 14.1, where the intentional reasons are provided already in the story blurb and comic picture.

Participants in the complex group were given the same storylines, but they had to come up with the intentional reasons themselves in order to explain the characters' actions in the story. Intentional reasoning for this group was elicited by putting an empty yellow thought bubble in the comic strip picture; this served as a prompt to reflect on and communicate why the character did a certain action. Figure 14.2 shows how this was done in the task input.

Figure 14.1 Card from cognitively simple task

Having to relay the intentional reasons of others' actions, whether as provided by the task input (simple group) or having to come up with the reasons themselves (complex group), naturally led to the use of the targeted linguistic item in this study: the Spanish past subjunctive.

Targeted linguistic item

The Spanish past subjunctive conforms naturally to the functional demands of +/– intentional reasoning. The subjunctive usage targeted in this study follows verbs of emotions or subjective reactions (i.e. she wanted, he was upset that, they could not believe that, etc.). When verbs of emotions or subjective reactions occur in an independent clause position, verbs in the dependent clause position must be marked with the grammatical mood in Spanish. The past subjunctive is formed by beginning with third-person plural verb forms of the preterit past tense. The past tense morpheme on these verbs is replaced with a subjunctive mood morpheme (i.e. comieron

Figure 14.2 Card from cognitively complex task

[they ate] → comie<s>ro</s>n → comie**ra**n [they ate-SUBJ]. An example of how this verb form occurs in the dependent verb position after a verb that relays an intentional, emotive state is: 'She shut the door loudly.' [action] 'Why?' '**She was angry**INDEPENDENT **that they ate-SUBJ**DEPENDENT all of the leftover cake'. [explanation of character's intentional reason; verb in dependent clause marked with subjunctive morphology]. Participants in this study had extensive practice forming predicates with independent and dependent clauses. They had also learned about the subjunctive concept in class and how to conjugate the subjunctive mood in the present tense. They had not learned past subjunctive morphology. To control for outside exposure, the past subjunctive form was removed from the curriculum at the time of the study, and participants' teachers were asked not to cover it in class. The tasks used in the present study were the same as those used in Baralt (2013), and proved to be successful at eliciting intentional reasoning in a two-way, interactive setting online, where the subjunctive was naturally required because of the demands of the tasks.

Assessment tasks

Three different assessment tasks were used to measure learning in this study. The first two were productive tasks carried out in the FTF and CMC modes. These were interactive story retells just as the treatment tasks were, but during which feedback was not provided on past subjunctive forms. Each assessment task had 10 obligatory instances where the Spanish past subjunctive needed to be produced. Three versions of both productive tasks were created, all with a different storyline, for the pre-test, post-test and delayed post-test data collection times. The third assessment was a multiple-choice test taken on a computer. It contained 15 obligatory uses of the past subjunctive. Three versions of the multiple-choice test were also made for each testing session. The order in which participants took the assessment task versions was randomized using a Latin square method. However, at each testing session, learners always took the multiple-choice test last so as to not be prompted with input before carrying out the FTF or CMC production tasks.

Working memory spans

As is recommended by Conway *et al.* (2005), three different memory span tasks were used to measure participants' WMC: an operation span task (OSPAN), a counting span task (CSPAN) and an RSPAN. All spans used were created by Dr Engle and associates at Georgia Tech University,[1] and were adapted for this study to be delivered to participants one-on-one with Microsoft PowerPoint. They contain a storage as well as a processing component, and their reliability and validity have been highly attested in the psychology literature. The OSPAN task (Engle *et al.*, 2005) required participants to calculate arithmetic problems aloud, judge a possible answer to the math problem and recall letters at the end of each mathematical string. The CSPAN task (Engle *et al.*, 1999) required participants to judge circles (as compared to squares of the same color), count them aloud and then recall the final count total of the circles in each set. Finally, the RSPAN task required participants to read sentences aloud, judge their semantic acceptability and recall letters at the end of each group of sentences. Together, these three tasks measure the executive component of working memory (with both a processing and a storage component), which is recommended by Wen (2012) in his integrated framework of working memory for SLA (see Wen [2012] for arguments on why the executive component of WMC is responsible for monitoring and noticing feedback).

Design

A pre-test-post-test-delayed post-test design was employed for this study. The 34 participants were randomly assigned to two different groups, one that performed the cognitively simple tasks and one that performed the cognitively complex tasks. Participants attended four sessions in total, each conducted one-on-one with the researcher. On Day 1, they carried out the three working memory spans and the three pre-test assessments: the FTF productive task, the CMC productive task and the multiple-choice receptive test. One week later, participants carried out the first treatment session. The next day, participants did the second treatment task, and also completed the three immediate post-tests. One week after that, participants did the delayed post-tests. Figure 14.3 provides a visual conception of how the study was implemented.

For the two treatment sessions, participants were given instructions and were also given a Mac laptop. Those in the simple group were told that they had to retell the story as best as they could to the researcher via iChat, using Spanish only and in the past tense. They were told not to worry about typing accent marks, and that if they had any questions about vocabulary, to ask the researcher via chat just as they would in a FTF conversation. Participants in the complex group were told the same thing, and in addition, were told that at times, they would have to reflect on what caused some of the story characters to do certain actions (i.e. their intentional reasons, their mental state, etc.). When the treatment session began, the researcher left the room and connected the participant's laptop to her own. All CMC interaction was conducted in this way in separate rooms, as opposed to sitting and typing in front of each other. This was for the purpose of eliciting the true nature of online language instruction. The CMC interaction was two-way in nature, with the researcher and participant working together to retell the story in Spanish. In both experimental conditions, whenever participants made an error on

Experimental procedure

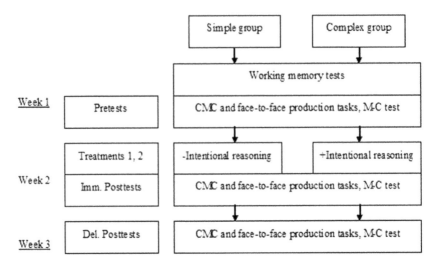

Figure 14.3 Experimental procedure

the past subjunctive form, the researcher provided them with a full recast (and without any typographical enhancement). An example of how this was done in iChat is provided in Figure 14.4.

The excerpt in Figure 14.4 shows a feedback episode between the researcher (in light font) and a participant (in black font). In the third line, the participant explains why the character did a certain action: '…she was happy that [Sra.] Gomez worked-IND for them'. The verb *trabajaba* (worked) is in the indicative mood and lacks subjunctive morphology. The researcher, in the next turn in iChat, provides a corrective recast, and changes the verb to '*trabajara*' which is marked with subjunctive morphology. Feedback was provided in this way in both treatment conditions.

The assessment tasks were done in the same way as the treatment tasks; however, no feedback was provided during these story retells. The CMC assessment tasks were also done via laptops and in separate rooms. The FTF assessment tasks were performed at a table with the researcher and participant sitting across from each other. After completing the two production tasks, the researcher then set up the participant's multiple-choice test, which he/she took online. All CMC interaction was recorded with the screen recording software iShowU and all FTF interaction was recorded with a digital audio recorder.

Figure 14.4 Example of recast done in iChat.
Figure 14.4 translation:

>**Participant:** She waited for sra. gomez and sra. martinez was smiling when sra. gomez arrived
>**Researcher:** Why?
>**Participant:** Because she was happy that sra. gomez worked-IND for them.
>**Researcher:** She was happy that Srta. Gómez worked-SUB for them. ←RECAST
>**Participant:** Yes
>**Researcher:** Alright, let's go to the next one!

Coding and analyses

Working memory data

Following the procedural recommendations of Conway *et al.* (2005), performance on all WMC span tasks (OSPAN, CSPAN, RSPAN) was first checked to ensure that participants achieved at least 85% accuracy in the processing component of the tasks (correct math calculations of the OSPAN, correct grammatical judgements of the RSPAN and correct counting during the CSPAN). This was critical to ensure that participants were actively engaged with the processing component of each task. Next, a partial-credit unit (PCU) scoring procedure was used to code and grade the spans, which Conway *et al.* (2005: 774) explain as 'mean proportion of elements within an item that were recalled correctly'. This method requires that one point be assigned to each correctly recalled element, regardless of its serial position. After scoring each task, scores were then averaged to create one composite score for each participant.

Assessment tasks

For both the FTF and CMC production assessment tasks, participants' production of the past subjunctive was scored using a weighted coding method in order to account for emerging incorporation of the subjunctive mood (e.g. Baralt, 2013; Norris & Ortega, 2009). A score of zero was assigned to indicative forms, 0.5 to present subjunctive forms and 1 to past subjunctive forms. Deviations (i.e. interlanguage forms), such as *tengaba(n)* (produced by four different learners), *fueron sean, estudieron, fuyera, hacera*, etc., were also given one full point. For the multiple-choice receptive tests, participants' selection of correctly answered past subjunctive forms was coded by assigning 1 point to correct items and 0 points to incorrect items.

Interrater reliability

A second SLA researcher coded and scored all of the working memory tests, as well as 20% of the CMC and FTF production tests. The working memory tests achieved 100% agreement and the production tests achieved 96% agreement. Both researchers met and discussed ways to deal with those interlanguage forms that were not coded equally until 100% rater agreement was achieved.

Statistical analyses

First, descriptive statistics (tallies, means and standard deviations) were calculated for participants' working memory span scores, as well as scores on the pre-tests, post-tests and delayed post-tests. Next, internal reliability (coefficient alphas) was assessed for each WMC span (OSPAN, RSPAN and CSPAN). A latent variable analysis was then conducted to divide the participants into learners of high and low working memory. Using SPSS version 20, correlation coefficients were calculated to explore the relationship between working memory and learning on each of the three post-tests. The analysis was done separately for the two experimental groups in order to test whether WMC was a moderating variable, i.e. whether working memory was related to learning and if learning outcomes were different for learners with low working memory compared to learners with high working memory, on both task types.

Results

This study was designed to investigate the moderating relationship between WMC and learning as a result of feedback provided during simple versus complex tasks in the computerized environment, and whether outcomes were different for low versus high working memory learners. Descriptive statistics are provided below for the provision of recasts during the treatments and learning outcomes as measured by the three assessments.

Number of recasts

The maximum number of recasts that a participant could receive during each treatment session was 10, for a total of 20 feedback opportunities. If the participant produced a past subjunctive form accurately, no recast was provided. Those participants who performed the simple task in CMC received an average of 6.88 recasts during the first treatment, and 4.24 recasts during the second treatment. Participants who performed the complex task needed an average of 8.88 and then 8.56 recasts during Treatment 1 and Treatment 2, respectively. This information is summarized in Table 14.1. Clearly, and especially by Treatment 2, the participants who received recasts alongside the cognitively simple task began incorporating the form earlier than those who did the complex task.

Learning outcomes

Learning of the past subjunctive form was measured with three assessments: two productive interactive tasks (in FTF and in CMC) and a receptive, multiple-choice test. Table 14.2 provides a summary of learners' scores from the pre-test to the delayed post-test. Similar to the mean number of recasts provided, a marked difference was observed between the simple group and the complex group. As can be seen from the development scores across time, and as measured by all of the assessments, the simple group learned more than the complex group.

Working memory

The correlation coefficient was first calculated for all three working memory spans, the OSPAN, RSPAN and CSPAN. All of the spans were significantly correlated with each other at the $p<0.001$ level: CPSPAN with OSPAN: $r(70)=0.59$, $p<0.001$; CPSAN with RSPAN: $r(70)=0.60$, $p<0.001$; OSPAN with RSPAN: $r(70)=0.77$, $p<0.001$. This confirmed that the three spans tapped the same construct and that further analyses could subsequently be performed. Descriptive statistics were then calculated to establish the mean composite score, which was 2.08. A new variable was subsequently calculated, which established the low working memory learners as those in the range of 0 to the mean (2.08) and the

Table 14.1 Provision of recasts to learners when feedback was needed

	Simple task group	Complex task group
Treatment session 1	6.88 (2.72)	8.88 (1.54)
Treatment session 2	4.24 (3.27)	8.56 (2.55)

Mean (standard deviation).

Table 14.2 Learner's development of the past subjunctive over time (mean scores)

	Simple task group			Complex task group		
	FTF task	CMC task	M-C test	FTF task	CMC task	M-C test
Pre-test	0.00	0.06	2.06	0.00	0.00	2.06
	(0.00)	(0.24)	(1.25)	(0.00)	(0.00)	(3.21)
Post-test	4.59	4.88	9.29	1.35	1.74	4.88
	(3.69)	(3.59)	(5.59)	(2.42)	(3.35)	(5.48)
D. post-test	4.06	4.79	10.59	0.59	1.12	4.82
	(3.50)	(3.53)	(5.25)	(1.30)	(2.63)	(5.49)

Mean (standard deviation).

high working memory learners as those in the range of the mean to the highest score.

Next, in order to determine if working memory moderated learning, bivariate correlations were conducted for each assessment at the post-test and delayed post-test times, with data output split for low versus high WMC learners. It was hypothesized that (1) working memory would be related to learning and that (2) there would be a difference between low versus high WMC learners, especially on the complex task (per the claims of the Cognition Hypothesis). Table 14.3 provides the results from the correlations.

Relationship between working memory and learning

A visual inspection of Table 14.3 reveals only one significant, albeit negative, relationship: learning outcomes on the immediate multiple-choice test for high working memory learners in the simple task group.

Table 14.3 Pearson's correlation results: Working memory as a moderator of learning

		Simple task group	Complex task group
FTF production task immediate post-test	Low WMC	−0.129	0.571
	High WMC	−0.596	−0.501
FTF production task delayed post-test	Low WMC	−0.237	−0.222
	High WMC	−0.731	−0.675
CMC production task immediate post-test	Low WMC	−0.183	0.001
	High WMC	−0.419	−0.428
CMC production task delayed post-test	Low WMC	−0.087	0.054
	High WMC	−0.526	−0.514
M-C receptive task immediate post-test	Low WMC	0.307	−0.296
	High WMC	−0.933**	0.116
M-C receptive task delayed post-test	Low WMC	−0.015	−0.497
	High WMC	−0.720	−0.276

$**p=0.002$.

Given that the relationship was negative however, working memory did *not* lead to more learning in this group (a negative inverse relationship would in fact imply that higher WMC would lead to worse developmental outcomes). As the remaining data in Table 14.3 show, WMC was not significantly correlated with learning on any of the other immediate or delayed assessments, in the simple or the complex groups. This applied regardless of whether learners had low or high WMC.

Results summary

Contrary to expectations, working memory was not related to learning in this study. As Pearson's correlations revealed, working memory also did not moderate learning differently for different types of learners. While participants did learn, the construct of working memory was not related to their benefitting from feedback in the CMC mode in this study, irrespective of whether it was provided during a cognitive simple or complex communicative task.

Discussion

The data from this study run counter to the findings by Payne and colleagues that (1) learners with higher working memory benefit from feedback more, and (2) CMC may help learners with lower WMC. In fact, this study found that working memory was not related to learning outcomes as a result of carrying out simple or complex tasks in the computerized chat environment. The findings from this study are more in line with those by Sagarra and Abdul (2013), who reported that there is no effect for WMC on *written* feedback efficacy in the computerized mode.

Payne and Whitney (2002) found a significant relationship between WMC and oral proficiency development after interacting in the CMC environment. Similarly, Payne and Ross (2005) found that lower phonological working memory learners produced significantly more output in CMC. However, these two studies did not look at working memory as it relates to feedback efficacy in CMC. Lai *et al.* (2008) did examine the relationship between working memory and noticing of feedback, and reported that higher working memory mediated the noticing of non-contingent feedback. Sagarra explored the relationship between working memory, feedback and learning in the CMC mode. She reported that WMC was significantly related to the recast group's learning, but learners in her study were provided with *oral* corrective recasts via a computer. Her findings corroborate with Mackey *et al.* (2002), who found that working memory predicts learning outcomes as a result of corrective feedback, but only if that feedback is provided orally. Sagarra and Abdul's (2013) findings also support this line of research:

WMC mediates learning and modified output production for learners who must process feedback auditorily, but not if it is written out for them in the CMC environment.

These data indicate that working memory does not play a role in learners' capacity to learn from feedback when it is provided in written form and in the computerized environment. Theoretically, this makes sense: the executive component of working memory is what permits learners to zoom in on and process specific relevant stimuli while blocking out irrelevant input. This is specific to the processing of auditory incoming L2 input, however. When oral corrective feedback is involved, and particularly recasts (which reformulate a learner's own form immediately after the form is said), working memory is the cognitive space in which an incorrect form is compared to the corrected form. If feedback is written out in chat, however, processing and comparison of forms in working memory is not necessary. This is because feedback in CMC is durable and permanent, and when contingent and written out, is very easy for learners to notice; its noticeability in CMC is not dependent on WMC. Contrarily, feedback in the FTF is ephemeral and temporary, and does depend on WMC.

One surprising result was the lack of a relationship between working memory and learning outcomes on both the cognitively simple and the complex tasks. The Cognition Hypothesis predicts that WMC will moderate task performance and learning as tasks increase in complexity. That notion was not supported here. In Baralt (2013), it was reported that the benefits associated with more complex tasks in mediating feedback efficacy may only apply in the FTF mode. Reflecting on type of task may also explain Lai *et al.*'s (2008) findings. Lai *et al.* (2008) reported a significant relationship between WMC and learners' accurate noticing of *non-contingent* feedback. However, the researchers used spot-the-difference tasks in their study, a type of task that is cognitively simple. In their study, working memory did not significantly moderate noticing of feedback that was contingent. The current study supports their finding in regard to the relationship between working memory and noticing of feedback during the cognitively simple task. In complex tasks in CMC however, the issue of error-feedback non-contingency is so problematic that it impeded learning (Baralt, 2013). That is, when learners have to reflect on the intentional reasons during a complex task, in addition to typing out, reading and sending messages in the CMC mode, their attentional resources are too dispersed to be able to process feedback – especially non-contingent feedback. In the cognitively simple task in CMC, feedback was very contingent with errors, and WMC did not matter in learners' noticing of the feedback.

Thus, task type could make a key difference in the moderating effect of WMC on feedback efficacy in online task-based learning. Cognitively complex tasks may not work in the CMC mode because of the attentional resources that they consume (Baralt, 2013).

What's more, feedback contingency may be more achievable alongside cognitively simple tasks in CMC. The current study and Lai *et al.* (2008) suggest that cognitively simple tasks in CMC do not depend on working memory because they so easily allow for error-feedback contingency. It would be very interesting to replicate the current study for additional cognitively simple versus cognitively complex tasks. It would also be worthwhile to replicate the study for the FTF mode. Learning, as reported here, was not dependent on WMC. It is reasonable to assume, however, that learning indeed would be moderated by working memory in more complex tasks in FTF interaction, which would support the claims of the Cognition Hypothesis.

Future studies should continue to examine how feedback is processed in both modes, and alongside different types of language teaching tasks. Another fruitful area of research is to examine interaction, feedback and task type in computerized video chat, such as Adobe® Connect. This is a medium available in almost all online language classes, and yet no research exists on how learners process feedback given in this environment. If working memory moderates feedback efficacy in FTF interaction, it seems reasonable to assume that it also does so in video-based interaction, given that feedback would be ephemeral and temporal in the video chat mode as well. Studies are also needed that examine how learners can best profit from feedback in this environment. Recent research has called for more studies on how to train learners to recognize and maximize how they use feedback in computerized learning environments (Gurzynski-Weiss & Baralt, 2014), and this is certainly an area that could be applied to video-based online language instruction.

Conclusion

The goal of this study was to examine whether working memory moderated feedback efficacy in task-based computerized interaction, and if the CMC mode might help learners with lower working memory (with no differences observed in the relationship between working memory and learning outcomes, as tasks increased in complexity). Working memory was not related to learning on simple or complex tasks. These data are in line with recent findings that working memory does not play a role on feedback efficacy when its mode of delivery is written (Sagarra & Abdul, 2013). Alongside cognitively simple task performance in CMC, the findings reported here also support those by Lai *et al.* (2008), where working memory is not indispensable in noticing contingent feedback. Working memory may only be relevant for feedback delivered when parsing of incoming auditory stimuli is required and/or for non-contingent recasts alongside cognitively simple tasks in CMC. Future studies are needed to examine these effects with different types of tasks, and especially with tasks that become increasingly complex for language learners. This line of research will inform what we know about how and where learners profit from corrective feedback in online language instruction.

Note

(1) Dr Engle graciously allowed his tests to be used for this study. The tests are available to researchers on his laboratory website: http://www.psychology.gatech.edu/renglelab/. Users must request a password and must cite the source of the span.

References

Baddeley, A.D. (2003) Working memory: Looking back and looking forward. *Nature Reviews Neuroscience* 4, 829–839.

Baddeley, A.D. (2007) *Working Memory, Thought, and Action*. Oxford: Oxford University Press.

Baralt, M. (2013) The impact of cognitive complexity on feedback efficacy during online versus face-to-face interactive tasks. *Studies in Second Language Acquisition* 35, 689–725.

Baralt, M., Gilabert, R. and Robinson, P. (2014) *Task Sequencing and Instructed Second Language Learning*. London: Bloomsbury.

Blake, R.J. (2011) Current trends in online language learning. *Annual Review of Applied Linguistics* 31, 19–35.

Conway, A., Kane, M., Bunting, M., Hambrick, D., Wilhelm, O. and Engle, R. (2005) Working memory span tasks: A methodological review and user's guide. *Psychonomic Bulletin & Review* 12, 769–786.

Ellis, R. (2003) *Task-Based Language Learning and Teaching*. Oxford: Oxford University Press.

Engle, R.W., Tuholski, S. W., Laughlin, J. E. and Conway, A. R. A. (1999) Working memory, short-term memory, and general fluid intelligence: A latent-variable approach. *Journal of Experimental Psychology: General* 128 (3), 309–331.

Gurzynski-Weiss, L. and Baralt, M. (2014) Exploring learner perception and use of task-based interactional feedback in FTF and CMC modes. *Studies in Second Language Acquisition* 36, 1–37.

Lai, C., Fei, F. and Roots, R. (2008) The contingency of recasts and noticing. *CALICO Journal* 26, 70–90.

Long, M.H. (2007) *Problems in SLA*. Mahwah, NJ: Lawrence Erlbaum Associates.

Mackey, A. (1999) Input, interaction and second language development: An empirical study of question formation in ESL. *Studies in Second Language Acquisition* 21, 557–587.

Mackey, A., Philp, J., Egi, T., Fujii, A. and Tatsumi, T. (2002) Individual differences in working memory, noticing of interactional feedback, and L2 development. In P. Robinson (ed.) *Individual Differences and Instructed Language Learning* (pp. 181–209). Philadelphia, PA: John Benjamins.

Mackey, A., Adams, R., Stafford, C. and Winke, P. (2010) Exploring the relationship between modified output and working memory capacity. *Language Learning* 60, 501–533.

Norris, J. and Ortega, L. (2009) Towards an organic approach to investigating CAF in instructed SLA: The case of complexity. *Applied Linguistics* 30, 555–578.

Payne, J.S. and Whitney, P.J. (2002) Developing L2 oral proficiency through synchronous CMC: Output, working memory, and interlanguage development. *CALICO Journal* 20, 7–32.

Payne, J.S. and Ross, B. (2005) Synchronous CMC, working memory, and L2 oral proficiency development. *Language Learning & Technology* 9, 35–54.

Roberts, L. (2012) Individual differences in second language sentence process. *Language Learning* 172–188.

Robinson, P. (2001a) Task complexity, cognitive resources, and syllabus design: A triadic framework for examining task influences on SLA. In P. Robinson (ed.) *Cognition and Second Language Instruction* (pp. 287–318). Cambridge: Cambridge University Press.

Robinson, P. (2001b) Task complexity, task difficulty, and task production: Exploring interactions in a componential framework. *Applied Linguistics* 22, 27–57.

Robinson, P. (2007) Task complexity, theory of mind, and intentional reasoning: Effects on L2 speech production, interaction, and perceptions of task difficulty. *International Review of Applied Linguistics in Language Teaching* 45, 191–213.

Robinson, P. (2010) Situating and distributing cognition across task demands: The SSARC model of pedagogic task sequencing. In M. Putz and L. Sicola (eds) *Inside the Learner Mind: Cognitive Processing in Second Language Acquisition* (pp. 239–264). Philadelphia, PA: John Benjamins.

Robinson, P. (2011) Second language task complexity, the Cognition Hypothesis, language learning, and performance. In P. Robinson (ed.) *Researching Task Complexity: Task Demands, Task-Based Language Learning and Performance* (pp. 3–38). Amsterdam: John Benjamins.

Robinson, P. and Gilabert, R. (2007) Task complexity, the Cognition Hypothesis and second language learning and performance. *International Review of Applied Linguistics in Language Teaching* 45, 161–176.

Sagarra, N. (2007) From CALL to face-to-face interaction: The effect of computer-delivered recasts and working memory on L2 development. In A. Mackey (ed.) *Conversational Interaction in Second Language Acquisition: A Collection of Empirical Studies* (pp. 229–248). Oxford: Oxford University Press.

Sagarra, N. and Abdul, R. (2013) Optimizing the noticing of recasts via computer-delivered feedback: Evidence that oral input enhancement and working memory help second language learning. *The Modern Language Journal* 97, 196–216.

Sauro, S. (2009) Computer-mediated corrective feedback and the development of L2 grammar. *Language Learning & Technology* 13, 96–120.

Schmidt, R. (1990) The role of consciousness in second language learning. *Applied Linguistics* 11, 129–158.

Swain, M. (2005) The output hypothesis: Theory and research. In E. Hinkel (ed.) *Handbook on Research in Second Language Teaching and Learning* (pp. 471–484). Mahwah, NJ: Lawrence Erlbaum.

Yilmaz, Y. and Yuksel, D. (2011) Effects of communication mode and salience on recasts: A first exposure study. *Language Teaching Research* 15, 457–477.

Wen, Z. (2012) Working memory and second language learning. *International Journal of Applied Linguistics* 22, 1–22.

15 Working Memory Measures and L2 Proficiency

Anne E. Mitchell, Scott Jarvis,
Michelle O'Malley and
Irina Konstantinova

Introduction

Working memory (WM), the ability to simultaneously store and process information, has been a popular topic of research for decades among cognitive psychologists and is now receiving increased interest among linguists and second language acquisition (SLA) researchers who wish to examine its role in language learning. Psychologists have developed several appropriate methods of measuring and discussing WM among first language (L1) speakers, and SLA researchers have been quick to apply these methods to the study of WM among second language (L2) learners. However, further examination of the nature and context of these methods suggests that they may be inappropriate for research with L2 participants.

A few researchers have already voiced concern over the way in which this research is being conducted. Gass and Mackey (2007: 69) point out that 'not much research has attempted to compare these tests of working memory for their appropriateness in the context of SLA research'. Similarly, Ellis (2005: 339) warns against 'circularity in interpretation and operationalization' of current WM measurements used in SLA research, specifically in studies examining a relationship between WM and L2 production.

Past studies have indicated that WM plays a very active role in the language learning process. More specifically, WM has demonstrated strong correlations with L2 proficiency levels. The present study seeks to further investigate this relationship and to determine whether the results of past studies examining WM and L2 proficiency may have been flawed by the utilisation of methods inappropriate for SLA research.

Literature Review

L2 proficiency

In an effort to determine how best to assess learner performance, SLA researchers have developed several models for conceptualising L2 learner proficiency. Jim Cummins (1979) first made a distinction between basic interpersonal communication skills (BICS) and cognitive academic language proficiency (CALP). Bachman's (1990) communicative competence model, divided into organisational competence and pragmatic competence, similarly discussed differing ways in which L2 learners employ their L2. In discussing L2 proficiency, we refer to Skehan's (1998) complexity, accuracy and fluency (CAF) model, which identifies three components of language proficiency. The first, complexity, refers to elaborate and varied language use (Ellis, 2003). The second, accuracy, measures a learner's ability to produce error-free speech. The third component, fluency, refers to a native-like language processing (Housen & Kuiken, 2009).

The validity of an L2 proficiency measurement may be determined by its ability to measure each of these three components. Unfortunately, convenience has often led researchers to use measurements that lack the complexity and the reliability to provide an accurate measurement. Some studies have used self-reports to determine proficiency levels (Rai *et al.*, 2010; Van den Noort *et al.*, 2006), the effects of which may be altered by a participant's tendency to over- or under-report his/her own proficiency levels. Other instruments have included word translation tasks (Van den Noort *et al.*, 2006) and simplified oral interviews (Payne & Whitney, 2002). These tasks measure only the accuracy component of proficiency and are incapable of measuring both the complexity and the fluency components, thus rendering them invalid measurements.

A widely recognised measurement of English proficiency is the test of English as a foreign language (TOEFL). Institutions in over 130 countries rely on the TOEFL as an accurate measurement of English L2 proficiency (ETS, 2011). Numerous research studies have demonstrated the TOEFL to be both highly reliable and highly valid and have determined that it measures both accuracy (Cohen & Upton, 2006) and complexity (Cumming *et al.*, 2006) of English production. It is important to note that the TOEFL provides a general measure of proficiency in academic English, but it may not be the best measurement of interpersonal communication skills. While no test is perfect, the current study proposes the use of TOEFL scores to serve as a more trustworthy measure of L2 proficiency than has been used in most of the relevant past research. This does not mean that we consider the TOEFL to be the ideal measure of English proficiency; we merely assert that it appears to be a far more reliable measure than most other measures of proficiency that have been used in investigations of the relationship between WM and language proficiency.

Working memory

Psychologists have developed multiple models of WM. The literature review will discuss two of the most widely recognised WM models: the Just and Carpenter (1992) model and the Baddeley and Hitch (1974) model. Both models identify two key components of WM: storage and processing. The Baddeley model, however, further dissects the storage component into finer elements.

Just and Carpenter (1992) developed a unitary model of WM that identified two interrelated capacities: storage and processing. Each of the two capacities was argued to make up the larger WM capacity (WMC) and to be 'fuelled' by the common commodity of activation, so that increased demand on one component resulted in decreased capacity in the other (Just & Carpenter, 1992: 123). Therefore, tasks that taxed processing ability would result in limited storage capacity. An individual's WMC was determined by the amount of available activation. Those with higher levels of available activation were able to store more items to be processed. When too many items were stored and there was insufficient activation to process them, some of these items would be displaced from WM.

Unsworth and Engle (2007) defined this relationship in a similar way using different terminology. They noted that WM must perform two tasks: maintenance and retrieval. Maintenance, according to the researchers, referred to the ability to hold information in an active state so that it may be retrieved when necessary. The authors also differentiated between two memory storage units: primary memory (PM) and secondary memory (SM). PM is where memory units are actively maintained to be utilised in ongoing processing, whereas SM is where memory units are stored and retrieved by WM when needed. The researchers held that PM had a capacity of four units. Any additional units would automatically be stored in SM and later retrieved when needed (Unsworth & Engle, 2007).

In an amendment to his 1974 publication (Baddeley & Hitch, 1974), Alan Baddeley (2000) proposed a model of WM that comprised four components: the central executive, the phonological loop, the visuospatial sketchpad and the episodic buffer. The central executive was defined as a supervisory system responsible for regulating its slave processes, shifting between tasks, and initiating attention and inhibition processes. The phonological loop was determined to store and process auditory information, as well as visually presented information that had been encoded into phonological information through a process of silent articulation. The visuospatial sketchpad was theorised to store visual and spatial information, and the most recently introduced component, the episodic buffer, was argued to be responsible for linking information across components to form integrated units of information (Baddeley, 2000).

Some researchers have argued that results of past research may have been skewed by the failure to make a distinction between WM and short-term memory (Conway *et al.*, 2002). Short-term memory refers to a simple storage structure, while WM is more complex in that it refers to both a storage and an activation component. Upon making this distinction, studies have confirmed that WM is a more significant predictor of fluid intelligence than short-term memory (Carpenter *et al.*, 1990; Conway *et al.*, 2002).

Measuring working memory

Researchers have developed a myriad of WM tests including listening span, reading span, digit span, speaking span, counting span and operation span tasks. These tasks may be considered 'simple' (measuring storage capacity only) or 'complex' (measuring storage and processing). Tasks designed to measure both the maintenance and retrieval components of WM must incorporate the transmission of information, which is then recalled by the participant on completion of a task that requires some form of cognitive processing.

The reading span task has been a favourite among WM researchers for decades (Daneman & Carpenter, 1980; Van den Noort *et al.*, 2006). This task requires participants to read a sentence, determine whether or not the sentence is plausible and store the final word of the sentence while moving on to the next sentence. At the end of a set of sentences, participants are asked to recall the final word of each sentence. Cognitive psychologists have used the reading span task and its variants, the listening span (Goo, 2010) and speaking span (Finardi & Weissheimer, 2008) tasks, as successful measurements of storage and processing capacity. An issue arises, however, when SLA researchers adopt the reading span task as a measurement of WMC among L2 learners. When the task is administered in the L2, it becomes difficult to determine whether the results measure WMC or L2 reading ability. The issue is further confounded by studies using this measurement to establish a correlation between WM and L2 proficiency (Van den Noort *et al.*, 2006).

The recalling of digits in a digit span task may be favoured for its resistance to influence from lexical knowledge (Harrington & Sawyer, 1992). Similar 'simple' span tasks, which measure only the storage component of WM, include free-recall tasks. Unsworth and Engle (2007) administered a free-recall task in which participants were presented with several sets of words and were subsequently asked to reproduce them in any order. Mackey and Sachs (2011) used a variant of this task in which participants were asked to recall non-words.

One task that remains popular among psychologists and SLA researchers as an effective measurement of both storage and processing components of WMC is the operation-span (O-span) task. Several recent studies have used a variant of this task in data collection (Goo, 2010; Pardo-Vázquez & Fernández-Rey, 2008; Weitz *et al.*, 2011). Goo (2010) used an O-span task in which participants were given a series of math problems to complete, followed by an L2 word. At the end of the sequence of math problems, participants were asked to recall the words in order. Engle *et al.* (1990) used a similar O-span task in which the words to be recalled were divided into high-frequency and low-frequency groups. Conway and Engle (1996) pre-tested participants' math ability to control the demand placed on processing capacity during an O-span task. Participants were required to recall a series of high-frequency, concrete nouns. Participants' storage capacities were measured by their ability to correctly recall the words.

Due to the language-independent processing component, the O-span seems to be one of the most appropriate WM measures for testing L2 participants. However, an O-span requiring the storage of L2 words may demonstrate effects similar to the reading span task, as it may be influenced by L2 proficiency levels. It is crucial, therefore, that the effects of L2 lexical knowledge be mitigated. This may be accomplished by presenting high-frequency words only or by presenting a non-lexical (i.e. monosyllabic letters) stimulus instead (Juffs & Harrington, 2011).

Working memory and SLA

The results of these studies have demonstrated that WM plays an active role in both L2 production and L2 processing. More specifically, WMC has been linked to L2 vocabulary development. Baddeley (2003) found that the phonological loop component contributed to learning L2 words. Further research has supported this link between the phonological loop and L2 vocabulary acquisition (French, 2006). On a related note, Service (1992) found that a higher WMC resulted in a more efficient system of acquiring L2 words.

WM may also play a part in language learning aptitude, which is considered by many SLA researchers to be a major determiner of successful L2 development. Miyake and Friedman (1998) discovered a significant correlation between WMC and syntactic comprehension ability, a large component of language learning aptitude. Another study found a correlation between WMC and inductive language learning ability (Safar & Kormos, 2008). In addition, WMC was found to be a predictor of L2 listening and reading ability (Andersson, 2010).

Trude and Tokowicz (2011) found that individuals with higher WM capacities were more successful in inhibiting negative L1 transfer and were able to produce L2 structures with more accuracy. Similarly, Finardi and Weissheimer (2008) posit that WM contributes directly to both the conceptualisation and the formulation of L2 speech production. They confirmed this hypothesis through a series of tasks in which WMC demonstrated a direct correlation with performance in L2 speech tasks.

Recent research has suggested that WM may be directly related to L2 proficiency levels. Van den Noort *et al.* (2006) utilised self-reports and a vocabulary translation test to determine participants' proficiency levels in German and Norwegian, correlating the results with O-span scores. The researchers reported findings consistent with past research, indicating that WM capacities were directly related to L2 proficiency levels and, thus, to L2 production. In addition, Payne and Whitney (2002) examined the relationship between oral proficiency interview (OPI) scores and reading span scores and found that the phonological loop component of WMC correlated with L2 oral proficiency.

However, as demonstrated, the current methods of measuring both WM and L2 proficiency in current research may be inappropriate for studies in SLA. In a recent publication, Gass and Lee (2011) measured the effect of L2 proficiency on performance in an L2 WM task. Results indicated that L2 proficiency influenced participant performance on L2 WM tasks 'with a small strength of association' (Gass & Lee, 2011: 72). The authors draw from these findings to discuss the methodological issues associated with performing WM tasks in the L2, concluding that researchers must carefully consider participant L2 proficiency levels when conducting WM research in the L2 (Gass & Lee, 2011).

High correlations between WM and L2 proficiency scores are interesting, of course, unless the WM tasks that are used turn out to be measures of L2 proficiency in and of themselves. WM tasks requiring the processing or storage of L2 text (reading span, O-span requiring storage of L2 words, etc.) may reflect a measurement of L2 proficiency rather than WM. In addition, word translation tasks and self-reports may not accurately measure the complexity of the L2 proficiency construct. Therefore, a study utilising language-independent WM scores and complex measurements of L2 proficiency may provide a more accurate portrayal of the relationship between WM and language proficiency. The current study sought to answer the following questions:

(1) Is there a statistically significant relationship between WMC and L2 proficiency?
(2) Which WM task demonstrates the strongest correlation with L2 proficiency scores?
(3) Which proficiency level (beginner, intermediate or advanced) demonstrates the strongest correlation with WM task scores?

Method

Participants

Participants in the study consisted of 36 undergraduate Chinese learners of English enrolled in an intensive English programme (IEP) at a Midwestern university. Participants were recruited by IEP instructors and members of the research team and were offered a small monetary compensation for their participation. The mean participant age was 22.31, ranging from 17 to 35 years old. All non-native participants had taken the TOEFL in paper-based or internet-based test (iBT) format within six months prior to participating in the study. Paper-based TOEFL scores were converted to iBT scores to provide consistency in scoring. Participant proficiency levels were categorised as beginner (0–40 iBT, $n=9$), intermediate (41–80 iBT, $n=23$) and advanced (81–120 iBT, $n=4$).

Instruments and procedure

A language background questionnaire was administered to ensure that high proficiency levels in a non-target non-native language would not interfere with task performance. Participants were asked to provide their current TOEFL score, IEP level, length of time studying English, age at which they began studying English and experience with any additional languages. Current TOEFL scores were also verified with permission from programme records.

To determine WMC, participants were administered both simple (digit span) and complex (O-span) WM tasks. The digit span task was administered in both the L1 (Chinese) and the L2 (English). These tasks required participants to listen to a prerecorded series of digits and repeat them in order when prompted. Digits were presented in increasing set sizes to determine capacity. The L1 digit span ranged in set sizes from 4 to 11 digits, and the L2 digit span set sizes ranged from 4 to 9 digits, as past research has indicated that participant performance on Chinese digit span tasks is consistently greater than performance on English digit span tasks (Stigler *et al.*, 1986).

Participants were then administered a relatively language-independent O-span task. During the task, participants were shown a completed two-step mathematical problem (e.g. [12/4]+6=9) and were prompted to identify the solution as correct or incorrect. Upon responding to the problem, participants were shown a monosyllabic letter (e.g. T) and were asked to say the letter aloud. Participants were then prompted to move on to another mathematical problem followed by another letter. At the end of each trial (i.e. set of problems), participants were prompted to recall the letters aloud in order. Trials were presented with increasing set sizes (two to six) to determine capacity.

In addition to the WM tasks, participants were administered elicited imitation and self-paced timed reading tasks to measure L2 production and processing. All tasks were programmed using Psyscope software and were administered with a Macintosh computer and a button box to record participant responses. Data collection sessions were audio-recorded to ensure accuracy in data analysis. In accordance with Wen's (2012: 12) argument that WM should be thought of as a 'continuous variable', all WM tasks were given a total span score (i.e. the total number of digits/letters that were recalled) rather than a level score (Conway *et al.*, 2005). Total span scores also result in greater sensitivity for statistical analysis.

Analysis and Results

Participants performed better on the L1 digit span (mean=14.92) than the L2 digit span (mean=6.03). The results show no significant correlation between iBT scores and L1 digit span or O-span totals. However, the L2 digit span was found to correlate moderately and significantly with iBT scores ($n=36$, $r=0.439$, $p=0.007$). These results support the hypothesis that performance on a WM task will be affected by proficiency in the language in which the task is administered (L1 or L2).

The initial absence of a significant correlation between iBT scores and L1 digit span and O-span scores is somewhat surprising. However, further analysis demonstrates differing trends among participants at different proficiency levels. When participants are divided into beginner (0–40 iBT), intermediate (41–80 iBT) and advanced (81–120 iBT) proficiency groups, we begin to see evidence of a more nuanced relationship between WM and proficiency scores. Beginner participants demonstrate no significant correlation between iBT and O-span ($n=9$, $r=0.263$, $p=0.495$), while advanced participants show a strong correlation that is nevertheless non-significant due to the low n ($n=4$, $r=0.775$, $p=0.225$). A converse effect was found for L1 digit span scores. Beginner iBT scores demonstrate a moderate correlation (but non-significant due to the low n) with L1 digit span totals ($n=9$, $r=0.651$, $p=0.058$), while advanced iBT scores show a weak correlation ($n=4$, $r=-0.316$, $p=0.684$). Non-parametric Spearman correlation coefficients are reported in Tables 15.1–15.3.

Discussion and Conclusions

Working memory measurements in SLA research

Digit span scores differed greatly between the L1 and the L2 task, despite the digit span's status as a relatively language-independent WM measure. This is evidence of the degree to which L2 proficiency levels may be inadvertently measured by researchers attempting to measure

Table 15.1 Correlations between L1 digit span scores and iBT scores

Proficiency level	n	r	p
Overall	36	0.017	0.923
Beginner	9	0.651	0.058
Intermediate	23	−0.106	0.632
Advanced	4	−0.316	0.684

WMC. Use of such WM tasks to investigate the role of WMC in language learning aptitude and proficiency may compromise the validity of the SLA studies that use them. Accordingly, it may be wise to consider language-independent measures, as they appear to yield more individually distinct results in research investigating L2 populations. Tasks that limit influence from L2 knowledge will provide a more accurate measurement of the individual cognitive processes that compose WMC.

An O-span task in which participants store letters, colours or shapes may provide an accurate index of an individual's WMC. A keyboard, touchscreen or response box could be used to record participant responses, so that participants are not forced to formulate responses in their L2. An additional language-independent task has been argued to be 'ideal' for L2 learners (Conway *et al.*, 2005: 773). The counting span task requires participants to count a number of shapes presented on a computer screen and to recall the totals of all groups of shapes at the end of each sequence. This task also taxes the inhibitory control component of WM by presenting distractors in the form of additional shapes that are to be ignored.

Interaction of working memory across proficiency levels

Results of the WM tasks demonstrate that learners at different proficiency levels may rely on various components of WM in different ways. One explanation may be that the role of WMC remains constant across proficiency levels, while influence from additional factors (aptitude, cross-linguistic influence, etc.) obscures their effects among lower-proficiency learners. This 'interplay' between WM and additional factors

Table 15.2 Correlations between L2 digit span scores and iBT scores

Proficiency level	n	r	p
Overall	36	0.439	0.007*
Beginner	9	0.263	0.495
Intermediate	23	0.170	0.439
Advanced	4	0.400	0.600

* Significant at P<0.05 level.

Table 15.3 Correlations between O-span scores and iBT scores

Proficiency level	n	r	p
Overall	36	−0.137	0.425
Beginner	9	0.325	0.394
Intermediate	23	−0.245	0.260
Advanced	4	0.775	0.225

could account for the failure of past studies to determine the role of WM in various SLA tasks (Wen, 2012: 13). For this reason, it has been argued that future studies examining WM in SLA should include these factors in their research design (Wen, 2012).

Another possible explanation for the disparity between beginner and advanced WM scores is offered by Juffs and Harrington (2011), who suggest that the effects of phonological memory (PM) are greater among lower-proficiency learners. If we consider the digit span to be a measurement of phonological WM (PWM; Baddeley, 2000), we may conclude that the results of the current study support this explanation. Beginner L1 digit span scores correlated more strongly with iBT scores than advanced digit span scores, suggesting that beginners' language development is more heavily dependent on PM. Moreover, if we consider the O-span to be a measurement of executive WM (EWM), we may conclude that higher-level learners' language development is more dependent on EWM than is the case for lower-level learners.

These distinct interactions across proficiency levels support the cautions of Wen (2012: 9), who argued that a composite WM score 'may obscure the distinctive functions of the two WM constructs (i.e. the PWM and the EWM)'. Simply put, a unitary model of WM may neglect to adequately represent the complex role of WM in language learning. Failure to make a distinction between components may result in faulty research design and distorted results.

This result, in fact, mirrors the process observed in young children (aged 4–6 years) acquiring their L1. Language development research suggests significant correlations between phonological loop functioning and vocabulary development in young children (e.g. Gathercole & Baddeley, 1989, 1990; Gathercole et al., 1992). Results of numerous studies, in fact, suggest that the phonological loop supports long-term learning of new sound patterns, i.e. new vocabulary, by allowing a child to begin to associate a meaning with these novel sound patterns. In addition to vocabulary development, the phonological loop has also been implicated in spoken language development.

The analogy between young children and adult novice users of an L2 is further expanded when one considers the nature of the WM construct in early childhood; it is not until age 12 that children are observed to perform WM tasks with the accuracy and comprehension capacities of adults (Riggs *et al.*, 2006). This highlights the activation of the phonological loop in early learning. As young children learning an L1 and adults learning an L2 progress, content acquired also progresses to include more complex linguistic forms and vocabulary of increased length and complexity of meaning. At these points, less phonological loop involvement is observed and language processing becomes a more complex task requiring activation of different cognitive constructs.

Specifically, regarding central executive activation during children's L1 spoken language comprehension, research indicates no executive involvement in comprehension of simple grammatical constructions (Montgomery, 2000a, 2000b). There *is* evidence, however, that the executive is involved in the comprehension of more complex linguistic content (Montgomery & Evans, 2009; Montgomery *et al.*, 2006). It is here that children and adult L2 users begin to present a similar profile when we investigate the process from the perspective of cognitively maturing children who are activating different components of WM as they perform language tasks that increase in complexity and, as they do, require less input from the loop and more activation/use of the executive. Children who haven't reached a certain age/level of cognitive maturity/WM development/language fluency, are not successful with more complex tasks. Adult L2 learners, likewise, are maturing in their language experience and knowledge and, as a result, are processing and using more complex language while activating, primarily, executive function components as opposed to phonological loop components (Montgomery *et al.*, 2006; Montgomery & Evans, 2009). What we would like to propose here is the term 'linguistic maturity' as a reflection of the cognitive systems' activation levels changing as a function of increased experience with/fluency in an L2.

In conclusion, it is evident that further research needs to be done in assessing WM measures for SLA research. To echo the suggestions of others (Juffs & Harrington, 2011; Wen, 2012), it seems best to work towards the standardisation of WM measures to facilitate cooperative efforts among SLA researchers. It is only through the use of instruments that have been proven to be both valid and reliable that we may continue to disentangle the intricacies of WM's role in language learning.

References

Andersson, U. (2010) The contribution of working memory capacity to foreign language comprehension in children. *Memory* 18 (4), 458–472.

Bachman, L. (1990) *Fundamental Considerations in Language Testing.* Oxford: Oxford University Press.

Baddeley, A. (2000) The episodic buffer: A new component of working memory? *Trends in Cognitive Sciences* 4 (11), 417–423.

Baddeley, A. (2003) Working memory and language: An overview. *Journal of Communication Disorders* 36 (3), 189–208.

Baddeley, A. and Hitch, G. (1974) Working memory. In G. Bower (ed.) *The Psychology of Learning and Motivation: Advances in Research and Theory* (pp. 47–87). New York: Academic Press.

Carpenter, P., Just, M. and Shell, P. (1990) What one intelligence test measures: A theoretical account of the processing in the Raven Progressive Matrices Test. *Psychological Review* 97, 404–431.

Cohen, A. and Upton, T. (2006) Strategies in responding to the new TOEFL reading tasks *(TOEFL Monograph No. MS-33)*. Princeton, NJ: Educational Testing Service.

Conway, A. and Engle, R. (1996) Individual differences in working memory capacity: More evidence for a general capacity theory. *Memory* 4 (6), 577–590.

Conway, A., Cowan, N., Bunting, M., Therriault, D. and Minkoff, S. (2002) A latent variable analysis of working memory capacity, short-term memory capacity, processing speed, and general fluid intelligence. *Intelligence* 30, 163–183.

Conway, A., Kane, M., Bunting, M., Hambrick, D., Wilhelm, O. and Engle, R. (2005) Working memory span tasks: A methodological review and user's guide. *Psychonomic Bulletin & Review* 12 (5), 769–786.

Cumming, A., Kantor, R., Baba, K., Eouanzoui, K., Erdosy, U. and James, M. (2006) Analysis of discourse features and verification of scoring levels for independent and integrated prototype writing tasks for new TOEFL *(TOEFL Monograph No. MS-30)*. Princeton, NJ: Educational Testing Service.

Cummins, J. (1979) Cognitive/academic language proficiency, linguistic interdependence, the optimum age question and some other matters. *Working Papers on Bilingualism* 19, 121–129.

Daneman, M. and Carpenter, P. (1980) Individual differences in working memory and reading. *Journal of Verbal Learning and Verbal Behavior* 19 (4), 450–466.

Ellis, N. (2005) At the interface: Dynamic interactions of explicit and implicit language knowledge. *Studies in Second Language Acquisition* 27, 305–352.

Ellis, R. (2003) *Task-Based Language Learning and Teaching*. Oxford: Oxford University Press.

Engle, R., Nations, J. and Cantor, J. (1990) Is 'working memory capacity' just another name for word knowledge? *Journal of Educational Psychology* 82 (4), 799–804.

Finardi, K. and Weissheimer, J. (2008) On the relationship between working memory capacity and L2 speech development. *Signotica* 20 (2), 367–391.

French, L.M. (2006) *Phonological Working Memory and L2 Acquisition: A Developmental Study of Francophone Children Learning English*. New York: Edwin Mellen Press.

Gass, S. and Mackey, A. (2007) *Data Elicitation for Second and Foreign Language Research* (1st edn). Mahwah, NJ/London: Lawrence Erlbaum Associates.

Gass, S. and Lee, J. (2011) Working memory capacity, inhibitory control, and proficiency in a second language. In M.S. Schmid and W. Lowie (eds) *Modeling Bilingualism: From Structure to Chaos: In Honor of Kees de Bot* (pp. 59–84). Amsterdam: John Benjamins.

Gathercole, S. and Baddeley, A. (1989) Evaluation of the role of phonological STM in the development of vocabulary in children: A developmental study. *Journal of Memory and Language* 28, 200–213.

Gathercole, S. and Baddeley, A. (1990) The role of phonological working memory in vocabulary acquisition: A study of young children learning new names. *British Journal of Psychology* 81 (4), 439–454.

Gathercole, S., Willis, C., Emslie, H. and Baddeley, A. (1992) Phonological working memory and vocabulary development during the early school years: A longitudinal study. *Developmental Psychology* 28 (5), 887–898.

Goo, J. (2010) Working memory and reactivity. *Language Learning* 60 (4), 712–752.

Harrington, M.W. and Sawyer, M. (1992) L2 working memory capacity and L2 reading skills. *Studies in Second Language Acquisition* 14 (1), 25–38.

Holmes, J., Gathercole, S.E., Place, M., Dunning, D.L., Hilton, K.A. and Elliott, J.G. (2010) Working memory deficits can be overcome: Impacts of training and medication on working memory in children with ADHD. *Applied Cognitive Psychology* 24 (6), 827–836. doi:10.1002/acp.1589.

Housen, A. and Kuiken, F. (2009) Complexity, accuracy, and fluency in second language acquisition. *Applied Linguistics* 30 (4), 461–473.

Juffs, A. and Harrington, M. (2011) Aspects of working memory in L2 learning. *Language Teaching* 44 (2), 137–166.

Just, M. and Carpenter, P. (1992) A capacity theory of comprehension: Individual differences in working memory. *Psychological Review* 99 (1), 122–149.

Kormos, J. and Safar, A. (2008) Phonological short-term memory, working memory and foreign language performance in intensive language learning. *Bilingualism: Language and Cognition* 11, 261–271.

Loosli, S.V., Buschkuehl, M., Perrig, W.J. and Jaeggi, S.M. (2012) Working memory training improves reading processes in typically developing children. *Child Neuropsychology* 18 (1), 62–78.

Mackey, A. and Sachs, R. (2011) Older learners in SLA research: A first look at working memory, feedback, and L2 development. *Language Learning* 1–37.

Miyake, A. and Friedman, N. (1998) Individual differences in second language proficiency: Working memory as language aptitude. In A. Healey and L. Bourne (eds) *Foreign Language Learning: Psycholinguistic Studies on Training and Retention* (pp. 339–364). Mahwah, NJ: Lawrence Erlbaum.

Montgomery, J. (2000a) Relation of working memory to off-line and real-time sentence processing in children with specific language impairment: Temporal processing or capacity processing deficit? *Applied Psycholinguistics* 23, 447–470.

Montgomery, J. (2000b) Verbal working memory and sentence comprehension in children with specific language impairment. *Journal of Speech, Language, and Hearing Research* 43, 293–308.

Montgomery, J., Magimairaj, B. and O'Malley, M. (2008) The role of working memory in children's complex sentence comprehension. *Journal of Psycholinguistic Research* 37 (5), 331–354.

Montgomery, J. and Evans, J. (2009) Complex sentence comprehension in children with specific language impairment: Influence of working memory. *Journal of Speech, Language, and Hearing Research* 52 (2), 269–288.

Pardo-Vázquez, J.L. and Fernández-Rey, J. (2008) External validation of the computerized, group administrable adaptation of the 'operation span task'. *Behavior Research Methods* 40 (1), 46–54.

Payne, J. and Whitney, P. (2002) Developing L2 oral proficiency through synchronous CMC: Output, working memory, and interlanguage development. *CALICO* 20 (1), 7–32.

Rai, M., Loschky, L., Harris, R., Peck, N. and Cook, L. (2010) Effects of stress and working memory capacity on foreign language readers' inferential processing during comprehension. *Language Learning* 61 (1), 1–32.

Richmond, L.L., Morrison, A.B., Chein, J.M. and Olson, I.R. (2011) Working memory training and transfer in older adults. *Psychology and Aging* 26 (4), 813–822.

Riggs, K., McTaggart, J., Simpson, A. and Freeman, R. (2006) Changes in capacity of visual working memory in 5- to 10-year-olds. *Journal of Experimental Child Psychology* 95, 18–26.

Safar, A. and Kormos, J. (2008) Revisiting problems with foreign language aptitude. *International Review of Applied Linguistics* 46, 113–136.

Sagarra, N. and Herschensohn, J. (2010) The role of proficiency and working memory in gender and number agreement processing in L1 and L2 Spanish. *Lingua* 120 (8), 2022–2039.

Service, E. (1992) Phonology, working memory and foreign-language learning. *Quarterly Journal of Experimental Psychology* 45 (1), 21–50.

Skehan, P. (1998) *A Cognitive Approach to Language Learning.* Oxford: Oxford University Press.

Stigler, J.W., Lee, S. and Stevenson, H.W. (1986) Digit memory in Chinese and English: Evidence for a temporally limited store. *Cognition: International Journal of Cognitive Science* 23 (1), 1–20.

Trude, A. and Tokowicz, N. (2011) Negative transfer from Spanish and English to Portuguese pronunciation: The roles of inhibition and working memory. *Language Learning* 61 (1), 259–280.

Unsworth, N. and Engle, R. (2007) The nature of individual differences in working memory capacity: Active maintenance in primary memory and controlled search from secondary memory. *Psychological Review* 114 (1), 104–132.

Van den Noort, M., Bosch, P. and Hugdahl, K. (2006) Foreign language proficiency and working memory capacity. *European Psychologist* 11 (4), 289–296.

Weitz, D., O'Shea, G., Zook, N. and Needham, W. (2011) Working memory and sequence learning in the Hebb digits task: Awareness is predicted by individual differences in operation span. *American Journal of Psychology* 124 (1), 49–62.

Wen, Z. (2012) Working memory and second language learning. *International Journal of Applied Linguistics* 22 (1), 1–22.

Appendix

Participant questionnaire   Gender _____ / Age _____ / TOEFL
_____ / OPI (Oral Proficiency Interview) level _____

1. Academic major (intended) _____
2. Current education level   _____
3. Length of time in US   _____
4. Length of time studying English   _____
5. Age when English study began   _____
6. What is your first language? _____
7. How many languages do you know? _____
    (a) Please list languages in order of skill (if applicable):
        (i)   _____
        (ii)   _____
        (iii)   _____
        (iv)   _____

8. Which countries have you lived in for 6 months or more?

    _____
    _____
    _____
    _____

9. How old were you when living in each area listed above?

    _____
    _____
    _____
    _____

    PL (L1) digit _____   Operations task _____
    PL (L2) digit _____   Elicited imitation _____
    PL (L2) non-word _____   Timed reading _____

16 Working Memory and L2 Development Across the Lifespan: A Commentary

Clare Wright

Introduction

As the contributions to this book clearly demonstrate, the exciting implications and applications of working memory (WM) research for second language (L2) development are now clearly recognized since the early studies of Juffs, Service and others in the 1990s. Understanding the complex nature of WM's involvement in second language acquisition (SLA), however, remains challenging across a range of theoretical and empirical dimensions, as shown throughout this volume, and particularly by Mitchell, Jarvis, O'Malley and Konstantinova in Chapter 15. As Mitchell *et al.* showed, some of the often contradictory findings from WM/SLA research may arise from fundamental problems in research design. WM tests themselves are not always reliably used as language-independent measures, which can produce a confounding effect of proficiency on WM scores if measured in the L2. Mitchell *et al.*, and other authors throughout this volume, also highlight the need to distinguish between the different WM constructs such as phonological short-term memory (PSTM) and executive WM (EWM). Then, as Mitchell *et al.* and others point out, SLA researchers also need to establish a robust logic for why each construct may apply to different aspects of language learning, rather than apply a general assumption of WM to L2 proficiency, without a clear identification of what is meant by proficiency. Mitchell *et al.* provide a useful introduction to thinking through the implications of how WM may work in different ways at different stages of language development – suggesting that PSTM may benefit earlier-stage learners, while EWM is associated with advanced learners.

This chapter seeks to reflect on Mitchell *et al.*'s work within the wider context of SLA and WM research, and, in particular, the claims of different effects of different aspects of WM as learners progress through stages of learning. Some of the challenges for SLA arising from the theoretical and empirical evidence of WM across the L2 lifespan will be presented, and the chapter finishes with implications and suggestions for where we can go from here.

Definitions of WM

It is worth starting off with some caveats about the definitions and models of WM used in this chapter. Much SLA research assumes that language learning shares similarities with skill development, shifting with enough practice from slow, controlled, consciously manipulated cognitive processes towards faster, automatic, unconscious processes. These two ends of the language learning spectrum are associated with constructs borrowed from information processing and psycholinguistics – the explicit/implicit learning distinction (Ellis *et al.*, 2009) and the declarative/procedural distinction (Ullman, 2004). Space precludes a detailed discussion here (but see, for example, Ellis [2005], Han and Finneran [2014] and Hulstijn [2005]). As such, WM is most usually associated with handling processes that involve controlled, conscious manipulation or attention (Levelt, 1989, 1993), which is especially the case in L2 production until the late stages of highly advanced automatised proficiency (Kormos, 2006). WM is therefore typically investigated for its involvement in language uses that benefit from consciously controlled explicit processes – such as vocabulary learning, or reading and interpreting ambiguous material that makes implicit automatic processing breakdown (Juffs & Harrington, 1995). This fits well into research questions that look at the role of WM for learners in the pre-automatic stage of learning, where it is clear that they are noticing, monitoring and using other explicit, consciously attended processes to control their language interpretation and production. However, the investigation of the involvement of WM in such learning contexts has not always distinguished between PSTM and EWM. In fact, in strict psycholinguistic terms, many of the complex language activities involving various aspects of WM, particularly EWM, must take place at preconscious levels of processing (Jackendoff, 2002). Therefore, it is worth carefully distinguishing between PSTM and EWM to clarify how they may also be involved in non-explicit processing, as procedural WM (Oberauer, 2010). This theoretical discussion of the nature of the broad scope of WM will need to be looked at in future research, at all stages of the lifespan. For now, to fit the scope of this chapter, I will assume the usual definition of PSTM and EWM as primarily assisting consciously monitored processing, including of explicitly learned, declarative linguistic knowledge. The interesting question addressed by Mitchell *et al.*, and reviewed here, is how far PSTM and EWM may play a differential role at various stages of the learning process, and across the lifespan.

WM in the Earliest Years of Linguistic Development

As many children grow up bilingual, or start learning an L2 from very young ages, it is logical to try and tease out how early in the lifespan WM (including PSTM) may be seen to have an effect on SLA. Traditionally, it was seen that infant learning was largely procedural or implicit, with little storage of explicit linguistic information beyond very simple words, and little capacity for executive control over declarative or explicit memory. WM was therefore assumed to have no major role in the earliest stages of first language acquisition, before about 3–4 years of age (Baddeley *et al.*, 2009). However, more sophisticated types of testing have now shown that even by one year of age, infants show evidence of explicit memory, remembering and applying learned information (Baddeley *et al.*, 2009), so this assumption may need to be revised, particularly in bilingual children. Very recent research into executive control in children suggests that there are effects of WM control which favour bilingual children even as young as 24 months (Poulin-Dubois *et al.*, 2011).

Most of the research on WM and children starts around 4 years of age upwards, when both storage and processing capacities begin to be identifiable using standard tests. The main area of work, to date, mainly in the US and the UK, has focused on Baddeley's multi-component model. Standardised tests for this age group are widely used to test PSTM (Gathercole & Baddeley, 1993), but often now also include an EWM component (Alloway & Gathercole, 2005). PSTM shows a steady increase in average item storage (including chunks of linked items) from around two items at the age of 5 years, to an adult average of six items by around 15–20 years, before starting to decline in middle age, and particularly after around 65 years (Alloway, 2011). Correlating this storage capacity with a range of school activities has found robust significant associations between PSTM and vocabulary development in children. Similarly, as executive control develops, EWM effects have been found on reading comprehension and the amount of information produced in storytelling tasks (Adams & Gathercole, 1996, 2000), as well as in spoken narrative comprehension (Montgomery *et al.*, 2009). There are identifiable effects in adults too, where PSTM has been identified as connected with novel word learning (Papagno & Vallar, 1995); in addition, the well-known WM effect on better reading comprehension (Daneman & Carpenter, 1980) has been found also in successful judgements on semantic ambiguity and syntactic complexity, such as in 'garden-path' sentence resolution (King & Just, 1991).

WM, especially PSTM, has therefore been very clearly found to be central to verbal development for monolingual acquisition, through school and into adulthood, particularly when using language in ways that require explicit and/or metalinguistic verbal knowledge, such as reading, vocabulary and analysing complex structures. However, as mentioned above, the assumption currently is that EWM has little significant part to play in the normal development of everyday monolingual grammatical language, especially for preschool children. There has been little research into young children's language – partly due to inherent problems in constructing reliable tests for preliterate participants, and partly because, theoretically, EWM control has not been assumed to relate to normal grammatical language – it would be simply impossible to manage normal fluent speech if all grammatical information had to be encoded consciously.

However, for people learning an L2, many of these assumptions need testing and challenging, and linking to a coherent model of how long-term memory (LTM) and STM are used in SLA (Juffs & Harrington, 2011). As mentioned above, a common assumption in current cognitive models of language (DeKeyser, 1995, 2003; Ellis, 2008; Housen *et al.*, 2012; Ullman, 2004) makes a distinction between implicit or procedural knowledge, and explicit or declarative knowledge. Implicit learning, where conscious awareness is not paid to the input, is associated with child SLA and naturalistic L2 learners (especially low-literate learners – Craats *et al.*, 2006; Tarone & Bigelow, 2005). It is argued that WM, for these kinds of language learners, as in young monolingual infants, does not play a major role in the implicit acquisition of grammar (Juffs & Rodriguez, 2006). This is most famously expressed in Newport's (1990) 'less is more' hypothesis, where younger children's lower levels of WM entail greater implicit learning of grammar. By comparison, post-puberty children and adults' greater WM capacities could override implicit mechanisms, in favour of explicit mechanisms such as use of longer memorised chunks and metalinguistic problem solving. Evidence that SLA, in the familiar setting of the instructed foreign language classroom, may often consist of explicit memorisation and problem solving, can therefore lead to the claim that WM is the 'key' to L2 development (Miyake & Friedman, 1998).

To date, most WM research has focused on adult SLA (see the very helpful and clear summary in Juffs and Harrington [2011]), but first I turn to WM research on child learners of an L2.

Child SLA and WM

How early and how widely can we see WM effects in L2 learners? Following the research into PSTM effects in monolingual child development, it was logical for early research in SLA to start by investigating PSTM effects in L2 acquisition. In these early studies, it was found that WM, particularly PSTM, predicted L2 proficiency across a range of measures of vocabulary and grammar (Ando *et al.*, 1992; Cheung, 1996; Service, 1992; Service & Kohonen, 1995). More recent research (e.g. French, 2006; Masoura & Gathercole, 2005) confirmed these strong PSTM effects on L2 proficiency.

Similarly to Mitchell *et al.* in this volume, these studies indicated threshold effects of PSTM in less proficient learners compared to more proficient learners – for example in Cheung's (1996) study of primary-age Hong Kong children, only participants with a below-mean vocabulary knowledge showed PSTM effects on their L2 vocabulary learning.

Closer inspection of the methodologies used in some of these studies suggests that the claim that PSTM supports general L2 development in child SLA may be problematic. The effects of PSTM on vocabulary are indeed robust; however, it seems, especially in Ando *et al.* (1992) and Service (1992), that the grammar tests used in these studies were more lexical than purely grammatical, and involved explicit metalinguistic knowledge rather than requiring implicit rule-based knowledge. Therefore, success on these grammar tests would be likely to be confounded by lexical knowledge rather than be a reflection of PSTM effects.

French and O'Brien (2008) specifically aimed to unpick the potential confound between lexical knowledge and grammatical learning, in their study of L2 French learners of English, aged around 11 years old, over an intensive learning programme of 5 months. Their careful, statistically rigorous research was able to identify a clear role for PSTM in learning grammatical knowledge, showing that PSTM scores, measured at the start of the study, accounted for nearly 30% of significant variance on the grammar scores, 'after taking into account L2 contact, nonverbal ability, earlier grammar skill, and most importantly, vocabulary knowledge' (French & O'Brien, 2008: 476).

Therefore, it does seem possible to claim that PSTM does indeed predict, or at least, mediate L2 learning in child SLA where the emphasis is on vocabulary or lexically driven grammar learning. It is less clear that EWM plays a role in complex language processing, as existing research shows contradictory findings, although there are very few studies using EWM specifically rather than PSTM.

One problem in comparing studies of EWM effects in child SLA, especially in processing complex grammar, is that so many aspects of language and cognition are still developing in child learners (Luciana *et al.*, 2005). First language grammatical development of complex structures such as relative clauses and passives are known to be acquired later, around the age of 7–9 years; other aspects of sociolinguistic, pragmatic and metalinguistic knowledge of language at discourse level may also not be fully developed until the teenage years (Karmiloff-Smith, 1986). WM capacity, as we saw earlier, is expected to increase up to a steady plateau until aged around 16. Given the additional cognitive load on bilingual use of language (Paradis, 2004), it is therefore not surprising to see varied findings in child SLA research. As learners reach the steady stage of WM capacity around 16 years, it ought to be possible to establish clear, robust tasks to measure WM in different L2 populations, and for different language purposes. So I turn now to offer a brief review of the research to date on WM effects on adult learners of an L2.

Adult SLA and WM

Even in adult SLA, there remain many problems in establishing clear WM effects. These problems are often due to variability in WM methodology (Juffs & Harringon, 2011). This variability then conflicts with the wide variety of stages of development in L2 among adult learners, from those who may have started learning the L2 at primary school to college *ab initio* learners. In addition, there is the question of researching WM effects in adults who are already multilingual, or those who may be bi/multilingual but non-literate (Juffs & Rodriguez, 2006), all of which creates different predictions for WM research, by broadening out the learnability implications beyond the standard instructed foreign language context.

There is also of course the rarely considered question of age-related effects of WM on language learning and development, as WM and cognitive capacity generally starts to decline beyond the mid-adult plateau. There is widely cited research on the benefits of existing bilingualism to offset aging effects on cognitive performance (e.g. Bialystok *et al.*, 2004). These are usually ascribed to the beneficial effects on executive function arising from the demands of controlling two or more languages. However, it remains to be seen how PSTM or EWM, rather than general measures of executive function, may interact with aging in bilinguals (Luo *et al.*, 2013). Furthermore, there is virtually no research on the impact of PSTM/EWM in older beginner learners of languages, who are often invisible in SLA research (Mackey & Sachs, 2012).

Despite so much variability in WM and L2 measures, some studies have found clear effects for PSTM and EWM in adult learners, as for younger learners. The two main claims from the monolingual and child L2 research, discussed above, are that PSTM is involved in learning novel verbal material and will therefore aid lexical learning and some aspects of grammatical rule-based learning; second, that WM supports complex management of verbal input and retrieval and will therefore aid sentence processing, reading comprehension and general language fluency, either in written or spoken form. A third strand of research suggests that EWM will aid executive control, which could be particularly important as learning progresses, in aiding learners to inhibit their L1 (Bialystok, 2002). Mitchell *et al.* in this volume have claimed, in line with other classic studies of WM effects in SLA, that PSTM aids less proficient earlier-stage learners, and EWM aids more proficient learners. Here, I highlight some specific studies that have provided evidence to support or contest these claims and so have important implications for future research into WM in SLA.

The first question is whether PSTM/EWM affects all learners, or has greater effects on early-stage learners. The prediction, based on child studies of acquisition such as Service (1992), was that PSTM/EWM effects would be evident in early learners, especially PSTM, in view of its role in helping build vocabulary. But it remained an open question as to whether there would be a ceiling effect at a certain point of L2 proficiency, or other threshold. Hummel (2009) studied a group of 77 adult upper-intermediate/advanced learners of English to look for PSTM effects on grammatical, lexical and reading scores in a proficiency test. After dividing out the group into lower and higher proficiency subgroups, PSTM emerged as a significant predictor of scores on the proficiency measures, especially for vocabulary, but only for the lower proficiency subgroup. Hummel takes this as evidence to support existing assumptions about the learning benefit of PSTM in younger, lower-level learners, but suggests this is due to lower levels of lexical knowledge, while the more advanced learners relied on greater lexical knowledge, combined perhaps with more advanced L1 analytic skills, rather than PSTM to help their performance on all the L2 proficiency tasks.

Similarly, O'Brien et al. (2006) tested PSTM effects as part of a range of grammatical and lexical measures in college-age participants, in the context of differing types of exposure (stay-at-home vs study abroad). They found PSTM to be linked to L2 vocabulary use and narrative production only in less proficient learners; interestingly, this effect was regardless of the type of exposure.

By comparison, other studies have also found effects only in higher proficiency groups, such as Kormos and Safar's (2008) study of Hungarian adolescents, at beginner and pre-intermediate stages, which found PSTM effects only at the higher-level, pre-intermediate stages.

Turning now to EWM, the key claim here is that EWM will benefit reading comprehension and sentence processing, most evidently in more advanced learners, in line with the monolingual research referred to earlier. Many of these studies have been referenced throughout this volume, but perhaps the seminal study remains that of Harrington and Sawyer (1992), who investigated advanced Japanese learners of English. Using a reading span test, they found significant effects for EWM between L2 reading ability and grammatical proficiency, but not when using simple PSTM storage measures of English digits and words. Other studies have also found beneficial effects of EWM on complex language processing (see, in particular, Miyake & Friedman, 1998), although as already noted, results can be very varied (Juffs & Harrington, 2011), particularly in less advanced stages of learning.

In recent research, Gilabert and Munoz (2010) report on EWM effects on a range of language proficiency measures for a cohort of 59 college-age learners of English, using reading span, and split into higher and lower achievers based on a general test of proficiency (the Oxford Placement Test). They found no EWM effects on general proficiency, nor on grammatical accuracy or complexity in a story-retelling task in either group; they did find significant, albeit weak, EWM effects on fluency and lexical diversity in the story-retelling task, but only in the higher proficiency group.

It therefore seems that proficiency level is not necessarily a key dividing point between the respective roles of PSTM and EWM (such as reading span) as claimed by Mitchell *et al.* in this volume. However, varying uses of proficiency measures need to be taken into account, as a relative split into lower or higher proficiency subgroups quickly obscures the actual level of proficiency in the group overall. Therefore, among other considerations, the assessment of proficiency level needs careful attention in future research, to avoid these apparent contradictions and ensure reliable comparability.

As well as proficiency differences, there are other potential confounding factors to be resolved to ensure comparability and reliability in WM studies. One such issue relates to how individual differences in WM may differentiate the rate of learning, rather than just the stage of learning. It is possible that there is an internal threshold effect arising from differing WM capacities, rather than a threshold based on L2 proficiency; this threshold is argued to relate to how learners process L2 input. Sunderman and Kroll (2009) used reading span to predict EWM effects on changes in lexical knowledge and processing time in learners of Spanish before and after time studying abroad; they only found beneficial effects for those with higher EWM. Sunderman and Kroll conclude that there might be a kind of internal threshold of EWM capacity which facilitates a quicker learning response to L2 input. Therefore, those with higher EWM capacity can benefit from a more intense type of input such as study abroad, while those with lower EWM may well feel generally cognitively overloaded during the added exposure of study abroad, so EWM *per se* does not make a significant difference. To my knowledge, there is no research testing different levels of PSTM in similar learning contexts to see if this threshold effect extends to PSTM.

A further question is whether PSTM/EWM effects are task specific, particularly in relation to WM processing and fluency. Logically, we would expect task performance to be affected by different cognitive loads (Robinson, 2001), in terms of differential levels of control; thus, WM could be expected to have a role in more complex cognitive tasks, which would require a greater executive capacity. Analysing WM effects on fluency, Fortkamp (1999) found positive significant effects of EWM on oral fluency in 16 advanced learners of English using a speaking span task. In order to test how far EWM may be task specific, Fortkamp also measured reading span and a reading-aloud task, and found significant correlations between these two scores, but no cross-correlations between EWM and proficiency between the two modes, speaking and reading. Fortkamp concluded from these data that EWM is task specific (Turner & Engle, 1989). Ahmadian (2012), studying 40 advanced learners of English, pursued the specific effects of time on task planning in oral production; he found that accuracy in a speaking task was mediated by EWM, measured by reading span, but only for the group allowed time for online planning (Yuan & Ellis, 2003).

These findings seem to echo Robinson's (2002) research into incidental vs intentional learning; he argues that EWM does play a role in L2 but in a task-specific way, so that correlations would be conditioned by task complexity and processing mode. This task effect would not logically be expected to relate to PSTM, but to my knowledge, there is very little research testing this hypothesis.

In addition, several studies have failed to find any effect for WM, contradicting the general claims about the benefits of WM on SLA (Miyake & Friedman, 1998). Wright (2013), in a longitudinal study of 32 Chinese learners of English, found that WM was significantly associated with grammatical development in a question production task, but only in the form of a novel story-recall task (specially designed to combine PSTM and listening span), and not for other standard EWM tasks, such as digits back or listening span. Sagarra (2000) found no effect for EWM using reading span on L2, looking at grammatical development for intermediate learners of Spanish. Mizera (2006) also found no relation between EWM and L2, using a variety of measures of fluency in early learners of Spanish.

This brief overview of research into SLA over the lifespan has shown that there are reasonably reliable effects for PSTM on learning, in terms of vocabulary and explicit metalinguistic grammatical knowledge. There is less clear reliable evidence for EWM effects on language processing or learning in more general terms. However, it is debatable that PSTM favours earlier learners *per se*, while EWM favours more advanced language learners, more that different aspects of WM may interact with different types of learning process, and the rate of learning.

It has been seen that the evidence of support for the effects of WM remains contradictory, largely due to the lack of comparability in methodology in research design. The theoretical basis for the predicted effects of PSTM on lexical development, and of WM on processing and fluency, has not been seriously challenged, and it remains a rich potential area to be validated through developing more robust and reliable methodologies, particularly for older learners, and in a wider range of learning settings. However, there are some theoretical and empirical issues which this overview has touched on, and I discuss them now in more detail.

Theoretical and Methodological Implications for Future WM Research

Some of the difficulties and contradictory findings may arise from the current range of tests used and the differences in participants involved. Major issues remain about the age effects at both ends of the lifespan, and about specific populations beyond the standard school-age foreign language learner, where we have little or no information about how WM may be expected to affect SLA. These would be fruitful and exciting areas to pursue.

However, I finish with a caveat about expecting too much from WM tests, span tests such as Daneman and Carpenter's reading span test and its variations for listening and speaking. This has been widely adopted as a suitable measure to test the effects of general WM capacity on proficiency, but may be flawed when being used to predict L2 proficiency, given the lack of robust evidence of benefits for aspects of proficiency, as well as potential task-specific effects noted above (e.g. Mizera, 2006; Sagarra, 2000). In addition, in view of the time lag involved during the test procedure between storage and recall, especially on the longer sentence sets, word recall may in fact be using some other kind of STM rather than the phonological loop (Mizera, 2006: 17). The phonological loop is assumed to be around 1–2 seconds, which would not be long enough to hold the information required in the longer sets of sentences. It is possible that successful recall could be tapping into some element of long-term WM (Ericsson & Kintsch, 1995), or it might be evidence of Baddeley's (2000) suggested episodic buffer, although this is purely speculation. Using measures combining PSTM and listening span, such as a story-recall task (Wright, 2013), could be one way of establishing a less task-dependent effect. Similarly, using a non-verbal task such as a mathematical task (Turner & Engle, 1986) would avoid any confound with verbal lexical or analytic skills, rather than WM *per se*.

One alternative is to pursue the claim that WM is domain specific (Caplan & Waters, 1999; Luo *et al.*, 2013), especially in terms of EWM rather than PSTM. Caplan and Waters (1999) follow Shah and Miyake (1996) in fractionating out the processing element of WM (the central executive) into verbal and visual components, and then into further sub-fractioned divisions between different types of verbal processing. Caplan and Waters (1999: 78) suggest that the 'interpretive processing' system, used for assigning syntactic structure and meaning to a sentence, is different to other verbal WM systems as used for long-term storage, planning actions and other 'post-interpretive' processing. This approach has been used in a few studies (e.g. for L2, Sunderman & Kroll, 2009), but has not been central to much of the research in language processing and WM.

It is easy to fall back on the typical shorthand view of WM, especially PSTM, as a part of the memory system, acting as a bottleneck to learning by limiting how much we can consciously notice and process at the same time. But we need to move on from this simplistic model. Miyake and Shah (1999: 445) concluded that WM should not be considered as a separate 'box' for short-term storage that is structurally distinct from other memory systems, but more as a set of processes that 'control' cognitive actions, and this should now include a discussion of procedural WM (Oberauer, 2010). We also need to better articulate how WM and LTM intersect in language learning and use, especially in retrieving linguistic knowledge in online performance, perhaps through a better integration of Ericsson and Kintsch's (1995) construct of LT-WM, and Cowan's (2005) view of WM as 'temporarily accessible' LTM. As yet, these psychological models, usually based on monolingual children or adults, do not always easily translate into linguistic models of language knowledge, storage, retrieval and processing which are relevant for SLA. Psychologists, linguists, language teachers and language learners all need to keep talking to each other to help tease out where the field will go from here.

Conclusion

It is clear that we are just at the start of beginning to understand how WM may or may not work in SLA across the lifespan. The priority is for greater clarity and reliability in WM methodology to distinguish between PSTM and EWM, and how the different roles of these constructs for storage, processing and control could be predicted to work in SLA. We need to clarify how best to test WM in different SLA populations at different stages of the lifespan. We must also specify more clearly what aspects of SLA we can logically expect to be supported by WM, given the recurring debates over the nature of SLA in terms of explicit vs implicit learning (Ellis, 2005; Han & Finneran, 2014) or knowledge vs performance (Housen et al., 2012) or as skill development (DeKeyser, 2003). This need for clarity is an inevitable product of a fertile cross-disciplinary overlap between linguistics, psychology and education, among other fields. But it does require care on the part of SLA researchers in what we can predict and test reliably.

There are still therefore many gaps in the theoretical and empirical literature to help us understand the role of WM in SLA across the lifespan. This book is a very welcome addition to the field, and it is hoped that many more studies will be inspired by the research described here to take this field forward.

References

Adams, A.-M. and Gathercole, S. (1996) Phonological working memory and spoken language development in children. *Quarterly Journal of Experimental Psychology* 49A, 216–233.

Adams, A.-M., and Gathercole, S. (2000) Limitations in working memory: Implications for language development. *International Journal of Language and Communication Disorders* 35, 95–116.

Alloway, T. (2011) *Improving Working Memory*. London: Sage Publications.

Alloway, T. and Gathercole. S. (2005) Working memory and short-term sentence recall in young children. *European Journal of Cognitive Psychology* 17 (2), 207–220.

Ando, J., Fukunaga, N., Kurahashi, J., Suto, T., Nakano, T. and Kage, M. (1992) A comparative study of the two EFL teaching methods: The communicative and grammatical approach. *Japanese Journal of Educational Psychology* (40), 247–256.

Baddeley, A. (2000) The episodic buffer: A new component of working memory? *Trends in Cognitive Sciences* 4 (11), 417–423.

Baddeley, A., Eysenck, M. and Anderson, M. (2009) *Memory*. Hove: Psychology Press.

Bialystok, E. (2002) Cognitive processes of L2 users. In V. Cook (ed.) *Portraits of the L2 User* (pp. 145–166). Clevedon: Multilingual Matters.

Bialystok E., Craik, F., Klein, R. and Viswanathan, M. (2004) Bilingualism, aging, and cognitive control: Evidence from the Simon task. *Psychology and Aging* 19 (2), 290–303.

Caplan, D. and Waters, G. (1999) Verbal working memory and sentence comprehension. *Behavioral and Brain Sciences* 22 (1), 77–94.

Cheung, H. (1996) Nonword span as a unique predictor of second-language vocabulary learning. *Developmental Psychology* 32 (5), 867–873.

Cowan, N. (2005) *Working Memory Capacity*. Hove: Psychology Press.

Craats, I., Kurvers, J. and Young-Scholten, M. (2006) Low-educated second language and literacy acquisition. In I. Craats, J. Kurvers and M. Young-Scholten (eds) *Low-Educated Second Language and Literacy Acquisition: Proceedings of the Inaugural LESLLA Symposium*. Netherlands Graduate School of Linguistics: LOT Publications.

Daneman, M. and Carpenter, P. (1980) Individual differences in working memory and reading. *Journal of Verbal Learning and Verbal Behavior* 19, 450–466.

DeKeyser, R. (1995) Learning second language grammar rules. *Studies in Second Language Acquisition* 17, 379–410.

DeKeyser, R. (2003) Implicit and explicit learning. In C. Doughty and M. Long (eds) *Handbook of Second Language Acquisition* (pp. 313–348). Oxford: Blackwell.

Ellis, N. (2005) At the interface: Dynamic interactions of explicit and implicit language knowledge. *Studies in Second Language Acquisition* 27, 305–352.

Ellis, R. (2008) Investigating grammatical difficulty in second language learning. *International Journal of Applied Linguistics* 18 (1), 4–22.

Ellis, R., Loewen, S., Elder, C., Erlam, R., Philp, J. and Reinders H. (2009) *Implicit and Explicit Knowledge in Second Language Learning, Testing and Teaching*. Bristol: Multilingual Matters.

Ericsson, K. and Kintsch, W. (1995) Long-term working memory. *Psychological Review* 102, 211–245.

Fortkamp, M. (1999) Working memory capacity and aspects of L2 speech production. *Communication and Cognition* 32 (3–4), 259–295.

French, L. (2006) *Phonological Working Memory and L2 Acquisition: A Developmental Study of Children Learning French in Quebec*. Lewiston, NY: Edwin Mellen Press.

French, L. and O'Brien, I. (2008) Phonological memory and children's second language grammar learning. *Applied Psycholinguistics* 29, 463–487.

Gathercole, S. and Baddeley, A. (1993) *Working Memory and Language.* Hillsdale, NJ: Lawrence Erlbaum.

Gilabert, R. and Munoz, C. (2010) Differences in attainment and performance in a foreign language: The role of working memory capacity. *International Journal of English Studies* 10 (1), 19–42.

Han, Z-H. and Finneran, R. (2014) Re-engaging the interface debate: Strong, weak, none, or all? *International Journal of Applied Linguistics* 24 (3), 370–389.

Harrington, M. and Sawyer, M. (1992) L2 working memory and L2 reading skill. *Studies in Second Language Acquisition* 14 (1), 25–38.

Housen, A., Kuiken, F. and Vedder, I. (2012) *Dimensions of L2 Performance and Proficiency: Complexity, Accuracy, Fluency.* Amsterdam: John Benjamins.

Hulstijn, J. (2005) Theoretical and empirical issues in the study of implicit and explicit second-language learning. *Studies in Second Language Acquisition* 27, 129–140.

Hummel, K. (2009) Aptitude, phonological memory, and second language proficiency in nonnovice adult learners. *Applied Psycholinguistics* 30, 225–249.

Jackendoff, R. (2002) *Foundations of Language: Brain, Meaning, Grammar, Evolution.* Oxford: Oxford University Press.

Juffs, A. and Harrington, M. (1995) Parsing effects in second language sentence processing. *Studies in Second Language Acquisition* 17 (4), 483–516.

Juffs, A. and Rodriguez, G. (2006) Second language sentence processing and working memory in college-educated and low-educated learners of English as a second language. Paper presented at EuroSLA, Antalya, Turkey.

Juffs, A. and Harrington, M. (2011) Aspects of working memory in L2 learning. *Language Teaching* 44 (2), 137–166.

Karmiloff-Smith, A. (1986) From meta-processes to conscious access: Evidence from metalinguistic and repair data. *Cognition* 23, 95–147.

King, J. and Just, M. (1991) Individual differences in syntactic processing: The role of working memory. *Journal of Memory and Language* 30, 580–602.

Kormos, J. (2006) *Speech Production and Second Language Acquisition.* Mahwah, NJ: Lawrence Erlbaum.

Kormos, J. and Safar, A. (2008) Phonological short-term memory, working memory and foreign language performance in intensive language learning. *Bilingualism: Language and Cognition* 11, 261–271.

Levelt, W. (1989) *Speaking: From Intention to Articulation.* Cambridge, MA: Bradford Books.

Levelt, W. (1999) Producing spoken language: A blueprint of the speaker. In C. Brown and P. Hagoort (eds) *The Neurocognition of Language* (pp. 83–154). Oxford: Oxford University Press.

Luciana, M., Conklin, H., Hooper, C. and Yarger, R. (2005) The development of nonverbal working memory and executive control processes in adolescents. *Child Development* 76 (3), 697–712.

Luo, L., Craik, F., Moreno, S. and Bialystok, E. (2013) Bilingualism interacts with domain in a working memory task: Evidence from aging. *Psychology and Aging* 28 (1), 28–34.

Mackey, A. and Sachs, R. (2011) Older learners in SLA research: A first look at working memory, feedback and L2 development. *Language Learning* 62 (3), 704–740.

Masoura, E. and Gathercole, S. (2005) Contrasting contributions of phonological short-term memory and long-term knowledge to vocabulary learning in a foreign language. *Memory* 13 (3–4), 422–429.

Miyake, A. and Friedman, N. (1998) Individual differences in second language proficiency: Working memory as language aptitude. In A. Healy and L. Bourne (eds) *Foreign Language Learning* (pp. 339–364). Mahwah, NJ: Lawrence Erlbaum.

Miyake, A. and Shah, P. (eds) (1999) *Models of Working Memory.* Cambridge: Cambridge University Press.

Mizera, G. (2006) Working memory and L2 oral fluency. PhD thesis, University of Pittsburgh.

Montgomery, J., Polunenko, A. and Marinellie, S. (2009) Role of working memory in understanding spoken narrative. *Applied Psycholinguistics* 30, 485–509.

Newport, E. (1990) Maturational constraints on language learning. *Cognitive Science* 14 (1), 11–28.

O'Brien, I., Segalowitz, N., Collentine, J. and Freed, B. (2006) Phonological memory and lexical, narrative and grammatical skills in second language oral production by adult learners. *Applied Psycholinguistics* 27, 377–402.

Oberauer, K. (2010) Declarative and procedural working memory: Common principles, common capacity limits? *Psychologica Belgica* 50 (3 & 4), 277–308.

Papagno, C. and Vallar, G. (1995) Verbal short-term memory and vocabulary learning in polyglots. *Journal of Experimental Psychology: Human Experimental Psychology* 48 (1), 98–107.

Paradis, M. (2004) *A Neurolinguistic Theory of Bilingualism.* Amsterdam/Philadelphia: John Benjamins.

Poulin-Dubois, D., Blaye, A., Coutya, J. and Bialystok, E. (2011) The effects of bilingualism on toddlers' executive functioning. *Journal of Experimental Child Psychology* 108 (3), 567–579.

Robinson, P. (2001) *Cognition and Second Language Instruction.* Cambridge: Cambridge University Press.

Robinson, P. (2002) Effects of individual differences in intelligence, aptitude and working memory on adult incidental SLA. In P. Robinson (ed.) *Individual Differences and Instructed Language Learning* (pp. 211–266). Amsterdam: John Benjamins.

Sagarra, N. (2000) The longitudinal role of working memory on adult acquisition of L2 grammar. PhD thesis, University of Illinois at Urbana-Champaign.

Service, E. (1992) Phonology, working memory, and foreign language learning. *Quarterly Journal of Experimental Psychology, Human Experimental Psychology* 45A (1), 21–50.

Service, E. and Kohonen, V. (1995) Is the relation between phonological memory foreign language learning accounted for by vocabulary acquisition? *Applied Psycholinguistics* 16, 155–172.

Shah, P. and Miyake, A. (1996) The separability of working memory resources for spatial thinking and language processing. *Journal of Experimental Psychology: General* 125, 4–27.

Sunderman, G. and Kroll, J. (2009) When study-abroad experience fails to deliver: The internal resources threshold effect. *Applied Psycholinguistics* 30 (1), 79–100.

Tarone, E. and Bigelow, M. (2005) Impact of literacy on oral language processing: Implications for second language acquisition research. *Annual Review of Applied Linguistics* 25, 77–97.

Turner, M. and Engle, R. (1989) Is working memory capacity task dependent? *Journal of Memory and Language* 28, 127–154.

Ullman, M. (2004) Contributions of memory circuits to language: The declarative/procedural model. *Cognition* 92, 231–270.

Wright, C. (2013) Investigation of working memory effects on oral grammatical accuracy and fluency in production questions in English. *TESOL Quarterly* 47 (2), 352–374.

Yuan, F. and Ellis, R. (2003) The effects of pre-task planning and on-line planning on fluency, complexity and accuracy in L2 monologic oral production. *Applied Linguistics* 24, 1–27.

Final Commentary

17 Working Memory in SLA Research: Challenges and Prospects

John Williams

The concept of working memory (WM) is usually traced back to the early models of Baddeley and Hitch, and then the more recent frameworks of Cowan, both of which are usefully laid out in this volume (Baddeley, this volume; Cowan, this volume). But interest in WM in second language acquisition (SLA) was also inspired by the work of Just and Carpenter (1992) who were the first to explore the involvement of what has been referred to in this volume as executive WM (EWM) in online language comprehension. It was probably their notion of WM 'capacity' (WMC), as determined by the amount of 'activation' available to be shared between processing and storage, that led to the idea that WMC might form an important cognitive component of language aptitude, and explain why some individuals are better second language (L2) learners and processors than others. Tests of WMC were quick and easy to administer, yet they tapped into what seemed to be deep and fundamental aspects of cognitive functioning. Given that people clearly differ in their performance on such tasks, even in their first language (L1), then surely, it seemed, this variability would relate to their L2 processing and learning ability. Practically speaking, tests of WMC could then provide a means for screening, streaming or tailoring language training to the individual in a theoretically informed and principled way.

The present volume presents a unique, varied and fascinating insight into the state of WM research in SLA, and it is becoming apparent that any hope that tests of WMC could form the cognitive bedrock of aptitude testing is probably misplaced. The relationship between WMC and L2 processing and learning is far more complex and nuanced than originally envisaged. There is now a clear recognition that WM has to be divided into separate components, most relevantly phonological storage and executive control, that the efficiency of each can vary independently and, as such, has to be measured independently. And there is growing recognition, as amply evidenced here, that the importance of these different components to learning and processing can, in principle, vary according to domain of language, mode of instruction, input and output modality, proficiency and age (Wen, this volume). From the perspective of the hope that WM tests would provide a quick and principled test of aptitude, one might despair. On the other hand, I would suggest that we should be inspired by this complexity, because it turns out that the study of the relationship between WM and SLA can provide real leverage in the exploration of underlying cognitive processes. We move beyond thinking of tests of WMC as a basis for aptitude, towards using them as a theoretical tool.

In fact, there is a current trend in the field to use individual differences as a means of distinguishing the contribution of different cognitive systems to learning. Interactions between age and instructional treatments or structures can be used to make inferences about underlying learning processes, as can interactions with aptitude (DeKeyser, 2012). Individual differences in the functioning of declarative and procedural memory, each measured by distinct tests, have been used as a means to explore the contribution of these systems to learning (e.g. Morgan-Short et al., 2014). The study of WMC therefore fits into this broader, theoretically motivated, style of research in which individual differences provide leverage to prise apart different components of learning and processing mechanisms.

Admittedly, we are at the early stages of this enterprise. In fact, one might say that we are still in an initial bottom-up phase in which evidence is accumulating concerning situations in which various WM measures do and do not correlate with various aspects of language processing and learning. The present collection provides invaluable input to this development. In some cases, the pattern of correlations may seem surprising. For example, EWM only does not correlate with learning from written feedback (Baralt, this volume), whereas it does with learning from spoken feedback (Sagarra & Abbuhl, 2013). WM correlates with gains from processing instruction when measured in production, not comprehension (Santamaria & Sunderman, this volume), or with the ability to detect grammatical patterns (but not ungrammatical ones) after training in an intentional mode (Tagiarelli et al., this volume). Such patterns of correlation, to the extent that they chime with past and future research, become valuable explananda for theories of WM and language processing and learning.

Perhaps we should be wary, though, of becoming overly constrained by the nature of the WM tasks themselves. If the goal is not so much to discover the basis of aptitude, but rather to understand underlying cognitive processes, then we should start with a careful analysis of the cognitive demands of the learning problem. WM models provide frameworks for thinking about the interplay between different forms of memory and limited attentional resources during online processing. The starting point for research should therefore be not 'which of the available WM tests do I think will explain individual variation in this learning or processing situation?', but rather 'how can I think about this learning situation in terms of this cognitive framework?'. Just and Carpenter's (1992) research provides a prime example of this kind of top-down approach. They targeted highly *specific* aspects of comprehension, such as anaphor resolution, syntactic complexity, and lexical ambiguity in a principled way, starting from an analysis of the nature of the processing problem, linking it to the components of the WM system and only then to the demands of the task used to measure the capacity of this system (namely the reading span test [RST]). Whatever we think now about their theoretical position, or the actual involvement of WM in online language processing as they conceived it (see for example Waters & Caplan [1996] for a critique) this seems like a good model of research practice.

With the benefit of emerging insights into the role of WM in SLA, researchers should now be in a position to take the kind of top-down approach exemplified by Just and Carpenter. The challenge is to frame research questions in terms of a detailed cognitive analysis of a specific learning or processing problem. This can then be used to motivate the selection of individual differences measures in order to test the validity of the cognitive analysis. The starting point for such an analysis should be a consideration of the targeted linguistic features or regularities. What type of information is critical to the learning problem? Clearly, phonology is important for vocabulary learning, but it is also important in certain areas of grammar too (e.g. in learning morphological paradigms, picking up on agreement regularities). Presumably, it is not so important for learning word order regularities, where more abstract syntactic and semantic information will be critical. In this case, we might consider the possibility that there is a separable semantic short-term memory (STM) capacity that is more relevant (Freedman & Martin, 2001; Martin et al., 1994). How important is order, as opposed to item information? The ability to retain sequence information is critical to learning novel word forms (as sequences of phonemes) and syntactic structures (as sequences of grammatical categories or meanings), and there is good evidence that, at least within phonological memory, the ability to retain item and order information can be dissociated and measured independently (Majerus et al., 2008). To what extent will the storage of item information be supported by existing long-term memory representations from the L1, or L2? Clearly, greater long-term memory support provides more opportunities for chunking.

With regard to the learning or processing task, how important is temporary maintenance of information in WM? Presumably storage demands will be high when the task involves listening or speaking (Skehan, this volume), but low when the task involves written input or output. WM storage demands will be high when learners are required to compare across instances of language to form hypotheses during continued online processing, but low when they rely on implicit learning to unconsciously extract regularities. We should therefore think about assessing the contribution of implicit and explicit learning processes, for example by using think-aloud procedures (Leow *et al.*, 2014) or measuring implicit and explicit knowledge (Rebuschat, 2013) in order to examine interactions with WM measures (see Tagarelli *et al.*, this volume, for an example).

How important is rapid attention switching, say between form and meaning? Possibly very important in learning through interaction, or attempting to learn vocabulary or grammar in a meaning-focused activity, assuming that the learning target depends on information at the level of form. Should we then be thinking about testing attention-switching ability (Unsworth & Engle, 2008)? How automated, or modularised, are the underlying processing operations that underpin the task? One reason for not finding correlations with WM, particularly in sentence processing, is because the underlying processes are automatised/proceduralised, and hence make minimal demands on resources. Could we include independent measures of automaticity (Segalowitz, 2003) in order to examine interactions with WM? Again, critical here is the relationship to the L1, because processing of L1-like structures is more native-like and automatic (van Hell & Tokowicz, 2010).

In all of this, we should not forget the importance of attention in models of WM (see Cowan, this volume; Bunting & Engle, this volume) and its pivotal role in both explicit (Schmidt, 2001) and implicit (Williams, 2013) learning. Critical to both forms of learning is the assumption that in order to forge new associations in memory, the relevant pieces of information need to be simultaneously active within the focus of attention (Cowan, this volume). When analysing learning situations, then, we need to consider, first, what the critical associations are (e.g. between forms and meaning, or forms and forms), the likelihood of bringing the relevant information into joint attentional focus (as determined, say, by the emphasis on form or meaning in the task, or by the distance between the relevant forms) and the role of different aspects of the WM system in bringing this about (e.g. rapid switching of attention between form and meaning, maintenance of phonological, syntactic or semantic information during online processing).

Given all of the above, it is perhaps not surprising that where relationships between EWM and learning have been found, it has been in relation to explicit, rather than implicit, learning situations (Kempe *et al.*, 2010; Mackey *et al.*, 2002; Martin & Ellis, 2012, Tagarelli *et al.*, this volume). This is presumably because EWM tasks tap the conscious maintenance of information during online processing in much the same way that explicit learning requires conscious maintenance of instances of input and hypotheses during listening and speaking tasks. This raises the question of what underlies variation in learning outcomes in implicit learning situations. Recent research suggests a connection between domain-general statistical learning ability and L1 processing (Conway et al., 2010) and L1 proficiency (Misyak & Christiansen, 2012). At present, though, it is unclear what underlies this ability, how it should be conceived of within our cognitive models or what contribution it makes to SLA. One would expect that the integrity of phonological storage would be relevant, at least for certain learning problems, because of the necessity to store the data from which generalisations are supposedly extracted. Although relationships between phonological STM and grammar learning have been obtained, these relate to situations where learning was likely to be explicit, rather than implicit (French & O'Brien, 2008; Martin & Ellis, 2012; Williams & Lovatt, 2003), although there is evidence for a correlation in the context of artificial grammar learning (Karpicke & Pisoni, 2004). In general, though, while the involvement of WM in explicit learning seems to be becoming established, the bases for variation in implicit learning remain largely open for further research.

Models of WM provide a framework for carrying out a detailed analysis of the cognitive processes underlying language learning and performance. WM tests provide a means of empirically testing these analyses through individual variation in the cognitive components that have been identified. As we progress, our analyses will suggest further aspects of WM that should be differentiated and measured, such as memory for order information, semantic STM or attention switching. We can also look for interactions between WM and other, independently measurable, cognitive factors such as the extent of relevant L1 and L2 knowledge, the automaticity of the targeted cognitive operations and the implicitness or explicitness of the learning process. Interactions with age and proficiency will become reduced to underlying cognitive factors. In this way, the study of WM provides real opportunities for deepening our understanding of the language learning process. As this volume amply illustrates, we are moving beyond the study of WM as a basis for aptitude, and towards using tests of WM, like individual differences more generally, to inform theory building. If WM is a 'language learning device' (Baddeley et al., 1998) then WM tests are tools for prising apart the device's components.

References

Baddeley, A.D., Gathercole, S.E. and Papagno, C. (1998) The phonological loop as a language learning device. *Psychological Review* 105, 158–173.

Conway, C.M., Bauernschmidt, A., Huang, S.S. and Pisoni, D.B. (2010) Implicit statistical learning in language processing: Word predictability is the key. *Cognition* 114, 356–371.

DeKeyser, R.M. (2012) Interactions between individual differences, treatments, and structures in SLA. *Language Learning* 62, 189–200.

Freedman, M. and Martin, R.C. (2001) Dissociable components of short-term memory and their relation to long-term learning. *Cognitive Neuropsychology* 18, 193–226.

French, L.M. and O'Brien, I. (2008) Phonological memory and children's second language grammar learning. *Applied Psycholinguistics* 29, 463–487.

Just, M.A. and Carpenter, P.A. (1992) A capacity theory of comprehension: Individual differences in working memory. *Psychological Review* 99, 122–149.

Karpicke, J.D. and Pisoni, D.B. (2004) Using immediate memory span to measure implicit learning. *Memory and Cognition* 32, 956–964.

Kempe, V., Brooks, P.J. and Kharkhurin, A. (2010) Cognitive predictors of generalization of Russian grammatical gender categories. *Language Learning* 60, 127–153.

Leow, R.P., Grey, S., Marijuan, S. and Moorman, C. (2014) Concurrent data elicitation procedures, processes, and the early stages of L2 learning: A critical overview. *Second Language Research* 30, 111–127.

Mackey, A., Philp, J., Egi, T., Fujii, A. and Tatsumi, T. (2002) Working memory, interactional feedback and L2 development. In P. Robinson (ed.) *Individual Differences and Second Language Instruction* (pp.181–209). Philadelphia, PA: John Benjamins.

Majerus, S., Poncelet, M., Van der Linden, M. and Weekes, B.S. (2008) Lexical learning in bilingual adults: The relative importance of short-term memory for serial order and phonological knowledge. *Cognition* 107, 395–419.

Martin, K.I. and Ellis, N.C. (2012) The roles of phonological short-term memory and working memory in L2 grammar and vocabulary learning. *Studies in Second Language Acquisition* 34, 379–413.

Martin, R.C., Shelton, J.R. and Yaffee, L.S. (1994) Language processing and working-memory: Neuropsychological evidence for separate phonological and semantic capacities. *Journal of Memory and Language* 33, 83–111.

Misyak, J.B. and Christiansen, M.H. (2012) Statistical learning and language: An individual differences study. *Language Learning* 62, 302–331.

Morgan-Short, K., Faretta-Stuttenberg, M., Brill-Scheutz, K.A., Carpenter, H. and Wong, P.C.M. (2014) Declarative and procedural memory as individual differences in second language acquisition. *Bilingualism: Language and Cognition* 17, 56–72.

Rebuschat, P. (2013) Measuring implicit and explicit knowledge in second language research. *Language Learning* 63, 595–626.

Sagarra, N. and Abbuhl, R. (2013) Optimizing the noticing of recasts via computer-delivered feedback: Evidence that oral input enhancement and working memory help second language learning. *The Modern Language Journal* 97, 196–216.

Schmidt, R. (2001) Attention. In P. Robinson (ed.) *Cognition and Second Language Instruction* (pp. 3–32). Cambridge: Cambridge University Press.

Segalowitz, N. (2003) Automaticity and second languages. In C. Doughty and M. Long (eds) *Handbook of Second Language Acquisition* (pp. 382–408). Oxford: Blackwell.

Unsworth, N. and Engle, R.W. (2008) Speed and accuracy of accessing information in working memory: An individual differences investigation of focus switching. *Journal of Experimental Psychology: Learning Memory and Cognition* 34, 616–630.

van Hell, J.G. and Tokowicz, N. (2010) Event-related brain potentials and second language learning: Syntactic processing in late L2 learners at different L2 proficiency levels. *Second Language Research* 26, 43–74.

Waters, G.S. and Caplan, D. (1996) The capacity theory of comprehension: Critique of Just and Carpenter (1992). *Psychological Review* 103, 761–772.

Williams, J.N. (2013) Attention, awareness, and noticing in language processing and learning. In Bergsleithner, J.M., Frota, S.N., and Yoshioka, J.K. (eds) *Noticing and Second Language Acquisition: Studies in Honor of Richard Schmidt* (pp. 39–57). Honolulu, HI: National Foreign Language Resource Centre.

Williams, J.N. and Lovatt, P. (2003) Phonological memory and rule learning. *Language Learning* 53, 67–121.

Index

Lightning Source UK Ltd.
Milton Keynes UK
UKHW02f0505110818
327079UK00004B/293/P